D1632069

Relationships in Organizations

Relationships in Organizations

A Work Psychology Perspective

Edited By

Rachel L. Morrison
Auckland University of Technology, New Zealand

Helena D. Cooper-Thomas
The University of Auckland, New Zealand

First published 2013 by
PALGRAVE MACMILLAN

Palgrave Macmillan in the UK is an imprint of Macmillan Publishers Limited,
registered in England, company number 785998, of Houndmills, Basingstoke,
Hampshire RG21 6XS.

Palgrave Macmillan in the US is a division of St Martin's Press LLC,
175 Fifth Avenue, New York, NY 10010.

Palgrave Macmillan is the global academic imprint of the above companies
and has companies and representatives throughout the world.

Palgrave® and Macmillan® are registered trademarks in the United States,
the United Kingdom, Europe and other countries

ISBN: 978-1-137-28063-3

This book is printed on paper suitable for recycling and made from fully
managed and sustained forest sources. Logging, pulping and manufacturing
processes are expected to conform to the environmental regulations of the
country of origin.

A catalogue record for this book is available from the British Library.

A catalog record for this book is available from the Library of Congress.

Contents

List of Tables and Figures

Tables

Figures

Acknowledgements

Rachel Morrison:
I would like to acknowledge the incredibly generous collegial support provided by so many members of my department within the Business School at AUT University. You comprise my own workplace relationship network and exemplify how great it is to have supportive and encouraging colleagues and friends at work. I would also like to acknowledge the Performance and Wellbeing Research group of the Work Research Institute (AUT).

Helena Cooper-Thomas:
I would like to acknowledge the support of colleagues both in the School of Psychology at the University of Auckland and in many other institutions around the world. My relationships with you make the process of work more pleasurable and the outputs better quality.

Notes on Contributors

Terry A. Beehr is a Professor and Director of the PhD Program in Industrial/Organizational Psychology at Central Michigan University. He earned his PhD in Organizational Psychology from The University of Michigan and previously worked at the Institute for Social Research and Illinois State University. He is currently an associate editor for three journals and on the editorial boards of two more. His research includes several topics related to the social psychology of organizations, such as work motivation and attitudes, occupational stress, older employees' retirement decisions, social support among employees, leadership, and careers in organizations.

Misty M. Bennett is currently Assistant Professor of the Management Department at Central Michigan University where she teaches Human Resources and Organizational Behavior classes. She earned her PhD in Industrial/Organizational Psychology from Central Michigan University. Her research areas include generational differences in workplace attitudes, aging-related workplace issues, social support from work and family sources, and work-family conflict. She is also the Program Director for the Women in Business Mentoring Program at CMU. She has consulting experience for a variety of organizations, both public and private, around staffing solutions and training and instructional design.

Jeffrey R. Bentley is a doctoral candidate in the School of Management at the State University of New York (SUNY) at Buffalo, and previously attained a Master's degree in Industrial/Organizational Psychology from New York University. Jeff's research revolves around personal growth at work and adaptation to challenges, and focuses specifically on the roles of self-concept and self-regulation, social and emotional aptitude, leadership, and victimization. He has coauthored 14 papers on organizational behavior presented at annual conferences including the *Academy of Management*, the *Society for Industrial & Organizational Psychology*, and the *Southern Management Association*.

Tim Bentley is Director of the New Zealand Work Research Institute at AUT University. Prior to taking up this role in mid-2012, Tim worked xii *Notes on Contributors*

at Massey University where he was Director of the Healthy Work Group, School Research Chair, and College of Business PBRF champion. Tim's major research interest is concerned with the role of organizational issues in occupational health, safety and well-being, and his current research includes studies on teleworking productivity and well-being, bullying and ill-treatment in the workplace, and the New Zealand Workplace Violence Survey. Tim has been a Principal Investigator for the Health Research Council of NZ on two occasions, and led a recently completed multidisciplinary government-funded project concerned with workplace bullying and stress in NZ workplaces.

Thomas A. Birtch is a Senior Research Fellow, Centre for Industry and Government, Cambridge University. His research regularly appears in leading business journals. His current research interests evolve around the performance of people and organizations, ethics and leadership, strategic decision-making, the transferability of management practices, and entrepreneurship. Thomas has taught widely at the graduate and undergraduate levels. His background in industry includes holding senior and executive level positions in the private sector and government spanning three continents. He has consulted in over 30 countries and is an advisor to a number of government bodies and professional associations.

Bevan Catley is Associate Head of the School of Management at Massey University and also a Director of the Healthy Work Group – a multidisciplinary team of researchers from Massey interested in psychosocial factors in workplace health and safety. He teaches introductory management and his research focus is on workplace violence and workplace bullying. Bevan has been involved in some of the first large scale research projects to investigate these two issues including the HRC-funded project examining workplace bullying in New Zealand workplaces.

Shaohui (Sophie) Chen is Senior Research Fellow and Lecturer in Management at the China Europe International Business School (CEIBS), People's Republic of China. Prior to the completion of her PhD at The University of Auckland in 2005, she worked as a senior executive in the Chinese securities and credit rating industry. Her research appears in leading academic journals and her teaching is focused on HRM and leadership development for MBA students at CEIBS, as well as executive development and consultancy.

Flora F. T. Chiang is a Professor in the Department of Management at Hong Kong Baptist University. She is an award winning educator and scholar. Flora has taught extensively on MBA, EMBA, MSc, MA, and BBA programs in Asia, Europe, and North America. Her primary research interests include employee behavior and performance, leadership, and cross-cultural management. Her publications regularly appear in leading international academic journals. She is Associate Editor of the *International Journal of Human Resource Management*. Prior to her academic career, Flora held senior management and directorate positions in public and private organizations and consulted internationally on all facets of employee performance and development.

Helena D. Cooper-Thomas is a Senior Lecturer and Director of Postgraduate Studies in Industrial Work and Organizational Psychology at the University of Auckland, New Zealand. Helena's research interests focus primarily on new employees and employee-employer relations. She publishes in the areas of newcomer adjustment and organizational socialization, the development of the psychological contract and person-organization fit, work engagement, and stress and bullying. She has published her research in a number of respected applied psychology, organizational behavior and human resources journals. Helena has also provided consulting to a range of private and public sector organizations in various countries.

Jennifer B. Farrell works in the Kemmy Business School at the University of Limerick. She recently graduated with her PhD from Dublin City University where the focus of her doctoral research was on the role of relationships in motivating proactive behavior. Her research interests lie in understanding how relational contexts influence workplace behavior with particular interest in the facets of social context which promote or inhibit proactivity.

Dianne Gardner is a registered psychologist and Senior Lecturer in Industrial/Organizational Psychology in the School of Psychology at Massey University in Auckland, New Zealand. She researches well-being and healthy work, in particular the positive and negative outcomes that can arise from work demands. She has published papers on research into work-life balance, coping, resilience, generational differences at work, the role of optimism, self-esteem and social support in work-related well-being and stress, emotional intelligence, the veterinary profession, learning from errors, and the effective management of hazards at work. She is particularly interested in researching effective solutions to the problem of workplace bullying.

Susan Geertshuis is Professor of Lifelong Learning in the Graduate School of Management at The University of Auckland, where she teaches on the MBA program. Prior to her appointment in 2012 Susan was Director of the University of Auckland's Centre for Continuing Education. Before moving to New Zealand from the UK, Susan was Professor of Organizational Studies at the University of Northampton Business School and Director of the Centre for Learning and Innovation in Organizations. Previous to this she led the Centre for Learning Research at the University of Wales, Bangor. Susan obtained her PhD in Cognitive Psychology from Nottingham University. Her current research interests are in corporate learning, influence, and decision-making.

Marcus Ho is a Senior Lecturer in HRM and entrepreneurship at Auckland University of Technology Business School in Auckland, New Zealand. He has a PhD from The University of Auckland Business School and has worked as a HR consultant and organizational psychologist. His current research interests are in high technology entrepreneurship and HRM issues in new ventures. He has published in leading journals such as *Entrepreneurship: Theory and Practice* and the *International Journal of Human Resource Management*.

Darl G. Kolb (PhD Cornell) is Professor of Connectivity in the Graduate School of Management at the University of Auckland. He is a pioneering theorist on socio-technical connectivity and has published articles on the metaphor and states of connectivity in *Organization Studies* and requisite connectivity in *Organizational Dynamics*. He is interested in connectivity's impact on performance and well-being, including recent work on smartphones and engagement (*Organizational Dynamics*), hyper-connectivity and "digital disruption". He discusses connects and disconnects on his blog, *Connectivity Corner*.

Kevin Lo is an Assistant Professor at the University of San Francisco, School of Management, Department of Organization, Leadership, and Communication. He completed his PhD in International Management in 2007 at the University of Hawaii. Prior to his current position, he lectured at The University of Auckland Business School. His research and teaching focus on cross-cultural management and organizational behavior. He is specifically interested in time orientation and interpersonal business relationships in a cross-cultural context.

Rachel L. Morrison runs the Organizational Behavior program within the Faculty of Business and Law, AUT University (New Zealand). She is an active and founding member of the Wellbeing and Performance Research Group within the NZ Work Research Institute (NZWRI). Her degrees are in Psychology and Organizational Psychology and she has previously taught within psychology departments at the University of Auckland and Massey University. She has published articles in a variety of academic Management and Psychology journals and coedited a previous, related volume *Friends and Enemies in Organizations: A Work Psychology Perspective*. Dr Morrison's research interests include workplace relationships, friendship formation, engagement, social capital and liability, and social networks.

Michael P. O'Driscoll is Professor of Psychology at the University of Waikato in New Zealand, where he convenes the postgraduate program in organizational psychology. His primary research interests focus on job-related stress (including the effects of bullying at work), coping and psychological well-being, work-life balance, and well-being of older workers. He is coauthor of several books and book chapters. He is associate editor of *Work & Stress*, *Stress & Health*, and the *Journal of Occupational & Organizational Psychology*, serves on the editorial boards of several international academic journals, and has provided consulting services to organizations on work stress and well-being.

Stephanie R. Seitz is a PhD student in the Organizational and Human Resources Department at the State University of New York at Buffalo. Her main research interests include leadership and followership, with particular attention to abusive supervision, transformational leadership, and implicit theories. As a licensed attorney, she is also interested in gender issues and discrimination. She has been commended for work in the areas of emotions and ethical performance with an award for best student paper in the Ethics, Social Issues, and Diversity Track of the Southern Management Association. She has also presented her research at conferences such as the Academy of Management and the Society for Industrial and Organizational Psychology.

Brooke A. Shaughnessy is a postdoctoral researcher for the Chair of Research and Science Management in the TUM School of Management at the Technische Universität München. Her research interests are on individual differences and diversity in the contexts of social influence, political skill, workplace victimization and bullying, leadership, negotiations and social networks. She has received recognition for her work on gender and negotiations having been awarded best doctoral paper in the Ethics/Social Issues/Diversity track for the Southern Management Association. Her research has been published in journals such as the *Journal of Managerial Psychology, International Journal of Human Resource Development and Management* and *American Business Journal*.

Deborah Shepherd is a Senior Lecturer in Management and International Business at The University of Auckland Business School. She is also a founding faculty member of The ICEHOUSE Growth Programmes and has facilitated Business Growth programs since 2001. Her research and teaching focuses on strategy, leadership, senior team development, change management and family business. She is coauthor of the business growth book *Changing Gears: How to take your Kiwi business from the kitchen table to the board room* (with Christine Woods, 2009, Auckland University Press). She holds a BA (Otago) in psychology, an MA (Hons) in psychology and management, and a PhD in management from the University of Auckland.

Karoline Strauss is an Associate Professor in Organizational Behavior at Warwick Business School. She holds a PhD in Organizational Psychology from the University of Sheffield. Karoline's primary research interests concern proactive behavior, in particular its boundary conditions and consequences. Her research on Future Work Selves investigates how proactive behavior can be guided by individuals' representations of themselves in the future. Karoline's research has been published in journals such as the *Journal of Applied Psychology* and the *Journal of Management*.

Valerie N. Streets is a doctoral student in Industrial/Organizational Psychology at Old Dominion University. She received her BSc in Psychology and Gender Studies from Towson University in Baltimore, Maryland in 2011. Her research is centered upon gender issues within organization, with special emphasis on the role of stereotyping and stereotype threat.

Darren C. Treadway is an Associate Professor of Organization and Human Resources at the State University of New York at Buffalo.

Dr. Treadway's research interests include social influence processes in organizations, with particular reference to organizational politics, political skill, workplace toxicity, and leadership. His research has been published in leading journals such as *Journal of Applied Psychology, Journal of Management, Leadership Quarterly, Journal of Organizational Behavior,* and *Human Relations.* Most recently, he coedited the Society for Industrial and Organizational Psychology Frontier Series book *Politics in Organizations: Theory and Research Considerations* with Gerald R. Ferris. Dr. Treadway's research has twice been awarded the Emerald Publishing *Citation of Excellence* as one of the top 50 business publications and has been awarded the *Journal of Management* Best Paper Award.

Linda Trenberth joined Birkbeck, University of London in 2000 and is currently Head of the Management Department, Acting Head of the Department of Organizational Psychology and Deputy Dean of the School of Business, Economics and Informatics. One area of Linda's work is on Sports Business Management and, together with colleagues, she set up the Birkbeck Sport Business Centre. A second area is work and well-being with a particular emphasis on the relationship between work-stress, leisure and coping. With her New Zealand colleagues, she has recently completed a large publicly-funded project on workplace bullying and stress, and is now leading an extension of this project throughout the ASEAN countries. Linda has published in a number of high quality peer reviewed international interdisciplinary journals.

Angela S. Wallace is a doctoral student in Organization and Human Resources in the School of Management at the State University of New York at Buffalo. She received her Master's of Science degrees from Embry-Riddle Aeronautical University and Syracuse University in Software Engineering and Engineering Management, respectively. She has worked as a software engineer for large corporations such as Lockheed-Martin and Eastman Kodak Company. Her research interests include psychological entitlement, narcissism, person-environment fit, and virtual teams.

Fiona M. Wilson is Professor of Organizational Behaviour in the Business School, University of Glasgow, Scotland. She has also been employed at the University of St Andrews, Bradford Management Centre and Manchester Business School. She has published two books – *Organizational Behaviour and Gender* and *Organizational Behaviour and*

Work as well as around 40 journal articles. Her current interests are focused on gender and disadvantage at work.

Marie Wilson is Professor of Management and Academic Dean at Griffith Business School, Griffith University in Brisbane, Queensland, Australia. Prior to her current role, she held a variety of senior roles at The University of Auckland, and executive roles in large multinational IT firms. Her research and teaching focus on people at work, particularly their identity, development and interaction with their organization and its context. She is particularly interested in discretionary effort and role identity across institutional and cultural contexts.

Barbara A. Winstead received her PhD in Personality and Developmental Psychology from Harvard University. She has been a faculty member at Old Dominion University, Norfolk, Virginia, for 34 years. She is currently Professor and Chair of the Department of Psychology. She is also a clinical faculty member with the Virginia Consortium Program in Clinical Psychology. Her research focuses on gender and relationships, including relationships in the workplace; the effects of relationships and self-disclosure on coping with stress and illness. Her research has resulted in more than 75 journal articles, chapters, and books and numerous conference presentations.

Christine Woods became interested in entrepreneurship and the small to medium business sector after working in Malawi as a small business advisor. Instead of catching malaria she caught the "entrepreneur bug", becoming "hooked" on the passion and energy that entrepreneurs bring to what they do. She returned to New Zealand and received her PhD in entrepreneurship from the University of Auckland. She is an Associate Professor in the Business School with research and teaching interests in entrepreneurship. Chris has also been involved with The ICEHOUSE Business Growth Programmes since their inception in 2001 and is a coauthor of the business growth book *Changing Gears: How to Take Your Kiwi Business from the Kitchen Table to the Board Room* (with Deborah Shepherd, 2009).

1
Maximizing the Good and Minimizing the Bad: Relationships in Organizations

Helena D. Cooper-Thomas[1] *and Rachel L. Morrison*[2]

Like them or loathe them we cannot escape the people we work with. Working adults spend around a third of their waking lives at work, and much of this time interacting with colleagues either directly or virtually. Further, our colleagues can become key players in our social life, through romantic liaisons, family links, or *guanxi* relationships that bridge organizational boundaries. Our colleagues can provide us with social support and advice, but they can also be a source of negative behaviors such as bullying. Thus, while we may seek to establish relationships with our colleagues, these work relationships will vary greatly in how and why they develop as well as in the outcomes they produce. Workers will form strong bonds with some colleagues that are enjoyable and mutually beneficial, while with other colleagues they may form more neutral or even negative relationships, and may try to avoid interactions where possible.

Our book has two main purposes. The first purpose is to present an up-to-date review of key issues around relationships in organizations, including both positive and negative elements of relationships, and also the context of relationships, including cultural and technological aspects. This follows on from the 2009 book *Friends and Enemies in Organizations: A Work Psychology Perspective* and widens the focus beyond friendships and enemyships to all manner of organizational relationships, from romantic liaisons to virtual relationships, from relationships with leaders to those with family members. The second purpose of this book is to have a positive impact for future relationships in organizations, through inspiring relevant future research to

[1] School of Psychology, The University of Auckland
[2] Management Department, AUT University

further explore these topics, as well as by encouraging best practice in achieving optimal workplace relationships. With regard to further research, there is plenty of scope for academics, researchers, and students to explore the myriad issues around workplace relationships, with the richest opportunities identified in each chapter. On the practical side, because relationships with colleagues are so pervasive to our experience of work, translating research knowledge into practice can have broad benefits to organizational members. This volume is relevant to both practitioners who may put policies or procedures in place to optimize workplace relationships (and minimize harmful ones), and also for individual employees looking for ideas on how to manage and ameliorate their relationships with colleagues, direct reports, and supervisors.

Why relationships in organizations are important

As we noted above, full-time employees spend a great many of their waking hours at work, often interacting and collaborating with colleagues to get their work done. For individual employees, the experience of work can be a source of happiness, engagement, and even joy, with colleagues often influencing each other to shape how enjoyable work is (Bakker & Xanthopoulou, 2009; Fisher, 2010). Moreover, how we feel about the experiences and relationships we have at work can spill over into our time out of work (Sonnentag et al., 2012); time spent with friends or family, or in leisure pursuits. Thus positive relationships at work may bring far reaching benefits.

Yet relationships may not always progress as we might hope. We may not establish the good working relationship with our manager that we want, or we may find that a particular colleague is persistently petty and undermining. Research on bullying shows that negative behaviors can have detrimental effects on individual employees leading to absenteeism, depression, and even suicide (see Chapter 10 by Gardner and colleagues). Clearly there are serious risks to bad workplace relationships.

For organizations also, positive relationships between colleagues have benefits. They may attract employees in the first place (Tews et al., 2012), and can support employees to act more supportively and collegially. The impact that friendships have on individual's experiences of work can be profound; improving satisfaction and commitment, increasing cohesion and reducing intentions to leave (Morrison, 2004; Morrison, 2009).

Organizations will also suffer when workplace relationships go sour. Colleagues who witness negative behaviors are affected by this, and experience lower well-being and report lower performance (Cooper-Thomas et al., 2011). For those on the receiving end of negative behavior within relationships, they are more likely to be absent, to feel disengaged, and eventually to leave the organization altogether (Morrison & Nolan, 2007), all considerable costs to organizations.

There are also new challenges to organizations, such as how virtual relationships develop and may be managed, as well as how supervisor-direct report (subordinate) relationships can best be improved, since it is at this level that individual performance is kept on track. With increasing numbers of women at all levels of the workforce, gender issues continue to be increasingly salient. The globalization of work also makes it important to develop productive relationships with colleagues from different cultures, for example when colleagues are immigrants, or when we are working away from our home culture.

Overview of the book

Our chapter contributors come from around the globe including Europe, the UK, China, Australasia, and North America. This provides a rich banquet of evidence-based ideas from diverse perspectives. All authors are successful academics and leaders in their field. Their expert summaries provide different perspectives on relationships in organizations.

In Chapter 2 Fiona Wilson tackles the often gossiped about, but seldom researched, topic of romance in workplaces. Romantic liaisons in the workplace are discussed in the context of organizational culture, power, and gender differences. Wilson then discusses the causes and effects of workplace romance; exploring why people are motivated to begin a romantic relationship at work, and the impact that these relationships can have on others in their social environment. She also looks at how organizations might respond to romance before outlining future research directions in this fascinating field of enquiry.

Chapter 3 explores the relational and organizational implications of *guanxi*; a construct that forms the basis for all social relationships in China but remains foreign, intriguing, and often confusing to outsiders. Kevin Lo, Shaohui Chen, and Marie Wilson collaborated on this chapter, and discuss how, why, and when *guanxi* impacts on organizational relationships and organizational functioning in a predominantly Chinese context. The authors both link and differentiate *guanxi* from concepts such as networking, relationship marketing, and mentoring. They discuss the ethics of *guanxi* and outline the practical implications of *guanxi* in doing business in China, providing useful insights for those in work relationships with Chinese colleagues. They highlight future research directions for *guanxi* including the impact of technology, as well as changing types and targets of *guanxi*.

The chapter on social influence and political skill (Chapter 4), by Darren Treadway and colleagues, introduces new ideas into this topic. Politically skilled behaviors are positioned as being socially astute when done well, and as necessary within many relationships. Treadway and colleagues introduce new ideas from other fields of psychology regarding how relationships develop, with an emphasis on dyads, bringing a fresh perspective to our understanding of political behavior. Using the two examples of performance management and leadership, Treadway and his colleagues outline how colleagues influence each other. These practically illustrate the intriguing and pervasive influence of political skill in workplace relationships. In a subsequent section, this chapter outlines how a greater consideration of politics can help deepen our understanding of various aspects of workplace relationships, including gender, ethnic minorities, motivation, and abuse. Importantly, they also provide practical suggestions of how to gain from the positive aspects of political behavior as well as how to reduce negative aspects, for team members and leaders.

Susan Geertshuis, along with the volume editors Rachel Morrison and Helena Cooper-Thomas describe the "influential subordinate" in Chapter 5, exploring how, why, and when subordinates can or should exert influence over their bosses or line managers. A review of relevant literature on social hierarchies and power in organizations precedes an analysis of subordinate-superior relationships. There is much to be learned by subordinates from their explanation of alternative sources of power and the ways in which subordinates can use these to influence others. An engaging vignette runs through the chapter and practically illustrates tactics that subordinates can employ to achieve behavior change in others.

Jennifer Farrell and Karoline Strauss tackle the role of proactive behavior in workplace relationships (Chapter 6). Proactive behavior is defined as being self-starting, change oriented, and future focused. Farrell and Strauss first discuss how relationships at work lead to psychological states of *can do*, *reason to*, and *energized to*, that lead to proactive work behavior. They then critically examine how relationships can influence perceptions of proactive behavior. As an example, a supervisor may negatively evaluate proactive behavior by a direct report if the proactive behavior is badly timed, seen as irrelevant, or perceived as threatening the supervisor's competence. On the flip side, when employees are viewed as prosocial, proactive behaviors are viewed as intended to benefit the collective and rated positively. Farrell and Strauss go on to discuss how proactive behavior can affect relationships, for example when new employees are proactive and begin to build relationships with colleagues. Towards the end of this chapter the authors discuss how to create relational contexts to support and enhance proactive behavior and its benefits, providing practical, research-based suggestions as to how to encourage proactive behavior and reap the rewards.

In Chapter 7 Barbara Winstead, along with her coauthor Valerie Streets, revisits her excellent chapter on gender differences in organizational relationships, which appeared in the 2009 book *Friends and Enemies in Organizations* (to which this current volume is a sequel). Not only do these authors update the research which is presented on gender as it relates to social networks, friendships, mentoring, and negative relationships, but they extend the content considerably. Winstead and Streets look at gender as it relates to the focus of several of the other chapters in this book. They examine gender and romance in the workplace, with content linking nicely with Fiona Wilson's chapter (Chapter 2) and go on to consider gender as it relates to leader/member relations; linking to Flora Chiang's chapter on leadership (Chapter 11). Gender differences in virtual work relationships are also examined and, again there are links with Darl Kolb's analysis of virtual work and perceived proximity (Chapter 8). Finally the impact and implications of gender and gender roles within family business is presented, and relates to the discussion of relationships in family firms by Marcus Ho and colleagues (Chapter 12).

In Chapter 8, Darl Kolb introduces ideas that are likely to be new to many readers, around the influence of technology on relationships. The mediums through which we communicate have a profound influence on what we communicate, with whom, and how often. It is fascinating to discover how virtual technology is influencing how we work with others. The model that Kolb presents is intriguing, with social and technical connectivity combining with context to determine choice of communication type (media, frequency, quantity) and, via connection and connective gaps, influencing perceived proximity. Kolb ends the chapter with practical suggestions for how to work across distance, and these are likely to be relevant to most readers who will have at least some relationships with colleagues where communication is principally electronic rather than face-to-face.

Misty Bennet and Terry Beehr explore collegial relationships in organizations in Chapter 9, focusing on the social support provided to and by organizational members. They begin by giving a theoretical background and defining the construct of social support. Bennet and Beehr go on to describe both individual and work-related outcomes of working in a supportive (or unsupportive) environment, as well as considering support in the context of individual differences such as age, gender and culture. The authors conclude with practical implications for social support interventions within organizations.

In their chapter on bullying at work (Chapter 10), Dianne Gardner and colleagues start with the stark details of two true bullying stories. In one case, the target of bullying took her own life; in the second case, as a result of bullying, the target experienced mental health problems including severe depression. From the outset, it is made clear that bullying is something that we should be concerned about, reflecting extremely negative relationships between colleagues. Gardner and colleagues note that, to be classified as bullying, negative behaviors have to be repeated, often involve an imbalance of power, and the target must feel unable to defend him or herself. They go on to highlight that, while some people may deliberately engage in bullying (the "predatory bully"), others are ignorant (the "unaware bully") or focused on results (the "purposeful bully"). Importantly, rather than just blaming individuals, they outline how the situation can encourage negative behavior, with leadership having a key role. In line with this, the best solutions focus on improving the situation through policy, training, mediation and counseling, and improving leadership and workplace climate.

In their chapter on ethical leadership (Chapter 11), Flora Chiang and Thomas Birtch outline the centrality of leaders relationships both with their direct reports (subordinates), but also with a range of other colleagues inside and outside of their employing organization. Drawing on notions of leadership, Chiang and Birtch outline how leader behaviors unfold both vertically within organizations, and also horizontally and externally. Throughout their chapter, they use the astonishing story of an unethical manager to illustrate some of the key ideas, alongside a direct report who displays highly ethical behaviors. The unethical manager manipulates information and, toward the end of the chapter, acts illegally to try and undermine his direct report. They helpfully outline many directions for future research.

In Chapter 12 Marcus Ho and his colleagues Chris Woods and Deborah Shepherd explore paradoxes that exist in family run business. They use the real-life case of Pacific Wide Group to describe the conflicts and tensions that are created by merging the roles of "family member" and "colleague". For example, the paradox of trust and commitment is described where, on the one hand, family business are seen as more trustworthy and often rely on trust as a governance mechanism but, on the other hand, they can also breed negative consequences such as nepotism, rivalries and jealousy; with members feeling imprisoned in their roles. Ho and his colleagues go on to describe ways to address the paradox in the family metasystem and provide four clear methods for working with paradox, relating the strategies back to the case of Pacific Wide Group.

Collectively these chapters bring together a plethora of new ideas about relationships at work, covering a wide range of situations and types of relationships. There are many new ideas here, which we hope both established researchers as well as newcomers to the field will find stimulating and useful. Enjoy!

References

Bakker, A. B. & Xanthopoulou, D. (2009). The crossover of daily work engagement: Test of an actor-partner interdependence model, *Journal of Applied Psychology*, *94*(6), 1562–1571. doi: 10.1037/a0017525

Cooper-Thomas, H. D., Catley, B. E., Bentley, T. A., Gardner, D. H., O'Driscoll, M. P., & Trenberth, L. (2011, June). *Is there a double whammy from being an observer and a target of workplace bullying?* In C. Caponecchia (Chair), Symposium conducted at the 9th Industrial and Organisational Psychology Conference, Brisbane, Australia.

Fisher, C. D. (2010). Happiness at work, *International Journal of Management Reviews*, *12*, 384–412. doi: 10.1111/j.1468-2370.2009.00270.x

Morrison, R. (2004). Informal relationships in the workplace: Associations with job satisfaction, organisational commitment and turnover intentions, *New Zealand Journal of Psychology*, *33*(3), 114–128.

Morrison, R. L. (2009). Organisational outcomes of friendships: in R. L. Morrison & S. Wright (eds) *Friends and Enemies in Organisations: A Work Psychology Perspective*. London: Palgrave Macmillan.

Morrison, R. L. & Nolan, T. (2007). Negative relationships in the workplace – A qualitative study, *Qualitative Research in Accounting and Management*, *4*(3), 203–221.

Sonnentag, S., Mojza, E. J., Demerouti, E., & Bakker, A. B. (2012). Reciprocal relations between recovery and work engagement: The moderating role of job stressors, *Journal of Applied Psychology*, *97*(4), 842–853. doi: 10.1037/a0028292

Tews, M. J., Michel, J. W., & Bartlett, A. (2012). The fundamental role of workplace fun in applicant attraction, *Journal of Leadership & Organizational Studies*, *19*(1), 105–114. doi: 10.1177/1548051811431828

2
Love is in the Air: Romantic Relationships at Work

Fiona M. Wilson[1]

Around Valentine's Day each year, magazine and newspaper articles talk about romance at work. For example, Adrian Furnham (Feb. 2012) a Professor of Psychology at University College London, discusses how up to a fifth of us meet our partners at work and a quarter to half of office romances lead to marriage. Online surveys and academic research over the last few decades have clearly illustrated the prevalence of workplace romance; it has been suggested that workplace romance has been on the rise over the last 50 years (Goudreau, 2012a). In a 2011 survey by CareerBuilder.com, 40% of respondents revealed they had dated a coworker, while a third said they had married the person they dated at work (Adams, 2011, 2012; see also SHRM, 2011). Dillard and Witteman (1985) report that nearly 75% of the individuals they interviewed had either observed or participated in a romantic relationship at work. Nearly a quarter of managers say they have been involved in such a relationship at least once during their career (Peak, 1995). Several studies from North America have shown that in universities approximately 17% of female graduate students say that they had a sexual relationship with at least one of their professors while at university (Bellas & Gossett, 2001; Pope et al., 1979; Glaser & Thorpe, 1986), 26% of male faculty reported sexual involvement with female students (Fitzgerald et al., 1988). Workplaces are now recognized to have an important sexual component (Kakabadse & Kakabadse, 2004; Fleming, 2007). Given the pervasive nature of romantic and sexual relationships, it is surprising that it is so rarely discussed as behavior that happens at work or considered as organizational behavior in textbooks on management.

---

[1]University of Glasgow

Workplace romances are defined by Pierce and Aguinis (2001, p. 206) as "mutually desired relationships involving sexual attraction between two employees of the same organization". Romantic behavior is often distinguished from sexually harassing behavior which is unwelcome so, for example, Pierce et al. (1996) refer to workplace romance as a consensual relationship between two partners of the opposite sex that does not constitute unwanted or harassing activity. Definitions tend to exclude those who are not heterosexual (e.g. Dillard and Witteman, 1985; Mainiero, 1986; Powell, 1993; Powell and Mainiero, 1990 and Quinn, 1977) and similarly the research literature has been largely silent on the topic of same sex romances (Powell & Foley, 1998). The exception to this is Rumens (2008) who researched gay men's friendship and intimacy at work.

Many newspaper and academic articles note how workplace romance has increased due to the influx of women into the workforce (e.g. Powell & Foley, 1998). The way this fact is presented in much of the writing could easily (and unfairly!) be interpreted as women being seen to be at fault for the increasing levels of workplace romance and the problems that managers face in dealing with it. For example Swartz et al. (1987, p. 22) talked of how this is "… upsetting traditional organizational behavior modes" while Goudreau (2012a) notes "… as women entered the workplace in greater numbers … people are together more at work. It creates potential issues for the employer". The increasing number of women in the workplace then leads to greater opportunity for individuals to form romantic relationships. Second, people are expected to work longer hours and so are spending more time at work and less time with family. Third, the higher divorce rate is likely to be related to a greater incidence of workplace romance (both through divorce allowing employees to become available for relationships, and also through divorce being a consequence of workplace romance).

Attraction at work tends to happen between those who work in close proximity, collaborate together to accomplish their work, are similar in attitude to each other and find it easy to interact (Byrne & Neuman, 1992; Quinn, 1977; Salvaggio et al., 2011). Working together fosters an increase in the interaction among coworkers as well as a sense of common purpose and goals which increases the likelihood of personal attraction. Sharing a subjective experience, such as a similar reaction to another person or event, can also lead to interpersonal attraction (Pinel et al., 2006).

Romance and workplace culture

While there has been comparatively little attention given to the context in which workplace romance occurs (Williams et al., 1999), research has found that slow-paced traditional and conservative organizational cultures (such as those found in banking and finance) are associated with fewer workplace romances while fast-paced liberal cultures (such as those found in advertising) are associated with more. Mainiero (1989, p. 279) asked her respondents to describe their company's culture as either "action oriented, creative, innovative" (liberal) or "reactive, conservative, traditional" (conservative). She found that there was stigma attached to office romances in conservative organizational cultures, for women employees in particular. Conservative cultures can threaten career advancement, again, particularly for women. In more liberal organizational cultures there were no stigmas attached to office romances (Bass, 1989).

Mano and Gabriel (2006) take a different tack and instead talk of hot and cold workplace climates. Romance is more likely in "hot" workplace climates, those characterized by a hedonistic orientation and a focus on physical attractiveness. An example would be a spa resort and hotel providing massage, sauna and other services (Mano & Gabriel, 2006). Jobs that are characterized by a sexual simmer (Giuffre & Williams, 1994) or a high level of sexual innuendo and flirtation offer a more hospitable climate for romance (Salvaggio et al., 2011). Jobs included in this category may include those in tourism, advertising, mass media, catering, and retail (Mano & Gabriel, 2006).

An example of love in a cold climate
A male employee working for a high tech company, part of a multinational organization and whose employees were mostly engineers, was relocated to work in the US where he met a woman who had been working for the same firm there; they began a romantic relationship. The firm saw their relationship as potentially damaging to the company and so assigned them to different team projects. Despite the company seeking to protect itself by keeping them apart, they married. (Adapted from Mano & Gabriel, 2006)

An example of love in a hot climate
This setting was a spa resort and hotel. There, a number of couples had met and married. In some cases a spouse was brought to work in the organization. Work was around the clock so close working contact over long hours was encouraged. A male assistant chef fell in love with a female shift manager and they got married. In order

to have a religious wedding, he changed his religion for her. (Adapted from Mano & Gabriel, 2006)

Such sexualized environments probably influence incidents of romance, as perceptions of coworkers as sexual beings are emphasized. Workers themselves often see sexual behaviors at work along a continuum ranging from pleasurable, to tolerable, to harassing (Williams et al., 1999). They may be more likely to tolerate sexualized interactions if they see it as a requirement of their jobs. For example service workers (e.g. bar staff) are subjected to sexual comments, leering, and touching from customers. Sexual behavior can be a requirement of the job. At one restaurant chain it was found that the female workers were hired to wait on mostly male customers; the women were required to wear skimpy uniforms, play with hula hoops, dance with customers, and placed orders by reaching up to a line in the kitchen (which exposed their midriffs) (Loe, 1996).

It is interesting to see worker's reactions to sexual advances, as we know that men and women see sexual behaviors and harassment differently. Men tend to view the same sexual behaviors at work as less offensive and harmful than do women (Berdahl, 2007) and hold more favorable attitudes towards romance and sexual intimacy at work (Pierce, 1998). Some men report wanting to experience more social behavior at work (Berdahl et al., 1996). This is probably because of gender differences in power; as men tend to have more power in organizations, be taller and stronger, earn higher salaries and hold higher ranks they are more economically and organizationally powerful. Sexual behavior initiated by men is therefore viewed as potentially more threatening and coercive than sexual behavior initiated by women (Berdahl & Aquino, 2009). Also reactions may differ depending on who workers find objectionable. In a study of restaurants, Giuffre and Williams (1994) found that waiters and waitresses eagerly engaged in flirtatious, sexual bantering with coworkers of the same race, ethnicity, class, and sexual orientation. However they defined identical behaviors by coworkers of different backgrounds a sexual harassment. This suggests that it is not the specific sexual behavior that some workers find objectionable but the combination of that behavior with the characteristics of the individual.

Sex and power

While sexual behavior at work primarily comes from peers (Gutek, 1985; US Merit Systems Protection Board, 1994), sexual behavior initiated by individuals with more power should be appraised as more threatening and coercive than that initiated by those with equal or less power (Bourgeois & Perkins, 2003). It is not surprising then that women, as the less powerful sex, may have more negative attitudes about their sexual experiences. In a study of sexual behavior at work (e.g. sexual jokes and propositions) Berdahl and Aquino (2009) found that some women and many men enjoyed sexual behavior at work. Over one quarter of survey respondents found it fun or flattering, while almost one half evaluated it as benign. Men tended to enjoy both ambient sexual behavior (sexual jokes, language) and direct sexual behavior (direct sexual comments and advances) but women tended to dislike both. Employees' work-related outcomes (withdrawing from work, neglecting tasks, and thinking about quitting) were worse the more they experienced sexual behavior in their workplaces, regardless of whether they disliked or enjoyed the behavior. The more frequently they experienced sexual behavior, the less they felt valued. These results suggest that sexual behaviors at work cause harm. A study by Collins (1983) also showed that many of the women felt that sexual liaisons at work had been harmful to their careers. Thus, sexual behaviors may or may not be considered "romantic".

Romance and gender

There do appear to be good reasons why women might be more cautious than men about being involved in a workplace romance. The experiences of women and men in workplace romance have been shown to be very different (Dillard & Miller, 1988; Powell & Foley, 1998; Quinn, 1977) at least in part due to their differences in power and status in organizations. If a woman's mentor is at a higher level in the organization, she can be unfairly accused of "sleeping her way to the top" (Quinn & Lees, 1984; Clawson & Kram, 1984). In addition there seems to be a belief that women will use, and lie about, sex; there is distrust towards women (Berebitsky, 2012; Goudreau, 2012b). Lower level participants in hierarchical romances are more likely to be relocated or terminated than higher level participants, especially if they are female (Pierce et al., 1996; Devine & Markiewicz, 1990; Quinn, 1977). Over 30 years ago Quinn (1977) found that women were twice as likely to be terminated by their companies as the men with whom they were involved. More recently Riach and Wilson (2007) found that employees believed that if a relationship between two people at different levels in the organization broke up, the more junior person should leave; this was usually the female. In addition women were construed as "over emotional" and "unstable" whereas men were "coping". Women have also been found to be more negatively evaluated than men in their motivation for participation in workplace romance (Anderson & Fisher, 1991; Anderson & Hunsaker, 1985; Morgan & Davidson, 2008; Quinn, 1977). Women are more likely to be perceived as being involved in a workplace romance to move up the organizational hierarchy whereas men are perceived as being involved to satisfy their ego needs (Anderson & Fisher, 1991). Women elicit more negative reactions from other organizational members than men who enter workplace romance for the same reasons (Dillard, 1987; Dillard et al., 1994). In addition women suffer from the negative stereotypes of slut, tart, and slag for being involved in a relationship at work, whereas men do not (Riach & Wilson, 2007). There is then a differential evaluation of women and men involved in workplace romances, reflecting the sex structuring of organizations where power remains in the hands of men. Powell and Foley (1998) argue that workplace romances may also be particularly hazardous for same sex couples due to negative reactions of fellow employees.

Reactions to romance

For those who choose to be involved in a workplace romance, historically most have tried to keep the romance a secret but fail to do so (Anderson & Hunsaker, 1985; Quinn, 1977; Quinn & Lees, 1984). Fewer people now keep their workplace romance secret (65% of workers are public with their workplace romance; Adams, 2011). There are however good reasons why the couple may try to keep their romance private. When the romance becomes public knowledge, it provokes reactions from others (Foley & Powell, 1999) and it stimulates substantial gossip (Dillard & Miller, 1988; Quinn, 1977). Romance at work can invoke discussions about love, sex, family, power, justice, ethics, and norms regarding acceptable behavior at work (Powell & Foley, 1998). Hierarchical romances stimulate more response as they raise issues of power and dependency (Mainiero, 1986). As career rewards (e.g. pay rises, favorable job assignments, and promotion) may be granted in exchange for personal favors in hierarchical romances, other organizational members may fear that the relationship is being exploited for personal gain; this then raises issues of equity and justice for non-participants (Greenberg, 1987). Reactions from coworkers are further intensified if the relationship is extra-marital – this is the case in about a third of romances (Mainiero, 1989). Dillard et al. (1994) found that workplace romances in which one or both participants were married led to greater deterioration of the work group's social climate. Powell (2001) examined coworkers' reactions to hierarchical romance between an older, married senior level executive and a younger single lower level employee, using a vignette (a paragraph of text in this case telling a story concerning making judgments about romantic relation-ships at work). He found that respondents regarded a hierarchical romance as representing a more serious problem for the organization when they believed that the lower level participant was motivated by job concerns. The most negative reactions were to a female participant at a lower level being involved with a male participant at a higher level. This is because coworkers fear that the romance will disrupt the conduct of work, affecting the productivity of individuals involved or fairness (for example, fearing that sex and power will be traded as male supervisors may show favoritism toward their female subordinate by providing lighter workloads, promotion, pay or other special benefits (Mainiero, 1986; Pierce et al., 1996)).

Causes and effects of workplace romance

Motives for romance

Research has identified a number of different motives for an employee's participation in a workplace romance. It may be (a) a sincere desire to seek a long-term companion or a spouse (a love motive) (b) a desire to seek adventure, excitement sexual experience or ego satisfaction (ego motive) or (c) a desire to seek advancement, secur-ity, power, financial rewards, lighter workloads or increased holidays time (job-related motive) (Anderson & Fisher, 1991; Brown & Allgeier, 1996; Dillard & Broetzmann, 1989; Quinn, 1977; Mainiero, 1986). Employees can have multiple motives for participation in the romance and each individual in a romantic pair may have different motives. However the focus of research has rarely been motivation and has usually been concerned with impact.

The impact of romance

Much of the research on organizational romance has a functionalist and managerial orientation focusing on whether or not romance impacts negatively on job productivity. A substantial proportion of the research literature shows that job productivity can be negatively affected by romance due to excessive chatting, long lunches and extended discussions behind closed doors, missed meetings, later arrivals, early departures, and costly errors (Quinn & Judge, 1978). Other negative effects include coworker disapproval, cynicism, and hostility (Anderson & Fisher, 1991) as well as concerns about whether there will be favoritism and employment benefits given to one party in the relationship by the other (Anderson & Hunsaker, 1985). Romantic relationships adversely affect those involved and the coworkers who observe them (Swartz et al., 1987). On the other hand research has also shown that employees involved in a romantic relationship can be more productive at work (Dillard, 1987; Dillard & Broetzmann, 1989; Pierce, 1998; Quinn & Lees, 1984). The level of productivity may be lower at the start of the relationship due to the large amounts of time and energy invested in it. After the initial excitement of the new romance diminishes, productivity tends to rise steadily; thus, the stage of romance appears to have an impact (Pierce et al., 1996).

The motive for the relationship also impacts on productivity. Those who participate with a "love" motive or a sincere desire for companionship tend to show an increase in productivity while those who participate with an "ego motive" or the desire for excitement, or with a "job related motive", or the desire for advancement, security, or power tend to show no change in performance (Dillard, 1987). Dillard explains that those who show a love motive fear the negative consequences of inadequate performance and so demonstrate increased effort in order to impress their supervisors. Job satisfaction and organizational commitment have also been shown to increase (Pierce & Aguinis, 2003). The extent to which an employee is satisfied with their personal life is positively associated with the extent to which they are satisfied with their job (Judge & Watanabe, 1993). Having a gratifying workplace romance may then create an emotional "spillover effect" in which the employees' positive emotional reactions from their romance spill over on their emotional reactions to their job (Pierce, 1998). Workplace romances that lead to marriage may help individuals to work to their maximum potential because their personal needs are being satisfied and so benefit performance (Mainiero, 1989). However, as Boyd (2010) notes, there is no benchmark evidence in the literature of any attempt to compare productivity gains or losses.

Alongside the positive and negative impacts of workplace romance on those in the romantic pair, there are a range of impacts on colleagues. For example Cole (2009) notes how workplace romance can energize workplace morale and motivate other employees, encourage creativity and increase innovation. It can soften work-related personality conflicts because the workplace romance parties are happier and easier to get along with. It can improve teamwork, communication, and cooperation. However it is interesting to note that, in Cole's (2009) study of coworkers who had observed workplace romance, none of the participants reported any positive effects of workplace romance on the performance of coworkers or on the work environment. When there was an impact, it was invariably negative. Negative outcomes include conflicts of interest, flawed or biased decision-making and other workplace inequities that have a negative impact on the individual and organizational performance and on the careers of one or both partners (Powell, 1993). One of the most negative outcomes of romance for one of the partners involved appears to be, according to the research, the accusation of sexual harassment.

Romance and sexual harassment

Workplace romance appears to be a major source of sexual harassment (Mainiero, 1989; Slovak, 1991). If a workplace romance breaks down, one partner's attempts at reconciliation may be perceived by the other former partner as harassment. The employer may be held responsible for not protecting that employee from such harassment. For example, 24% of respondents in one survey indicated that sexual harassment claims had occurred in their organization as a direct result of workplace romance (Society for Human Resource Management, 1998). About 10% of women have left a job because of sexual harassment (Gutek et al., 1990). Knowing that nearly 48% of workplace romances dissolve (Henry, 1995), perhaps we should better understand the conditions under which such terminated relationships result in sexually harassing behaviors at work. Pierce and Aguinis (2009) estimate that there will be one incidence of harassment for every 704 romances. In 2001 they proposed that a number of factors play a critical role in increasing the likelihood that terminated romances lead to sexually harassing behavior. These include the type of romance (for example how genuine the love motive is), the partner's social power (for example if one person in the relationship is a supervisor who can exchange a reward such as a lighter workload for sexual favors), who initiated the dissolution of the romantic relationship, the male partner's sexual proclivity and the organization's tolerance for sexual harassment. They predict, for example that dissolved flings have a relatively low likelihood of leading to sexually harassing behaviors as the parties involved would move onto a novel romantic relationship.

Organizational responses to romance

Given the link between terminated workplace romance and sexual harassment, it might be argued that it is surprising not many organizations develop policies for managing workplace romance, particularly given the extensive debate in the law journals about the degree to which an employer may legitimately constrain an employee's liberty in matters of romance (Boyd, 2010). Yet relatively few organizations have written policies on workplace romance (Appelbaum et al., 2007). Research from the Society for Human Resource Management (1998) demonstrated that only 13% of organizations had a workplace romance policy; by 2006 less than 30% had policies (Parks, 2006). Most policies cover only the most blatant instances in which workplace romance may disrupt the conduct of work. The most frequent restrictions are bans on romance between supervisors and subordinates and public displays of affection (SHRM, 1998). Researchers and practitioners argue that more organizations need to develop and enforce policies to manage romantic relationships at work, particularly those relationships that are hierarchical and involve a social power differential (Pierce & Aguinis, 1997, 2009; Paul & Townsend, 1998). On the other hand it may be argued that if workplace romance is being managed fairly and consistently, there may be no need for a formal policy. The majority (70%) of Fortune 500 chief executive officers surveyed said that workplace romances are none of the company's business (Fisher, 1994) which probably explains why such a small percentage have a policy on romance. While professional HR managers may seek to avoid intervening in workplace romances, those employees who do not engage in workplace romances believe that HR intervention is needed more frequently than indicated by HR practitioners (Michelson et al., 2010). This may be because, if romances are kept secret or considered a private affair by managers who have no policy on romance, abuses of power may go unnoticed and undealt with by management. This would be a concern for coworkers and others. Fairness of managerial action does seem to be the main concern for both coworkers (Cole, 2009; Riach & Wilson, 2007) and job seekers (Pierce et al., 2012).

An organization that tried to ban romance

Wal-Mart, as an organization, felt it had a moral duty to protect its employees from sexuality in the workplace, and specifically to prevent the possibility of adultery by married employees. Laurel Allen (23) and Sam Johnson (20) had been working together at

Wal-Mart in New York for a few months when they began dating in January 1992. They were employed in different departments and neither was a supervisor. In February the store manager fired both of them. The reason she gave was that Laurel, though legally separated from her husband, was not yet divorced and the romance was inconsistent with the company's "strongly held belief in and support of the family unit" (Dworkin, 1997; Schaner, 1994).
Adapted from Fortune (1993) and Boyd (2010)

Organizations have varied considerably in their response to consensual relationships at work. Some, such as Wal-Mart in Germany have tried to introduce an ethics policy to ban romantic liaisons at work (Personnel Today, 2005). Prior to 1994 (when they lost a court battle) Wal-Mart was well known for its anti-fraternization policy in the US. In 1993 they fired an employee who acknowledged committing adultery (see case above and Amaral, 2006; Boyd, 2010; Halverson, 1993). Wal-Mart later revised its policy to exclude any reference to married employees but to ban dating between supervisors and individuals who report directly to them (Powell & Foley, 1998) only to lose its court appeal in Germany when it tried to ban these relationships there (Personnel Today, 2005). Other organizations to introduce strict nonfraternization policies include Staples (an office supplies retail chain) and Lloyd's of London (Schaefer & Tudor, 2001).

Some employers have introduced consensual dating agreements requiring a dating couple to sign a document affirming that their workplace romance is consensual, that they will not engage in favoritism and neither will take legal action against the employer or each other if the relationship founders. While Schaefer and Tudor (2001) and Wilson et al. (2003) provide examples of specimen contracts, Kramer (2000) and others question if these contracts are possible violations of the privacy rights of employees.

Other organizations such as Southwest Airlines, AT & T, Xerox (Budak, 2012) and Ben & Jerry's have a more positive view and actively promote romance. Southwest Airlines boasts 1,200 married couples out of its staff of 35,000 (Budak, 2012). Ben & Jerry's human resource manager is quoted as saying "We expect that our employees will date, fall in love, and become partners. If a problem comes up, we encourage employees to let us know and we'll talk about it" (Loftus, 1995, p. 8; Amaral, 2006, p. 10). The current advice to employers appears to be to establish a policy or guidelines about workplace romance and ensure that all employees understand the potential consequences (Colby, 1991;

Paul & Townsend, 1998). In the research I conducted with Kathleen Riach, in the public house sector (bars and pubs), we discovered informal "house rules" about romance at work (Riach & Wilson, 2007).

The literature advises organizations to be cautious of overly strict anti-fraternization policies (Amaral, 2006). Policy makers in most organizations believe that workplace romances cannot be banned and should be ignored unless they present a serious threat to the conduct of work or group morale (Powell & Foley, 1998). Hierarchical and utilitarian romances (where a lower rank employee has a job related motive and a higher rank employee has an ego motive) are thought to present the greatest threat (Powell & Foley, 1998; Powell, 2001). Even those organizations who have a positive view of workplace romance may wish to try to manage hierarchical romances. For example Southwest Airlines employ a policy of reassigning one party in a couple where there is a supervisor-subordinate relationship (Budak, 2012).

Future directions

The vast majority of the research is US-based. Boyd (2010) notes that of the 400 articles on workplace romance, there is just one article from outside the US for every 10 articles originating from the US. It would be interesting to know more about a variety of countries and cultures in which workplace romance occurs. For example Nadeem (2009) begins to explore amorous relationships in an Indian call centre. The research to date has tended to use surveys (either mail or telephone) as well as case studies. It has been assumed that because of the sensitive nature of the topic, obtaining interviews with those actually involved in romance at work will be problematic. Most studies are conducted with convenience samples such as MBA students or executives waiting in airports and have used closed-end surveys (Williams et al., 1999). As a result the samples are unrepresentative in terms of gender (for example 85.6% of Harrison and Lee's (1986) sample were male) as well as class and status. Most investigators have used third party observations of romantic behavior (Anderson & Hunsaker, 1985; Harrison & Lee, 1986; Quinn, 1977); these individuals may or may not have had firsthand experience of workplace romance. Research should now concentrate on firsthand experience as there is very little reliable information about what is actually taking place in organizations and why (Williams et al., 1999).

Little is known about policies, particularly informal policies that attempt to manage intimate relationships such as the ones we uncovered

(Riach & Wilson, 2007). We also know very little about workers' reactions to workplace policies and their implementation (for example requiring one member of the couple to move jobs), and if this is still happening. As much of what is known about workplace romance is now as much as 20 or 30 years old, we need to know whether or not companies are still terminating the employment of one party in the romance, how pervasive workplace policies on romance are (both formal and informal), how consistently they are enforced and their impact on the behavior of different groups. Little has been done to clarify the ethical issues involved in consensual sexual relationships in the workplace (Irvine, 2000; Bowes-Sperry & Powell, 1999). Are women still being more negatively evaluated than men in their motivation for participation in workplace romance? Although research on sex stereotypes shows "remarkable durability" over time and place (Burgess & Borgida, 1999), it would be interesting to see if this was still the case with sex stereotypes such as women tend to be warm, caring, and deferential in relationships at work whereas men are strong and controlling. Or if myths endure such as "it is women who sleep their way to the top". Very little research has looked at how sexual intimacy with a superior is used to enhance career status (the exception is Harris and Ogbonna (2006) who found that four out of 112 interviewees admitted to enhancing their careers through sexual intimacy with a superior). Future research requires more interview-based research with parties in romance. Very little research has used face-to-face interviews with those who have actually been involved in workplace romance to better understand romantic relationships. Where they have been used, some interesting findings have emerged. For example it would be interesting to see if Cole's (2009) results showing no positive impact of organizational romance on coworkers would be replicated in a different study.

Tourigny and Dougan (2004) suggest that researchers have typically focused on a relationship between two individuals. However individuals often form networks of relationships and a partner could be experiencing more than one intimate relationship at a time. In addition there is little conceptualization and empirical investigation of relationships involving infidelity and extra-marital affairs; researchers have carefully avoided the treatment of extramarital affairs as an organizational phenomenon perhaps because this has been seen as an area too sensitive for research. Tourigny and Dougan also point out that homosexual relationships tend to be ignored; these too should have a greater focus of attention in the future. More research is needed to better understand how romantic relationships affect others who are not themselves involved in relationships but who are aware of them (Bellas & Gossett, 2001). We also need to know more about the contexts of romance; in particular how it is viewed and unfolds in blue collar and non-professional settings (Riach & Wilson, 2007) as, to date, most of the research has been in white collar, office settings.

What is missing from the research to date is an understanding of what the couple themselves think about how they are being treated. For example do people at work treat them as an invincible duo with extra power bestowed on them as they are a couple, rather than two separate individuals with more limited power? Do their work colleagues assume that if one feels strongly on a particular work issue, the other will agree? If one of them goes to a meeting, when both are on the invitation list, is that seen as acceptable? Do couples affect how information is shared; for example do their colleagues fear "pillow talk" and therefore trust the individuals in the couple less with sensitive information?

Another area ripe for research is an understanding of the inconsistency of espoused views on romance and actual behavior. For example research has found that while a manager might advise their assistants against having romantic relationships with their subordinates, they may actually be "serial romancers" themselves (see Wilson & Riach, 2008). Also we know very little about the norms of behavior that are considered acceptable, the rules of engagement (Wilson & Riach, 2008), who can do what to whom and the effect of hierarchy, class, and gender on this.

A dangerous liaison
One workplace romance may have been the cause of the loss of lives. In 2006 a ferry ran aground and sank in Canadian waters while navigating a narrow and hazardous passage. Alone together in the bridge were the male fourth officer and the female quartermaster who were known to have had a relationship. No course corrections or speed changes were made for the thirty minutes before the ferry ran aground (Boyd 2010).

Conclusions

The literature appears to have followed a very particular course where surveys have shown the extent of romance and the researchers have examined some of the positive and negative impacts of romance, warning of some of the dangers which managers should be aware of. However there are wide areas of romance at work that we still know very little about and so it remains an area ripe for research.

Given the emphasis in the literature on the need for managers to ensure fair treatment in organizations when romance occurs, it is not surprising that there are recommendations for managers to follow. The most extreme involve attempting to ban romance. The anthropologist Margaret Mead says unequivocally "you don't make passes or sleep with people you work with" (Mead, 1980, p. 55). Prohibition may be required for some employees where there are clear conflicts of interest, for example managers may want to prohibit prison officers or those in the police service dating known felons. Managers may wish to ban romances in all types of organizations in an attempt to stop the potential for the abuse of power differential between superior and subordinate or the threat of loss of productivity due to resentment of coworkers if they perceive favorable treatment given to the subordinate partner in the romance, or sexual harassment lawsuits resulting from dissolved relationships. However they may then be accused of breaching human rights, as Wal-Mart discovered in Germany (Personnel Today, 2005).

Some companies, rather than ban romance, have tried to manage it through consensual dating agreements or "love contracts" (Economist, 2005) as noted earlier. As an alternative, Pierce and Aguinis (2009) recommend a written workplace romance policy that is clearly communicated to employees; the policy should be part of the organization's ethical code of conduct. It should, at minimum, state and justify the types of romances that are permitted or encouraged (e.g. between peers from different departments), the types that are discouraged (e.g. extramarital affairs), and the types that are prohibited (e.g. direct reporting supervisor/subordinate relationships, senior level executives, and lower level employees). Managers are advised to intervene when the romance causes work disruption or participants' job performance drops. The challenge for managing romance is balancing the employer's liability for harassment against employees' rights for privacy (Wilson et al., 2003). Boyd (2010) suggests that future research should further examine the consequences of adopting managerial policies and procedures to manage workplace romance. Given the pervasiveness of workplace romance all year round, not just in February, and the relative lack of research, it is a topic where there is much more to be learned.

References

Adams, S. (2011). *How to have a successful office romance*, Forbes.com, 31st August, p. 12. Found at http://www.forbes.com/sites/susanadams/2011/08/31/how-to-have-a-successful-office-romance/

Adams, S. (2012). *The state of the office romance 2012*, Forbes.com, 10th February, p. 31. Found at http://www.forbes.com/sites/susanadams/2012/02/10/the-state-of-the-office-romance-2012/

Amaral, H. P. (2006). *Workplace romance and fraternization policies*, Schmidt Labor Research Center Seminar Research Series. Found at http://www.uri.edu/research/lrc/research/papers/Amaral_Fraternization.pdf

Anderson, C. J. & Fisher, C. (1991). Male-female relationships in the workplace: Perceived motivations in office romance, *Sex Roles*, *25*, 163–180.

Anderson, C. I. & Hunsaker, P. L. (1985). Why there's romancing at the office and why it's everybody's problem, *Personnel*, *62*(2), 57–63.

Appelbaum, S., Marinescu, A., Klenin, J., & Bytautas, J. (2007). Fatal attractions: The (mis) management of workplace romance, *International Journal of Business Research*, *7*(4), 31–43.

Bass, S. L. (1989). Connecticut Q &A: Lisa Ma Mainiero; "There's potential for exploitation", *New York Times*, 25th June. Found at http://www.nytimes.com/1989/06/25/nyregion/connecticut-q-a-lisa-a-mainiero-there-s-potential-for-exploitation.html?pagewanted=all&src=pm

Bellas, M. L. & Gossett, J. L. (2001). Love or the "lecherous professor": Consensual sexual relationships between professors and students, *The Sociological Quarterly*, *42*(4), 529–558.

Berdahl, J. L. (2007). The sexual harassment of uppity women, *Journal of Applied Psychology*, *92*, 425–437.

Berdahl, J. L., Magley, V. J., & Waldo, C. R. (1996). The sexual harassment of men: Exploring the concept with theory and data, *Psychology of Women Quarterly*, *20*, 527–547.

Berdahl, J. L. & Aquino, K. (2009). Sexual behavior at work: Fun or folly, *Journal of Applied Social Psychology*, *94*(1) 34–47.

Berebitsky, J. (2012). *Sex and the Office: A History of Gender, Power and Desire*. Yale: Yale University Press.

Bourgeois, M. J. & Perkins, J. (2003). A test of evolutionary and socio-cultural explanations of reactions to sexual harassment, *Sex Roles*, *49*, 343–351.

Bowes-Sperry, L. & Powell, G. (1999). Observers' reactions to social-sexual behavior at work: An ethical decision making perspective, *Journal of Management*, *25*(6), 779–802.

Boyd, C. (2010). The debate over the prohibition of romance in the workplace, *Journal of Business Ethics*, *97*(2), 325–338.

Brown, T. J. & Allgeier, E. R. (1996). The impact of participant characteristics, perceived motives, and job behaviors on coworkers' evaluations of workplace romances, *Journal of Applied Social Psychology*, *26*, 577–595.

Budak, J. (2012). Love among the cubicles, *Canadian Business*, *85*(8), 24–28.

Burgess, D. & Borgida, E. (1999). Who women are, who women should be: Descriptive and prescriptive gender stereotyping in sex discrimination, *Psychology, Public Policy and Law*, *5*(3), 665–692.

Byrne, D. & Neuman, J. H. (1992). The implications of attraction research for organizational issues: in K. Kelley (ed.) *Issues, Theory and Research in Industrial/ Organizational Psychology*. North Holland, Amsterdam (pp. 29–70).

Clawson, J. G. & Kram, K. E. (1984). Managing cross-gender mentoring, *Business Horizons, 27*(3), 22–32.

Colby, L. (1991). Regulating love, *Personnel, 68*(6), 23.

Cole, N. (2009). Workplace romance: A justice analysis, *Journal of Business Psychology, 24*, 363–372.

Collins, E. A. (1983). Managers and lovers, *Harvard Business Review* (September–October), 142–153.

Devine, I. & Markiewicz, D. (1990). Cross-sex relationships at work and the impact of gender stereotypes, *Journal of Business Ethics, 9*, 333–338.

Dillard, J. P. (1987). Close relationships at work: Perceptions of the motives and performance of relational participants, *Journal of Social and Personal Relationships, 4*, 179–193.

Dillard, J. P. & Broetzmann, S. M. (1989). Romantic relationships at work: Perceived changes in job-related behaviors as a function of participant's motive, partner's motive and gender, *Journal of Applied Social Psychology, 19*, 93–110.

Dillard, J. P., Hale, J. L., & Segrin, C. (1994). Close relationships in task environments: Perceptions of relational types, illicitness and power, *Management Communication Quarterly, 7*(3), 227–255.

Dillard, J. P. & Miller, K. I. (1988). Intimate relationships in task environments: in S. W. Duck (ed.) *Handbook of Personal Relationships*. New York: Wiley (pp. 449–465).

Dillard, J. P. & Witteman, H. (1985). Romantic relationships at work: Organizational and personal influences, *Human Communication Research, 12*, 99–116.

Dworkin, T. M. (1997). It's my life-leave me alone: Off-the-job employee association rights, *American Business Law Journal, 35*(1), 47–103.

Economist (2005). The end of the office affair? *Economist*, 12th March, *374*(8417), 82.

Fisher, A. B. (1994). Getting comfortable with couples in the workplace, *Fortune, 130*(October 3), 138–144.

Fitzgerald, L. F., Weitzman, L. M., Gold, Y., & Ormerod, M. (1988). Academic harassment: Sex and denial in scholarly garb, *Psychology of Women Quarterly, 12*(3), 329–340.

Fleming, P. (2007). Sexuality, power and resistance in the workplace, *Organization Studies, 28*(2), 239–256.

Foley, S. & Powell, G. N. (1999). Not all is fair in love and work: Coworkers' preferences for and responses to managerial interventions regarding workplace romances, *Journal of Organizational Behavior, 20*, 1043–1056.

Fortune (1993). *Can smoking or bungee jumping get you canned?* 9th August. Found at http://money.cnn.com/magazines/fortune/fortune_archive/1993/08/09/78170/index.htm

Furnham, A. (2012). On your head: Don't be surprised to find cupid among the cubicles, *The Sunday Times*, 12th February. Found at http://www.thesundaytimes.co.uk/sto/public/Appointments/article870552.ece

Giuffre, P. A. & Williams, C. L. (1994). Boundary lines: Labelling sexual harassment in restaurants, *Gender Soc*, 8, 378–401.

Glaser, R. D. & Thorpe, J. S. (1986). Unethical intimacy: A survey of sexual contact and advances between psychology educators and female graduate students, *American Psychologist*, 41, 43–51.

Goudreau, J. (2012a). *Would you sign a love contract … with your employer?* Forbes.com, 14th February. Found at http://www.forbes.com/sites/jennagoudreau/2012/02/14/would-you-sign-love-contract-with-employer-workplace-romance/

Goudreau, J. (2012b). *Sex at the office: Why so little has changed in 150 years*, Forbes.com, 22nd May. Found at http://www.forbes.com/sites/jennagoudreau/2012/05/22/sex-and-the-office-why-little-has-changed-in-150-years/

Greenberg, J. A. (1987). A taxonomy of organizational justice theories, *Academy of Management Review*, 12, 9–22.

Gutek, B. A. (1985). *Sex and the Workplace: The Impact of Sexual Behavior and Harassment on Women, Men and Organizations*. San Francisco: Jossey-Bass.

Gutek, B. A., Cohen, A. G., & Konrad, A. M. (1990). Predicting social-sexual behavior at work: A contact hypothesis, *Academy of Management Journal*, 33(3), 560–577.

Halverson, H. (1993). *Wal-Mart cited for dating policy leading to firing of employees.* Found at http://findarticles.com/p/articles/mi_m3092/is_n15_v32/ai_14334706/

Harris, L. C. & Ogbonna, E. (2006). Approaches to career success: An exploration of surreptitious career-success strategies, *Human Resource Management*, 45(1), 43–65.

Harrison, R. & Lee, R. (1986). Love at work, *Personnel Management*, January, 20–24.

Henry, D. (1995). Wanna date? The office may not be the place, *HR Focus*, 72(4), 14.

Irvine, W. B. (2000). Beyond sexual harassment, *Journal of Business Ethics*, 28, 353–360.

Judge, T. A. & Watanabe, S. (1993). Another look at the job satisfaction-life satisfaction relationship, *Journal of Applied Psychology*, 78(6), 939–948.

Kakabadse, N. & Kakabadse, A. (2004). *Intimacy: International Survey of the Sex Lives of People at Work*. Basingstoke: Palgrave.

Kramer, G. M. (2000). Limited license to fish off the company pier: Towards express employer policies on supervisor-subordinate fraternization, *Western New England Law Journal*, 22(1), 77–147.

Loe, M. (1996). Working for men – At the intersection of power, gender and sexuality, *Sociological Inquiry*, 66, 399–421.

Loftus, M. (1995). Frisky business – Romance in the workplace, *Psychology Today*, http://www.psychologytoday.com/articles/200910/frisky-business?page=8

Mainiero, L. (1986). A review and analysis of power dynamics in organizational romances, *Academy of Management Review*, 11, 750–762.

Mainiero, L. (1989). *Office Romance: Love, Power and Sex in the Workplace*. New York: Rawson Associates.

Mano, R. & Gabriel, Y. (2006). Workplace romances in cold and hot organizational climates: The experience of Israel and Taiwan, *Human Relations*, 59, 7–35.

Mead, M. (1980). A proposal: We need taboos on sex at work: in A. Neugarten and J. M. Shafritz (eds) *Sexuality in Organizations* (3rd edn). Oak Park, Ill.: Moore Publishing Company.

Michelson, G., Hurvy, R., & Grunauer, C. (2010). Workplace romances and HRM: A private matter or organizational concern? *International Journal of Employment Studies, 18*(2), 117–149.

Morgan, L. M. & Davidson, M. J. (2008). Sexual dynamics in mentoring relationships – A critical review, *British Journal of Management, 19*, S120–S129.

Nadeem, S. (2009). Macaulay's cyber children: The cultural politics of outsourcing in India, *Cultural Sociology, 3*(1), 102–122.

Parks, M. (2006). *Workplace Romance: Poll Findings*. Alexandria, VA: Society for Human Resource Management.

Paul, R. J. & Townsend, J. B. (1998). Managing the workplace romance: Protecting employee and employer rights, *Review of Business, 19*(2), 25–30.

Peak, M. H. (1995). Cupid in a three piece suit, *Management Review, 84*(4), 5.

Personnel Today (2005). *Court approval for liaisons in the workplace*, 22nd November. Found at http://www.personneltoday.com/articles/2005/11/22/32670/court-approval-for-liaisons-in-the-workplace.html

Pierce, C. A. (1998). Factors associated with participating in a romantic relationship in a work environment, *Journal of Applied Social Psychology, 28*, 1712–1730.

Pierce, C. A. & Aguinis, H. (1997). Bridging the gap between romantic relationships and sexual harassment in organizations, *Journal of Organizational Behavior, 18*, 197–200.

Pierce, C. A. & Aguinis, H. (2001). A framework for investigating the link between workplace romance and sexual harassment, *Group and Organization Management, 26*, 206–229.

Pierce, C. A. & Aguinis, H. (2003). Romantic relationships in organizations: A test of a model of formation and impact factors, *Management Research, 1*, 161–169.

Pierce, C. A. & Aguinis, H. (2009). Moving beyond a legal-centric approach to managing workplace romances: Organizationally sensible recommendations for HR leaders, *Human Resource Management*, May, 48(3), 447–464.

Pierce, C. A., Byrne, D., & Aguinis, H. (1996). Attraction in organizations: A model of workplace romance, *Journal of Organizational Behavior, 17*, 5–32.

Pierce, C. A., Karl, K., & Brey, E. T. (2012). Role of workplace romance policies and procedures on job pursuit intentions, *Journal of Managerial Psychology, 27*(3), 237–263.

Pinel, E. C., Long, A. E., Landau, M. J., Alexander, K., & Pyszczynski, T. (2006). Seeing I to I: A pathway to interpersonal connectedness, *Journal of Personality and Social Psychology, 90*, 243–257.

Pope, K., Levenson, H., & Schover, L. (1979). Sexual intimacy in psychology training: Results and implications of a national survey, *American Psychologist, 34*, 682–689.

Powell, G. N. (1993). *Women and Men in Management*, 2nd edition. Newbury Park, CA: Sage.

Powell, G. N. (2001). Workplace romances between senior-level executives and lower-level employees: An issue of work disruption and gender, *Human Relations, 54*, 1519–1544.

Powell, G. N. & Foley, S. (1998). Something to talk about: Romantic relationships in organizational settings, *Journal of Management*, 24(3), 421–448.
Powell, G. N. & Mainiero, L. A. (1990). What managers need to know about office romances, *Leadership and Organizational Development Journal*, 11, i–iii.
Quinn, R. E. (1977). Coping with Cupid: The formation, impact and management of romantic relationships in organizations, *Administrative Science Quarterly*, 22(1), 30–45.
Quinn, R. E. & Judge, N. A. (1978). The office romance: No bliss for the boss, *Management Review*, July, 43–49.
Quinn, R. E. & Lees, P. L. (1984). Attraction and harassment: The dynamics of sexual politics in the workplace, *Organizational Dynamics*, 13, 35–46.
Riach, K. & Wilson, F. (2007). Don't screw the crew: Exploring the rules of engagement in organizational romance, *British Journal of Management*, 18, 79–92.
Rumens, N. (2008). Working at intimacy: Gay men's workplace friendship, *Gender, Work and Organization*, 15(1), 9–30.
Salvaggio, A. N., Hopper, J. E., Streich, M., & Pierce, C. A. (2011). Why do fools fall in love (at work)? Factors associated with the incidence of workplace romance, *Journal of Applied Social Psychology*, 41(4), 906–937.
Schaefer, C. M. & Tudor, T. R. (2001). Managing workplace romances, *SAM Advanced Management Journal*, 66(3), 4–10.
Schaner, D. J. (1994). Romance in the workplace: Should employers act as chaperones? *Employee Relations Law Journal*, 20(1), 47–71.
SHRM (Society for Human Resource Management) (1998). *Workplace romance survey* (Item no 62.17014). Alexandria, VA: Public Affairs Department.
SHRM (Society for Human Resource Management) (2011). *Every day is Valentine's for some workers*, 2nd November. Found at http://www.shrm.org/Publications/HRNews/Pages/ValentinesDay.aspx
Slovak, P. C. (1991). Sex in the workplace: From romance to harassment, *The Human Resources Professional*, 3(3), 9–12.
Swartz, R. A., Warfield, A., & Wood, D. (1987). Coworker romances: Impact on the work group and on career oriented women, *Personnel*, 64(5), 22–35.
Tourigny, L. & Dougan, W. L. (2004). *More than love and work: A critique of existing treatments of organizational romance*, Proceedings of the 2004 Annual meetings of the Midwestern Academy of Management, Minneapolis, USA.
US Merit Systems Protection Board, (1994). *Sexual Harassment in the Federal Workplace: Trends, Progress, Continuing Challenges*. Washington, DC: US Government Printing Office.
Williams, C. L., Giuffre, P. A., & Dellinger, K. (1999). Sexuality in the workplace: Organizational control, sexual harassment and the pursuit of pleasure, *Annual Review of Sociology*, 25, 73–93.
Wilson, F. & Riach, K. (2008). *Organizational romance: Deviancy and discourse, where "Love Conquers All"*, Invited paper given to Women in Science Conference organized by the Network of Female Professors at Radboud University, Nijmegan, Netherlands on 6th March.
Wilson, R. J., Filosa, C., & Fennel, A. (2003). Romantic relationships at work: Does privacy trump the dating police? *Defense Counsel Journal*, 70(1), 78–88.

3
Guanxi in Organizations: Cross-Cultural Perspectives on an Enduring Construct

Kevin Lo[1], Shaohui Chen[2], and Marie Wilson[3]

Haier is now a global brand in major home appliances, but it was not always so. In 1984, Zhang Ruimin was appointed as the director of Qingdao General Refrigerator Factory, Haier's predecessor. The factory was running at a loss and the banks of the time were not allowed to lend money to non-state-owned enterprises. Zhang had to borrow the funds from locals so that employees could have a decent Spring Festival.

Zhang recruited new leadership to turn this small collectively-owned factory around. Zhang knew a young technical officer from the local government bureau and recruited her to the company on the basis of her observed studiousness and sense of accountability: "you expect 2 from her, but she will get 10 for you". For Yang Mianmian, accepting the invitation meant her life path changed from a traditional public sector employee to a company leadership position in China's transition to a market economy. She reflects that "assisting Zhang's effort was a great opportunity for me ... following him I could think boldly, ... and success [would follow] eventually". She gave up her existing career path, and worked countless days and hours to move the company toward competitiveness.

In 1985, in order to arouse quality awareness among the employees, Zhang publically destroyed 76 Haier refrigerators that did not meet quality requirements. The value of each refrigerator was more than two years' salary of an ordinary factory employee, so that was a

---

[1] School of Management, University of San Francisco
[2] Management, China Europe International Business School
[3] Dean of Griffith Business School

moment of "hammer with tears". Yang not only followed Zhang by making deductions from wages for quality problems, but also enhanced the quality orientation by introducing a quality control system and culture. In the ensuing 27 years, Yang was a consistently loyal follower of Zhang's brand strategy and vision, bringing Zhang's management philosophy to every corner of Haier, and spending years bringing the message to every Haier employee. An independent director of Haier notes: "without Yang Mianmian's work, it would be impossible to execute Zhang's initiatives. She is very good at [putting] policy into practice". It is impossible to imagine Haier's success without Yang's commitment and contribution.

In China, the story of Haier's leadership duo is seen as a classic example of *guanxi*. The relationship is long term, involves loyalty, sacrifice and commitment, and is based on mutual respect, contribution, and affective (rather than instrumental) ties. In the context of organizations, it is also clearly focused on the success of the company, although it also impacts the success of the individuals involved. With Haier's success, Yang rose to become the President of Haier Group, and Zhang remained as CEO. The two are referred to as the "golden partners", as both have done well through their roles, but also exemplify a positive partnership.

Understanding *guanxi*

Taken together, *guanxi* translates to "network", "connection", or "relationship" (Chen & Chen, 2004; Luo, 2000; Yang, 1994), and forms the basis for all social relationships in China (Luo, 2000). Liang (1949) argues that the Chinese are neither individual-based nor society-based, but rather are relationship-based. Chinese people cultivate and maintain close *guanxi* relationships and leverage them for information and favors (Luo, 1997; Xin & Pearce, 1996; Yang, 1994), and good *guanxi* is central to accomplishing anything in China, for Chinese and non-Chinese alike (Farh et al., 1998; Tsang, 1998; Wall, 1990).

While Westerners may regard *guanxi* as an ancient principle, in reality – much like "networking", *guanxi* is a product of the recent past. The term, *guanxi* (关系), was used in colloquial speech nearly a century ago (Chen & Chen, 2004; Luo, 1997). However, the word is not found in either of the classic Chinese dictionaries *Ciyuan* "Word Source" or *Cihai* "Word Sea". The classical term *lun* (伦), found in Confucian writings, captures the essence of relationships (Yang, 1994). Linguistically, *guanxi* is comprised of the two monosyllabic Chinese words; guan and xi. *Guan*, as a noun, originally meant "door/gate", which referred to a strategic pass or junction in wartime. As a verb, it means "to close". *Xi* is a verb meaning "to tie up" or "to have bearing on".

The traditional roots of *guanxi* are primarily located in two sources: Confucian morals and the tradition of wandering knights. According to Pye (1982), the Confucian virtues of filial piety (孝), loyalty (忠), and trust (信) form the cultural roots of *guanxi,* with their emphasis on relationships. Confucian philosophy prescribed codes of conduct for a variety of social contexts. His writings outlined behaviors for properly fulfilling social obligations, etiquette for extending both congratulations and condolences, giving and receiving gifts, and proper reciprocation for social etiquette (Yang, 1957). Modern day *guanxi* still retains many of these implicit understandings, which make them all the more complex for the non-Chinese individual to understand.

The practice of repaying debts also stems from the knight errant tradition that emerged during the Period of Warring States (Yang, 1994). This era was characterized by widespread social unrest. As a result, many knights were without patrons to support them. In an effort to survive without patrons, these knights looked out for and protected each other. Deep male friendships evolved, and a code of honor developed. It was during these times that the bonds of male friendship became stronger as the knights looked out for each other, abiding by this code of honor that included loyalty and self-sacrifice (Yang, 1994). This tacit code formed the basis for modern day *guanxi* and the practices of rendering favors and repaying debts.

In China, *guanxi* remains central to social capital. Liu (2011) notes three types of *guanxi*: The first is power-based, and the foundation of complex political networks in Chinese organizations; the second is benefit-based, which can be seen widely in supportive professional and social networks; the third is personality-based, or friendship networks. The rationale for establishing and maintaining the first two types of *guanxi* is social capital and social exchange, but the third type relies on emotional and affective ties, and fit between personality and personal values. These bases for *guanxi* can overlap, for example, a power-based relationship may also lead to a friendship developing over time, or a friendship may exist but one party then gets power so the relationship shifts to have several bases for *guanxi*.

It is important to highlight that *guanxi* is not a simple or universally agreed concept, even within China. Yang (1994) details the four current conceptualizations of *guanxi*. One is the "official" Communist

Party rhetoric; the remaining three are "unofficial" and come up in conversations with ordinary people. The "official", Communist Party view argues that *guanxi* corrupts proper Communist Party ideology and the socialist ethics upon which it is based. The Communist Party sees *guanxi* as a bourgeois practice with roots in feudal China with little applicability to contemporary times. Although Yang (1994) does not go into greater detail, we can extrapolate why this may be the case. The preponderance of research on *guanxi* prior to modern times examines *guanxi* and its use from the period from 1949 (when the People's Republic of China was established) through the 1970s, which included the Cultural Revolution and the Great Leap Forward, and into the 1980s in which China remained closed to the outside world. During this period, scarce resources forced people to rely on *guanxi* to procure extra commodities for themselves and their families. However, because China has a centrally planned state economy, such a practice suggested inefficiency in the Communist Party, a possible problem that they would not readily acknowledge. Thus, it is not difficult to understand why the Communist Party might condemn *guanxi*, as its practice discredits governmental efficiency and solvency.

The remaining three views on *guanxi*, the "unofficial" ones, place *guanxi* in varying lights. First, some view *guanxi* as anti-social because it compels actors into social exchanges and suppresses emotions, thus emphasizing utility over affect. People who hold this view, whom Yang (1994) notes are most frequently women, are weary of indebtedness to others and the ongoing needs both to keep score and reciprocate favors. Interestingly, her book finds that women are also more adept at the art of *guanxi*, however, they also most quickly grow tired of leveraging it to maneuver through society. The second perspective on *guanxi* suggests that it serves a necessary social function because it has its own morality. As such, it captures both the ethical and unethical, thus allowing actors to find means of doing the unacceptable in a more acceptable fashion (we discuss the ethics of *guanxi* later in this chapter). The third and final view places *guanxi* as morally neutral. Under this view, societal restrictions, such as the aforementioned scarcity of resources, can force people to engage in certain behaviors out of a need for survival. From this perspective, human nature is essentially good, but certain restrictions act as external pressures causing people to behave differently.

These four views on *guanxi* illustrate how varied perspectives are within Chinese culture, and leads to further difficulty for non-Chinese to understand this construct. To assist in our understanding of *guanxi*,

this handbook chapter examines *guanxi* in the workplace with particular attention to the following questions:

1. How do historical or traditional conceptions of *guanxi* differ from
   modern ones?
2. What implications do differences between traditional and modern
   guanxi have for cross-cultural work and international business, particularly with regard to subtle differences between *guanxi* and
   Western concepts of networking and mentoring?
3. Is *guanxi* becoming more or less valuable in contemporary Chinese
   society, and how is the concept evolving? and
4. How do the ethics of *guanxi* differ from ethics within conceptualizations of relationships in a non-Chinese context?

To commence our inquiry into *guanxi* in the workplace, we highlight
its importance, strictly in a Chinese context, to conducting successful
business. Chen and Chen (2004) note that business management
scholars have validated the importance of *guanxi* as an important construct by no longer translating it into English. This suggests that non-
Chinese people are familiar with the term, even if the nuances and
complexities are still elusive.

Guanxi in the workplace

In contemporary business research, the importance of good *guanxi* is
frequently highlighted. For example, Luo, (2000) calls it the "lifeblood
of both the macro-economy and micro-business contact" and that
"[no] company can go far unless it has extensive *guanxi* networks in
this setting" (p. 1). Park and Luo (2001) extend this thought by suggesting that both Chinese and non-Chinese need to understand and be
able to use *guanxi* for business to be successful.

Possession of good *guanxi* has been shown to have a positive relationship with firm performance (Wong, 1988). He presents several
models that integrate *guanxi* (as relationships) which emphasize the
importance of relationships on firm performance. The motivation for
Wong's research was to offer theoretical frameworks for known phenomena and create a research agenda that would allow for empirical
testing. While, to our knowledge, these specific models have not yet
been empirically tested, the suggestion remains that there is a strong
relationship between *guanxi* and performance in business.

Because of the lack of empirical evidence for the relationship
between *guanxi* and business success, Yeung and Tung (1996) addressed

this gap by conducting semi-structured interviews to extract factors leading to business success in China. In a sample of 19 business executives (who were head of operations for China in their respective organizations), the single theme (out of 11) that emerged consistently as an important factor for success was *guanxi*. However, they do qualify their findings. First, having *guanxi* was critical to successful business, but having *guanxi* alone would not ensure success. Rather, *guanxi* is important in the early stages of a business venture and declines with the life cycle of the business. In addition, older executives more than younger ones placed a priority on *guanxi*. Finally, small- and medium-sized firms emphasized the importance of *guanxi* more than larger firms. The first finding suggests a generational gap in conceptualizations of *guanxi*. Perhaps the older executives value *guanxi* more highly because their experiences required them to rely on *guanxi* to achieve their business success. Younger executives, on the other hand, might be more familiar with an international business climate in which relationships are both created and broken more easily. Related to the second finding, larger firms might have access to more resources that small- and medium-sized firms do not. Thus, the small- and medium-sized firms might need to rely on *guanxi* more to compensate for this lack of resources.

Guanxi cultivation is determined by an organization's institutional, organizational, and strategic characteristics (Park & Luo, 2001). They used quantitative methods in a survey of 128 firms to clarify different firms' need and capacity for *guanxi* building. They found that *guanxi* leads to higher firm performance but only with respect to expanding sales, not to higher profits. In addition, only factors of an institutional (ownership structure and location) or strategic (market orientation) nature were significant when using *guanxi* with government agencies. Finally, there were two benefits of using *guanxi* when considering a firm with respect to its external environment: *Guanxi* was found to have a positive effect on market expansion as well as strategic positioning. However, *guanxi* was not found to have a significant effect on the internal workings of an organization.

At the personal, individual level, Xin and Pearce (1996) found that the lack of a legal infrastructure made private sector executives more heavily reliant on *guanxi* than executives in the government or state owned enterprises. Without formal institutional support, private sector executives overall had more business connections and placed a higher value on them than did executives in other sectors. In addition, they trusted these connections more and depended on them for protection.

In human resources management, Chen et al. (2004) found tensions between *guanxi* and procedural justice. In a sample of 94 executives, *guanxi* practices in an organization were found to reduce trust in management. However, perceptions of procedural justice were found to mediate this effect. Thus, *guanxi* affected both procedural justice and trust in management, and procedural justice affected trust in management. When taken together, procedural justice still retained a significant effect on trust in management, but *guanxi* practices did not. Furthermore, not all *guanxi* practices had the same magnitude of effects. According to these authors, *guanxi* practices that favored a family member (e.g. a nephew) or an individual from the same hometown, reduced trust in management. However, *guanxi* practices that favored a former classmate or a close friend did not lower trust in management. Overall, these findings lend further support to Yang's (1994) findings that perceptions of types of *guanxi* differ. While it is valuable to investigate further the complexities of *guanxi*, it is difficult to argue definitively regarding its nature, use, or perceptions.

Guanxi and networking

Because of the linguistic similarity between *guanxi* and networking, it is easier to understand the two constructs through each other, particularly *guanxi* as it is less familiar to a non-Chinese audience. However, we must exercise caution not to collapse any cultural differences between the two. Shenkar (2004) argues that a surface level understanding of *guanxi* as networking precludes a grasp of more subtle emic (culture-specific) differences. To differentiate *guanxi*, business researchers have drawn distinctions highlighting what *guanxi* is not. It is not relational demography (Farh et al., 1998; Tsui & Farh, 1997), leader-member exchange (Law et al., 2000), or relationship marketing (Wang, 2007). All of these are important constructs in Western business ideology. However, these authors make specific cases that these constructs are different from *guanxi*. We now examine each of these studies in slightly more detail to ascertain a better picture of how and why *guanxi* is different from each of these constructs.

Guanxi has been shown to differ from relational demography (Farh et al., 1998; Tsui & Farh, 1997). First, Tsui and Farh (1997) propose a theoretical framework to differentiate between *guanxi* and relational demography. Drawing from previous literature, their first suggestion is that the social basis from which individuals secure mutual commonalities differ between the two constructs. For example, shared experiences such as being former classmates or from the same geographic region form a basis for *guanxi*. In contrast, relational demography looks at personal characteristics such as age, gender, and socioeconomic standing. In addition, the authors emphasize the importance of a shared past in *guanxi*, while relational demography is built of current, existing features.

Farh et al. (1998) further this work empirically by testing for contexts in which *guanxi* and relational demography are of significant importance and whether there is congruence between these contexts. Their findings imply that the "old boys network", which is highly suggestive of *guanxi* relationships, is actually a cultural universal. However, they provide empirical evidence that bases of social identification and similarity attraction fundamentally differ between Eastern and Western cultures, as Tsui and Farh's (1997) theoretical framework suggests. To this end, kinship, shared place of birth, and being neighbors are supported as points of similarity that are of significance in China but not in Western contexts. In addition, while both *guanxi* and relational demography were found to be important with respect to a subordinate's trust in a superior (a vertical relationship), only *guanxi* was important for an executive's trust in their business connections (a horizontal relationship). These findings suggest culture specific characteristics of *guanxi* that relational demography fails to capture, thus preventing researchers from substituting or merging the two constructs.

Guanxi has also been found to differ from two Western superior-subordinate constructs: leader-member exchange (LMX) and commitment to supervisor (Law et al., 2000). These authors examine the superior-subordinate relationship in China citing a significant number of *guanxi* relationships of that nature. With respect to LMX, they argue that LMX differs from *guanxi* because LMX is strictly within the work context and about work-related exchanges. In contrast, they argue that *guanxi* exchanges often extend outside of the workplace and are often of a social nature. They find empirical support (through different factor structures) for their hypothesis that LMX is theoretically different from *guanxi*. With respect to commitment to supervisor being different from superior-subordinate *guanxi*, the authors argue the difference as being from the subordinate to the supervisor in the case of commitment to supervisor, but of bi-directional exchanges in the case of superior-subordinate *guanxi*. As in the case of LMX, the authors found empirical support for a hypothesized theoretical difference between the two through factor analysis.

The field of relationship marketing, which evolved from the framework for developing buyer-seller relationships (Dwyer et al., 1987), emphasizes long-term customer retention over sales and transactions. Wang (2007) differentiates theoretically between *guanxi* and relationship marketing, arguing that the fundamental mechanisms of each are different. More specifically, the trust on which relationship marketing is built is fundamentally different as a construct from the reciprocal obligations borne out of *renqing* (a distinctly Chinese construct referring to the emotional responses to life's situations) in *guanxi*. Furthermore, while relationship marketing is more impersonal (Morgan & Hunt, 1994) and driven by legal prescriptions (Arias, 1998), *guanxi* is personal, affective, and driven by contextual social norms. Finally, he differentiates between *guanxi* as particularistic relationships as contrasted to universalistic relationships in relationship marketing.

The nature of *guanxi* that emerges from business research led many scholars and practitioners to attempt to relate *guanxi* to networking and/or mentoring. As we detail below, there are both similarities and differences between these constructs.

In their work comparing networking and *guanxi*, Yeung and Tung (1996) suggest a six part framework to identify differences. The following table summarizes their model.

Table 3.1 Comparison of *Guanxi* and Networking

	Guanxi	Networking
Motives	Role Obligations	Self-Interest
Reciprocation	Self-Loss	Self-Gain
Time Orientation	Long Term	Short Term
Power Differentiation	*Xia* (helping disadvantaged)	Power (no obligation)
Nature of Power	Personal Power	Institutional Authority
Sanction	Shame	Guilt

Source: Yeung & Tung, 1996.

These findings present a starting point for assessing potential differences between *guanxi* and networking. We offer the caution regarding these findings that *guanxi* and networking might not be at opposite ends of the relationship spectrum as this categorical framework might suggest. Indeed, different Chinese sub-cultures, with varying exposure to Confucian or other influences, may hold differing views on many cultural elements (Lin & Ho, 2009).

Rather than exclusive categories, we suggest that the Yeung and Tung model may be conceptualized as domains in a Venn diagram with two partially overlapping circles. The area of overlap between the two circles would indicate general, or etic, properties that are possessed by Western networking and Chinese *guanxi*. The unique areas of each circle, to Chinese and non-Chinese cultures respectively, would indicate culture specific, also known as emic, characteristics. A codification of behaviors and values that are either etics (universals) of relationships or emics of *guanxi* has not been well established.

To begin to fill this gap, Lo (2009) conducted semi-structured interviews with ten Chinese-American individuals who could speak specifically to differences between networking and *guanxi*. The three themes that emerged from these interviews were all specific to the uniqueness of *guanxi* and included: An emphasis on reciprocity, a long-term orientation, and culture specific etiquette for building *guanxi*. Further quantitative investigation corroborated a Chinese preference for a long-term orientation when cultivating *guanxi*. In addition, there was further empirical support for culturally specific behaviors for cultivating *guanxi* and networks, respectively. Chinese business etiquette for building *guanxi* included giving gifts, hosting banquets, rendering small favors, and visiting people in their homes. In contrast, American behaviors for building networks included offering handshakes as well as exchanging phone calls, emails, and business cards.

In addition to the subtle but pervasive differences between *guanxi* and networking, we should highlight differences within each of these domains. As highlighted above, many Chinese do not necessarily agree on what *guanxi* is, its nature, or its utility. Similarly, networking has a variety of forms (Winstead & Morganson, 2009) and meanings, including affective and instrumental forms, and increasingly sociotechnical transformations of the term to include software applications and digitally intermediated social and work-related communication. An increased focus on specific types of networks and their closer relationship to *guanxi* at work may be helpful. If we examine the sponsorship and developmental aspects of the Haier example that opens this chapter, we might see this as more akin to mentorship than "networks", per se. However, the emergence of the concept of developmental networks (Kram, 1985) within the mentoring literature may offer additional insights into *guanxi*'s comparative differences with Western workplace relationships, with respect to both networks and mentoring.

Guanxi and Mentoring

A student from the US, studying in China, relates his introduction to the importance of *guanxi* in gaining access to the labor market:

It was already a sticky, hot summer in Beijing. I discovered that the Chinese academic calendar runs for slightly longer than in the

United States. It was already July and I had been in my summer program classes for nearly a month, but the Chinese students were just starting to prepare for exams.

One evening, one of the Chinese students, Zhang Chi, came to my room looking visibly distraught. I figured the stress of exams was getting to him. "*Ni fuxi zemmayang?*" ("How's your review going?") I asked.

He shook his head. "*Fuxi mei wenti.*" ("The review is no problem.") Given his response, I didn't really understand why he looked so upset. All the other Chinese students that I had met were approaching their exam preparations with extreme seriousness. I studied him for a while as he sat there looking anxious. Finally I asked him, "*Nani weishemma nemma bugaoxing?*" (So why are you so unhappy?")

I listened to him explain how his family is very poor and needed money and that summer vacation was an excellent time to earn money with a part-time job.

"So why don't you get a part-time job?" I asked innocently.

"*Meiyou guanxi!*" ("I don't have *guanxi*!") he wailed.

Guanxi is seen as critical to career development in China, influencing access to good jobs, and progress within companies and industries. This parallels the Western concepts of mentoring and sponsorship. Similar stories emerge throughout China's business elite. In addition to the "golden partnership" between Haier's CEO and President, even more extensive ties may be seen in the relationship between senior managers at Lenovo. Liu Chuanzhi, the founder of Lenovo Group, emphasized *guanxi* principles of loyalty for leadership succession, and likened the relationships with trusted senior managers to a marriage. Taking this metaphor further than most, Liu announced in public in 2011 that he happily married his daughter (Lenovo Group) to the capable son-in-law, Yang Yuanqing, the CEO and chairman of Lenovo Group, a trusted employee since 1989, and someone that Liu had coached and mentored over the years.

Traditionally, the Western concept of mentoring has been conceptualized as a dyadic developmental relationship between individuals of unequal status in which the more powerful individual, the mentor, provides career development and support (career and personal) for the less powerful individual, the protégé (see Kram, 1985). There is a substantial body of research on protégés and mentors, and satisfaction with, stages of, and types of support provided in mentoring relationships (Armstrong et al., 2002; Mullen & Noe, 1999). The relationship is seen as leading to enhanced career advancement, rewarding both mentor and protégé with improved career outcomes and social capital (Ibarra, 1993; Kram & Isabella, 1985). The expectation is that the relationship is "strictly business", although similarity biases often result in affinity and affective ties. In China, the unilateral and unequal nature of mentoring and protégés is not an inherent characteristic of *guanxi*, nor is an exclusive emphasis on career outcomes, though these may be included. Despite the long-term orientation of *guanxi*, and emphasis on affinity and affective ties, deep personal relationships, particularly sexual or familial ties, are seen as "taboo" particularly in cross-gender relationships (see Winstead & Morganson, 2009).

Using the model developed by Yeung and Tung (1996) to compare *guanxi* and networking, we can adopt a similar framework (with similar caveats) for *guanxi* and mentoring (see Table 3.2).

Table 3.2 Comparison of *Guanxi*, Mentoring, and Developmental Networks

	Guanxi	Mentoring	Developmental Networks
Motives	Role Obligations*	Self-Interest	Self-Interest of protégé
Reciprocation	Self-Loss*	Self-Gain	Not expected
Time Orientation	Long Term*	Long Term	Long Term
Power Differentiation	*Xia* (helping disadvantaged)* Not hierarchically defined	Producing advantage for the protégé Hierarchical	Producing advantage for the protégé Peer and hierarchical
Nature of Power	Personal Power*	Institutional Authority	Relational
Ties	Social, familial and organizational	Organizational; employment-based	Social, familial and organizational
Spillover between work and social domains	Expected	Sanctioned	Varies by initial relationship

* Content adapted from Yeung & Tung, 1996.

While there are notable differences between mentoring and *guanxi*, as summarized in Table 3.2, the contemporary career development literature is increasingly merging the fields of networking and mentoring through the concept of developmental networks (see Molloy, 2005, for a review).

Developmental networks are defined as multiple, simultaneous relationships that are specifically improvement-focused (Kram, 1985). That is, in contrast to mentoring's dyadic exclusivity, developmental networks occur as the protégé maintains concurrent relationships with multiple "developers" – some of whom may be peers rather than superiors, but all of whom are interested and act to advance the protégé's career (see Higgins & Kram (2001) for an extended discussion of the differences between traditional mentoring relationships and developmental networks). Within the protégé's developmental network, the nature of the relationship with each "developer" may vary in terms of the strength of the relationship (Higgins & Kram, 2001), and the length of the relationship (de Janasz & Sullivan, 2004). The relational and supportive nature of developmental networks may be more similar to *guanxi*, but there are still emic differences with regard to reciprocity and instrumentality.

Guanxi – Tradition and contemporary practices

Although generally speaking *guanxi* is a concept deeply embedded in the Chinese mindset, which influences their manner of interaction and the nature of their relationships, there are some new facets of *guanxi* that have emerged as contemporary social changes in Chinese society impact on personal and organizational life.

Market economy

Confucianism's emphasis on hierarchy and socialism's planned economy are seen as the two critical ingredients in traditional *guanxi* – one providing the social structure of relationships and obligation, the other creating the necessity for alternative means of exchange and influence. However, after almost 30 years of market economy emergence in China, *guanxi* is seen as less relevant (Huang, 2008; Zhou & Tong, 2002). Jobs are gained through an open labor market process, and the state no longer controls individual careers or personal and professional relationships. Both in business and in personal life, formal contracts have replaced relational bonds. The resulting interpersonal and organizational competition creates a transactional or utilitarian network ethos, potentially overshadowing the emotional ties and loyalty of *guanxi* (Huang, 2008; Su, 2004; Wang & Le, 2001; Zhou & Tong, 2002).

Generational change

Gen Y and the millennials of China were born during the emergence and growth of the market economy (Su, 2004; Zhou & Tong, 2002). Many Chinese born in the last three decades come from a one-child family, enjoy focused attention from their elders, and have improved educational resources and living standards. Many have international experience in education or work, and formative exposure to other cultures, exhibiting greater individualism and weakened relational ties (Wang & Le, 2001). As younger Chinese develop a stronger sense of independence and self-importance, their values center more on personal competency and capability rather than benefits from traditional *guanxi*. The emphasis on self, rather than relationships, may cause them to devalue *guanxi*, and experience shame or embarrassment if it is seen that their success arises from family *guanxi* rather than their own ability.

Ironically, the younger generation also seems to recognize the importance of *guanxi* in China's transitional society. Their voices can be heard in public media: When new graduates find it difficult to get the best jobs, they lament not having a "powerful daddy", or as the prior case notes: "*Meiyou guanxi*". With increasing mobility in the Chinese labor market, moving to a new location poses problems as well, as there is no local *guanxi* to access in establishing potential work relationships.

The exposure to Western influences and comparisons to networking and mentoring may also result in different approaches to relationships, resulting in far more transactional or instrumental interactions, with much shorter timeframes. This view implicitly rejects the emic character of *guanxi* in favor of etic instrumentalism. Younger Chinese sometimes describe this new approach to relationships as "subjectively for self-interest but objectively benefits to others" (Wang & Le, 2001, p. 110; Zhou & Tong, 2002). The impression management implied by this phrase suggests that there is still awareness that others, particularly older Chinese, regard *guanxi* in the traditional way, as creating value for others.

Communication technology

The changing attitudes of the young are compounded by the advent of digital communication and social media. Technological development allows greater freedom, and speed of connection and communication, but also increases the risk of fraud, cheating, and dangerous interactions in the virtual world. In terms of its impact on Chinese *guanxi*, it makes the maintenance of existing *guanxi* easier, but restricts establishment of *guanxi*, because of the fast but shallow interaction which impedes building trust and credibility (Su, 2004).

Guanxi – More, less or more of the same?

Is *guanxi* use increasing, declining, or remaining the same in modern Chinese society as contrasted with previous times? Most researchers argue that *guanxi* is so firmly rooted in Chinese culture that it will neither disappear nor decline (Chen & Chen, 2004; Hall & Xu, 1990; Jacobs, 1980; Luo, 1997, 2000; Tsang, 1998; Tsui & Farh, 1997; Xin & Pearce, 1996; Yang, 1994). However, a minority of scholars argue that the development of a more solid legal system and increased free market competition will usher in a decline of *guanxi* because of more institutionalized means of getting things done in contrast to relying on interpersonal relationships (Guthrie, 1998, 2002; Peng, 2003). Still others argue that *guanxi* can coexist with institutionalized markets because *guanxi* offers transaction cost advantages beyond those allowed by market mechanisms alone (Standiford & Marshall, 2000). While these three alternatives do not offer a succinct answer by themselves, Luo (2000) summarizes this debate with the following four points: 1) Blood-based *guanxi*, as contrasted to socially-based *guanxi*, is deeply rooted in Chinese culture and is, therefore, less subject to changes in the institutional environment. 2) *Guanxi* with local government officials, as contrasted with central government officials, will become more important as the state affords local governments more autonomy. Standiford and Marshall (2000) also make the same argument for the growing importance of *guanxi* with local government workers. 3) Long-term *guanxi*, as contrasted to short-term *guanxi*, will remain important. Short-term *guanxi* may decline in importance with the strengthening of the free market economy. However, over the long-term, *guanxi* may still be valuable to navigate through the system. 4) Finally, there will be greater diversity of *guanxi* with respect to individuals and organizations. As the economy shifts from one in which demand exceeds supply to one characterized by greater free market competition and a higher service orientation, *guanxi* will also be more diverse in nature. Growing cultural diversity within China will heighten this diversity (Lin & Ho, 2009).

The ethics of *guanxi*

To return to the ethical issues raised earlier, it is important to clarify the differences between *guanxi* and what would be considered bribery in a Western context. First, the *raison d'etre* for the relationship differs fundamentally between *guanxi* and bribes. In a bribery relationship, the relationship only exists because of the bribe. Any relationship comes out of utility, as contrasted to affect. In *guanxi*, however, the relationship comes into existence first, and then the exchange is made subsequently. *Ganqing,* or emotions, are central to *guanxi* relationships (Chen & Chen, 2004; Yang, 1994). Thus, in a *guanxi* relationship, there is both a need to develop an emotional connection as well as to have a long-term orientation. Because of differences in levels of commitment, as well as rational versus relational differences, bribery relationships are far less enduring than *guanxi* relationships.

In addition to the existence or absence of an emotional connection, the nature of what is exchanged in bribery also differs. In a bribe, the exchange is that of money for either a good or service. However, quite rarely would the object exchanged in a *guanxi* relationship be money. Rather, as the title of Yang's (1994) book *Gifts, Favors, and Banquets: The Art of Social Relationships in China* suggests, an exchange in a *guanxi* relationship could be a gift, banquet, or favor. Money is viewed as a lesser gain and less stable than social investments that incur obligation and indebtedness, thus requiring reciprocity (Yang, 1994). As stated previously, reciprocity is central to *guanxi*.

Implications and future research

It is clear that *guanxi* is still an important part of workplace relationships and doing business in China. Managers and professionals engaged in cross-national work must understand its importance, and its differences from Western concepts of networking and mentoring. The importance of long-term social investments remain essential for business success, even as social change may be leading to questions regarding *guanxi*'s meaning and continuing importance.

While this handbook chapter did not make levels of analysis a salient focal point, there are suggestions that confusion arises out of differences between *guanxi* at the interpersonal level, *guanxi* at the firm level, and the interplay between the two levels (Chen & Chen, 2012). Future research might be geared towards exploring how *guanxi* at these various levels differ from each other so that a more comprehensive understanding of the broad construct can be reached.

Future research may investigate the emergence of new social trends, including the impact of technology and increasing workplace diversity on *guanxi* and its meaning in Chinese society. Current research on differences in distinct Chinese sub-cultures and nationalities (e.g. Lin & Ho, 2009) may be extended to *guanxi*. As career patterns change and organizational HR practices evolve, the international joint venture and China-based multinational enterprise may give rise to new expressions of *guanxi*. This may lead to empirical tests of Luo's (2000) social predictions regarding the relative importance of different types and targets of *guanxi*. Overall, *guanxi* presents an under-researched, and increasingly complex, facet of Chinese society; one that will influence relationships at work for many years to come.

References

Arias, J. T. G. (1998). A relationship marketing approach to guanxi, *European Journal of Marketing*, *32*(1/2), 145–156.

Armstrong, S., Allinson, C., & Hayes, J. (2002). Formal mentoring systems: An examination of the effects of mentor/protégé cognitive styles on the mentoring process, *Journal of Management Studies*, *39*(8), 1111–1137.

Chen, C. C., Chen, Y. R., & Xin, K. (2004). Guanxi practices and trust in management: A procedural justice perspective, *Organization Science*, *15*, 200–209.

Chen, X. P. & Chen, C. C. (2012). Chinese guanxi: The good, the bad and the controversial: in X. Huang & M. H. Bond (eds) *Handbook of Organizational Behavior: Integrating Theory, Research and Practice* (pp. 415–435). Massachusetts: Edward Elgar.

Chen, X. P. & Chen, C. C. (2004). On the intricacies of the Chinese guanxi: A process model of guanxi development, *Asia Pacific Journal of Management*, *21*, 305–324.

de Janasz, S. & Sullivan, S. (2004). Multiple mentoring in academe: Developing the professorial network, *Journal of Vocational Behavior*, *64*(2), 263–283.

Dwyer, F. R., Schurr, P. H., & Oh, S. (1987). Developing buyer-seller relationships, *Journal of Marketing*, *51*(2), 11–27.

Farh, J. L., Tsui, A. S., Xin, K. R., & Cheng, B. S. (1998). The influence of relational demography and *guanxi*: The Chinese case, *Organization Science*, *9*, 471–487.

Guthrie, D. (1998). The declining significance of *guanxi* in China's economic transition, *The China Quarterly*, *154*, 254–282.

Guthrie, D. (2002). Information asymmetries and the problem of perception: The significance of structural position in assessing the importance of guanxi in China: in T. Gold et al. (eds) *Social Connections in China Institutions, Culture, and the Changing Nature of Guanxi* (pp. 37–55). Cambridge, UK: Cambridge University Press.

Hall, R. H. & Xu, W. (1990). Run silent, run deep: Cultural influences on organizations in the Far East, *Organization Studies*, *11*, 569–576.

Higgins, M. & Kram, K. (2001). Reconceptualizing mentoring at work: A developmental network perspective, *Academy of Management Review*, *26*(2), 264–288.

Huang, X. (2008). The analysis of interpersonal relationship under contemporary Chinese society-based on social exchange theory, *Journal of Huinan Vocational and Technical College*, *3*, 60–62.

Ibarra, H. (1993). Personal networks of women and minorities in management: A conceptual framework, *Academy of Management Review*, *18*(1), 56–87.

Jacobs, J. B. (1980). The concept of guanxi and local politics in a rural Chinese cultural setting: in S. L. Greenblatt, R. W. Wilson, & A. A. Wilson (eds) *Social Interaction in Chinese Society* (pp. 209–236). New York: Praeger.

Kram, K. (1985). *Mentoring at Work: Developmental Relationship in Organizational Life*. Glenview, IL: Scott, Foresman and Company.

Kram, K. E. & Isabella, L. A. (1985). Mentoring alternatives: The role of peer relationships in career development, *Academy of Management Journal*, *28*(1), 110–132.

Law, K. S., Wong, C. S., Wang, D., & Wang, L. (2000). Effect of supervisor-subordinate *guanxi* on supervisory decisions in China: An empirical investigation, *International Journal of Human Resource Management*, *11*(4), 751–765.

Liang, S. M. (1949). *The Essential Meanings of Chinese Culture*. Hong Kong: Zheng Zhong Press.

Lin, L-H. & Ho, Y. L. (2009). Confucian dynamism, culture and ethical changes in Chinese societies – A comparative study of China, Taiwan and Hong Kong, *International Journal of Human Resource Management*, *20*(11), 2402–2417.

Liu, G. (2011). Thoughts on relationship management, *China Electric Power Enterprises Management*, *2*, 89.

Lo, K. D. (2009). *Anglo-American Networking and Chinese Guanxi*. Germany: VDM Verlag Dr. Müller.

Luo, Y. D. (1997). *Guanxi:* Principles, philosophies, and implications, *Human Systems Management*, *16*(1), 43–52.

Luo, Y. D. (2000). *Guanxi and Business*. Singapore: World Scientific Publishing Co. Pte. Ltd.

Molloy, D. C. (2005) Development networks: Literature review and future research, *Career Development International*, *10*(6/7), 536–587.

Morgan, R. M. & Hunt, S. D. (1994). The commitment – Trust theory of relationship marketing, *Journal of Marketing*, *58*, 20–38.

Mullen, E. J. & Noe, R. A. (1999). The mentoring information exchange: When do mentors seek information from their protégés? *Journal of Organizational Behavior*, *20*(2), 233–242.

Park, S. & Luo, Y. D. (2001) Guanxi and organizational dynamics: Organizational networking in Chinese firms, *Strategic Management Journal*, *22*, 455–477.

Peng, M. (2003). Institutional transitions and strategic choices, *Academy of Management Review*, *28*(2), 275–296.

Pye, L. (1982). *Chinese Commercial Negotiating Style*. Massachusetts: Oelgeschlager, Gunn & Hain, Publishers, Inc.

Standiford, S. S. & Marshall, R. S. (2000). The transaction cost advantage of guanxi based-business practices, *Journal of World Business*, 35(1), 21–42.

Shenkar, O. (2004). Organizational behavior: in K. Leung & S. White (eds) *Handbook of Asian Management* (pp. 295–315). Boston: Kluwer Academic Publishers.

Su, H. (2004). Three characteristics of the development of Chinese interpersonal relationship, *Heihe Journal*, 110, 65–67.

Tsang, E. W. K. (1998). Can *guanxi* be a source of sustained competitive advantage for doing business in China? *Academy of Management Executive*, 12, 64–73.

Tsui, A. S. & Farh, L. J. L. (1997). Where *guanxi* matters: Relational demography and *guanxi* in the Chinese context, *Work and Occupations*, 24, 56–79.

Wall, J. A. (1990). Managers in the People's Republic of China, *Academy of Management Executive*, 4(2), 19–32.

Wang, C. L. (2007). *Guanxi* vs. relationship marketing: Exploring underlying differences, *Industrial Marketing Management*, 36, 81–86.

Wang, X. & Le, G. (2001). Cultural change in contemporary Chinese interpersonal relationship, *Journal of Social Science Research*, 2, 105–110.

Winstead, B. A. & Morganson, V. (2009). Gender and relationships at work: in S. L. Wright & R. L. Morrison *Friends and Enemies in Organizations: A Work Psychology Perspective* (Ch. 8, pp. 141–167). Sydney: Palgrave Macmillan.

Wong, S. L. (1988). *Emigrant Entrepreneurs: Shanghai Industrialists in Hong Kong*. Hong Kong: Oxford University Press.

Xin, K. R. & Pearce, J. L. (1996). *Guanxi*: Connections as substitutes for formal institutional support, *Academy of Management Journal*, 39, 1641–1658.

Yang, L. S. (1957). The concept of pao as a basis for social relations in China: in J. K. Fairbank (ed.) *Chinese Thought and Institutions*. Chicago: University of Chicago Press.

Yang, M. M. H. (1994). *Gifts, Favors, and Banquets: The Art of Social Relationships in China*. Ithaca: Cornell University Press.

Yeung, I. Y. M. & Tung, R. L. (1996). Achieving business success in Confucian societies: The importance of *guanxi* (connections), *Organizational Dynamics*, Autumn, 54–65.

Zhou, J. & Tong, X. (2002). Social transformation and the structural change of interpersonal relationship: From emotional relationship structure to rational one, *Journal of Southern Yangtze University (Humanities & Social Sciences)*, 1(5), 48–52.

4
Relationships and Organizational Politics

Darren C. Treadway[1], Jeffrey R. Bentley[1], Angela S. Wallace[1], Stephanie R. Seitz[1], and Brooke A. Shaughnessy[2]

> The fundamental concept in social science is Power, in the same sense that Energy is the fundamental concept in physics ... The laws of social dynamics are laws which can only be stated in terms of power.
>
> (Russell, 1938, p. 10)

It has been suggested that the most motivating and fundamental force in social life is interpersonal power. Organizational politics represents the contextual and behavioral manifestations of power in the workplace, and researchers have invested a great deal of energy into framing the most fundamental relationships in organizations through the power and politics lens. From leadership to performance appraisal, organizational politics has demonstrated itself to be a valuable framework to investigate. Despite the abundance of research on politics in organizations, very little of that research has attempted to fully integrate political and relational perspectives.

In the current chapter, we advance thought toward that goal. We explore the reciprocal effects relationships and organizational politics have on one another by discussing: (1) the nature and development of interpersonal relationships, (2) the means through which relationships are leveraged for political gain at work, (3) the importance of political skill in leveraging relationships and politics effectively, (4) two of the most salient contexts in which politics can affect relationships, (5) the broader ramification of relationships and politics on one's

---

[1] State University of New York at Buffalo
[2] Technische Universität München

perceptions of the work environment, and (6) conclusions and directions for future work integrating politics and relationships.

Politics in organizations

Workplace politics is something that few admit they engage in at work,
but everybody loves to talk about. While researchers often view politics
as, at best, a necessary evil, most practitioners view it as the way things
get done. Perhaps due to the negative connotations researchers have
about the construct, there is often misunderstanding regarding the
precise nature of politics in organizations. In order to more clearly
discuss the topics throughout this chapter, we offer the following
description of our key constructs.

First, organizational politics, in general, is the use of power and
social influence to affect organizational functioning, decision-making,
and individual behavior while achieving goals in the face of uncertainty (Drory & Romm, 1988; Ferris et al., 2002; Ferris et al., 1989;
Gandz & Murray, 1980; Pettigrew, 1973; Pfeffer et al., 1976). Although
politics can be damaging and divisive (Gandz & Murray, 1980;
Madison et al., 1980), Mintzberg (1983) asserted that it is ultimately
just another system of influence that arises out of necessity as people
seek to organize themselves to coordinated action, similar to authority
or proscribed ideology. Organizational politics are more common in
environments or situations that are ambiguous or have limited
resources worth competing over. This is because goals and scarce
resources are often obtained in such situations through the use of
social influence behavior.

In the workplace, social influence behaviors are typically referred to
as political behaviors, and are actions that guide another individual's
thoughts or behaviors towards meeting one's own self-serving or
organization-serving ends (Ferris et al., 1989; Tedeschi & Melburg,
1984). When influencing others directly, political behaviors often take
the form of influence tactics that engender in a target individual
various levels of commitment to a particular task or behavior (Kipnis
et al., 1980; Yukl & Tracey, 1992). For instance, inspiring a target to
engage in a behavior by making it appear personally relevant may
enhance a target's commitment to a task or goal, while overtly pressuring them may cause resistance (Yukl et al., 1996). When seeking to
affect others indirectly, however, political behavior may take the more
subtle form of managing one's impression in the eyes of others.
Individuals may, for instance, render favors or give compliments in an

effort to appear ingratiatory and thus likeable and deserving of favors, or may exemplify the ideal traits of an employee in their organization in an effort to appear devoted and thus deserving of trust and rewards (Jones & Pittman, 1982). While there are other, related forms of proactive and reactive political behavior (e.g. Tedeschi & Melburg, 1984), they all revolve around controlling the behavior of others to meet one's own goals.

With the fulfillment of personal objectives being the motivating force behind political behaviors, it is no surprise that environments characterized as "political" are those that appear to be highly self-serving (Kacmar & Baron, 1999). The perception of politics is the extent to which an individual perceives others' actions in their work environment to be characterized by self-serving motives and behavior (Ferris & Kacmar, 1992; Ferris et al., 1989). One will perceive his or her environment to be increasingly political to the extent that they believe: 1) others' behavior is increasingly self-serving, 2) others are simply going along with potentially dysfunctional political norms or expectations to personally get ahead, and 3) there are biases in pay and promotion procedures (Kacmar & Carlson, 1997; Zhou & Ferris, 1995). Perceptions of politics, however, are ultimately a subjective experience rather than an objective descriptor, and different individuals will perceive different environments as political (Ferris & Kacmar, 1992; Gandz & Murray, 1980) based on their personal traits, aspects, and opportunities in their work or job environment, and the characteristics of their organization (Ferris et al., 2002).

At its root, organizational politics are built on the enactment of political behaviors. Those who most adeptly enact political behavior are politically skilled, which is "the ability to effectively understand others at work, and to use such knowledge to influence others to act in ways that enhance one's personal and/or organizational objectives" (Ferris et al., 2005, p. 127). Politically skilled individuals excel because they are socially astute (e.g. able to deduce motives, aware of social cues, etc.), able to interpersonally influence others, cultivate strong, and resource-rich social networks, and appear sincere and genuine when taking action (Ferris et al., 2007a). Those who are politically skilled have a distinct advantage in politicking as they have been found to more effectively engage in political behaviors (Harris et al., 2007) while at the same time not appearing politically motivated (Treadway et al., 2007). Having defined the fundamental political constructs in the past few paragraphs, we now move forward and discuss their integration with relationships.

Organizational politics as relationship science

Relationship science explores "the oscillating rhythm of influence observed in the interaction of two people" (Berscheid, 1999, p. 261) by determining the antecedents, dynamics, and consequences of such social interactions (Berscheid, 1999; Reis et al., 2000) as they pertain to effective interpersonal relationships. According to Reis and colleagues (2000), relationship scientists generally agree on four guiding assumptions. First, people are involved in relationships from the moment they are born. Second, the nature and productivity of any given relationship is unique and determined by the combination of individual goals and experiences of both partners (Reis & Collins, 2004). Third, relationships are embedded within a stable and predictable physical system (e.g. one's home, one's office), as well as within an ambiguous and dynamic social system. Finally, one's unique combined place in those systems is in turn embedded in a larger system of society and culture.

As expected, the more that an individual's primary human needs for autonomy, competence, and relatedness (Downie et al., 2008) are satisfied by a relationship, the higher the quality of that relationship. In the work environment, these high quality relationships most often manifest in interpersonal trust and civility which, in turn, predict relationship effectiveness (Ferris et al., 2009). Effective relationships in organizations benefit employees' mental health, subjective well-being, overall behavioral functioning, and social capital (Downie et al., 2008; Gui & Stanca, 2010; Reis et al., 2000). For example, the mutual exchange inherent in high quality relationships between leaders and subordinates tends to result in positive outcomes for both members of the leadership dyad (Gerstner & Day, 1997). However, incidents or situations that incite self-serving motives and aggressive tendencies among the relationship partners may generate harmful relationships such as abusive supervision or workplace bullying (Aryee et al., 2007; Tepper et al., 2011).

The current chapter offers a novel view of relationships in organizations; specifically that these relationships are a conduit through which employees interpret and enact their environment and constantly strive to advance their personal and organizational objectives. Although social influence behaviors are among the primary means through which the quality and nature of relationships are shaped in the social system (Berscheid, 1999), they have not been explicitly framed as such in the organizational sciences. Below we discuss politics as it effects relationship development and the importance of political skill within relationships.

Relationship development

Relationship partners respond to each other's wishes, concerns, abilities, and emotional expressions in different ways depending on their intent (e.g. to strengthen the relationship vs. to break the relationship; Reis & Collins, 2004). A unique baseline of reciprocity in relationships develops slowly (Barry & Crant, 2000) as partners increasingly influence one another's behavior (Reis, 2007) while learning to account for actions of the other; a unique level of interdependence forms for each relationship and acts as the basis for future interactions. Partners are typically in relationships to fulfill goals or needs of some kind (conscious or otherwise) and engage in social influence or political behaviors that guide them to those ends. Relationships grow and take on new qualities (e.g. trust, cohesion, affect) through development in four interrelated domains: dyadic communication, expectations, responsiveness, and emotions.

Dyadic communication

The quantity and quality of communication between partners affects the overall quality, development, and utility of the relationship (Barry & Crant, 2000; Souerwine, 1978). Communication shapes the impression partners have of one another and, to gain trust, partners often seek to appear open, cooperative, and willing to suspend self-interest or at least balance it with a desire to help one's partner (Ferris et al., 2005; Souerwine, 1978). As partners communicate more they learn about one another's motives and habits and develop a system of shared meaning (Barry & Crant, 2000) that further facilitates communication and allows them to more easily influence one another (Willits, 1968). The richness of information and influence derived from effective communication can build or deteriorate trust and reciprocity within the relationship. By communicating effectively, partners not only begin to accurately predict their behavior, but also negotiate expectations for their relationship.

Dyadic expectations

Formed through various sources (e.g. direct or vicarious experiences, third-party reports, stereotypes, and personality-based proclivities; Reis et al., 2000), expectations provide behavioral guidelines that aid in modifying one's behavior to gain the favorable outcomes in a relationship (Reis et al., 2000). If a cued response from an expectation (e.g. being prepared with detailed information when one expects one's partner to immediately question one's new method) serves a functional purpose for both entities, a self-reinforcing feedback loop is slowly created that embeds an ongoing behavioral pattern in the relationship. Expectations, however, may endanger a relationship (Souerwine, 1978) if they are formed on biased information, their meaning is altered by intervening social forces, or a partner changes in a way that falls out of line with the expectation. Such misconceptions are, in part, detrimental because they reduce the perceived responsiveness of one's partner (Reis, 2007), which is an important facet that can endanger reciprocity and threaten shared meaning.

Perceived partner responsiveness

Partners are perceived to be responsive when they engage in behaviors that enhance a relationship, yet unresponsive when they act in ways that impair or threaten a relationship (Reis, 2007). Perceived, rather than objective, partner responsiveness is critical for facilitating well-being in a relationship (Reis, 2007), and is enhanced by: (1) communicating a sense of understanding, (2) validating one's partner, and (3) caring about one's partner. Perceptions of responsiveness are in large part subjective as they are influenced by individual differences in self-concept. People often seek out relationships in which others acknowledge their positive self-concepts (Reis, 2007), and are often not concerned with the accuracy of their self-conception, only that their self-conception is lauded or affirmed. This highlights the importance of relationships in facilitating emotional regulation for partners.

Emotions

Emotions that are deemed beneficial to the relationship, even if not necessarily positive ones (e.g. anger towards a common enemy, remorse over a mistake), enhance perceptions of relationship value; while those deemed detrimental to the relationship reduce that value (Gui & Stanca, 2010). People often regulate their emotion, using both suppression and expression, to ensure desired outcomes in a relationship or adhere to accepted situational norms (Reis et al., 2000), however the overall intensity of felt emotion is rooted in the strength of the relationship (Reis & Collins, 2004). Stronger relationships are often characterized by more detailed expectations than weak relationships, and expectation confirmation and disconfirmation are major drivers of emotional reactions in relationships. In order to adapt one's expectations and communication style to generate facilitative emotions for the relationship, it is important for partners to be responsive to the feelings and emotional desires of one another in the first place (Souerwine, 1978).

Political skill in work relationships

Communication, expectations, perceived responsiveness, and emotions are all shaped by partners' ability to understand one another in a given social context. Work relationships refer to patterns of interactions between two employees that accomplish common objectives and goals within an organizational context; it is the context of these relationships that make them unique (Ferris et al., 2009). According to Ferris and his colleagues (2009) there are various types of work relationships that have received extensive coverage in management literature.

Many work relationships are derived from an organization's formal hierarchy or organizational structure, meaning that partners must interact with one another to achieve work-related goals such as favorable performance evaluations, promotions, and so forth, whether they chose their partners or not. In order to achieve favorable outcomes in these relationships, political skill is essential (Ferris et al., 2012; Ferris et al., 2005; Ferris et al., 2007a). Those who possess political skill are able to accurately assess their work environments, understand others' motives, and recognize the impact of their own behavior. This allows them to more effectively influence others through the use of political behavior that is appropriate for the dyadic partner and the relational context. Critical to the success of politically skilled employees is their ability to have others perceive their behaviors as generated from a genuine concern for the relationship rather than for their own personal gain (Ferris et al., 2005; Treadway et al., 2007). Taken together, these capacities lead the politically skilled to "... develop and maintain vast networks of individuals that can ultimately help them achieve their goals" (Ferris et al., 2012, p. 492).

Relational contexts in which politics is salient

To this point, we have offered that political behavior and assumptions are at the core of how employees interpret and enact their work relationships. In the current section, we shall discuss those areas of organizational research in which political considerations have been shown by researchers to have a most direct impact on relationships in the workplace: promotions, performance appraisal, and leadership. Whereas the research discussed demonstrates that politics is an integral part of employment relationships, there are several other ways in which politics affects work relationships that have yet to be empirically assessed and we will offer some discussion of those later in the chapter.

Promotions and performance appraisal

Perhaps no other event provides as clear a signaling environment for the employee and their supervisor than does an employee's performance appraisal. It is an event in which both parties attempt to mold the relationship to achieve their own personal objectives. Indeed, research has shown that a leader's objective is seldom to accurately reflect a subordinate's performance, but is rather to use the performance appraisal to influence their subordinate's behavior (Longenecker et al., 1987). Given the importance of the performance appraisal context, it is not surprising that a great deal of research has been conducted surrounding this event.

The majority of performance appraisal research has focused on subordinates' use of political behavior and has shown that some behaviors are simply more useful than others for obtaining positive performance appraisals. Higgins et al.'s (2003) meta-analytic findings indicated that both ingratiation and rationalization lead to higher performance appraisal ratings (Higgins et al., 2003). Scholars have consistently suggested that the positive impact is attributed to the elevated level of affect that targets experience when these political behaviors are employed (Gordon, 1996). As noted previously, perceived partner responsiveness may also be at the core of this positive impact because these behaviors would be seen as enhancing the relationship (Reis, 2007).

Treadway and colleagues (2007) also posited that higher performance ratings were directly due to supervisors being effectively ingratiated, such that higher affect was created. Using Balance Theory they articulated that politically skilled subordinates were less likely to have their self-reported ingratiation detected by supervisors and less politically skilled subordinates (perhaps engaging in very similar behaviors) would be seen as investing in ingratiation for self-serving purposes. When supervisors felt they were ingratiated by the less skilled employees, those employees received lower performance ratings. Similarly, Kolodinsky et al. (2007) found that rational behaviors enacted by politically skilled subordinates achieved higher performance ratings.

There is also evidence to suggest that politics are effective in gaining promotions. Judge and Bretz (1994) examined the impact of politics on career success. These authors found that supervisor-focused political behavior tactics were positively related to promotions. In addition, Thacker and Wayne (1995) found that ingratiation had a weak positive relationship with promotion, but combined with assertiveness had a negative effect on promotions. Taken together, these studies imply that, although political behavior plays a role in ratings of promotability and promotions, it is the enactment of specific political behaviors that leads to a positive outcome.

The intersection of gender and political behavior has also been a focus in explaining promotions and performance appraisals. In a study of upward influence tactics, Kipnis and Schmidt (1988) demonstrated that performance appraisals were most positive for men who used tactical influence mechanisms (i.e. rational persuasion, leveraging expert power) whereas women benefitted from using ingratiatory and bystander influence tactics. Similarly, Shaughnessy et al. (2011) found that politically skilled women were more likely to be liked, and thus perceived as promotable, when they engaged in behavior typically stereotyped as female (i.e. ingratiation). However, when women used political behavior that was not considered stereotypically female, such as assertiveness, their supervisors liked them less, and thus perceived them as less promotable, regardless of their level of political skill.

Leadership

Ferris and Judge (1991) described politics in organizations as the management of shared meaning. They noted that "[r]ather than inherent properties of situations, meanings are the result of our responses to those situations and our subsequent responses … The idea is to manage the meaning of the situation to produce the outcomes desired" (Ferris & Judge, 1991, p. 450). Leadership also has, at its core, the function of managing shared meaning (Smircich & Morgan, 1982), and it can thus be recognized as a political process. As we will illustrate in this section, leaders manage shared meaning through political behaviors.

Ammeter et al. (2002) argued for a political theory of leadership that would go beyond traditional theories of leadership that "have labored under implicit assumptions of rationality" (p. 753). Their conceptualization focused on leader political behavior, its antecedents, and its consequences. They proposed that leader antecedents, such as political will, social capital, and interpersonal style, together with target antecedents, such as status and personality, influence the type of political behaviors in which the leader engages. Examples of the forms that these political behaviors can take include proactive and reactive political behaviors and symbolic influence. These behaviors are then linked to outcomes for the leader and the follower. For the leader, this could include performance evaluations, promotion, and power. For the follower, this may include affective and cognitive reactions, attitudes, and performance.

Although this section focuses on politics and leadership, it should be noted that politics is not simply a top-down process. Followers as well as leaders exhibit political behavior, which makes the entire cycle of the leadership process a context in which politics is salient. Organizational members use influence tactics in all directions: laterally, upward, and downward. These influence tactics have varying levels of effectiveness depending on the direction in which they are used (Yukl & Tracey, 1992). As such, leadership is an element of the political context not only because leaders use political behaviors, but because followers use political behaviors to influence leaders as well. Much like the performance management process, the enactment of leadership is replete with political behavior and feeds the general perception of politics in the organization. Such perceptions are at the root of what make an organization "political", and strongly affect the development of relationships at work.

Given the relational nature of the leadership context, it is not surprising that political skill researchers have set forth a number of models and studies reviewing the role political skill plays in leadership effectiveness. The first of these models discussed a cross-level model of leader-member exchange. Treadway et al. (2010) explained how leaders and followers use political skill to assess both their relationship and their relative positioning within the social networks in the organization. Once assessed, this skill is utilized to effectively gain entrance to valuable social networks. Moving forward to explore a more relational viewpoint, Treadway et al. (2012) take a process perspective wherein the political skill is the means by which leaders and followers exert control over the effects of their political behaviors on one another's views of the partner's self, which ultimately determines relational quality.

Researchers have also empirically demonstrated the utility of political skill for both leaders and followers. From the leader's perspective, political skill has been found to increase trust and reduce cynicism of followers (Treadway et al., 2004). Ahearn et al. (2004) found that team leader political skill was directly related to increased performance of teams, while Douglas and Ammeter (2004) and others (e.g. Ferris et al., 2005) found that leader political skill is linked to increased ratings of leader effectiveness by subordinates. Political skill, however, is also beneficial to followers. Breland et al. (2007) found that followers in low quality leader-member relationships were more likely to have higher perceptions of career success if they were politically skilled. Similarly, Brouer et al. (2009) found that followers in demographically dissimilar dyads were more likely to have high quality leader-member relations if they were politically skilled.

Perceptions of politics

As illustrated above, relationships are one of the primary conduits through which impressions at work are managed and political goals are realized. The experience of politics in an organization is a subjective process however, and one's experience with politics and political behavior in relationships can bleed beyond the dyad to affect one's overall perceptions of the work environment as a whole. Perceptions of politics are subjective since, based on their own characteristics or conditions (e.g. power, personal style, etc.), different individuals will view different actions as less or more political (Drory & Romm, 1988; Ferris & Kacmar, 1992; Gandz & Murray, 1980) and react in different ways (Ferris et al., 1989; Drory, 1993). Accepting that the experience of workplace politics was a subjective one and that employees acted not on political behavior but on their perception of such behavior, Ferris et al. (1989) set forth the first comprehensive model of organizational politics, the evolution of which will be explored while discussing the integration of politics and relationships for the rest of this section.

Given that both the perception of politics and relationships are inter-twined with social influence, the two interact in three major ways. First, relational quantities directly affect politics perceptions, and vice-versa, within the same relational level. Second, the politics within relationships and social interactions in large part determine the nature of the broader political environment, thus shaping a higher-level context that affects lower-level politics perceptions. Lastly, relational qualities exert not only a main effect on politics perceptions, but are also a boundary condition on the effects of politics on outcomes that may affect the work environment as well as future relationships. Although, there is not yet a significant body of research specifically exploring the linkage between relationships and politics perceptions, we have isolated and integrated work that touches upon the relational context of political perceptions.

Perception of politics and dyadic relationships

Relationships have a strong impact on perceptions of politics when considered at the dyadic-level (Ferris et al., 2002). For instance, Ferris and Kacmar (1992) found that employees in higher quality working relationships with their leaders tended to perceive their leader's behavior as being non-political. In contrast, others have found that group- or organization-level perceptions of politics were mainly related to behavioral, rather than relational, factors (Maslyn & Fedor, 1998). Other studies support the inverse effect of relationship quality on politics perceptions at the supervisor-level (Kacmar et al., 1999; Valle & Perrewé, 2000) and peer-level (Andrews & Kacmar, 2001; Parker et al., 1995). Lack of ambiguity and a strong sense of control or certainty are theorized to reduce perceptions of politics (Ferris et al., 1989; Ferris et al., 2002), and may indeed be facilitated by the positive characteristics associated with strong leader-member relationships (e.g. trust, resource exchange, loyalty; Graen & Uhl-Bien, 1995; Sparrowe & Liden, 1997).

The effect flows both ways, though, since perceptions of politics may also affect relationships. For instance, Hochwarter et al. (2003) found that politics varied across levels of an organization, and that politics at the coworker level negatively predicted job satisfaction beyond that predicted by politics at the supervisor level, while politics at the supervisory level negatively predicted leader-member relationship quality. Moreover, Cropanzano et al. (1997) found that perceptions of politics can lead to enhanced tension, anxiety, and fatigue, while Vigoda (2002) found that perceptions of politics can stress people, even to the point of aggression. Moreover, since such negative work behaviors, and some negative political behaviors (e.g. self-promotion; Ferris et al., 2000; Wayne & Liden, 1995), may signal to others that an individual is threatening and dangerous or merely self-serving, politics perceptions may also indirectly influence workers' likelihood of forming or maintaining relationships. In sum then, relationships and politics perceptions affect one another most strongly when considered within the same relational level, for better or worse. These findings represent the strongest direct linkages between politics and relationships, but do not explain the full story.

Perceptions of politics in the broader social environment

The nature of politics in interpersonal relationships shapes the nature of politics in the broader work context. The work environment, over time, affects individuals' choices of behaviors, which in turn shape the political characteristics of relationships. In other words, politicized relationships will politicize the environment, which causes political behaviors that further politicize relationships. For instance, Christiansen et al. (1997) found that, by asking employees to report the types of political behavior they experienced or witnessed their coworkers performing the most, they were able to distinguish between different types of subjective political environments. Those employees whose preferences for exhibiting certain types of political behavior, matched the types of political behavior prevalent in their work environment, experienced more positive outcomes (e.g. satisfaction with coworkers, trust in management, etc.) which would, over time, reinforce the political nature of the environment in their minds.

Further work by Ferris and colleagues (2000) found that perceptions of politics only caused political behavior among employees who had longer tenure in the organization. These authors proposed that, because of their time in the organizational environment, high tenure employees had become socialized into the political norms of the organization and began acting in line with those norms. As mentioned above, political behaviors can often signal threat or lack of trustworthiness, and by shaping a political environment, politics within relationships may lead to the degradation of future relationships. The tendency for people to engage in political behavior in order to cope with political environments is documented elsewhere (e.g. Harrell-Cook et al., 1999) as well. Treadway et al. (2005) demonstrated that the formation of political sub-climates is based in large part on employee social interaction patterns. Treadway and colleagues found that socialization and group membership patterns, based on department membership and organizational membership before an acquisition, led to the development of different amounts of politics within various groups.

Taking into account the work by Treadway et al. (2005) and Christiansen et al. (1997), as well as general work on the effects of politics perceptions, it is becoming apparent that relationships and social interactions shape the political nature of the work environment. That environment in turn shapes employees' perceptions of politics and their political behavior, which then comes full circle to reinforce the baseline political environment. Politics can almost be viewed as a trap, wherein relationships and social interactions characterized by political social influence simply incur further political behavior and politicized relationships.

Perceptions of politics: Relationships as buffers

Organizational life is not as simple as a straightforward downward or upward spiral. While relationships form the foundation and set the direction of politics formation, they also act as a check to moderate fluctuations in politics. Ferris et al. (1996) found evidence to suggest that the socializing relationships of white males helped provide them with the understanding and ability to survive the politics of organizations, and inhibited the negative effects of supervisor political behavior and political policies on attitudes and anxiety. Such understanding also nullified the detrimental effects of coworker political behavior on personal anxiety in women. There were no moderating effects for minority employees, seemingly because their relationships were not strongly integrated into the dominant coalitions that shaped politics in the organization.

Similar results were found by Gilmore et al. (1996) investigating the moderating effects of tenure on the impact of politics perceptions on attendance (Ferris et al., 1994). Moreover, linking back to leader-member relationships, Harris and Kacmar (2005) found that indicators of the quality of subordinate-supervisor relations (i.e. leader-member exchange, participative decision-making, and communication) weakened the positive effect of politics perceptions on job strain, while Witt (1998) found that leader-member goal congruence weakened the negative effects of perceptions of politics on subordinate commitment. These three factors all have the potential to increase subordinates' understanding and perceived control in political environments, and thus reduce the negative effects of politics perceptions that have already formed. Whereas control and understanding can reduce politics, they also serve as a moderating function on existing political perceptions.

In the above scenarios, relationships helped to socialize some employees or provide the tools necessary for suppressing the negative effects of politics perceptions on outcomes. Thus although relationships and politics can reinforce one another and lead to an ever-increasingly political or apolitical environment, relationships in a different form moderate that process and can restrict politics to a range that neither completely destroys relationships nor nullifies their essential function as a form of informal control.

Toward a relational understanding of politics

In this section we will discuss several aspects of relationships where the evaluation of political concerns should provide deeper insights. Specifically, we look at gender, ethnic minorities, motivation, and abuse. We offer not only a summary of the current research, but also some brief ideas towards possible research extensions.

Gender, politics, and relationships

There is a nascent body of literature dedicated to understanding gender differences in political behavior and relationships at work. Much of the foundation of the study of gender in social contexts reflects on the notion that gender is inherently socially constructed and can operate as a characteristic of an actor, a target, or the dyad (Winstead & Morganson, 2009). It is through the interactions between societal members that the social construction of gender is realized (West & Zimmerman, 1987). Resulting from these interactions are the expectations that men will engage in behaviors that will maintain their independence while women will conduct themselves in a manner that connects them to others. Given that our understanding of gender develops from our interactions with others, and both men and women are increasingly taking on the jobs, roles, or professions historically associated with the other, gender is having an increasingly notable effect on politics in relationships and organizations.

Previous research has established that the gender of the actor modifies the impact of the political behavior employed. More specifically, one's gender role expectations provide a lens through which the targets interpret actor influence behavior. When influence behavior is incongruent with gender role expectations, an observed actor incurs social or economic sanctions (Rudman, 1998). Tepper et al. (1993) found that, when engaging in upward-, or supervisor-, directed influence behavior, men who employed aggressive tactics were recognized as better performers than those who used weaker tactics, such as friendliness. Alternatively, women who engaged in weaker upward influence tactics received more psychosocial support and resources than those who engaged in stronger tactics (Tepper et al., 1993).

Other research has shown that political skill (Shaughnessy et al., 2011) or positive affect (Castro et al., 2003) enhances the positive effects of influence behavior that is consistent with gender role expectations. As social ability is necessary for positive interpersonal relationships, it is proposed that future research consider not only the gender and political behavior of actors but also how socially able actors leverage their gender and related social expectations to effectively cultivate relationships within organizations.

Ethnic minorities, politics, and relationships

A more developed understanding of politics is available in relation to the experience of ethnic minorities, yet little work has examined the functioning of political skill and political behavior. Conceptually, political skill may be effective at a different time during an ethnic minority person's career than during the career of majority members. Social effectiveness for ethnic minorities may begin with first building trust in the eyes of organizational members. Ethnic minorities have to work at establishing trust more so than majority members because three factors that inhibit trust are stereotypically associated with them. These three factors are low status, lack of self-disclosure, and lack of conformity (Brass, 1985; Ilgen & Youtz, 1986; Williams & O'Reilly, 1998). If one's dyadic partner does not trust the other then interpersonal skills have very little impact on the interpersonal relationship.

Some researchers have demonstrated the difficulty ethnic minorities experience when dealing with organizational politics, in that minorities often may not have access to the reservoir of political knowledge and resources held by members of the majority and dominant coalition (e.g. Ferris et al., 1996). As hinted above, minority members may enhance their learned political skill by breaking into the coalition or tapping into such knowledge, a task that is both challenging and often times undesirable for fear of losing one's identity. Much of the difficulty for minority members arises because of negative associations attached to their ascribed status (status associated with demographic characteristics) that overshadows their achieved status (status associated with performance). Since certain ascribed characteristics tend to generate negative attributions of minority members' intelligence, competence, or other work-related characteristics, minority members often enter organizations feeling that majority members do not trust them. This lack of trust can impair relationship development.

However, unlike ascribed status, which is difficult to change, achieved status can be changed. Ragins (1997) suggested that ethnic minorities who achieve at a "superachiever"-level are likely to increase their achieved status to a level that is greater than that of their majority counterparts. Unfortunately, some suggest that only when this level of achieved status is met, will mentoring from majority members occur, meaning that ethnic minorities must first overcome stereotypical attributions (Ragins, 1997). Building on worries about one's ascribed characteristics, minority members may be further unlikely to self-disclose because it may bring to light more stereotypical, and thus negatively viewed, characteristics of oneself (Phillips et al., 2009). As a result, minority members may be likely to fake conformity (e.g. Hewlin, 2003) in order to try to build trust. Self-disclosure and conformity can, however, be enacted effectively, but minority employees face challenges to such enactment that majority members may never experience.

Although it is yet unknown, minority members may have to leverage different aspects of their political skill or context, than do majority members, when seeking to thrive at work. Working relationships between minority and majority members may begin with an air of distrust and tension as the minority member strives to convince the other that he or she is more capable than any other employee. At this point, social astuteness and apparent sincerity may become key, as opposed to interpersonal influence and networking, in drawing attention to one's abilities and intentions. From there, influence may help minority members perform well using those abilities, and thus illicit the support of the majority partner that garners both instrumental and emotional resources and mentoring. There are many opportunities for future research to confirm or deny the above suppositions, and explore the way that political behavior functions in minority-majority partner relationships rather than majority-majority ones, especially in the developmental stages.

Relationships and the motivation to engage in politics (political will)

With all of the work that has been done within the realm of organizational politics, one particular area that is relevant to organizational scientists that has been relatively neglected is motivation. Mintzberg (1983) suggested that it was not enough to have the skill to engage in political behavior, one must also possess the motivation to engage in the influence process. Political behavior is inherently risky for the individual engaging in the behavior. Until recently the idea of motivation and political behavior was not fully developed beyond Mintzberg's initial discussion. However, some recent work has shed greater light on the role of political will in organizations.

Treadway (2012) elaborated on the concept of political will in organizations; offering the first definition of the construct in organizational settings. He posited political will to be "the motivation to engage in strategic, goal-directed behavior that advances the personal agenda and objectives of the actor that inherently involves the risk of relational or reputational capital" (p. 533). From this definition, Treadway proposed that political will was guided by the focus of one's concern and the nature of the outcome one was advancing.

The nature of the outcome deals most closely with relationships. Treadway (2012) suggested that individuals could be driven by two opposing motivations. Specifically, employees can be driven by either instrumental or relational outcomes. That is, either trying to gain self-serving outcomes or trying to preserve and/or protect the capital inherent in an interpersonal relationship. This interpretation acknowledges both the traditional view of political activity as being solely based on tangible outcomes, but also includes the role of relationships in developing one's career and identity.

The focus of concern also gets to the idea of relationships in organizations. Again, Treadway (2012) argues that there are two competing motivations at play: self versus others. Political activity has always been tainted because of the view that it is a selfish behavior that has little, if any, concern for others in the organization. Certainly this aspect of human nature is evident in the workplace. However, any social change movement requires that individuals engage in political activity to be successful. Thus, a concern for others is also a possible motive for engaging in such behavior.

We feel that developing a better understanding of political will as a motivation construct offers one way to integrate long standing confusion with regard to the differentiation of political behavior, impression management behavior, and citizenship behavior. It is our contention that most organizational behaviors are political by nature: they are designed to influence others to achieve outcomes that are, in some way, personally rewarding for the actor. From this view, what is critical then is what the actor directs their attention toward. When a politically skilled individual is motivated to do bad things, she or he will do them very well. We see this as a critical underpinning of understanding bullying and other abusive behaviors as strategic and political rather than haphazard and uncontrolled. Examples can be seen in the literature on bullying and leadership.

Abusive behavior and politics

It has long been suggested that abusive relationships and abusive behavior are, at some level, about the power within those relationships. If viewed as a means of developing or establishing power, abusive behavior must be seen as political. Thus, it is not surprising that recent scholarly work has discussed such relationships as strategic in nature. Ferris et al. (2007b) offered a model of strategic bullying in organizations. They argued that leaders strategically bully their subordinates to achieve desired outcomes. Critical to their discussion was that political skill allowed bullies to choose the right targets in organizations. Furthermore, politically skilled bullies should be better at uncovering which mechanisms or tactics will be most effective in bullying their targets and inflicting the most damage.

Few empirical studies have assessed politics in abusive organizational relationships. Treadway et al. (2013) investigated the relationship between bullying behavior and performance. Building on Crick and Dodge's (1994) model of social competence, they found that bullies who were politically skilled were likely to achieve higher performance ratings; whereas bullies who were political skill deficient were likely to have lower performance ratings as their bullying behavior increased. This article suggests that, contrary to popular belief, some bullies are very socially skilled and may use intimidation to their benefit.

At the other end of the spectrum, more recent work on the relationship between workplace victimization and job performance found that political skill serves to buffer the effects of a victimizing climate. Specifically, Bentley et al. (2011) found, through a three-study replication, that politically skilled employees performed better on work tasks and engaged in more positive work behaviors when they perceived victimization in their work environment than did less politically skilled employees. They postulated that when victimization becomes embedded in a work environment, it becomes intertwined with the social functioning of that environment that in part affects an employee's job performance. Since politically skilled employees are more perceptive of social cues and are better able to control such an environment, they can cope better and use their social aptitude to maintain higher levels of performance as well.

Moving forward we feel it is important to fully expand the boundaries of political behavior to include abusive behaviors and contexts. In doing so, we would hope that political behaviors and political skill would no longer be viewed within the falsely dichotomous lens of "good vs. bad" but rather viewed as simply tools through which organizational participants can achieve their desired outcomes. It is these outcomes that define whether an employee is operating in functional or dysfunctional manner.

Conclusion and recommendations for practice

The present chapter offers an interpretation of the role of politics and political behavior in the development and leveraging of relationships in the workplace. We began by reviewing the nature and development of interpersonal relationships. Next, we argued that work relationships tend to revolve around social influence, and those who are more politically skilled tend to more effectively manage work relationships. We then illustrated the politicization of work relationships using two well-researched examples, performance management and leadership, and described how politics and relationships overlap with one another with respect to the broader political environment of an organization. We will end with a brief discussion of the practical implications of politics in relationships.

First and foremost, it is important to view work relationships as different from familial or social friendship relationships. Being inherently constrained and permeated by work-related goals and systems, work relationships necessarily involve social influence behavior; recognizing this fact helps reduce the stigma of "politics" at work, and may let people more effectively interact with one another and meet mutual goals. Enacting political behavior can not only benefit oneself, but also one's organization. Practitioners can benefit from encouraging people to influence one another to meet benevolent goals that satisfy self, partner, and organization, and in doing so may create more dynamic and adaptable organizations. Again, people and relationships are the conduits through which work happens, and the more they are growing to meet the needs and goals of the organization, the more effective that organization will be. Employees should be encouraged to engage in ethical and productive political behaviors, not to be afraid of them.

Second, as we discussed above, political skill is consistently linked both to enhanced productivity and performance, but also personal well-being and effective coping. There is recent work suggesting that it may be an excellent tool for personnel selection (Blickle & Schnitzler, 2010), and Ferris and colleagues (2007a; Ferris et al., 2002; Ferris et al., 2005) insist that political skill, at least in part, can be trained and developed. Employees and practitioners would do well to engage in formal or informal training, development, mentoring, or coaching activities that help them enhance their awareness of their social surrounding, and the meaning indicated therein, as well as their capacity to influence others, build strong social networks, and appear sincere.

While this may sound like a daunting task, political skill is rooted in part in tacit knowledge (Ferris et al., 2002; Sternberg, 1997), which suggests that employees may actually become more politically skilled the more they become involved in the social dynamics of their organization, or learn from experienced members. Challenging oneself to learn new perspectives, engage in influence behaviors, seek feedback, and model one's behavior after skilled others can leverage basic human tendencies for learning socially from others and hopefully enhance political skill. Moreover, mentoring and coaching relationships may be of great benefit, as work in other domains finds that employees in high quality relationships with their leaders or mentors tend to become integrated into those leaders' or mentors' social networks (Sparrowe & Liden, 1997, 2005). Assuming those individuals are politically skilled or have developed resource-rich networks, integration may enhance one's overall social capital and provide access to more advanced mentors, developmental opportunities, or power and influence capacity (Blickle et al., 2009).

Finally, our above discussion on relationships and politics perceptions also has ramifications for both employees and leaders in organizations. First, while perceiving politics in one's environment is typically very stressful, such stress can be alleviated by believing one has control over one's environment, especially the political aspects of it. Taking time to develop supportive and trusting relationships can do just that; employees who spend extra effort cultivating work relationships may find themselves more robust when they perceive a hostile and self-serving organizational climate. Second, from the perspective of leaders, perceptions of politics will likely arise among their employees based on the types of influence behaviors prevalent in working relationships. Taking steps to ensure that such influence behaviors are more positive (e.g. ingratiation, rational persuasion, inspiration, consultation; Falbe & Yukl, 1992; Yukl et al., 1996) than negative (e.g. pressure, coalitions, upwards appeals), can cultivate an environment where social influence flows easily and leads to effective interactions, rather than taxes the emotional and performance resources of employees.

In sum, politics and relationships are perpetually intertwined in the work environment. With social influence as a driving force behind change and progress, often detrimentally, organizations, leaders and followers alike can't help but act politically towards one another. This is not necessarily a bad thing as much as it is an apparent reality. The key to success for both individuals and organization, then, lies in cultivating effectiveness in social influence and politics, while managing the broad-level effects such influence behaviors have on work as a whole. An ideal balance of personal and organizational politicization can be achieved that can enhance rather than stymie performance, and it is something worth striving towards.

References

Ahearn, K. K., Ferris, G. R., Hochwarter, W. A., Douglas, C., & Ammeter, A. P. (2004). Leader political skill and team performance, *Journal of Management*, *30*, 309–327.

Ammeter, A. P., Douglas, C., Gardner, W. L., Hochwarter, W. A., & Ferris, G. R. (2002). Toward a political theory of leadership, *Leadership Quarterly*, *13*, 751–796.

Andrews, M. C. & Kacmar, K. M. (2001). Discriminating among organizational politics, justice, and support, *Journal of Organizational Behavior*, *22*, 347–366.

Aryee, S., Chen, Z. X., Sun, L. Y., & Debrah, W. A. (2007). Antecedents and outcomes of abusive supervision: Test of a trickle-down model, *Journal of Applied Psychology*, *92*, 191–201.

Barry, B. & Crant, J. M. (2000). Dyadic communication relationships in organizations: An attribution/expectancy approach, *Organization Science*, *11*, 648–664.

Bentley, J. R., Treadway, D. C., Yang, J., Shaughnessy, B. A., & Williams, L. V. (2011). Thriving in the face of oppression: The moderating effect of political skill on the perceived victimization-performance relationship, a three-study replication. Poster presented at the annual meeting for the Society for Industrial and Organizational Psychology, Chicago, IL.

Berscheid, E. (1999). The greening of relationship science, *American Psychologist*, *54*, 260–266.

Blickle, G. & Schnitzler, A. K. (2010). Is the political skill inventory fit for personnel selection? An experimental field study, *International Journal of Selection and Assessment*, *18*, 155–165.

Blickle, G., Witzki, A. H., & Schneider, P. B. (2009). Mentoring support and power: A three year predictive field study on protégé networking and career success, *Journal of Vocational Behavior*, *74*, 181–189.

Brass, D. J. (1985). Men's and women's networks: A study of interaction patterns and influence in an organization, *Academy of Management Journal*, *28*, 327–343.

Breland, J. W., Treadway, D. C., Duke, A. B., & Adams, G. L. (2007). The interactive effects of leader-member exchange and political skill on subjective career success, *Journal of Leadership & Organizational Studies*, *13*, 1–14.

Brouer, R. L., Duke, A., Treadway, D. C., & Ferris, G. R. (2009). The moderating effect of political skill on the demographic dissimilarity – Leader-member exchange quality relationship, *Leadership Quarterly*, *20*, 61–69.

Castro, S. L., Douglas, C., Hochwarter, W. A., Ferris, G. R., & Frink, D. D. (2003). The effects of positive affect and gender on the influence tactics-job performance relationship, *Journal of Leadership & Organizational Studies*, *10*, 1–18.

Christiansen, N., Villanova, P., & Mikulay, S. (1997). Political influence compatibility: Fitting the person to the climate, *Journal of Organizational Behavior*, *18*, 709–730.

Crick, N. R. & Dodge, K. A. (1994). A review and reformulation of social-information-processing mechanisms in children's social adjustment, *Psychological Bulletin*, *115*, 74–101.

Cropanzano, R., Howes, J. C., Grandey, A. A., & Toth, P. (1997). The relationship of organizational politics and support to work behaviors, attitudes, and stress, *Journal of Organizational Behavior*, *18*, 159–180.

Douglas, C. & Ammeter, A. P. (2004). An examination of leader political skill and its effect on ratings of leader effectiveness, *Leadership Quarterly*, 15, 537–550.

Downie, M., Mageau, G. A., & Koestner, R. (2008). What makes for a pleasant social interaction? Motivational dynamics of interpersonal relations, *Journal of Social Psychology*, 148, 523–534.

Drory, A. (1993). Perceived political climate and job attitudes, *Organization Studies*, 14, 59–71.

Drory, A. & Romm, T. (1988). Politics in organization and its perceptions within the organization, *Organization Studies*, 9, 165–179.

Falbe, C. M. & Yukl, G. (1992). Consequences for managers of using single influence tactics and combinations of tactics, *Academy of Management Journal*, 35, 638–652.

Ferris, G. R., Adams, G., Kolodinsky, R. W., Hochwarter, W. A., & Ammeter, A. P. (2002). Perceptions of organizational politics: Theory and research directions: in F. J. Yammarino & F. Dansereau (eds) *Research in Multi-Level Issues, Volume 1: The Many Faces of Multi-Level Issues* (pp. 179–254). Oxford, UK: JAI Press/Elsevier Science.

Ferris, G. R., Anthony, W. P., Kolodinsky, R. W., Gilmore, D. C., & Harvey, M. G. (2002). Development of political skill: in C. Wankel & R. DeFillippi (eds) *Rethinking Management Education for the 21ˢᵗ Century, A Volume in: Research in Management Education and Development* (pp. 3–25). New York: Information Age Publishing.

Ferris, G. R., Davidson, S. L., & Perrewé, P. L. (2005). *Political Skill at Work: Impact on Work Effectiveness*. Mountain View, CA: Davies-Black Publishing.

Ferris, G. R., Fedor, D. B., & King, T. R. (1994). A political conceptualization of managerial behavior, *Human Resource Management Review*, 4, 1–34.

Ferris, G. R., Frink, D. D., Bhawuk, D. P. S., Zhou, J., & Gilmore, D. C. (1996). Reactions of diverse groups to politics in the workplace, *Journal of Management*, 22, 23–44.

Ferris, G. R., Harrell-Cook, G., & Dulebohn, J. H. (2000). Organizational politics: The nature of the relationship between politics perceptions and political behavior: in S. B. Bacharach & E. J. Lawler (eds) *Research in the Sociology of Organizations* (Vol. 17, pp. 89–130). Stamford, CT: JAI Press.

Ferris, G. R. & Judge, T. A. (1991). Personnel/human resources management: A political influence perspective, *Journal of Management*, 17, 447–488.

Ferris, G. R. & Kacmar, K. M. (1992). Perceptions of organizational politics, *Journal of Management*, 18, 93–116.

Ferris, G. R., Liden, R. C., Munyon, T. P., Summers, J. K., Basik, K. J., & Buckley, M. R. (2009). Relationships at work: Toward a multidimensional conceptualization of dyadic work relationships, *Journal of Management*, 35, 1379–1403.

Ferris, G. R., Perrewé, P. L., & Douglas, C. (2002). Social effectiveness in organizations: Construct validity and research directions, *Journal of Leadership and Organization Studies*, 9, 33–50.

Ferris, G. R., Russ, G. S., & Fandt, P. M. (1989). Politics in organizations: in R. A. Giacalone & P. Rosenfeld (eds) *Impression Management in the Organization* (pp. 143–170). Hillsdale, NJ: Lawrence Erlbaum.

Ferris, G. R., Treadway, D. C., Brouer, R. L., & Munyon, T. P. (2012). Political skill in the organizational sciences: in G. R. Ferris & D. C. Treadway (eds)

Politics in Organizations: Theory and Research Considerations (pp. 487–528). New York: Routledge/Taylor & Francis.

Ferris, G. R., Treadway, D. C., Kolodinsky, R. W., Hochwarter, W. A., Kacmar, C. J., Douglas, C., & Frink, D. D. (2005). Development and validation of the political skill inventory, *Journal of Management*, *31*, 126–152.

Ferris, G. R., Treadway, D. C., Perrewé, P. L., Brouer, R. L., Douglas, C., & Lux, S. (2007a). Political skill in organizations, *Journal of Management*, *33*, 290–320.

Ferris, G. R., Zinko, R., Brouer, R. L., Buckley, M. R., & Harvey, M. G. (2007b). Strategic bullying as a supplementary, balanced perspective on destructive leadership, *Leadership Quarterly*, *18*, 195–206.

Gandz, J. & Murray, V. V. (1980). The experience of workplace politics, *Academy of Management Journal*, *23*, 237–251.

Gerstner, C. R. & Day, D. V. (1997). Meta-analytic review of leader-member exchange theory: Correlates and construct issues, *Journal of Applied Psychology*, *82*, 827–844.

Gilmore, D. C., Ferris, G. R., Dulebohn, J. H., & Harrell-Cook, G. (1996). Organizational politics and employee attendance, *Group and Organization Management*, *21*, 481–494.

Gordon, R. A. (1996). Impact of ingratiation on judgments and evaluations: A meta-analytic investigation, *Journal of Personality and Social Psychology*, *71*, 54–70.

Graen, G. B. & Uhl-Bien, M. (1995). Development of leader-member exchange (LMX) theory of leadership over 25 years: Applying a multi-level multi-domain perspective, *Leadership Quarterly*, *6*, 219–247.

Gui, B. & Stanca, L. (2010). Happiness and relational goods: Well-being and interpersonal relations in the economic sphere, *International Review of Economics*, *57*, 105–118.

Harrell-Cook, G., Ferris, G. R., & Dulebohn, J. H. (1999). Political behaviors as moderators of the perceptions of organizational politics – Work outcomes relationships, *Journal of Organizational Behavior*, *20*, 1093–1106.

Harris, K. J. & Kacmar, K. M. (2005). Easing the strain: The buffer role of supervisors in the perceptions of politics-strain relationship, *Journal of Occupational and Organizational Psychology*, *78*, 337–354.

Harris, K. J., Kacmar, K. M., Zivnuska, S., & Shaw, J. D. (2007). The impact of political skill on impression management effectiveness, *Journal of Applied Psychology*, *92*, 278–285.

Hewlin, P. F. (2003). And the award for best actor goes to ...: Facades of conformity in organizational settings, *Academy of Management Review*, *28*, 633–642.

Higgins, C. A., Judge, T. A., & Ferris, G. R. (2003). Influence tactics and work outcomes: A meta-analysis, *Journal of Organizational Behavior*, *24*, 89–106.

Hochwarter, W. A., Kacmar, K. M., & Treadway, D. C., & Watson, T. (2003). It's all relative: The distinction and prediction of politics perceptions across levels, *Journal of Applied Social Psychology*, *33*, 1995–2016.

Ilgen, D. R. & Youtz, M. A. (1986). Factors affecting the evaluation and development of minorities in organization, *Research in Personnel and Human Resources Management*, *4*, 307–337.

Jones, E. E. & Pittman, T. S. (1982). Toward a general theory of strategic self-presentation: in J. Suls (ed.) *Psychological Perspectives on the Self* (Vol. 1, pp. 231–262). Hillsdale, NJ: Lawrence Erlbaum.

Judge, T. A. & Bretz, R. D., Jr. (1994). Political influence behavior and career success, *Journal of Management, 20*, 43–65.

Kacmar, K. M. & Baron, R. A. (1999). Organizational politics: The state of the field, links to related processes, and an agenda for future research: in G. R. Ferris (ed.) *Research in Personnel and Human Resources Management* (Vol. 17, pp. 1–39). Stamford, CT: JAI Press.

Kacmar, K. M., Bozeman, D. P., Carlson, D. S., & Anthony, W. P. (1999). A partial test of the perceptions of organizational politics model, *Human Relations, 52*, 383–416.

Kacmar, K. M. & Carlson, D. S. (1997). Further validation of the Perceptions of Politics Scale (POPS): A multi-sample approach, *Journal of Management, 23*, 627–658.

Kipnis, D. & Schmidt, S. M. (1988). Upward influence styles: Relationship with performance evaluations, salary, and stress, *Administrative Science Quarterly, 33*, 528–542.

Kipnis, D., Schmidt, S. M., & Wilkinson, I. (1980). Intraorganizational influence tactics: Explorations in getting one's way, *Journal of Applied Psychology, 65*, 440–452.

Kolodinsky, R. W., Treadway, D. C., & Ferris, G. R. (2007). Political skill and influence effectiveness: Testing portions of an expanded Ferris and Judge (1991) model, *Human Relations, 60*, 1747–1777.

Longenecker, C. O., Sims, H. P., & Gioia, D. A. (1987). Behind the mask: The politics of employee appraisal, *Academy of Management Executive, 1*, 183–193.

Madison, D., Allen, R., Porter, L. W., Renwick, P., & Mayes, B. (1980). Organizational politics: An exploration of managers' perceptions, *Human Relations, 33*, 79–100.

Maslyn, J. & Fedor, D. B. (1998). Perceptions of politics: Does measuring different foci matter? *Journal of Applied Psychology, 84*, 645–653.

Mintzberg, H. (1983). *Power In and Around Organizations.* Englewood Cliffs, NJ: Prentice-Hall.

Parker, C., Dipboye, R., & Jackson, S. (1995). Perceptions of organizational politics: An investigation of antecedents and consequences, *Journal of Management, 5*, 891–912.

Pettigrew, A. (1973). *The Politics of Organizational Decision Making.* London: Tavistock.

Pfeffer, J., Salancik, G. R., & Leblebici, H. (1976). The effect of uncertainty on the use of social influence in organizational decision making, *Administrative Science Quarterly, 21*, 227–245.

Phillips, K. W., Rothbard, N. P., & Dumas, T. L. (2009). To disclose or not to disclose? Status distance and self-disclosure in diverse environments, *Academy of Management Review, 34*, 710–732.

Ragins, B. R. (1997). Diversified mentoring relationships in organizations: A power perspective, *Academy of Management Review, 22*, 482–521.

Reis, H. T. (2007). Steps toward the ripening of relationship science, *Personal Relationships, 14*, 1–23.

Reis, H. T. & Collins, W. A. (2004). Relationships, human behavior, and psycho-logical science, *Current Directions in Psychological Science*, *13*, 233–237.

Reis, H. T., Collins, W. A., & Berscheid, E. (2000). The relationship context of human behavior and development, *Psychological Bulletin*, *126*, 844–872.

Rudman, L. A. (1998). Self-promotion as a risk factor for women: The costs and benefits of counterstereotypical impression management, *Journal of Personality and Social Psychology*, *74*, 629–645.

Russell, B. (1938). *Power: A New Social Analysis.* London: Allen & Unwin.

Shaughnessy, B. A., Treadway, D. C., Breland, J. A., Williams, L. V., & Brouer, R. L. (2011). Influence and promotability: The importance of female political skill, *Journal of Managerial Issues*, *26*, 584–603.

Smircich, L. & Morgan, G. (1982). Leadership: The management of meaning, *Journal of Applied Behavioral Science*, *18*, 257–273.

Souerwine, A. H. (1978). Career strategies: Planning for personal achievement, *Management Review*, *65*, 55–62.

Sparrowe, R. T. & Liden, R. C. (1997). Process and structure in leader-member exchange, *Academy of Management Review*, *22*, 522–552.

Sparrowe, R. T. & Liden, R. C. (2005). Two routes to influence: Integrating leader-member exchange and social network perspectives, *Administrative Science Quarterly*, *50*, 505–535.

Sternberg, R. J. (1997). Managerial intelligence: Why IQ isn't enough, *Journal of Management*, *23*, 475–493.

Tedeschi, J. T. & Melburg, V. (1984). Impression management and influence in the organization: in S. B. Bacharach & E. J. Lawler (eds) *Research in the Sociology of Organizations* (Vol. 3, pp. 31–58). Greenwich, CT: JAI Press.

Tepper, B. J., Brown, S. J., & Hunt, M. D. (1993). Strength of subordinates' upward influence tactics and gender congruency effects, *Journal of Applied Social Psychology*, *23*, 1903–1919.

Tepper, B. J., Moss, S. E., & Duffy, M. K. (2011). Predictors of abusive supervi-sion: Supervisor perceptions of deep-level dissimilarity, relationship conflict, and subordinate performance, *Academy of Management Journal*, *54*, 279–294.

Thacker, R. A. & Wayne, S. J. (1995). An examination of the relationship between upward influence tactics and assessments of promotability, *Journal of Management*, *21*, 739–756.

Treadway, D. C. (2012). Political will in organizations: in G. R. Ferris & D. C. Treadway (eds) *Politics in Organizations: Theory and Research Considerations* (pp. 529–554). New York: Taylor & Francis Group.

Treadway, D. C., Adams, G. L., & Goodman, J. M. (2005). The formation of political sub-climates: Predictions from social identity, structuration, and symbolic interaction, *Journal of Business and Psychology*, *20*, 201–219.

Treadway, D. C., Breland, J. W., Adams, G. L., Duke, A. B., & Williams, L. A. (2010). The interactive effects of political skill and future time perspective on career and community networking behavior, *Social Networks*, *32*, 138–147.

Treadway, D. C., Breland, J. W., Williams, L. A., Yang, J., & Williams, L. (2012). Political skill, relational control, and the self in relational leadership processes: in M. Uhl-Bien & S. M. Ospina (eds) *Advancing Relational Leadership Research: A Dialogue Among Perspectives* (pp. 381–420). New York: Information Age Publishing.

Treadway, D. C., Ferris, G. R., Duke, A. B., Adams, G. L., & Thatcher, J. B. (2007). The moderating role of subordinate political skill on supervisors' impressions of subordinate ingratiation and ratings of subordinate interpersonal facilitation, *Journal of Applied Psychology, 92*, 848–855.

Treadway, D. C., Hochwarter, W. A., Ferris, G. R., Kacmar, C. J., Douglas, C., Ammeter, A. P., & Buckley, M. R. (2004). Leader political skill and employee reactions, *Leadership Quarterly, 15*, 493–513.

Treadway, D. C., Shaughnessy, B. A., Breland, J. W., Yang, J., & Reeves, M. (2013). Political skill and the job performance of bullies, *Journal of Managerial Psychology, 28*, 273–289.

Valle, M. P. & Perrewé, P. L. (2000). Do politics perceptions relate to political behaviors? *Human Relations, 53*, 359–386.

Vigoda, E. (2002). Stress-related aftermaths to workplace politics: The relationships among politics, job distress, and aggressive behaviors in organizations, *Journal of Organizational Behavior, 23*, 571–591.

Wayne, S. J. & Liden, R. C. (1995). Effects of impression management on performance ratings: A longitudinal study, *Academy of Management Journal, 38*, 232–260.

West, C. & Zimmerman, D. H. (1987). Doing gender, *Gender & Society, 1*, 125–151.

Williams, K. Y. & O'Reilly, C. A. (1998). Demography and diversity in organizations: A review of 40 years of research, *Research in Organizational Behavior, 20*, 77–140.

Willits, R. D. (1968). Company performance and interpersonal relations, *Industrial Management Review, 8*, 91–107.

Winstead, B. A. & Morganson, V. (2009). Gender and relationships at work: in R. L. Morrison & S. L. Wright (eds) *Friends and Enemies in Organizations: A Work Psychology Perspective*. UK: Palgrave Macmillan.

Witt, L. A. (1998). Enhancing organizational goal congruence: A solution of organizational politics, *Journal of Applied Psychology, 83*, 666–674.

Yukl, G., Kim, H., & Falbe, C. M. (1996). Antecedents of influence outcomes, *Journal of Applied Psychology, 81*, 309–317.

Yukl, G. & Tracey, J. B. (1992). Consequences of influence tactics used with subordinates, peers, and the boss, *Journal of Applied Psychology, 77*, 525–535.

Zhou, J. & Ferris, G. R. (1995). The dimensions and consequences of organizational politics perceptions: A confirmatory analysis, *Journal of Applied Social Psychology, 25*, 1747–1764.

5

The Influential Subordinate: An Oxymoron or a Daily Necessity?

Susan Geertshuis[1], Rachel L. Morrison[2], and
Helena D. Cooper-Thomas[3]

Naomi was recruited to restructure the administrative systems within a company. Her new line manager provided Naomi with the company's vision for how this should be done and provided her view on the system that would bring about the desired efficiency gains. Naomi's manager did not have a background in administration but had been in the company for many years and so knew everyone and was an experienced user of the old systems. Over a period of months Naomi and her manager got to know each other and Naomi also built up her knowledge of the company's systems and a network of her own contacts. Naomi was keen to make a good impression on her new boss, she worked hard, and discussed her evolving ideas for the restructure with her manager. Unfortunately, Naomi's manager seemed to reject most of Naomi's reasoning and ideas. She discounted the evidence Naomi provided and asked Naomi to stick with the original vision. Naomi felt that her boss had not given her, or her ideas, proper regard. She was concerned that her manager was wedded to solutions that would be expensive and inefficient. Can Naomi influence her boss? What should she do? Who should she involve?

The above story illustrates the dilemmas that all of us have experienced at one time or another as we have pondered the likely consequences of seeking to influence our boss. Perhaps more poignantly, if you are in a leadership role, it may illustrate the dilemmas that those who report to

---

[1] Graduate School of Management, The University of Auckland
[2] Management Department, AUT University
[3] School of Psychology, The University of Auckland

you wrestle with as they contemplate the need to communicate a different view or approach to you.

As subordinates, we are expected to contribute to, follow, and support decisions rather than to take a lead. As subordinates we can choose to intervene or not, and can do so in a number of ways. Each possible intervention involves both risks and potential benefits to our reputation and relationships as well as to the issue in hand. For example, an effort to introduce facts pertinent to a decision may be welcomed and our expertise recognized or it may be received as an inappropriate and worthless intrusion from someone who should know their place. This chapter explores the subordinate position and how it manifests in the workplace. We examine the nature of the relationship subordinates have with their immediate superiors at work and the ways subordinates may seek to influence decisions and situations.

Social hierarchies

Magee and Galinsky (2008, p. 354) define social hierarchy as "an implicit or explicit rank order of individuals or groups with respect to a valued social dimension". Social hierarchies are ubiquitous, they emerge spontaneously or can be imposed, and are resistant to efforts to subvert or suppress them (Leavitt, 2005). Higher positions in the hierarchy are valued, awarded, rewarded, and signified in numerous ways; they necessarily involve subordinates with, typically, a greater number of subordinates than superiors (Mintzberg, 1979). In the sections that follow we describe the nature of formal and informal hierarchies and the purpose they serve in organizations. We explore the bases of position in a hierarchy and the constraining and enabling effects they have on subordinates.

Few workplaces of any size exist without formal and explicit hierarchical structures as depicted by titles, reporting lines, and organizational charts. Hierarchies, it is argued, provide a superior opportunity for coordination compared to other forms of organization, and are believed to enhance performance (Groysberg et al., 2011; Halevy et al., 2012). They appear to serve a number of organizational purposes: They create order and stability, define roles, facilitate coordination and communication, limit and enable actors, and motivate members who strive for higher positions (Magee & Galinsky, 2008). Formal structures also serve individuals well, setting the behavior of subordinates and their superiors and so creating certainty, clarity, and more satisfying encounters (Tiedens et al., 2007).

So pervasive are hierarchies that if they are not set formally, they will arise spontaneously (Anderson et al., 2001). On the basis of multiple cues relating to behavior, perceived competence, and position rankings are established and reinforced (Fiske & Ofshe, 1970; Hall et al., 2005; Schmid Mast & Hall, 2004). These informal social processes are also likely to be active within formal hierarchies generating nuances which layer over more simplistic and explicit formal hierarchical structures.

The very fabric of an organization, its subunits, its reporting lines, committee structures, and approval processes serve to signify, reinforce, and sustain the hierarchy and to determine who makes decisions, how, and about what (Lueger et al., 2005; Schreyogg & Sydow, 2011). There are also psychological pressures in favor of the status quo; low ranking individuals internalize and accept that they do not have legitimate claims to power and status, and that those higher up are more deserving and able (Jost et al., 2004; Liviatan & Jost, 2011). The sustainability of hierarchies can also be attributed to having access to opportunity: Superiors have greater opportunities to perform well and justify their elevated positions whereas subordinates are more likely to be weighed down by undesirable tasks (Ashforth & Kreiner, 1999). As an example that might resonate, senior professors are awarded sabbaticals and grants so they can spend time on research. They consequently generate substantial research outputs which justifies their elevated position in the hierarchy and greater time allocation for research. Junior researchers, on the other hand, are squeezing in their research between marking, tutoring, administrative duties, and lecturing. Small wonder that subordinates, even those of superior ability, tend not to overtake their superiors within an organization. Collectively, hierarchical position, structures, psychological pressures, and limited opportunities appear to define and curtail subordinates. In efforts to influence upwards, subordinates must "swim against the tide", they must seek audience, win hearts and minds, secure commitment, and possibly resources, within systems which appear to be structured neither to listen nor obey. How is this done?

Power

Influence derives not only from position in the social hierarchy but also from power, and the relationship between the two is so close that influence is sometimes seen as integral to definitions of power. By these definitions an agent has power to the extent that they can get a target to do something that they would not otherwise be inclined to do

(French & Raven, 1959; Pfeffer, 1981). Simon (1953) identifies this definition as tautological, with propositions that must be so by definition rather than on the basis of proof. It is not safe to assume power is influence and we should establish whether this is so.

An alternative view is that powerful people have control over outcomes or resources that others want to gain or avoid (Fiske & Berdahl, 2007; Pfeffer & Salancik, 1978). Within this conception powerful people do not have to have the intention of influencing. Influence is not power or status, it is a consequence of both and possibly, in a symbiotic process, may contribute to both (Magee & Galinsky, 2008). This view is intuitively appealing; it is substantiated by the findings that power does not inevitably lead to influence and it enables researchers to unpack the power-to-influence relationship. Subordinates, in general, are more dependent on superiors for access to resources than superiors are dependent on subordinates. The degree of power imbalance depends upon the degree to which the subordinate can access valued "rewards" and avoid unwelcome "punishments" only through their superior or whether alternatives exist by either working independently or via other relationships. Sources of power are many and varied and are not all valued equally by all subordinates. For example a superior's power to allocate a subordinate a challenging and high profile task may be seen by different subordinates as highly positive, highly negative or met with indifference. Subordinates also have control over resources and so can be powerful, at least in the short term. For example, we are all familiar with the manager who struggles to function without his secretary to operate the "new-fangled" office technologies. Knowledge workers in particular may create a reverse dependency. For example, an accountant may be subordinate to the directors but his/her control of access to information and ability to translate it renders him/her powerful.

In seminal work on power, French and Raven (1959) identified the sources of power as being: Reward (support, benefits, favors), coercive (abuse, annoyance, cause problems), information (persuasion, logic, evidence), expert (reputation for knowledge, experience, judgment), legitimate (the right to direct, duty to obey), and referent (vision, ideals, principles). Within the resource dependency approach described above the capacity to reward or sanction are the means by which power is exercised; they are "power in action" and the remaining categories describe alternative resources that the more powerful have greater control over. Sources of superiors' power include power over physical outcomes, economic outcomes, and social outcomes. Social outcomes include belonging, understanding, responsiveness and predictability, enhancing, and respecting (Baumeister & Leary, 1995; Fiske, 2004).

Status and power are sometimes used interchangeably but they should be distinguished. Social status is related to power and is the degree to which an individual or group is respected or admired (Magee & Galinsky, 2008). Generally higher status individuals have enhanced social influence (Fiske & Berdahl, 2007). Status is subjective and determined solely through the perceptions of others. It is a reflection of perceptions of competence, stature, and characteristics that are deemed to confer status, such as race, height, dress, class, education, or gender (Anderson et al., 2001; Carli, 2001). While power is based on the resources an individual actually has, status lies in the eyes of others. Powerful people have status only if they are respected by others. A stock room employee may have power in that they control access to valuable resources but may have more or less status depending on their ability and willingness to locate items at short notice and on the value others place on this function of their job. On the other hand, a technical expert may have status and be respected for his or her ability to diagnose faults but have no control over valued resources such as spare parts and so have little power.

As an added complexity, and one that subordinates might be able to turn to their advantage, power and status are signaled in the way we behave. Subordinates are less likely to express their personal opinions (Berdahl & Martorana, 2006), talk for shorter periods than do superiors and tend neither to interrupt (Brown & Levinson, 1987) nor to override others' views (Briñol et al., 2007) and, in fact, may actually let superiors shape their views. Subordinates attend more to emotional expressions and take more account of others' experience and knowledge (Galinsky et al., 2006). Subordinates tend to attend more to details, while managers look at the bigger picture (Trope & Liberman, 2003). Keltner et al. (2003) argue that this extends to our neurobiological systems with high power individuals having a primary "approach" orientation and low power individuals a primary "inhibit" orientation, giving them differing perspectives on the same issues. However, at least some of these behaviors appear to be amenable to training, which means subordinates can learn to behave in ways that indicate power and status (Brown et al., 1990). Although this can backfire and subordinates who do not conform to expectations and act as if they have more status than they do may find themselves socially sanctioned (Anderson et al., 2008).

When Naomi joined her company she was told who she would report to and how often they would meet. Naomi is aware that her new boss can either help her in her new role or make her life more difficult. It hasn't occurred to Naomi that she too can choose to reward her boss nor that she has the power to withdraw her productivity and her social approval. Naomi is proud of her expertise and expects it to be valued.

In conversations Naomi expresses her views cautiously and does not argue with her boss. Naomi tries to make her capability and expertise clear. She presents specific evidence that supports her ideas but her boss is more focused on the vision and pays scant regard to detail.

As Naomi settles into her new job she creates her own network of contacts and becomes less dependent on her boss for information, support, contacts, and direction. She is building her own power base and gaining a greater appreciation of her manager's relative status and position within the company.

We have established that, although subordinates tend to be disadvantaged relative to superiors, they are not without power. Being capable, and being recognized as such, is a critical source of both power and status. Improving networks of powerful others, getting assigned to specialist roles, and gaining privileges are all strategies a subordinate can use to increase access to restricted resources and so increase their powerbase without moving within a formal hierarchy.

Subordinate – Superior relationships

We now turn to relationships within hierarchies, more specifically, the relationship between subordinates and their immediate superior. We begin by looking at what constitutes *good* relationships and go on to identify their precursors and consequences. We will then be in a position to look at how subordinates' relationships with their superiors may affect their ability to influence.

Having a wide network of contacts and close relationships with important people can be looked at as a source of power (Ferris et al., 2005) and is partially captured by French and Raven's (1959) conception of referent power. Referent power though seems unidirectional and is the extent to which subordinates identify with, admire or emulate the leader and want to maintain or form a relationship

(French & Raven, 1959). This is an overly narrow view and more recent work has also focused on reciprocity and mutual affect.

Reciprocity in trust appears to be critical to all relationships whether they occur in our personal, educational or working lives (Simpson, 2006). Trust is signified by a sense of confidence in a group member (Meyer et al., 1998) and by a willingness to be vulnerable to another group member (Kramer & Carnevale, 2001; Sweeney et al., 2009). In new relationships, interdependence models of relationships suggest that through demonstrating competence and dependability and through exhibiting trust, a trusting relationship will emerge (Holmes & Rempel, 1989; Thibaut & Kelley, 1959).

Trust ties leaders and followers together and is a measure of leader legitimacy (Bennis & Nanus, 1985). Trust in relationships is associated with cooperation (Jones & George, 1998) and the greater the trust a subordinate has in their superior, the greater the level of influence the subordinate will accept (Sweeney et al., 2009; Zand, 1972). Zand (1972) demonstrated that this worked both ways and that subordinates who were trusted more were better able to influence their superiors than subordinates whose superiors reported lower levels of trust. It seems that subordinates who establish trust-based relationships with their bosses will find their superiors more amenable to influence attempts. To build such trust-based relationships, subordinates need to demonstrate competence, dependability, and their own trustworthiness.

Leader Member Exchange (LMX) theory concentrates exclusively on dyadic relationships between leaders and followers and includes trust. LMX theory holds that leaders develop close, trusting and informal relationships with a limited number of subordinates who will constitute an "in" group, privileged with increased access to resources and better able to influence each other (Dansereau et al., 1975; Graen & Cashman, 1975). Other subordinates remain in an "out" group and have a more formal relationship with their superior. Relationships develop through reciprocity and social exchange. LMX has origins in both role theory and social exchange theory. Role theory explains how relationships develop based on mutual dependencies within evolving roles (Dienesch & Liden, 1986). Social exchange theory describes the interdependence that forms between two parties based on benefits exchanged, which may include elements of power and influence (Molm et al., 1999). Leaders and followers may test each other to see if they can safely develop a trust-based relationship. If exchanges are satisfying they will be repeated and a relationship will develop (Dansereau et al., 1975; Dienesch & Liden, 1986; Graen et al., 1990). Over time, as the relationship deepens, trust may be afforded based on affect and caring rather than on a more rational evaluation (McAllister, 1995).

Graen and Uhl-Bien (1995) suggest that LMX is comprised of three dimensions: Mutual respect of capabilities, reciprocated trust, and a sense of work-related obligation to one another. Liden and Maslyn (1998) recognize that a broader base of factors may contribute to relationship quality and suggest four dimensions: Contribution, affect, liking and professional respect. Studies also identify support, liking, loyalty, attention, and latitude as components of LMX (Schriesheim et al., 1999). Again, it follows that a relationship with these components is likely to be one where participants are willing to listen to, trust and be influenced by one another.

A number of variables have been identified as antecedents or as co-occurring with LMX which potentially indicate how readily a relationship can be built (Dulebohn et al., 2011). In superiors they include: trustworthiness (Brower et al., 2009; Brower et al., 2000; Gomez & Rosen, 2001), positive expectations of subordinates (Wayne et al., 1997), and agreeableness (Bernerth et al., 2008; Erdogan & Liden, 2002) and in subordinates they include: goal orientation (Chiaburu, 2005; Janssen & Van Yperen, 2004), effort (Maslyn & Uhl-Bien, 2001), liking (Engle & Lord, 1997; Liden & Maslyn, 1998; Wayne et al., 1997), similarity (Deluga, 1998; Murphy & Ensher, 1999), and positive expectation (Liden et al., 1993; Wayne et al., 1997).

There are multiple favorable consequences for both organizations and individuals that derive from trust-based relationships. LMX has an impact on subordinate behavior in that subordinates in high LMX relationships are more likely to be dedicated, hard-working and proficient (Dansereau et al., 1975; Liden & Graen, 1980; Yukl, 1989). In addition, subordinates who trust their superiors and feel they will be listened to are more likely to attempt to influence their superiors and share ideas that benefit the organization (Dutton et al., 1997). Not only do subordinates in high LMX relationships receive higher performance appraisals, they are allowed greater room for influence (Graen et al., 1990; Yukl, 1989). Additionally, successful upward influencing attempts are associated with favorable attributions of subordinates (Liden & Mitchell, 1988). In good relationships partners accentuate the positive and attenuate the negative (Murray et al., 1993). That is, they are attuned in their perceptions to evidence that sits comfortably with preconceptions. Thus in a good relationship, subordinates could benefit from a virtuous cycle where their target of influence is open to influence, allows them opportunity to influence and is likely to interpret their messages in a positive way, and then regards the subordinate still more favorably. Of course credibility can be lost and subordinates who are unsuccessful in influencing or use overly assertive tactics may damage relationships and appraisals of their performance (Christensen, 2011; Gupta & Case, 1980; Maslyn et al., 1996).

> Naomi's boss seems to have a strong and established network of trusted colleagues and Naomi has not become one of them. Their conversations, though amicable, relate only to Naomi's work and on a personal level they don't seem to have much in common. Naomi has demonstrated trust and commitment by working hard and sharing her ideas but isn't feeling that she is trusted in return. Naomi's boss has listened to her in their regular but rather brief formal meetings but has not agreed with, contributed to, or taken on any of Naomi's suggestions. Naomi's boss wonders whether Naomi is up to the job, as she cannot see much value in Naomi's ideas which run counter to her own views.

To summarize, subordinates in high trust or high LMX relationships are advantaged: They have superiors who are inclined to view them positively and are more willing to accept influencing attempts. They have closer relationships, more contact and more freedom to speak and so have more opportunity to influence. However, influencing attempts viewed as overly harsh may damage the relationship, reduce LMX, and lose hard-won advantages.

Influencing behavior

The research and practice context

So far we have considered hierarchy, social power, and relationships. We have established that position, power, and relationship quality determine how influential a subordinate may be. Influencing upwards is undertaken in an effort to bring about a change in a superior's attitudes, decision-making or behavior. We now look to how such attempts to influence might be executed. It is likely that some of the principles identified as predictive of successful change management and persuasive communication (Kenton, 1989; King, 2010) also have relevance to upward influence and may offer models and novel interpretations regarding how subordinates might bring about changes in their superiors. To the extent that influencing upwards is one of many forms of persuasive communication, then these general principles are likely to provide useful guidance to subordinates seeking influence.

We know that bringing about change is difficult, with as few as 30% of attempts to lead change being successful (Meaney & Pung, 2008). Change threatens people's social identity, power, and status, and the response to threat is often resistance (Diefenbach, 2007). In addition, change requires careful planning and management (Appelbaum et al., 2012; Kotter, 1996). Language is not merely the vehicle in which most efforts to influence are delivered, it is a source of influence itself. An engaging story, a succinct exposition of evidence or an impassioned plea cannot be equated with this same information delivered in a rambling and bored manner, even if the bald contents remain the same. Linguistic tactics (such as pitch) and non-verbal behavior (such as eye contact) almost invariably influence targets and add or detract weight from messages (Cesario & Higgins, 2008; Drake & Moberg, 1986; Imada & Hakel, 1977; Stewart et al., 2008). Strategic communication research suggests that while clarity and authenticity are usually goals of effective communication, ambiguity is sometimes used to maintain position and can also be effective in achieving goals (Tregaskis, 2003). Research into teaching and learning tells us that understanding is built, not given, and that must be pitched at a learner's current levels of understanding (Hummel & Holyoak, 2003). We also know the importance of motivating our learners; we know that active involvement facilitates learning (Pintrich, 2003) and that power differentials can make learning more difficult (Bunderson & Reagans, 2011). From the field of social influence, Cialdini and Goldstein (2004) define six strategies or tools that can be used purposefully to add strength to verbal and non-verbal persuasive messages. They are; *reciprocation*, people receiving a favor often feel obliged to return it; *consistency*, once assent is indicated targets feel an obligation to deliver on this commitment however fleeting it was; *social proof*, people tend to act a lot like sheep and do what others do; *authority*, people tend to do as they are told if it is someone in authority who is speaking; *liking*, people are persuaded by people they like; and *scarcity*, the risk of failure or loss motivates.

Collectively, these fields of study would suggest that subordinates who wish to influence superiors should be skilled communicators, prepared to devote time and energy to planning and executing their efforts to influence. They should be attuned to and deliver messages that resonate with their superiors. In the next section we look at behaviors associated with attempts to influence upwards.

Identifying influencing tactics

The proactive behaviors one uses to influence others are commonly known as "influence tactics", succinctly defined by (Castro et al., 2003) as "goal-oriented behaviors that individuals use to obtain desired outcomes" (p. 1). This section begins with an account of alternative influencing tactics and their dimensions. The motivations behind, and the antecedents of, tactic use are explored and the effects and effectiveness of different strategies are examined.

Kipnis is thought of as the pioneer of work in this area, with his thinking derived from his earlier contributions to the power literature. Kipnis et al. (1980) identified distinct influencing tactics used by individuals within organizations. They proposed eight tactics in their early work and later reduced this to six. In their 1980 paper, Kipnis et al. analyzed essays written by managers describing instances when they "succeeded in getting 'the target' to do something they wanted" (p. 440) and conducted a survey telling respondents "this questionnaire is a way of obtaining information about how you go about changing your boss's mind so that he or she agrees with you" (p. 443).

The tactics identified through factor analysis were:

Assertiveness included demanding, ordering, and setting milestones.
Ingratiation included showing humility, and making the target feel important.
Rationality was categorized as explaining and developing plans.
Exchange of benefits included offering to make sacrifices.
Upward appeal involves seeking the support of more senior staff.
Coalition is characterized by efforts to obtain through garnering the support of coworkers and subordinates.

Subordinates used both ingratiation and rationality much more frequently than any of the other tactics. Superiors' frequency of tactics use was somewhat higher, suggesting that frequency of use was related to the relative power of the respondent and target. Assertiveness was reported as being used by superiors at almost twice the rate it was reported as being used by subordinates but, this aside, no other marked differences were discernible in the relative frequency of tactic use. The measures developed by Kipnis and colleagues (1980) have been further refined by subsequent research (Barbuto & Moss, 2006; Hochwarter et al., 2000; Schriesheim & Hinkin, 1990). Other researchers have independently developed alternative measures of influencing tactics (Yukl & Falbe, 1990), although these show considerable overlap, as would be expected.

Numerous variables have been associated with tactic use, providing evidence both for commonalities and differences in antecedents and consequences. Examples of findings in relation to the most researched tactics are summarized in Table 5.1 but this is not an exhaustive list. What is not clear from the table is the range in findings, with some researchers reporting strong relationships and others negligible relationships between the same variables (Barbuto & Moss, 2006). In part this may arise from the variety of ways in which some tactics can be delivered. For example, coalition could be used by subordinates and could be perceived by a superior as a clear display of power, exerting extreme pressure, but it could also be used in a neutral or even encouraging way. Evidence for associations with some tactics is also slight, possibly because they are infrequently used which affects both research interest in them and statistical power when they are assessed. Machiavellianism seems to predict high use of tactics almost irrespective of type, perhaps indicating a general willingness to influence others. External locus of control predicts assertiveness and ingratiation while internal locus of control predicts rationality. Social identity is associated inversely with assertiveness and upward appeals, but positively with ingratiation.

The inconsistent relationships between predictor variables and tactic use could well reflect important moderator variables at work, and there is ample evidence of situational factors impacting on tactic use. For example, LMX, position, and autonomy have been associated with contrasting results for a number of tactics. To illustrate, Frese et al. (1999) note that while rational argument forms part of voice and therefore influential communication, autonomous workers may not need to explain themselves to their superiors and so may exhibit low levels of rationality. Some researchers have gone so far as to suggest that influencing tactics can only be understood within the context in which they are executed (Lueger et al., 2005). A further group of moderators might be goal or purpose: Kipnis et al. (1980) reported that tactics were executed for a variety of purposes, which were categorized as follows: To gain assistance on own job, to get others to do their jobs, to obtain personal benefits, and to initiate changes in work to improve the target's performance. Subordinate influence attempts were most commonly reported as having the goals of obtaining personal benefits from their superior, improving superior's performance, or initiating a change. When the goal was self-interest, the tactics used most commonly were self-presentation and negative actions which included becoming a nuisance and slowing down work. When the goal was to

Table 5.1 Influencing Tactics, Their Characteristics, and Associated Variables

Influence Tactic	Characteristics	Strength	Previous Research	Associated variables	Measures Used
Assertiveness	Demanding, ordering, setting deadlines, and making repeated requests (Kipnis et al., 1980).	Hard	No significant directional difference, and used more often in large organizations Kipnis et al. (1980). Often coercive and controlling in nature (van Knippenberg & Steensma, 2003). Labelled pressure tactics by Yukl and Falbe (1990).	Preceded by person centred or softer tactics (Kipnis et al., 1980); Machiavellianism (Vecchio & Sussman, 1989); extrinsic motivation, impression management, self-monitoring (Hochwarter et al., 2000); external locus of control (Ringer & Boss, 2000); perception of interpersonal skills (Wayne et al., 1997) and inversely with social identity (Hochwarter et al., 2000) and intrinsic motivation (Barbuto & Scholl, 1999); extrinsic measures of success (Higgins et al., 2003); LMX (Deluga & Perry, 1991; Dockery & Steiner, 1990; Krishnan, 2004; Yukl & Michel, 2006); promotability (Thacker & Wayne, 1995); performance assessments (Higgin et al., 2003).	Profile of Organizational Influence Strategies, Form M (Kipnis & Schmidt, 1988). Schriescheim and Hinkin (1990) refinement of Kipnis et al. (1980) subscales.
Coalitions	Using pressure for conformity (Kipnis et al., 1980) by gathering support from others and creating a "ganging-up" effect to influence (Barbuto & Moss, 2006).	Soft/Hard	Initially stated as a characteristic of rationality (Kipnis et al., 1980), thus classed as a soft tactic. However, the characteristics of this tactic are similar to that of Upwards Appeal, classified as a hard tactic. No significant directional differences (Yukl & Falbe, 1990).	Preceded by person centred or softer tactics (Kipnis et al., 1980); impression management and extrinsic motivation (Hochwarter et al. 2000); self-monitoring (Caldwell & Burger, 1997); intrinsic motivation (Barbuto & Scholl, 1999) and external locus of control (Ringer & Boss, 2000).	Profile of Organizational Influence Strategies, Form M (Kipnis & Schmidt, 1988). Schriescheim and Hinkin (1990) refinement of Kipnis et al. (1980) subscales.

Table 5.1 Influencing Tactics, Their Characteristics, and Associated Variables – *continued*

Influence Tactic	Characteristics	Strength	Previous Research	Associated variables	Measures Used
Exchange	Offering an exchange of positive benefits, or offering to make personal sacrifices (Kipnis et al., 1980). May include reminding the target of past favors (Barbuto & Moss, 2006).	Soft/Hard	Used to influence superiors (Kipnis et al., 1980). There is relatively little research on this influence strategy.	External locus of control, Machiavellianism, self-monitoring; (Hochwarter et al., 2000); intrinsic motivation (Barbuto et al., 2002) and inversely with perception of interpersonal skills (Wayne et al., 1997).	Yukl and Falbe (1990) Influence tactic taxonomy. Schriescheim and Hinkin (1990) refinement of Kipnis et al. (1980) subscales.
Ingratiation	Attempts to increase own attractiveness in another person's eyes, involving flattery, open support of targets opinion, false modesty, and smiling (Treadway et al., 2007).	Soft	Emerges at all target levels – upward, lateral, and downward (Kipnis et al., 1980).	Impression management (Deluga & Perry, 1994; Hochwarter et al., 2000); self-monitoring (Kumar & Beyerlain, 1991); external locus of control (Ringer & Boss, 2000; Canary et al., 1986); social identification (Harrison et al., 1998); intrinsic motivation (Barbuto & Scholl, 1999) and extrinsic motivation (Harrison et al., 1998); LMX/relationship (Deluga & Perry, 1994; Wayne & Ferris, 1990; Dockery & Steiner, 1990; Yukl & Michel, 2006; Wayne & Green, 1993, Colella & Varma, 2001; Farmer et al., 1997; Kacmar et al., 2004; Poppe et al., 1999, Furst & Cable, 2008); political skill (Treadway et al., 2007); performance assessment and extrinsic success (Higgins et al., 2003); inversely with self esteem (baumeister et al., 1989; Kacmar et al., 2004); promotability (Thacker & Wayne, 1995 but see Judge & Bretz, 1994; Orpen, 1996; Liden & Mitchell, 1988); need for power (Kacmar et al., 2004).	Influence Behavior Questionnaire (Furst & Cable, 2008). Schriescheim and Hinkin (1990) refinement of Kipnis et al. (1980) subscales.

Table 5.1 Influencing Tactics, Their Characteristics, and Associated Variables – *continued*

Influence Tactic	Characteristics	Strength	Previous Research	Associated variables	Measures Used
Rationality	Uses logic, factual evidence, and thorough explanations to persuade others to conform (Kolodinsky et al., 2007).	Soft	Initially found by Kipnis et al. (1980) to be used more in upwards influence, however Yukl & Falbe (1990) results were inconsistent with this, finding no significant directional differences.	Impression management (Deluga, 1991); self-monitoring (Hochwarter et al., 2000); intrinsic motivation (Blickle, 2000); internal locus of control (Ringer & Boss, 2000; Canary et al., 1986); job status (Kipnis et al., 1980); LMX (Dockery & Steiner, 1990; Yukl & Michel, 2006); promotability (Thacker & Wayne, 1995); gender – preferred by females (Schermerhorn & Bond, 1991); work outcomes (Higgins et al.,2003); political skill (Kolodinsky et al., 2007)	Schriescheim and Hinkin (1990) refinement of Kipnis et al. (1980) subscales.
Upwards Appeal	Making formal appeals to, and gaining informal support from, higher levels than the target (Kipnis et al., 1980).	Hard	Used by subordinates to influence superiors (Kipnis et al., 1980). There is relatively little research on this influence strategy.	Preceded by person centred or softer tactics (Kipnis et al., 1980); external locus of control and extrinsic motivation (Hochwarter et al., 2000); self esteem (Savard and Rogers, 1992); Machiavellianism (Vecchio and Sussman, 1989); self monitoring (Calwell & Burger, 1997); inversely with social identity (Hochwarter et al., 2000).	Yukl and Falbe (1990) Influence tactic taxonomy. Schriescheim and Hinkin (1990) refinement of Kipnis et al. (1980) subscales.

initiate change, subordinates tended to use self-presentation in conjunction with evidence and coalitions with others. When faced with resistance, tactics shifted to increasing levels of persistence and negative actions. Other theorists have classified influencing behaviors in terms of the goal of the behavior, with self-oriented and organization-oriented goals being associated with harder and softer tactics respectively (Kipnis et al., 1980; Schmidt & Kipnis, 1984; Wayne & Ferris, 1990).

The picture is equally complex when the consequences rather than antecedents of tactic use are examined. Following their meta-analysis of studies examining the associations between influencing tactic use and work outcomes, Higgins et al. (2003) conclude that the literature displays very little consensus. Using Kipnis et al.'s classification of tactics plus self-promotion, they concluded that only rationality and ingratiation had a consistent relationship with work outcomes but noted a wide range of findings in the literature they examined. They report that subjective measures of work outcome, such as performance appraisal, bore a stronger relationship with tactic use than did objective measures, such as salary.

Both ingratiation and rationality have been examined by workers in related fields. Ingratiation, defined as attempts by individuals to increase their attractiveness in the eyes of others (Wortman & Linsenmeier, 1977), is the most researched of all the tactics and has been reported to improve not only performance appraisal ratings (Wayne & Kacmar, 1991), the likelihood of interview offer (Kacmar et al., 2006), but also supervisor-subordinate relationships (Deluga & Perry, 1991). It is important to note that there are almost as many reports of negative association between ingratiation and subordinate outcomes as there are positive, and many positive results derive from analyses of encounters prior to or at the beginning of employment which, of course, usually precedes opportunities to form relationships with superiors. For example, the ingratiator tactic of self-promotion has been found to have a positive effect at interview but a negative impact on subsequent supervisor ratings of subordinates (Higgins et al., 2003).

In other research regarding ingratiation, Kacmar et al. (2004) report that high LMX positively predicts other-focused ingratiation (such as opinion conformity, other-enhancement and giving favors) but not self-focused ingratiation (such as self-enhancement or self-promotion) (Varma et al., 2006). Gurevitch (1984) showed that ingratiation attempts by subordinates in low LMX relationships are regarded with suspicion and are ineffective (Ralston and Elsass, 1989). Treadway et al. (2007) suggest that ingratiation, if it is identified as such, is regarded negatively but welcomed if the target believes it to be genuine.

To summarize ingratiation tactics are used frequently by those with relatively low status and with the aim of influencing the target's opinion. They are more likely to be effective if the relationship between the agent and target is in its infancy, is positive and if the effort is interpreted as genuine. While flattery and self-promotion might get you a job, it is unlikely to keep you in it!

Rationality (influencing through the use of evidence and logic) is the tactic most consistently associated with positive outcomes. It is reported that rationality is associated with improved performance assessments (Higgins et al., 2003) and supervisor liking of subordinates (Kolodinsky et al., 2007). Work within the fields of voice and issue selling provides insight into the selective and timely use of rationality tactics (Dutton et al. 2001; Bansal, 2003). Issue selling involves a subordinate selling or persuading key decision-makers (Ashford et al., 1998; Morrison & Phelps, 1999) and has been likened to a lengthy process of situational sense-making and the gradual accumulation of assets such as formal authority, knowledge, and contacts (Howard-Grenville, 2007). As an example, in one study issue selling involved presenting a business plan reinforced with clear structures, data and charts; this is an example of a rationality-based tactic use (Dutton et al., 2001). Thus in this context rationality is not a tactic executed in isolation but reflects rationality embedded within sense making and strategic communication, relationship building and attention to power differentials.

Some researchers investigating performance evaluations and subordinates' use of rationality and ingratiation suggest that it is not *what* tactics a subordinate uses that determine success but rather *how* tactics are used (Dutton et al., 2001). So getting the timing, delivery style, and leveraging right might be as important as which tactics are used. Political skill is defined by Ahearn and colleagues as "the ability to effectively understand others at work, and to use such knowledge to influence others to act in ways that enhance one's personal and/or organizational objectives" (Ahearn et al., 2004, p. 311). Almost by definition, therefore, we would expect to find close associations between political skill and the use of tactics. However, Kolodinsky et al. (2007) report that political skill predicted rationality but did not predict five other upward influencing tactics. Geertshuis et al. (forthcoming) report that political skill positively predicted upward influencing, perhaps by virtue of the politically skilled's rich network of contacts, but no association was found for the five other upward influencing tactics, including rationality. Harris et al. (2007) found political skill increased the effectiveness of certain influencing techniques which in turn led to higher ratings of performance by supervisors. Chapter 4 by Treadway and colleagues explores political skill in greater detail.

Yukl and colleagues (Yukl, 1989; Yukl & Falbe, 1990; Yukl et al., 2008; Yukl & Tracey, 1992) have developed and validated an alternative instrument measuring influencing tactic use which assesses the use of eleven tactics: Five of Kipnis et al.'s original six along with six additional ones. Upward appeal was dropped as it was reported to be a category within coalition rather than being a tactic in its own right (Yukl et al., 1992). Respondents are asked to rate how much each tactic is used "in an effort to influence" (Yukl et al., 2008, pp. 618–619) and they are not asked to rate tactics that are used to change minds. The additional tactics identified are: Apprising, inspirational appeals, collaboration, personal appeal, legitimizing, and consultation, which were derived from leadership and power studies.

> *Apprising* involves explaining how a task could benefit the target;
> *Inspirational appeals* is the enthusiastic and positive presentations of new ideas;
> *Collaboration* is where assistance is offered with tasks that the agent wishes the target to complete;
> *Personal appeals* are where a target is asked to do something in the name of friendship;
> *Legitimizing tactics* are where the agent explains it is acceptable and within role for the request to be made;
> *Consultation* is inviting a target's participation in making a decision.

Some of these tactics are clearly more appropriately delivered by superiors but Yukl and Falbe (1990) report that consultation is used as often by subordinates as is rationality and ingratiation. Of their 11 tactics, they report that rational persuasion, consultation, and ingratiation were the tactics used most, with the most capable subordinates using each of these tactics more than the least capable ones (Yukl et al., 2008).

Still more tactics have been identified but again little researched. For example, in considering Eastern cultures, Fu and Yukl (2000) introduce gift giving and face giving in a cross-cultural context. The importance of affect appears to be emerging in influencing, as in other areas of interpersonal behaviors. Related to findings supporting the importance of inspirational appeals, Staw and Barsade (1993) report that subordinates displaying positive emotions at work were more likely to be rated as high performers by their superiors. Negative affect is associated with intimidation as a tactic (Gallagher et al., 2008). Interestingly, in a series of experiments, Forgas (2007) showed that people in a negative mood produced arguments perceived as more persuasive than did people in a positive mood.

Tactics along dimensions and in combination

Some workers have looked at dimensions of tactics used and at the way tactics may be clustered or combined. It may be that, in such an approach, the fundamental underlying constructs can be unearthed and the confusing array of variables that have been posited to predict or flow from tactics can be made sense of. This line of research goes some way to recognizing that influencing communications are more likely to feature the use of a variety tactics in fluid, complex, and interdependent combinations and over a period of time.

Influencing strategies are often classified by tactic strength (Tepper et al., 1993; Van Knippenberg & Steensma, 2003) and analyzed on a continuum from soft to hard. The differentiation of strength is decided by the degree of control that an influence tactic has over the situation and target. Assertiveness, coalitions, and upward appeal are "harder" tactics and involve behaviors such as demanding, gathering support to exert pressure, and going over the superior's head to gain support. Hard tactics may place strain on the agent-target relationship. "Softer" tactics place less strain as they allow the target more latitude in deciding whether to comply. Soft tactics include ingratiation, rationality, and coalitions, which involve behaviors such as flattery, logic, and offering personal sacrifices respectively. The soft-hard dimension has been extended by Ralston and Pearson (2003) to include additional hard tactics such as espionage, blackmail, and bribery. They confirmed the psychological validity of the soft-hard dimension across 30 cultures and noted that ethical differences across cultures determine which tactics are regarded as acceptable. Moreover, soft tactics appear to be used more frequently than hard. This may be because hard tactics strain relationships with superiors, hence subordinates are generally more reluctant to use them (Van Knippenberg & Steensma, 2003).

There appear to be many different antecedents of hard versus soft tactics including: Position in a hierarchy (Yukl & Tracey, 1992), self-esteem (Raven, 1992), status (Stahelski & Paynton, 1995), competence (Van Knippenberg et al., 1999), Machiavellianism (Farmer et al., 1997), need for cognitive closure (Arnold, 2007; de Dreu et al., 1999; De Grada et al., 1999), unionization (Kipnis et al., 1980), and education (Farmer et al., 1997). Collectively these reflect the close relationship between power and influence. Those with power are more likely to use influencing tactics and also to use harder tactics. In addition, different types of power are associated with different types of influencing tactics; referent and expert power are associated with softer tactics and formal power with harder tactics.

Understanding the relative frequency of use of tactics may be primarily of theoretical value. From a practical perspective, however, we are likely to be more interested in which tactics are effective and when, rather than how often other people use them. Falbe and Yukl (1992) found that soft tactics were more effective than hard, and combining two soft tactics or a soft tactic and rationality was more effective than any single tactic. In an experimental situation, Barry and Shapiro (1992) found that combining soft tactics with hard is less effective than using soft tactics alone. Yukl et al. (2008) say that the tactics most likely to bring about commitment rather than compliance are rational persuasion, consultation, inspirational appeals, and collaboration, which are generally considered "soft" tactics.

In an investigation of Western and Eastern cultures by Fu et al. (2004), three dominant approaches were reliably found: persuasive strategy, assertive strategy, and relationship-based strategy. Consistent with early work, they report that managers view gentle persuasion (a mix of ingratiation, persuasion, and reasoning or fact presentation) as being the more effective strategy while contingent control (retaliation, exchange of benefits, coalition formation, and assertiveness) brought about superficial yielding but no true commitment (Leong et al., 2007). They also report that females view gentle persuasion as more effective in all situations, and that males are more likely to favor contingency control in downward but not upward influencing.

> We began this chapter with Naomi's story and have followed her as she encountered the hierarchical, power and relationship-based constraints on her ability to influence. Despite these constraints, Naomi has at her disposal a number of influencing tactics and uses them in combination. She favors softer tactics and resists using more risky hard tactics as she does not think they would work. Here are two of many possible endings.

Ending 1

Naomi got to know the political and cultural landscape in which she was operating. She worked out how things got done in her unit. She found out who would be affected by her work and what they wanted. She found out who her boss trusted and what they thought. Instead of attempting to persuade her boss directly, Naomi asked lots of questions. Informed by the views of other contacts and her greater understanding of their views and of her boss's concerns and priorities, Naomi inspired her boss with an even better vision, one that could be operationalized. Together they worked out how to take a high level description of the solution to senior management.

Ending 2

Naomi continued to work on her solution and tried to make friends with her boss. Naomi asked her peers for support and disclosed her difficulties. Her peers were sympathetic but not inclined to get involved. Naomi found it hard to keep going. Naomi produced increasingly detailed analyses proving her point but sometimes she wondered if her boss even read them. Ultimately, Naomi decided that influencing upwards is not just about being right and nice, it's a risky business and a strategic withdrawal was going to be less costly than a fight. She decided to move on to another role.

Further thoughts

Of course these two endings are not the only possible ways that Naomi's story could have concluded. Naomi could have been more or less forceful, involved more or fewer colleagues, and used a wider or a narrower range of tactics. In thinking of alternative approaches and outcomes, readers might like to relate Naomi's experiences to their own and to think how subordinate influence is shaped by the people involved and the situations they find themselves in.

Further research

The tendency to examine individual tactics in isolation has probably exhausted its utility, especially for practitioners. Future research needs to recognize the situated and ongoing nature of influencing and work when considering upward influence. Such approaches would appreciate the interactive and codependent nature of influence. Employees are situated within complex cultures and embedded in evolving relationships with varying degrees of autonomy over their actions and this needs to be captured by our research efforts.

Subordinates, in contemplating an effort to influence, have simultaneous goals or priorities. Goals can relate to the current situation, and may be relatively trivial, such as a problem to solve or a favor to ask. Subordinates also have longer-term goals. These may include: the preservation or improvement of positive relationships, personal work and career goals, and ambitions for the company and their superior. Day-by-day opportunities to further or frustrate these ambitions are available, interpreted as such or not, and acted upon or ignored. Research to date does not fully recognize this.

We do not know the extent to which influencing upwards is a unique form of communication or whether it can be regarded as one of a group of similar behaviors. Researchers in the field tend to regard it as unique and do not stray far in their references to the wider literature. For example, researchers frequently define influencing as a proactive behavior but do not relate influencing tactic use to the more general literature on proactivity and have not yet established whether influencing tactics are used in ways that are consistent with the proactivity literature.

Similarly, influence, power, trust, and relationship quality are codependent. When trust is lost, access to resources is withdrawn and influence and relationships suffer. There is little evidence on how a dyad can recover from this position, although the wider literature on recovery from breaches of trust may offer some pointers which could be of value.

Conclusion

It is probably safe to say that subordinates who lack credibility, competence, and trustworthiness are unlikely to be successful in influencing upwards. These attributes are seen to contribute to status, reputation, perceived power, relationship quality, and influencing behaviors. In addition, political awareness, good relationships, socially skilled, persuasive, and evidence-based communication will determine whether a subordinate will successfully influence their boss's thinking.

In seeking to influence, subordinates taking a long-term view can approach from three directions: they can seek to make themselves more influential, they can seek to improve the effectiveness of their influencing efforts, or they can seek to render the target more readily influenced. Becoming influential can be regarded as an effort to build a power base or gain access to resources that others value. This can be achieved by acquiring formal roles and authorities, building expertise, managing information, fitting in (or, more accurately, being the same but better), indicating that status is warranted in behavior and dress, getting to know powerful others, or becoming more capable and expert. While positions in social hierarchies may be relatively stable, power balance and relative status fluctuate over time, between people and by task. Subordinates may want to assess whether they are likely to be regarded as being influential in a given situation, before seeking to influence others.

To improve the effectiveness of influencing strategies a subordinate should use harder tactics very sparingly and softer tactics with skill. Culturally appropriate ways of communicating need to be adopted. Ingratiatory tactics perceived as contrived or manipulative are risky and may backfire but politeness and expressions of genuine appreciation are likely to be necessary. Carefully prepared reasoning that is consultative, collaborative, and strategically structured is likely to be more effective than other approaches. A reasoned approach should draw attention to an issue, establish it as a priority as well as propose a solution. This is unlikely to be achieved in a single meeting let alone by a single tactic. However skillful the delivery of an effort to influence is, it can never be likened to a well-aimed sniper's bullet destined for it chosen target; it is always more of a scatter bomb, having positive knock-on effects and negative collateral damage that may not be predicted.

Finally, a subordinate may try to render the task of influencing easier by enhancing the receptiveness of targets. Superiors are more receptive to ideas from trusted, liked, and capable employees, and those who are perceived as loyal and committed to their superiors and the organization. Building a good relationship with a superior has many and varied (but almost exclusively positive) outcomes for a subordinate. Track record is important too: Successful influencing in the past is likely to make superiors more receptive to being influenced in the future. Unsuccessful attempts in the past may have the opposite effect. It follows that subordinates should not risk too many failures since failure may affect perceptions of capability, performance, trust, and relationship quality. Subordinates should enter the murky and swirling waters of influencing upwards cautiously, with vigilance, taking one step at a time.

References

Ahearn, K. K., Ferris, G. R., Hochwarter, W. A., Douglas, C., & Ammeter, A. P. (2004). Leader political skill and team performance, *Journal of Management, 30*, 309–327. doi: 10.1016/j.jm.2003.01.004

Anderson, C. P., Ames, D. R., & Gosling, S. D. (2008). Punishing hubris: The perils of status self-enhancement in teams and organizations, *Personality and Social Psychology Bulletin, 34*, 90–101. doi: 10.1177/0146167207307489

Anderson, C., John, O. P., Keltner, D., & Kring, A. M. (2001). Who attains social status? Effects of personality and physical attractiveness in social groups, *Journal of Personality and Social Psychology, 81*(1), 116–132.

Appelbaum, S. H., Habashy, S., Malo, J., & Shafiq, H. (2012). Back to the future: Revisiting Kotter's 1996 change model, *Journal of Management Development, 31*(8), 764–782.

Arnold, J. A. (2007). The influence of the need for closure on managerial third-party dispute intervention, *Journal of Managerial Psychology, 22*(5), 496–505.

Ashforth, B. E. & Kreiner, G. E. (1999). How can you do it?: Dirty work and the challenge of constructing a positive identity, *Academy of Management Review, 24*(3), 413–434.

Ashford, S. N., Rothbard, S., Piderit, S., & Dutton, J. (1998). Out on a limb: The role of context and impression management in selling gender issues, *Administration Science Quarterly, 43*, 23–557.

Bansal, P. (2003). From issues to actions: The importance of individual concerns and organizational values in responding to natural environmental issues, *Organization Science, 14*(5), 510–527.

Barbuto Jr, J. E., Fritz, S. M., & Marx, D. (2002). A field examination of two measures of work motivation as predictors of leaders' influence tactics, *The Journal of Social Psychology, 142*(5), 601–616.

Barbuto Jr, J. E. & Scholl, R. W. (1999). Leaders' motivation and perception of followers' motivation as predictors of influence tactics used, *Psychological Reports, 84*(3c), 1087–1098.

Barbuto, J. E. & Moss, J. A. (2006). Dispositional effects in intra-organizational influence tactics: A meta-analytic review, *Journal of Leadership and Organizational Studies, 12*(3), 30–48. doi: 10.1177/107179190601200303

Barry, B. & Shapiro, D. L. (1992). Influence tactics in combination: The interactive effects of soft versus hard tactics and rational exchange, *Journal of Applied Social Psychology, 2*(18), 1399–1480. doi: 10.1111/j.1559-1816.1992.tb00958.x

Baumeister, R. F. & Leary, M. R. (1995). The need to belong: Desire for interpersonal attachments as a fundamental human motivation, *Psychological Bulletin, 117*, 497–529.

Baumeister, R. F., Tice, D. M., & Hutton, D. G. (1989). Self-presentational motivations and personality differences in self-esteem, *Journal of Personality, 57*(2), 547–579.

Bennis, W. & Nanus, B. (1985). *Leaders: The Strategy for Taking Charge.* New York: Harper & Row.

Berdahl, J. L. & Martorana, P. (2006). Effects of power on emotion and expression a controversial group discussion, *European Journal of Social Psychology, 36*(4), 497–509.

Bernerth, J. B., Armenakais, A. A., Feild, H. S., Giles, W. F., & Walker, J. J. (2008). The influence of personality differences between subordinates and supervisors on perceptions of LMX: An empirical investigation, *Group and Organization Management, 33*(2), 216–240.

Blickle, G. (2000). Do work values predict the use of intraorganizational influence strategies? *Journal of Applied Social Psychology, 30*, 196–205.

Briñol, P., Petty, R. E., Valle, C., Rucker, D. D., & Becerra, A. (2007). The effects of message recipients' power before and after persuasion, *Journal of Personality and Social Psychology*, *93*(6), 1040–1053.

Brower, H. H., Lester, S. W., Korsgaard, M. A., & Dineen, B. R. (2009). A closer look at trust between managers and subordinates: Understanding the effects of both trusting and being trusted on subordinate outcomes, *Journal of Management*, *35*, 327–347.

Brower, H. H., Schoorman, F. D., & Tan, H. H. (2000). A model of relational leadership: The integration of trust and leader-member exchange, *Leadership Quarterly*, *11*, 227–250.

Brown, J. H., Dovidio, J. F., & Ellyson, S. L. (1990). Reducing sex differences in visual displays of dominance: Knowledge is power, *Personality and Social Psychology Bulletin*, *16*, 358–368.

Brown, P. & Levinson, S. C. (1987). *Politeness: Some Universals in Language Usage* (Vol. 4). Cambridge University Press.

Bunderson, J. S. & Reagans, R. E. (2011). Power, status, and learning in organizations, *Organization Science*, *22*(5), 1182–1194.

Caldwell, D. F. & Burger, J. (1997). Personality and social influence strategies in the workplace, *Personality and Social Psychology Bulletin*, *23*(10), 1003–1012.

Canary, D. J., Cody, M. J., & Marston, P. J. (1986). Goal types, compliance-gaining and locus of control, *Journal of Language and Social Psychology*, *5*(4), 249–269.

Carli, L. L. (2001). Gender and social influence, *Journal of Social Issues*, *57*(4), 725–741.

Castro, S. L., Douglas, C., Hochwarter, W. A., Ferris, G. R., & Frink, D. D. (2003). The effect of positive affect and gender on the influence tactics – Job performance relationship, *Journal of Leadership and Organizational Studies*, *10*(1), 1–18.

Cesario, J. & Higgins, E. T. (2008). Making message recipients "feel right": How non verbal cues can increase persuasion, *Psychological Science*, *19*, 415–420.

Chiaburu, D. S. (2005). The effects of instrumentality on the relationship between goal orientation and leader-member exchange, *The Journal of Social Psychology*, *145*(3), 365–357.

Christensen, M. D. (2011). *Does Agreement Matter? How Supervisor-Subordinate Influence Behavior Agreement/Disagreement Contributes to Supervisor Ratings of Subordinate Defectiveness*. Sacramento: California State University.

Cialdini, R. B. & Goldstein, N. J. (2004). Social influence: Compliance and conformity, *Annual Review of Psychology*, *55*, 591–621. doi: 10.1146/annurev.psych.55.090902.142015

Colella, A., & Varma, A. (2001). The impact of subordinate disability on leader-member exchange relationships, *Academy of Management Journal*, *44*(2), 304–315.

Dansereau, F., Graen, G., & Haga, W. J. (1975). A vertical dyad linkage approach to leadership within formal organizations: A longitudinal investigation of the role making process, *Organizational Behavior and Human Performance*, *13*(1), 46–78. doi: 10.1016/0030-5073(75)90005-7

de Dreu, C. K. W., Koole, S. L., & Oldersma, F. L. (1999). On the seizing and freezing of negotiator inferences: Need for cognitive closure moderates the use of heuristics in negotiation, *Personality and Social Psychology Bulletin*, *25*(3), 349–362.

De Grada, E., Kruglanski, A. W., Mannetti, L., & Pierro, A. (1999). Motivated cognition and group interaction: Need for closure affects the contents and processes of collective negotiations, *Journal of Experimental Social Psychology*, 35, 346–365.

Deluga, R. J. (1991). The relationship of upward-influencing behavior with subordinate-impression management characteristics, *Journal of Applied Social Psychology*, 21(14), 1145–1160.

Deluga, R. J. (1998). Leader-member exchange quality and effectiveness ratings: The role of subordinate-supervisor conscientiousness similarity, *Group & Organization Studies*, 23, 189–216.

Deluga, R. J. & Perry, J. T. (1991). The relationship of subordinate upward influence behavior, satisfaction and perceived superior effectiveness with leader-member exchanges, *Journal of Occupational Psychology*, 64(3), 239–252.

Deluga, R. J. & Perry, J. T. (1994). The role of subordinate performance and ingratiation in leader-member exchanges, *Group & Organization Studies*, 19(1), 67–86. doi: 10.1177/1059601194191004

Diefenbach, T. (2007). The managerialistic ideology of organizational change management, *Journal of Organizational Change Management*, 20(1), 126–144.

Dienesch, R. M. & Liden, R. C. (1986). Leader-member exchange model of leadership: A critique and further development, *Academy of Management Review*, 11(3), 618–634.

Dockery, T. M. & Steiner, D. D. (1990). The role of the initial interaction in leader-member exchange, *Group & Organization Studies*, 15(4), 395–413.

Drake, B. H. & Moberg, D. J. (1986). Communicating influence attempts in dyads: Linguistic sedatives and palliatives, *Academy of Management Review*, 11, 567–584.

Dulebohn, J. A., Bommer, W. H., Liden, R. C., Brouer, R. L., & Ferris, G. R. (2011). A met-analysis of antecedents and consequences of leader-member exchange: Integrating the past with an eye toward to future, *Journal of Management*. doi: http://dx.doi.org/10.1177/0149206311415280

Dutton, J. A., Ashford, S. J., O'Neill, R. M., Hayes, E., & Wierba, E. E. (1997). Reading the wind: How middle managers assess the context for selling issues to top managers, *Strategic Management Journal*, 18(5), 407–425.

Dutton, J. E., Ashford, S. J., O'Neill, R. M., & Lawrence, K. A. (2001). Moves that matter: Issue selling and organizational change, *The Academy of Management Journal*, 44(4), 716–736.

Engle, E. M. & Lord, T. G. (1997). Implicit theories, self-schemas, and Leader-Member Exchange, *Academy of Management Journal*, 40(4), 988–1010.

Erdogan, B. & Liden, R. C. (2002). Social exchanges in the workplace: A review of recent developments and future research directions in leader-member exchange theory: in L. L. Neider & C. A. Schriesheim (eds) *Leadership* (pp. 65–114). Greenwich, CT: Information Age.

Falbe, C. M. & Yukl, G. (1992). Consequences for managers of using single influence tactics and combinations of tactics, *Academy of Management Journal*, 35(3), 638–652. doi: 10.2307/256490

Farmer, S. M., Maslyn, J. M., Fedor, D. B., & Goodman, J. S. (1997). Putting upward influence strategies in context, *Journal of Organizational Behavior*, 18, 17–42. doi: 10.1002/(SICI)1099-1379(199701)

Ferris, G. R., Davidson, S., & Perrewe, P. (2005). *Political Skill at Work: Impact on Work Effectiveness*. Palo Alto, CA: Davies-Black Publishing. Retrieved from http://proquest.umi.com/pqdlink?did=931257361&Fmt=7&clientId=13395&R QT=309&VName=PQD

Fiske, M. H. & Ofshe, R. (1970). The process of status evolution, *Sociometry*, *33*(3), 327–346.

Fiske, S. (2004). *Social Beings: A Core Motives Approach to Social Psychology*. New York: Wiley.

Fiske, S. T. & Berdahl, J. (2007). Social power: in A. W. Kruglanski & H. T. Higgins (eds) *Social Psychology: Handbook of Basic Principles* (pp. 678–692). New York: Guilford.

Forgas, J. (2007). When sad is better than happy: Negative affect can improve the quality and effectiveness of persuasive messages and social influence strategies, *Journal of Experimental Social Psychology*, *43*(4), 513–528.

French, J. R. & Raven, B. (1959). *The Bases of Social Power*. Ann Arbor MI: University of Michigan Press.

Frese, M., Teng, E., & Wijnen, C. J. D. (1999). Helping to improve suggestion systems: Predictors of making suggestions in companies, *Journal of Organizational Behavior*, *20*, 1139–1155.

Fu, P. P., Kennedy, J., Tata, J., Yukl, G., Bond, M. H., Peng, T. K., Cheosakul, A. (2004). The impact of societal cultural values and individual social beliefs on the perceived effectiveness of managerial influence strategies: A meso approach, *Journal of International Business Studies*, *35*(4), 284–305.

Fu, P. P. & Yukl, G. (2000). Perceived effectiveness of influence tactics in the United States and China, *The Leadership Quarterly*, *11*(2), 251–266. doi: doi.org/10.1016/S1048-9843(00)00039-4

Furst, S. A. & Cable, D. M. (2008). Employee resistance to organizational change: Managerial influence tactics and leader-member exchange, *Journal of Applied Psychology*, *93*(2), 453–462.

Galinsky, A. D., Magee, J. C., Inesi, M. E., & Gruenfeld, D. H. (2006). Power and perspectives not taken, *Psychological Science*, *17*(12), 1068–1074.

Gallagher, V. C., Harris, K. J., & Valle, M. (2008). Understanding the use of intimidation as a response to job tension: Career implications for the global leader, *Career Development International*, *13*(7), 648–666.

Gomez, C. & Rosen, B. (2001). The leader-member exchange as a link between managerial trust and employee empowerment, *Group & Organization Management*, *26*, 53–69.

Graen, G. & Cashman, J. (1975). A role-making model of leadership in formal organizations: A development approach: in J. G. Hunt & L. L. Larson (eds) *Leadership Frontiers* (pp. 143–165). Kent, OH: Kent State University.

Graen, G. B. & Uhl-Bien, M. (1995). Relationship-based approach to leadership: Development of leader-member exchange (LMX) theory of leadership over 25 years: Applying a multi-level multi-domain perspective, *The Leadership Quarterly*, *6*(2), 219–247.

Graen, G. B., Wakabayashi, M., Graen, M. R., & Graen, M. G. (1990). International generalizability of American hypotheses about Japanese management progress: A strong inference investigation, *The Leadership Quarterly*, *1*(1), 1–24.

Groysberg, B., Polzer, J. T., & Elfenbein, H. A. (2011). Too many cooks spoil the broth: How high-status individuals decrease group effectiveness, *Organization Science*, *22*(3), 722–737. doi: 10.1287/orsc.1100.0547

Gupta, S. & Case, T. L. (1980). Managers' outward influence tactics and their consequences: An exploratory study, *Leadership and Organization Development Journal*, *20*(6), 300–308.

Gurevitch, Z. D. (1984). Impression formation during tactical self-presentation, *Social Psychology Quarterly*, *47*(3), 262–270.

Halevy, N., Chou, E. Y., Galinsky, A. D., & Murnighan, J. K. (2012). When hierarchy wins: Evidence from the national basketball association, *Social Psychological and Personality Science*, *3*(4), 398–406. doi: 10.1177/1948550611424225

Hall, J. A., Coats, E. J., & LeBeau, L. S. (2005). Nonverbal behavior and the vertical dimension of social relations: A meta-analysis, *Psychological Bulletin*, *131*(6), 898–924.

Harris, K. J., Kacmar, K. M., Zivnuska, S., & Shaw, J. D. (2007). The impact of political skill on impression management effectiveness, *Journal of Applied Psychology*, *92*(1), 278–285. doi: 10.1037/0021-9010.92.1.278

Harrison, A. W., Hochwarter, W. A., Perrewe, P. L., & Ralston, D. A. (1998). The ingratiation construct: An assessment of the validity of the Measure of Ingratiatory Behaviors in Organizational Settings (MIBOS), *Journal of Applied Psychology*, *83*(6), 932.

Higgins, C. A., Judge, T. A., & Ferris, G. R. (2003). Influence tactics and work outcomes: A meta-analysis, *Journal of Organizational Behavior*, *24*, 89–106. doi: 10.1002/job.181

Hochwarter, W. A., Pearson, A. W., Ferris, G. R., Perrewe, P. L., & Ralston, D. A. (2000). A reexamination of Schreisheim and Hinkin's (1990) measure of upward influence, *Educational and Psychological Measurement*, *60*(5), 755–771.

Holmes, J. G. & Rempel, J. K. (1989). Trust in close relationships: in C. Hendrick (ed.) *Close Relationships* (pp. 187–220). Newbury Park, CA: Sage.

Howard-Grenville, J. A. (2007). Developing issue-selling effectiveness over time: Issue selling as resourcing, *Organization Science*, *18*(4), 560–577.

Hummel, J. E. & Holyoak, K. J. (2003). A symbolic-connectionist theory of relational inference and generalization, *Psychological Review*, *110*(2), 220–264. doi: 10.1037/0033-295X.110.2.220

Imada, A. S. & Hakel, M. D. (1977). Influence of nonverbal communication and rater proximity impressions and decisions in simulated employment interviews, *Journal of Applied Psychology*, *62*, 295–300.

Janssen, O. & Van Yperen, N. W. (2004). Employees' goal orientations, the quality of leader-member exchange, and the outcomes of job performance and job satisfaction, *Academy of Management Journal*, *47*, 368–384.

Jones, G. R. & George, J. M. (1998). The experience and evolution of trust: Implications for cooperation and teamwork, *Academy of Management Review*, *23*(3), 531–546.

Jost, J. T., Banaji, M. R., & Nosek, B. A. (2004). A decade of system justification theory: Accumulated evidence of conscious and unconscious bolstering of the status quo, *Political Psychology*, *25*(6), 881–920.

Judge, T. A. & Bretz, R. D. (1994). Political influence behavior and career success, *Journal of Management*, *20*(1), 43–65.

Kacmar, K. M., Carlson, D. S., & Bratton, V. K. (2004). Situational and disposi-tional factors as antecedents of ingratiatory behaviours in organizational settings, *Journal of Vocational Behavior*, 65, 309–331. doi: 10.1016/j.jvb.2003.09.002

Kacmar, K. M., Delery, J. E., & Ferris, G. R. (2006). Differential effectiveness of applicant impression management tactics on employment interview deci-sions, *Journal of Applied Social Psychology*, 22(16), 1250–1272.

Keltner, D., Gruenfeld, D. H., & Anderson, C. (2003). Power, approach and inhi-bition, *Psychological Review*, 110(2), 265–284.

Kenton, S. B. (1989). Speaker credibility in persuasive business communication. A model which explains gender differences, *Journal of Business Communication*, 26(2), 143–157.

King, C. L. (2010). Beyond persuasion: The rhetoric of negotiation in business communication, *The Journal of Business Communication*, 47(1), 69–78.

Kipnis, D. & Schmidt, S. M. (1988). Upward-influence styles: Relationship with performance evaluation, salary, and stress, *Administrative Science Quarterly*, 33(4), 528–542.

Kipnis, D., Schmidt, S. M., & Wilkinson, I. (1980). Intraorganizational influence tactics: Explorations in getting one's way, *Journal of Applied Psychology*, 65(4), 440–452. doi: 10.1037/0021-9010.65.4.440

Kolodinsky, R. W., Treadway, D. C., & Ferris, G. R. (2007). Political skill and influence effectiveness: Testing portions of an expanded Ferris and Judge (1991) model, *Human Relations*, 60(12), 1747–1777. doi: 10.1177/0018726707084913

Kotter, J. P. (1996). *Leading Change*. Boston, MA: Harvard Business School Press.

Kramer, R. M. & Carnevale, P. J. (2001). Trust and intergroup negotiation: in R. Brown & S. Gaertner (eds) *Blackwell Handbook of Social Psychology: Intergroup Processes* (pp. 431–450). Malden, MA: Blackwell.

Krishnan, V. R. (2004). Impact of transformational leadership on followers' influence strategies, *Leadership & Organization Development Journal*, 25(1), 58–72.

Kumar, K. & Beyerlain, M. (1991). Construction and validation of an instrument for measuring ingratiatory behaviors in organizational settings, *Journal of Applied Psychology*, 76, 619–627.

Leavitt, H. J. (2005). *Top Down: Why Hierarchies are Here to Stay and How to Manage Them More Effectively*. Boston, MA: Harvard Business School Press.

Leong, J. L. T., Bond, M. H., & Fu, P. P. (2007). Perceived effectiveness of influence strategies among Hong Kong managers, *Asia Pacific Journal Manage*, 24, 75–96.

Liden, R. C. & Graen, G. (1980). Generalizability of the vertical dyad linkage model of leadership, *The Academy of Management Journal*, 23(3), 451–465.

Liden, R. C. & Maslyn, J. (1998). Multidimensionality of leader-member exchange: An empirical assessment through scale development, *Journal of Management*, 24, 43–72.

Liden, R. C. & Mitchell, T. R. (1988). Ingratiatory behaviors in organizational settings, *Academy of Management Review*, 13(4), 572–587.

Liden, R. C., Wayne, S. J., & Stilwell, D. (1993). A longitudinal study on the early development of leader-member exchanges, *Journal of Applied Psychology*, 78(4), 662–674. doi: 10.1037/0021-9010.78.4.662

Liviatan, I. & Jost, J. T. (2011). Special issue: System justification theory motivated social cognition theory in the service of the status quo, *Social Cognition*, 29(3), 231–237.

Lueger, M., Sander, K., Meyer, R., & Hammerschmid, G. (2005). Contextualizing influence activities: An objective hermeneutical approach, *Organization Studies*, 26, 1145–1168.

Magee, M. C. & Galinsky, A. D. (2008). Social hierarchy: The self-reinforcing nature of power and status, *The Academy of Management Annals*, 2(2), 351–398.

Maslyn, J. M., Farmer, S. M., & Fedor, D. B. (1996). Failed upward influence attempts: Predicting the nature of subordinate persistence in pursuit of organizational goals, *Group & Organization Management*, 21(4), 461–480.

Maslyn, J. M. & Uhl-Bien, M. (2001). Leader-member exchange and its dimensions: Effects of self-effort and other's effort on relationship quality, *Journal of Applied Psychology*, 86, 697–708.

McAllister, D. J. (1995). Affect and cognitive based trust as foundations for interpersonal cooperation in organizations, *Academy of Management Journal*, 38, 24–59.

Meaney, M. & Pung, C. (2008). McKinsey global results: Creating organizational transformations, *The McKinsey Quarterly*, August, 107.

Meyer, R. C., Davis, J. H., & Schoorman, F. (1998). An integrative model of organizational trust, *Academy of Management Review*, 20.

Mintzberg, H. (1979). *The Structuring of Organizations: A Synthesis of the Research*, Englewood Cliffs, NJ: Prentice-Hall.

Molm, L. D., Peterson, G. & Takahashi, N. (1999). Power in negotiated and reciprocal exchange, *American Sociological Review*, 64, 876–890.

Morrison, E. W. & Phelps, C. C. (1999). Taking charge at work: Extra-role efforts to initiate workplace change, *Academy of Management Journal*, 42(4), 403. doi: Retrieved from http://www.jstor.org/stable/257011

Murphy, S. E. & Ensher, E. A. (1999). The effects of leader and subordinate characteristics in the development of leader-member exchange quality, *Journal of Applied Social Psychology*, 29(7), 1371–1394. doi: 10.1111/j.1559-1816.1999.tb00144.x

Murray, S. L., Holmes, J. G., & Griffin, D. W. (1993). The benefits of positive illusions: Idealization and the construction of satisfaction in close relationships, *Journal of Personality and Social Psychology*, 70(1), 79–98.

Orpen, C. (1996). Dependency as a moderator of the effects of networking behavior on managerial career success, *The Journal of Psychology*, 130(3), 245–248.

Pfeffer, J. (1981). *Power in Organizations*. Marshfield, MA: Pitman.

Pfeffer, J. & Salancik, G. R. (1978). *The External Control of Organizations: A Resource Dependence Perspective*. New York: Harper Row.

Pintrich, P. R. (2003). A motivational science perspective on the role of student motivation in learning and teaching contexts, *Journal of Educational Psychology*, 95(4), 667–686.

Poppe, M., van der Kloot, W., & Valkenburg, H. (1999). The implicit structure of influence strategies and social relationships, *Journal of Social and Personal Relationships*, 16(4), 443–458.

Ralston, D. A. & Elsass, P. M. (1989). Ingratiation and impression management in the organization: in R. A. Giacalone and P. Rosenfeld (eds) *Impression*

Management in the Organization (pp. 235–249). Hillsdale, NJ: Lawrence Erlbaum Associates.

Ralston, D. A. & Pearson, A. (2003). Measuring interpersonal political influences in organizations: The development of a cross-cultural instrument of upward influence strategies: in L. Weatherly (ed.) *Southern Management Association Proceedings*. Retrieved from http://www.southernmanagement.org/meetings/2003/proceedings/flashpop.htm

Raven, B. H. (1992). A power/interaction model of interpersonal influence: French and Raven thirty years later, *Journal of Social Behaviour and Personality*, *7*, 217–244.

Ringer, R. C. & Boss, R. W. (2000). Hospital professionals' use of upward influence tactics, *Journal of Managerial Issues*, *7*, 92–108.

Savard, C. J. & Rogers, R. W. (1992). A self-efficacy and subjective expected utility theory analysis of the selection and use of influence strategies, *Journal of Social Behavior and Personality*, *7*(2), 273–292.

Schermerhorn Jr., J. R. & Bond, M. H. (1991). Upward and downward influence tactics in managerial networks: A comparative study of Hong Kong Chinese and Americans, *Asia Pacific Journal of Management*, *8*(2), 147–158.

Schmid Mast, M. & Hall, J. A. (2004). Who is the boss and who is not? Accuracy of judging status, *Journal of Nonverbal Behavior*, *28*(3), 145–165.

Schmidt, S. M. & Kipnis, D. (1984). Managers' pursuit of individual and organizational goals, *Human Relations*, *37*, 781–794.

Schreyogg, G. & Sydow, J. (2011). Organizational path dependence: A process view, *Organization Studies*, *32*(3), 321–335. doi: 10.1177/0170840610397481

Schriesheim, C. & Hinkin, T. (1990). Influence tactics used by subordinates: A theoretical and empirical analysis and refinement of the Kipnis, Schmidt, and Wilkinson subscales, *Journal of Applied Psychology*, *75*, 246–257.

Schriesheim, C. A., Castro, S. L., & Cogliser, C. C. (1999). Leader-Member Exchange (LMX) research: A comprehensive review of theory, measurement and data-analytic practices, *Leadership Quarterly*, *10*, 63–113.

Simon, H. (1953). Notes on the observation and measurement of political power, *Journal of Political Power*, *15*, 500–516.

Simpson, E. (2006). *Muslim Society and the Western Indian Ocean: The Seafarers of Kachchh*. London; New York: Routledge.

Stahelski, A. J. & Paynton, C. F. (1995). The effects of status cues on choices of social power and influence strategies, *The Journal of Social Psychology*, *135*, 553–560.

Staw, B. M. & Barsade, S. (1993). Affect and managerial performance: A test of the sadder-but-wiser vs. happier-and-smarter hypotheses, *Administrative Science Quarterly*, *38*, 304–331.

Stewart, G. L., Dustin, S. L., Barrick, M. R., & Darnold, T. C. (2008). Exploring the handshake in employment interviews, *Journal of Applied Psychology*, *93*(3), 1139–1146.

Sweeney, P. J., Thompson, V., & Blanton, H. (2009). Trust and influence in combat: An interdependence model, *Journal of Applied Social Psychology*, *39*(1), 235–264.

Tepper, B. J., Brown, S. J., & Hunt, M. D. (1993). Strength of subordinates' upward influence tactics and gender congruency effects, *Journal of Applied Social Psychology*, *23*(22), 1903–1919. doi: 10.1111/j.1559-1816.1993.tb01072.x

Thacker, R. A. & Wayne, S. J. (1995). An examination of the relationship between upward influence tactics and assessments of promotability, *Journal of Management*, 21, 739–756.

Thibaut, J. W. & Kelley, H. H. (1959). *The Social Psychology of Groups*. New York: Wiley.

Tiedens, L. Z., Unzueta, M. M., & Young, M. J. (2007). An unconscious desire for hierarchy? The motivated perception of dominance complementarity in task partners, *Journal of Personality and Social Psychology*, 93(3), 402–414.

Treadway, D. C., Ferris, G. R., Duke, A. B., Adams, G. L., & Thatcher, J. B. (2007). The moderating role of subordinate political skill on supervisors' impressions of subordinate ingratiation and ratings of subordinate interpersonal facilitation, *Journal of Applied Psychology*, 92(3), 848–855. doi: 10.1037/0021-9010.92.3.848

Tregaskis, O. (2003). Learning networks, power and legitimacy in multinational subsidiaries, *International Journal of Human Resource Management*, 14(3), 431–447.

Trope, Y. & Liberman, N. (2003). Temporal construal, *Psychological Review*, 110(3), 403–421.

Van Knippenberg, B. & Steensma, H. (2003). Future interaction expectation and the use of soft and hard influence tactics, *Applied Psychology: An International Review*, 52(1), 55–67. doi: 10.1111/1464-0597.00123

Van Knippenberg, B., Van Knippenberg, D., Blaauw, E., & Vermunt, R. (1999). Relational considerations in the use of influence tactics, *Journal of Applied and Social Psychology*, 29, 806–819.

Varma, A., Toh, S. M., & Pichler, S. (2006). Ingratiation in job applications: Impact on selection decisions, *Journal of Managerial Psychology*, 21(3), 200–210.

Vecchio, R. P. & Sussman, M. (1989). Preferences for forms of supervisory social influence, *Journal of Organizational Behavior*, 10(2), 135–144.

Wayne, S. J. & Ferris, G. R. (1990). Influence tactics, affect, and exchange quality in supervisor-subordinate interactions: A laboratory experiment and field study, *Journal of Applied Psychology*, 75, 487–499.

Wayne, S. J. & Green, S. A. (1993). The effects of leader-member exchange on employee citizenship and impression management behavior, *Human Relations*, 46(12), 1431–1440.

Wayne, S. J. & Kacmar, K. M. (1991). The effects of impression management on the performance appraisal process, *Organizational Behavior and Human Decision Processes*, 48, 70–88.

Wayne, S. J., Liden, R. C., Graf, I. K., & Ferris, G. R. (1997). The role of upward influence tactics in human resource decisions, *Personnel Psychology*, 50, 979–1006.

Wayne, S. J., Shore, L. M., & Liden, R. C. (1997). Perceived organizational support and leader-member exchange: A social exchange perspective, *Academy of Management Journal*, 40(1), 82–111.

Wortman, C. B. & Linsenmeier, J. A. (1977). Interpersonal attraction and techniques of ingratiation in organizational settings: in B. M. Staw & G. R. Salancik (eds) *New Directions in Organizational Behavior* (pp. 133–178).

Yukl, G. (1989). Managerial leadership: A review of theory and research, *Journal of Management*, 15(2), 251–289. doi: 10.1177/014920638901500207

Yukl, G. & Falbe, C. M. (1990). Influence tactics and objectives in upward, downward, and lateral influence attempts, *Journal of Applied Psychology*, 72(2), 132–140. doi: 10.1037/0021-9010.75.2.132

Yukl, G., Lepsinger, R., & Lucia, A. (1992). Preliminary report on development and validation of the influence behavior questionnaire: in K. Clark, M. B. Clark, & D. Campbell (eds) *Impact of Leadership, Center for Creative Leadership* (pp. 417–427). Greensboro: NC.

Yukl, G. & Michel, J. W. (2006). Proactive influence tactics and leader member exchange: in C. A. Schriesheim & L. L. Neider (eds) *Power and Influence in Organizations: New Empirical and Theoretical Perspectives* (pp. 87–104). Miami, FL: Information Age Publishing Inc.

Yukl, G., Seifert, C., & Chavez, C. (2008). Validation of the extended influence behavior questionnaire, *The Leadership Quarterly, 19*(5), 609–621.

Yukl, G. & Tracey, J. B. (1992). Consequences of influence tactics used with subordinates, peers and the boss, *Journal of Applied Psychology, 77*, 525–535.

Zand, D. (1972). Trust and managerial problem solving, *Administrative Science Quarterly, 17*, 230–239.

6

The People Make the Place, and They Make Things Happen: Proactive Behavior and Relationships at Work

Jennifer B. Farrell and Karoline Strauss

George Bernard Shaw famously observed that there are three kinds of people: those who make things happen, those who watch what happens, and those who wonder what happened. Proactive behavior is about making things happen. It involves taking initiative to bring about a different future, for oneself, for one's team, or for the organization as a whole (Parker et al., 2010). From extensive research we know that people do indeed vary in their propensity to "make things happen" (Bateman & Crant, 1993; Fuller & Marler, 2009). Those with a proactive personality are particularly likely to take charge and initiate change (Bateman & Crant, 1993). But while those people may sometimes override the influence of their environment, they are by no means independent of their context. Like most work behaviors, proactive behavior depends on the interplay of individual dispositions and factors in the work environment. Making things happen does not occur in a social vacuum: Those who "watch what happens" will, for example, make it more or less risky to speak up with suggestions. Their reactions will determine whether efforts to initiate change will be successful, and whether these efforts will have positive or negative consequences for the individual, for example in relation to his or her image, performance evaluation or career success.

We begin our chapter by defining proactive behavior. Next we discuss the complex interplay between proactive behavior and relationships at work. As part of our dynamic model (see Figure 6.1) we

---

[1] Kemmy Business School, University of Limerick
[2] Warwick Business School

108

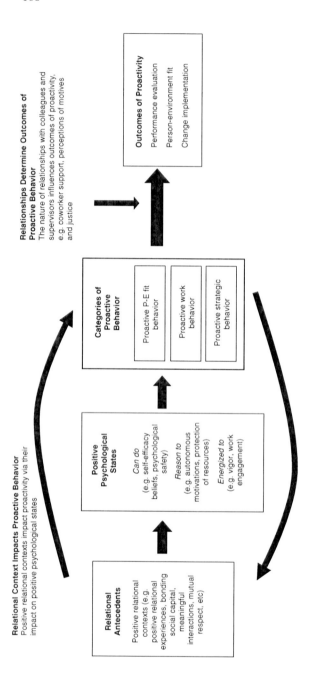

Figure 6.1 Dynamic Model of Work Relationships and Proactive Behavior

propose that relationships with others at work interact with proactive behavior in three different ways: first, we discuss how relational aspects of the workplace act as antecedents of proactive work behavior, via their influence on more proximal psychological states. Second, we examine how relationships determine the outcomes of proactive behavior, for example as others resist or support individuals' efforts to bring about change. Third, we discuss how relationships are also influenced by proactive behavior, for example during organizational entry when individuals may proactively seek to build relationships with their peers or supervisors. We then outline ways in which organizations can shape positive relational contexts to promote and sustain proactive behavior. Finally, we propose a number of directions for future research.

What is proactive behavior?

Traditionally research on work behaviors and attitudes has predominantly focused on the influence of factors in the work environment on individuals, treating individuals themselves as relatively "passive, reactive respondents to their context" (Parker et al., 2010, p. 828). However, over the last few decades researchers have become increasingly interested in the more active role individuals play in shaping their work environment, rather than just reacting to it (Bandura, 1982, 2006). The concept of proactive behavior reflects this view of individuals in organizations as active agents of change who take initiative and challenge the status quo. Following a period of relatively dispersed research on different phenomena that reflect a more proactive approach to work in different domains (for reviews see Crant, 2000; Grant & Ashford, 2008), there is now a growing consensus on a more general definition of proactive behavior. Proactive behavior has three key attributes: it is self-starting, change oriented, and future focused (Grant & Ashford, 2008; Parker et al., 2010). In other words, it involves taking action to bring about an envisioned future outcome. Researchers have identified that these envisioned future outcomes can be classified into three higher order categories (see Figure 6.1; Parker & Collins, 2010):

1. Proactive person-environment (P-E) fit behavior aims at achieving a greater match between one's own preferences, needs, and abilities on the one hand, and the organizational environment on the other hand. This may involve proactively seeking feedback to obtain

information on one's behavior and performance (Ashford & Black, 1996; Ashford et al., 2003); negotiating specific terms of employment (Rousseau, 2005; Rousseau et al., 2006); changing aspects of one's job to make it more personally meaningful (Wrzesniewski & Dutton, 2001) or creating more job resources such as autonomy or support (Tims et al., 2012); or actively shaping one's career, for example, by developing skills and networks (Claes & Ruiz-Quintanilla, 1998; Tharenou & Terry, 1998).

2. Proactive work behavior refers to "taking control of, and bringing about change within, the internal organizational environment" (Parker & Collins, 2010, p. 636). This captures behaviors such as trying to initiate change in the workplace to improve the functioning of the organization (Morrison & Phelps, 1999), making suggestions for change and improvements (Van Dyne & LePine, 1998), identifying opportunities and implementing ideas (Scott & Bruce, 1994), and finding long-term solutions for work problems to prevent them from recurring (Frese & Fay, 2001; Parker & Collins, 2010; Parker et al., 2006).

3. Proactive strategic behavior involves improving the strategic fit between the organization and its environment, such as by actively scanning the environment for potential future threats and opportunities (Parker & Collins, 2010), and by making others aware of particular issues (Dutton & Ashford, 1993; Dutton et al., 2001).

Relational antecedents of proactive behavior

The long-term focus of proactive behavior implies that individuals are unlikely to reap immediate benefits. Instead, they often have to forego more immediate gains in order to invest time, energy and resources into bringing about the envisioned future. Whether they will indeed succeed in bringing about this future and whether, if achieved, this future will be what they hoped for is uncertain. Since proactive behavior cannot be as easily explained by short-term rewards and pre-set goals as other work behaviors, researchers have been particularly interested in how proactive behavior is motivated, and a considerable amount of research has explored its antecedents, the factors that drive proactive behavior. Parker et al. (2010) have proposed a model of proactive motivation that explains how individual differences and contextual factors influence proactive behavior. Even individuals with a proactive personality are not proactive all the time and in all domains of their life. Rather than focusing on personality as the main driver of proactive behavior, we need to consider how proactive behavior is motivated in a given social context. Individual differences such as proactive personality and contextual factors such as social processes influence proactivity via their influence on positive psychological states. Personality factors and contextual factors in turn motivate individuals to set and pursue proactive goals. Drawing on previous research on motivation, three different forms of critical psychological states have been identified (Parker et al., 2010). As depicted in Figure 6.1, these are, "can do" states, "reason to" states, and "energized to" states.

"Can do" states capture individuals' beliefs that they can be successful in their proactive behavior, including the belief that they will be able to deal with the consequences of their proactive behavior (Bandura, 1997; Parker, 2000). "Can do" states include individuals' feelings of capability, as well as their perceptions of the risks associated with engaging in proactive behavior and the availability of psychological resources.

An abundance of research has linked perceived capability to proactive behavior. Particularly important for proactive behavior is role breadth self-efficacy which refers to "one's perceived capability of carrying out a range of proactive, interpersonal and integrative activities beyond the prescribed technical core" (Parker & Collins, 2010, p. 641). Role breadth self-efficacy has been shown to predict a variety of proactive behaviors including proactive job performance (Griffin et al., 2007), proactive problem solving (Parker et al., 2006), a range of strategic proactive behaviors and some P-E fit proactive behaviors (Axtell et al., 2000; Parker & Collins, 2010).

The risk of engaging in proactive behavior is strongly determined by the extent to which individuals feel confident that others will not embarrass, punish or reject them for speaking up with a suggestion. This sense of "psychological safety stems from mutual respect between colleagues" (Edmondson, 1999, p. 354). Psychological safety has been found to predict personal initiative (Vennekel, 2000: as cited in Fay & Frese, 2001), voice (Edmondson et al., 2001), and enhanced motivation for quality improvements. These studies suggest that psychological safety has a powerful influence on "can do" states because it alleviates individuals' concerns regarding the negative consequences of their proactive behavior.

Proactive behaviors require energy and effort (Grant et al., 2011) and the belief that one has the physical, emotional, and cognitive resources to invest in such behaviors is likely to affect the decision to be proactive. Psychological availability refers to individuals' beliefs that they have the resources to invest themselves fully in their work roles (Kahn, 1990). Employees may face a variety of preoccupations and distractions in the course of doing their jobs, such as the emotional demands of the job, more information processing than an individual can handle, a heightened self-consciousness about how others perceive them, or excessive physical demands. When employees lack psychological availability at work they may feel unable to cope and are prevented from dedicating their full attention to their work roles. When individuals experience psychological availability they have a clear mind and are able to direct their attention and efforts towards developing and improving their work tasks. Individuals with a sense of psychological availability are better equipped with the resources required to generate new ways of approaching their work and to persist in the face of setbacks (Binyamin & Carmeli, 2010; Vinarski-Peretz & Carmeli, 2011) and are consequently more likely to take a proactive approach to their work.

"Reason to" states capture the value or utility of engaging in proactive behavior. Parker et al. (2010) draw on self-determination theory (Deci & Ryan, 1985, 2002) to explore individuals' different reasons to be proactive. Individuals may engage in proactive behavior because they find it enjoyable or challenging (intrinsic motivation); because it fulfills life goals and/or is connected to their sense of self, and/or because they identify strongly with their organization or team and thus feel ownership for proactively improving it (integrated motivation); or because they recognize that initiating a change is important to them personally or to their team or organization (identified motivation). These three forms of motivation are autonomous motivations, characterized by a sense of volition and choice (Ryan & Deci, 2000). Although it has been argued that not all proactive behaviors are necessarily autonomously motivated, when compared to external or controlled motivations, autonomous motivation is more likely to stimulate proactive behaviors that lead to successful change for individuals and their organizations (Strauss & Parker, forthcoming). Empirical research has found that autonomous motivation results in greater performance in tasks that require discipline and determination (Koestner & Losier, 2002), and involve flexibility, creativity and determination (Gagne & Deci, 2005) – characteristics associated with a range of proactive endeavors. Autonomous motivation is thus likely to be a key driver of effective proactive behavior (Strauss & Parker, forthcoming).

"Energized to" states refer to high-activation positive emotions such as enthusiasm and joy (Bindl et al., 2012). Drawing on Fredrickson's (1998) "broaden and build" theory of emotions, researchers have suggested that positive affect positively influences proactive behavior. Parker (2007) proposed that when individuals experience positive affect they generate broader, future oriented and more challenging goals associated with proactive motivation. It is also argued that when an individual is engaged in proactive action, positive affect helps to promote goal striving by supporting individuals in staying the course even in the face of negative events or resistance they may encounter (Parker, 2007). There is an abundance of research evidence to suggest that positive affect influences a range of proactive concepts such as personal initiative (Den Hartog & Belschak, 2007), proactive work behavior (Fritz & Sonnentag, 2009) and strategic proactive behaviors (Parker et al., 2008; cited in Bindl & Parker, 2010). High activated positive moods such as excitement and enthusiasm have also been found to be positively related to all phases of proactive goal regulation including envisioning, enacting, and reflecting (Bindl et al., 2012). Work engagement, "a positive, fulfilling, work related state of mind that is characterized by a persistent positive, affective motivational state of fulfillment" (Maslach et al., 2001, p. 417), has also been found to be positively and significantly related to personal initiative (Sonnentag, 2003) and proactive work behavior (Salanova & Schaufeli, 2008; Warshawsky et al., 2012).

The notion of energy is captured in a number of strands of research which identify it as a driving force behind workplace behavior (Csikszentmihalyi, 1990; Peterson et al., 2009; Spreitzer et al., 2005). High levels of energy at work are an important psychological resource required for setting and striving towards challenging proactive goals. In line with this, research has shown, for example, that thriving, i.e. "the psychological state in which individuals experience both a sense of vitality and a sense of learning at work" (Spreitzer et al., 2005, p. 538), stimulates proactive work behaviors such as problem solving (Ashby et al., 1999) and innovative behavior (Carmeli & Spreitzer, 2009), and is important in generating and implementing creative and new ideas to problems (Kark & Carmeli, 2009).

As captured in our dynamic model, it is at least in part via their impact on these positive psychological states that relational antecedents influence proactive behavior. We now explore how positive work relationships promote "can do", "reason to" and "energized to" states that have been found to stimulate proactivity.

Positive work relationships promote "can do" states

Positive work relationships contribute to "can do" states in a number of different ways. Below we discuss how characteristics of relational context influence individuals' beliefs that they can be successful in being proactive and that they can deal with the consequences of their proactive endeavors. Positive workplace relationships play a role in enhancing individuals' beliefs about their ability to carry out proactive actions. Generally, positive relationships enable people to feel competent at work. Research has shown that subjective relational experiences, that is, the extent to which people experience positive regard, mutuality, and vitality in their workplace relationships, lead to greater engagement in innovative work behaviors by enhancing individuals' self-beliefs about their ability to generate novel ideas, solve problems creatively, and develop the ideas of others (Vinarski-Peretz et al., 2011).

Positive regard and mutuality have a direct influence on individuals' sense of capability. Positive regard reflects a sense of being known or loved. This is key for one's own positive self-regard (Rogers, 1951), which in turn determines self-efficacy at work (Chen et al., 2001). Experienced mutuality reflects a sense that the people in the relationship are both engaged and actively participating. It provides opportunities for growth and development. Individuals learn from each other and develop new skills, and consequently feel more capable (Vinarski-Peretz et al., 2011).

Positive relationships may also impact self-efficacy beliefs indirectly via their impact on positive emotions. Positive relational experiences provide a sense of vitality and positive emotions, broadening thought-action repertoires and enhancing individuals' perceptions of their ability to approach their job in innovative and creative ways (Vinarski-Peretz et al., 2011).

Positive relational contexts are also important in terms of individual perceptions of the interpersonal risk associated with their behavior. The nature of relationships between work colleagues plays a crucial role in building interpersonal climates where individuals feel safe enough to engage in proactive action. In particular, mutual respect between work colleagues reduces the likelihood of negative reactions which undermine efforts to change or improve work processes. Even if the potential benefits of proactive behavior are not appreciated or recognized by others who could be affected by it, mutual respect enhances the possibility of a professional response from colleagues, such as constructive criticism of the initiative rather than a response which is punitive in nature. Social capital, which reflects "the sum of actual and potential resources embedded within, and available through the network of relationships possessed by an individual or social units" (Nahapiet & Ghoshal, 1998, p. 243), has also been found to predict perceptions of psychological safety (Carmeli, 2007). These findings are echoed in research on high quality interpersonal relationships (Carmeli et al., 2009b), which found that such relationships enhanced psychological safety by reducing interpersonal risks, resulting in greater engagement in feedback seeking and experimentation.

Finally, positive work relationships contribute to "can do" states by freeing up psychological resources required for proactive action. When individuals believe that organizational members or coworkers care for them, they experience a greater sense of security and feel more confident knowing that should they require their coworkers' support it will be forthcoming. This enhances their psychological availability and boosts the resources they need to be innovative in the way they approach their work (Vinarski-Peretz & Carmeli, 2011). In this sense positive relationships are resource giving rather than resource depleting (Dutton & Heaphy, 2003). Employees who experience positive work relationships have more psychological resources available to dedicate to shaping their proactive ideas, which in turn serves to enhance their readiness to implement such ideas (Vinarski-Peretz & Carmeli, 2011).

Positive work relationships promote "reason to" states

Positive work relationships may also provide a compelling "reason to" be proactive. Firstly, as discussed above, autonomous motivation has been suggested as a key driver of proactive behavior. Positive relationships contribute to "reason to" states by enhancing autonomous motivation through their positive effect on psychological need satisfaction. Although positive relationships at work are important for functional purposes, they also satisfy fundamental psychological needs such as the need for relatedness. Relatedness needs refer to the desire to feel connected to others, to love and care for others, and to feel loved and cared for. According to self-determination theory, positive relational contexts which support the satisfaction of this need are more likely to promote the expression of autonomous motivation, which is required for proactivity resulting in positive change (Deci & Ryan, 2000; Gagne & Deci, 2005). Furthermore, as part of a dynamic model of autonomously regulated proactivity, Strauss and Parker (forthcoming) argue that individuals who find that their psychological needs are met

experience personal growth resulting in the raising of their expectations for themselves and their jobs, which provides further reason to
set and pursue proactive goals.

Positive work relationships may also influence "reasons to" be proactive by motivating the protection of relational resources. Conservation
of resources theory (Hobfoll, 2002) proposes that people are motivated
to acquire and protect the things they value. Positive workplace relationships constitute relational resources that have value for the people
engaged in them. For example, if individuals work as part of a team
that is rich in relational resources, individuals may be motivated to initiate support for the team by suggesting improvements to the team's
functioning. Similarly, individuals who are engaged in positive relationships may be motivated to proactively develop these relationships
in order to ensure that they are sustained in the long term (for
example, via proactively supporting colleagues, or by building their
own unique networks of relationships). This highlights that not only
do positive relational contexts boost the psychological states necessary
to motivate proactivity, many proactive endeavors may also serve to
build and develop these relational resources. We elaborate on this reciprocal effect at a later stage in this chapter.

Positive work relationships promote "energized to" states

Workplace relationships directly contribute to the level of energy that
individuals experience at work. In particular, research on workplace
vigor has shown that positive work relationships provide a contextual
backdrop against which vigor flourishes. Vigor refers to a set of interrelated affective states, comprising energy and vitality, experienced at
work (Carmeli et al., 2009a). Research has shown that meaningful
interactions with others is one of the most frequently cited work-
related antecedent of vigor (Shraga & Shirom, 2009). Bonding social
capital between group members has also been identified as an
antecedent of vigor (Carmeli et al., 2009a). The concept of social
capital has been defined as the resources embedded in one's internal
and external network of relationships (Nahapiet & Ghoshal, 1998).
Bonding social capital focuses specifically on internal networks and
refers to the extent of high-quality relationships among members of a
group that enhance collaboration, cooperation, and trust. Carmeli and
colleagues (2009a) found that individuals who reported high levels of
bonding social capital experienced greater energy and vitality on the
job which in turn led to enhanced job performance.

The importance of relationships for workplace energy is also high-lighted in research on thriving at work. As discussed earlier, thriving describes a psychological state characterized by a sense of vitality and learning at work (Spreitzer et al., 2005). From a relational perspective, positive social contexts contribute to thriving in that learning does not happen in isolation; rather it occurs through interactions with others in the course of work (Spreitzer et al., 2005). Relational theories on self-development (Miller & Stiver, 1997) also submit that vitality is gener-ated through relational connections with others. In support of these arguments, Niessen et al. (2012) found that relational resources were positively related to thriving at work in a sample of social workers.

Finally, social resources are likely to enhance "energized to" motiva-tion for proactive behavior by supporting engagement at work. Job resources such as social support have been identified as one of the most predictive antecedents of work engagement because, as argued above, they contribute to psychological need satisfaction (Hakanen & Roodt, 2010) which in turn also contributes to engagement (Van den Broeck et al., 2008). Although studies that specifically focus on the role of rela-tional resources alone are limited, a number of empirical studies have found support for the link between positive relational contexts, such as those characterized by organizational support (Saks, 2006), high quality interpersonal relationships (Warshawsky et al., 2012), and work engagement. Furthermore, a lack of social support has consistently been found to be related to work burnout, the antipode of work engagement (Maslach et al., 2001). Taken together, these studies high-light the importance of positive relationships for enhancing "energized to" motivations for proactive behavior.

Thus far we have focused attention on how positive relational con-texts support positive psychological states which motivate proactive behavior. However, given that many proactive behaviors by their nature have implications for others who may be affected by them, we now turn our attention to how workplace relationships influence the outcomes of proactivity.

How relationships determine the outcomes of proactive behavior

Proactive behavior is expected to be critical for organizational perfor-mance, particularly in uncertain and dynamic organizational environ-ments where it is not possible to specify and anticipate exactly how employees can contribute to organizational effectiveness (Griffin et al.,

2007). Studies exploring the outcomes of proactive behavior have primarily focused on its benefits. Proactive behavior has been found to be associated with greater job performance (Crant, 1995; Thompson, 2005), career success (Seibert et al., 2001), and job satisfaction (Wanberg & Kammeyer-Mueller, 2000). Individuals with a proactive personality also seem to be more satisfied with their lives, partially because the goals they are pursuing reflect their authentic personal interests and values and allow them to satisfy their psychological needs (Greguras & Diefendorff, 2010). Furthermore, entrepreneurs with a proactive personality have been found to positively impact levels of innovation within the small firms they are leading (Kickul & Gundy, 2002).

However, more recently scholars have noted the possibility of negative consequences of proactive behavior. Under certain circumstances proactive behavior may not be successful and even detrimental (e.g. Belschak et al., 2010; Bolino et al., 2010; Cooper-Thomas & Burke, 2012; Strauss & Parker, forthcoming) As indicated by the latter phases of our dynamic model (Figure 6.1), we argue that relationships and social factors are likely to be key factors that influence the outcomes of proactive behavior, both for the individual and for the organization. Below, we discuss how relationships determine the effects of proactive behavior on performance evaluation, the responses to P-E fit behaviors from those who may be affected by it, and individuals' ability to successfully implement the changes they initiate.

Effects on performance evaluation

Researchers generally propose a positive relationship between proactive behavior and job performance, arguing that it should result in increased productivity (Thompson, 2005). This, however, does not take into account the social context in which proactive behavior occurs. Whether proactive behavior does indeed lead to increased performance evaluations will depend on the perceptions and expectations of others. Supervisors in particular do not always evaluate proactive behavior positively (Fuller et al., 2012; Grant et al., 2009), and may see employees' proactive behavior as a threat (Frese & Fay, 2001). Employees raising questions about the effectiveness of current procedures may cause supervisors to feel embarrassed or incompetent, which could have a negative impact on their relationship. Supervisors may also see proactive behavior as a self-serving impression management strategy (Bolino, 1999), or as a distraction, particularly when it is badly timed (Chan, 2006).

Whether supervisors value proactive behavior and consequently "reward" it with higher performance evaluations is likely to depend on a range of different factors, including the perceived motives and intentions of the employee, characteristics of the employee such as their ability to accurately judge how and when to engage in proactive behavior, and characteristics of the supervisor.

One way in which supervisors form impressions about the intentions and motives underlying proactive behavior is by observing which values and emotions employees express (Grant et al., 2009). Employees with strong prosocial values, that is, values that are benevolent, altruistic, and other-oriented (Schwartz & Sagiv, 1995), are likely to be seen as engaging in proactive behavior for the benefit of others rather than out of self-serving motives. When employees have strong prosocial values, proactive behavior is positively linked to performance evaluations (Grant et al., 2009). When accompanied by prosocial values, proactive behavior is likely to be seen as contributing to collective goals over and above what is expected, and this will likely foster positive relationships between the respective employee and his or her peers and superiors. Employees' emotions may also inform others' judgments about the motives underlying proactive behavior. Employees who have an enduring tendency to express negative emotions and moods (c.f. Watson et al., 1988) could be seen as complaining when they voice suggestions for improvements, and they are likely to appear overburdened by their efforts to bring about change (Grant et al., 2009). In line with these arguments, Grant and his colleagues (2009) found, across two different studies, that proactive behavior was only positively associated with supervisors' evaluations of performance if employees were low in negative affect.

Supervisors' evaluations of, and reactions to, proactive behavior are also likely to depend on whether supervisors generally see proactive behavior as valuable. Fuller and colleagues found that supervisors who were high in proactive personality gave high performance evaluations to employees who engaged in proactive behavior (Fuller et al., 2012). However, whether supervisors and employees were similar in their personality (proactive versus passive) did not influence supervisor ratings of performance or proactive behavior (Fuller et al., 2012).

Finally, supervisors' judgment on whether proactive behavior is useful is also likely to depend on the characteristics of the individual employee, such as their perceived competence (Den Hartog & Belschak, 2012). When employees are not meeting the prescribed requirements of their job, proactive behavior that goes beyond their job role is likely to be seen as a distraction. In support of this idea, Chan (2006) found that employees high in proactive personality only received positive evaluations of job performance from their supervisors if these employees were perceived as capable of making effective judgments about the appropriate response to work situations.

Effects on P-E fit

As employees take action to achieve a better fit between their own needs and preferences and their work environment, their relationships with colleagues are likely to determine the extent to which such colleagues support these efforts, and affect whether the proactive individual actually succeeds in achieving better P-E fit.

While coworker reactions to employees' proactive behavior have received relatively little attention in the literature, scholars have acknowledged that coworker reactions can determine the outcomes of employees' proactive efforts to negotiate employment conditions and working arrangements (Lai et al., 2009; Rousseau, 2005; Rousseau et al., 2006). Negotiating an idiosyncratic deal (or "i-deal", Rousseau, 2005) can be seen as a proactive behavior aimed at increasing the fit between the needs and desires of the individual and the working conditions offered by the organization. I-deals may be negotiated prior to employment (ex ante i-deals), or once on the job (ex post i-deals) (Rousseau et al., 2006). I-deals create different working conditions for the individual and may also have implications for his or her coworkers. Whether i-deals are effective, that is, whether they meet the individual's need for a desirable working arrangement and the employer's need for retaining an employee who constitutes a valuable asset, is also influenced by the individual's coworkers (Rousseau, 2005). For example, an employee may negotiate compressed working hours and work four ten-hour days to have the fifth day of every week off. However, if this arrangement is met with resentment by coworkers and colleagues who consequently regularly schedule important meetings on the fifth day, this will mean that the individual will not succeed in implementing their i-deal arrangement and may leave the organization if attractive alternatives are available.

I-deals may have a negative instrumentality for coworkers (Lai et al., 2009). Particularly if resources are constrained, coworkers are likely to experience a loss when a colleague successfully negotiates an i-deal (Rousseau et al., 2006). Drawing on conservation of resources theory (Hobfoll, 2002), Bolino and colleagues similarly proposed that proactive behavior may help some employees acquire more resources while simultaneously threatening their peers' current or future resources (Bolino et al., 2010). For example, successfully negotiating flexible working hours may increase the workload of others. Those who manage to secure developmental assignments through proactive behaviors may cause colleagues to miss out on these opportunities; these colleagues are then potentially less likely to be promoted, and may find their own needs for challenging work thwarted. Because individuals are habitually more sensitive to losses than to gains when resources are constrained (Kahneman & Tversky, 1979), coworkers are likely to be particularly sensitive to the losses they may experience as a consequence of a peer's proactive behavior (Rousseau et al., 2006).

The relationship between the person engaging in P-E fit proactivity and their coworkers at least in part determines their peers' reactions. If coworkers have close relational ties with the person engaging in proactive behavior, the benefits this person subsequently enjoys can be personally satisfying for the coworkers themselves (Rousseau, 2005). Lai et al. (2009) studied employees' reactions to coworkers i-deals in a sample of 65 research scientists and research managers in a US-based research and development firm and found that coworkers were more likely to accept and support an i-deal if the person in question was a close personal friend. Similarly, supervisors are more likely to support and facilitate employees' efforts to shape their working arrangements if they have a high quality relationship with the employee, characterized by mutual trust (Hornung et al., 2010; Rousseau et al., 2006). Taken together, these studies provide initial support for the idea that relationships at work clearly have implications for whether or not others will support proactive P-E fit behavior.

Effects on the implementation of change

By its very nature, proactive behavior involves initiating change. The quality of the relationship between the person engaging in proactive behavior and those affected by it is likely to ultimately determine whether proactivity is actually effective in bringing about the envisioned change. Rallying support for one's idea and getting the right people involved are important aspects of facilitating the implementation of innovative ideas (Howell et al., 2005; Mumford & Licuanan, 2004; Mumford et al., 2002) and individuals working towards the implementation of innovative ideas appear to have more influence on others' behavior if they have a good relationship with them (Markham, 1998).

Where relationships between colleagues reflect high levels of coordination, individuals may be better able to enact and sell their initiatives to those likely to be affected, thus making successful implementation of change more likely. Relational coordination emphasizes the relational dimensions of shared goals, shared knowledge, and mutual respect – supported by timely and frequent communication – as key components of effective coordination between interdependent work roles (Gittell, 2002). Where employees share common goals, proactive ideas can likely be planned and enacted with greater confidence and greater potential for success. Similarly, if individuals working together have shared knowledge regarding colleagues' work roles, they have greater understanding of the interconnections between these roles. This knowledge is important for assessing the impact of proactive work behaviors on the roles of others, and consequently, their reaction to the proactive behavior. As such, individuals who know their coworkers' roles well may be better equipped to sell their proactive ideas in ways that emphasize how the changes will result in improvements in work processes and valued outcomes. This is in line with research by Dutton et al. (2001), which highlights the value of normative knowledge for the successful implementation of proactive ideas. In addition, frequent and timely interactions also provide the employee engaging in proactive behavior with more opportunities to convince others of the benefits of the change he or she is trying to implement.

Finally, coworkers are more likely to attribute benevolent motives to a proactive peer they have a good relationship with, and may feel more confident that their own needs and interests will be taken into consideration. These positive attributions, in turn, make it more likely that initiatives focused on implementing change will find greater support and consequently be more successful.

Effects of proactive behavior on the relational context

Proactive behavior can have both positive and negative effects on the relational context in organizations. First, as mentioned above, individuals may extend their proactivity to relationships at work. By actively shaping social interactions and relationships (Grant & Ashford, 2008), they thus contribute to a positive relational context. For example, they may decide to help others not only if they are asked to, but also in proactive ways, driven, for example, by prosocial motives (Rioux & Penner, 2001). In order to help a colleague or subordinate, they may even decide to violate organizational policies and regulations (Morrison, 2006).

Individuals may proactively seek to increase their social job resources at work (Tims et al., 2012), such as by asking others for feedback and advice (Ashford et al., 2003). Particularly during organizational entry, individuals may proactively try to build relationships with their supervisor, which in turn contributes to their job performance (Ashford & Black, 1996). They may aim to enhance their understanding of the relational context by seeking social information from their new colleagues (Morrison, 1993). They may actively seek out opportunities to interact with others (Reichers, 1987), for example by initiating social get-togethers, stopping by others' offices, contributing to online discussion forums within the organization, connecting with more distal colleagues on professional networking sites or by taking part in more formal social activities (Ashford & Black, 1996), which in turn contributes to a positive relational context.

Individuals may also be proactive in alleviating the potential negative effects of their proactive behavior in other domains of their relationships with others. Individuals engaging in proactive P-E fit behavior may try to manage its impact (and the impact of its consequences) on colleagues. For example, they may try to offer an explanation for the particular working arrangements they have crafted or negotiated for themselves to enhance their colleagues' perceptions of fairness, or downplay the differences in working arrangements (Rousseau et al., 2006). They may also try to proactively help coworkers who face additional workload or demands as a consequence of their own proactive behavior.

Proactive behavior may, however, also have negative effects on the relational context in organizations. First, it may increase demands upon peers, as discussed above. Individuals' efforts to bring about change in their organization may, if successful, result in an environment that others perceive as characterized by frequent change. Frequent change in turn can increase uncertainty, and may consequently result in lower job satisfaction and increased turnover intention of those affected (Rafferty & Griffin, 2006). Particularly proactive work behavior and proactive strategic behavior are likely to require the support of others, and may make it necessary for others to adapt their ways of working, and potentially develop new skills to cope with new ways of working (Griffin et al., 2007). For example, introducing a new open-source application for sharing files electronically may save the organization money and make collaborations across teams easier, but it will require others to learn the new software and change the way they are working. Coworkers may consequently resent their peer, who they may perceive as contributing to frequent change, requiring them to constantly adapt and making it more difficult for them to meet performance expectations.

Second, proactive employees may be seen as violating group norms for acceptable performance by their peers, and may consequently face social sanctions, ranging from criticism to more severe forms of hostility (Van Dyne & Ellis, 2004). According to conservation of resources theory (Hobfoll, 2002), individuals are motivated to obtain and protect the resources they value. Threat to, or depletion of these resources causes stress. Proactive behavior can help some employees to acquire resources while simultaneously depleting or threatening the resources of others. For example, Bolino and colleagues (2010) argue that less proactive employees may attempt to pressure their more proactive peers to decrease their proactive behavior so that they themselves have to put in less effort and are able to conserve their own resources. Similarly, more proactive employees may attempt to "share the load" and pressure others to engage in more proactive behavior. These processes are likely to increase interpersonal tension (Bolino et al., 2010), and may have negative consequences for relationships in organizations.

Third, proactive behavior may negatively affect relationships through its impact on justice perceptions. Particularly if the proactive behavior is covert, for example if negotiations about i-deals occur in secret, it is likely to be judged as less fair (Rousseau et al., 2006), and may jeopardize the justice climate in the organization (Lai et al., 2009; Lind & Tyler, 1988; Rousseau, 2005). Organizations' reactions to employees' proactive behavior provide a further potential source of conflict. If organizations reward proactive behavior, this can potentially affect justice perceptions (Bolino et al., 2010). In jobs with low levels of autonomy, proactive behavior is more difficult to enact (Grant & Ashford, 2008; Parker et al., 2006). Consequently, different jobs offer varying opportunities to engage in proactive behavior. If organizations reward proactive behavior without taking into account that not all employees have the same opportunities to engage in proactivity, this could instill a sense of injustice in some employees (Bolino et al., 2010). This could not only affect the justice climate in the organization but also relationships between employees, as employees in more restrictive jobs may resent those whose jobs allow them to engage in proactive behavior and gain rewards for it (Bolino et al., 2010).

Creating relational contexts that support proactive behavior and enhance its benefits

This chapter highlights the value of positive relationships in the workplace for proactive behavior by articulating how, as part of a dynamic model, such relationships influence motivations to be proactive via their impact on positive psychological states. We have also addressed how the nature of relationships at work can impact the outcomes of proactivity for the individual, and how proactivity can affect the relational context in organizations. These issues have clear implications for organizations aiming to foster positive relational contexts that are likely to support the development of a proactive workforce.

First, organizations should give consideration to how work is structured. Providing employees with opportunities for interdependence and enabling them to develop attachments to work groups and teams may help to satisfy psychological needs and thus promote the autonomous motivation required for successful implementation of self-initiated change.

Second, organizational managers and leaders are well positioned to serve as role models for positive relational interactions. Such positive role modeling can potentially change workplace relationships, constructing positive relational contexts. In practice this could involve providing skills-based training and coaching in relationship-building and collaborative practice for leaders and managers. They may themselves display positive regard for others, engage respectfully in their interactions, and encourage collaboration and open communication between employees. This in turn signals to the workforce that these skills are valued and reflect expected ways of interacting.

The human resource function within an organization is well positioned to contribute to the development of high quality relationships amongst employees through the recruitment of employees. When relational skills form part of the selection criteria, organizations are likely to recruit individuals who are capable of building high quality relationships with others (Baker & Dutton, 2006). Furthermore, organizations should also select for, and reward, cross-functional teamwork, which has been found to be particularly important in strengthening relational coordination (Gittell et al., 2010). By selecting people with an orientation towards teamwork or with proven past experience of successfully working as part of a cross-functional team, organizations can strengthen relational coordination between different employee groups and in so doing enhance the capacities of individuals to envision, enact, and sell their proactive ideas to the colleagues whose roles or tasks they may affect.

Organizations also play an important role in alleviating the potential negative impact proactive behavior may have on the relational context in the organization. In particular, they need to prevent the potential negative effects of proactive behavior on justice perceptions in the organization. By conducting negotiations with employees aiming to enhance their P-E fit through an i-deal in a transparent way, they may prevent a negative impact on the organization's justice climate.

Organizations also need to be mindful of potential inequalities arising from individuals' proactive behavior and ensure that they acknowledge and potentially compensate for an unequal distribution of resources. This, however, does not mean that organizations should aim to prevent and stifle individual employees' efforts to maximize their own resources. Rather they should aim to minimize inequalities in the opportunity to engage in proactive behavior among employees at the same hierarchical level, enabling all employees to shape their work context wherever possible to achieve a better fit with their needs and preferences. When there are potential differences in the opportunities afforded to individuals to engage in proactive behavior, organizations need to ensure they account for these when providing formal and informal rewards for proactive behavior.

Finally, organizations need to be aware of the potential negative interpersonal consequences of "demanding" proactive behavior from their employees (Bolino et al., 2010). Instead, they should encourage autonomously motivated proactive behavior which is likely to have greater benefits for the individual as well as the organization (Strauss & Parker, forthcoming).

Future directions

Given that previous research highlights the values of a positive relational context for stimulating and sustaining proactive behavior, we propose that future research agendas should give focused attention to how to create environments where the positive workplace relationships required for effective proactive behavior can flourish. For example, future research may investigate how best to foster workplace relationships that inspire or develop personal beliefs in one's ability to take proactive action, or explore how relationships boost the resources required to persist and follow through on implementing proactive ideas. As discussed above, one potential avenue for investigation is the role of leaders in shaping the relational context. For example, promising work by Carmeli et al. (2009a) has identified the role of relational leadership in shaping bonding social capital between coworkers.

Although within this chapter we have focused on the ways in which positive relationships motivate proactivity, future research might also consider when and how positive work relationships can potentially stifle proactive goal motivation. For example, if relationships are characterized by closeness and cohesion, this may cultivate climates in which the status quo is valued. Attempts to initiate change to work practices could then potentially "upset the apple cart" and individuals invested in these relationships may thus refrain from engaging in proactive behavior. Future research could test for a curvilinear relationship between relational constructs and proactivity such that, while positive relationships may have a positive impact on proactivity to a point, at some level very tightly knit relationships may in fact have a detrimental impact on proactivity.

We suggest that future research aimed at enhancing our understanding of the dynamic interplay between relational resources, positive psychological states, proactive behavior and its outcomes should adopt longitudinal research designs. Such an approach would help to explore the reciprocal relationships between positive work relationships and proactivity, and uncover potential gain spirals between these constructs (Xanthopoulou et al., 2009). For example, research could examine the proposition that positive reactions of coworkers and supervisors may signal to the employee that proactive action is worth it; the resulting positive self-perceptions and positive affect would lead the individual to evaluate their social resources more positively and feel more capable of building and exploiting these resources in the future. Broadening networks of relationships, providing more support to coworkers in need of help, and searching out new collaborations in turn serve to build the relational resources required to motivate and facilitate further proactive action. Additionally, as part of a longitudinal research design using diary studies, future research might also explore how positive or negative interactions with colleagues on a daily basis influence the frequency of proactive behavior at the day-level. This would enable researchers to understand how brief interactions with colleagues impact fluctuations in psychological states which have potential to impact on daily proactive behavior.

We also advocate further empirical research on the interpersonal consequences of proactive behavior for the individual. Although research on supervisor evaluations of proactivity is gathering pace, less empirical research has been conducted to investigate how proactive behaviors influence individuals' relationships with their coworkers.

Although we have made a strong case for the value of focusing on understanding how relational contexts can shape motivations for proactive behavior and determine the outcomes of this behavior, we acknowledge that individual traits may interact with the relational context. They may influence individuals' motivations to behave proactively and shape how they deal with the consequences of their behavior (Mischel & Shoda, 1995). For example, it is possible that the effects of positive work relationships on proactive behavior are amplified for individuals with a dispositional tendency towards neuroticism. For these individuals, supportive and caring relationships provide an important buffer against worry and anxiety, allowing individuals to focus their emotional and cognitive resources directly on a more proactive approach to their work.

Although we have largely focused on more conventional workplace relationships where colleagues are largely collocated we acknowledge that today work in many contexts is carried out at least in part via communication technologies which enhance connectivity between both collocated and distributed employees (Dixon & Panteli, 2010; Kolb et al., 2012). These connective technologies are likely to influence the extent to which individuals can successfully "make things happen". For example, where organizations employ online discussion forums or internal networking sites in order to facilitate knowledge sharing and collaboration amongst employees, such media may serve as a platform for instant feedback on proactive ideas. In this way connectivity of this nature may not only help individuals to build on their proactive ideas, it may also help generate the crucial momentum and energy needed to implement ideas. Widespread participation in employee blogging may also foster a sense of community and identification with the organization facilitating "reason to" motivations to be proactive. Networking sites (e.g. LinkedIn) may serve to enhance professional connections between individuals internally and externally, facilitating information exchange, while simultaneously providing employees with the opportunity to proactively build their own unique networks of relationships. Notwithstanding the many potential benefits of new communication technologies, researchers might also explore the potential negative side effects of these media. For example, where organizations rely heavily on social media, this may displace time spent on face-to-face interactions between employees. In such situations it is possible that increased online communication technologies actually result in employees substituting strong relationships (based on more face to face interpersonal contact) for weak ones (based primarily on online communications). Given these possibilities, future research might explore how social media and/or networking platforms influence the nature and quality of relational context and its impact on proactive behavior.

Finally, in considering the impact of relationships on proactive behavior we have primarily focused on the effect of positive relationships on pro-organizational forms of proactive behavior. However, it is also possible that relationships trigger counterproductive forms of proactive behavior. In line with this argument, Searle and Kelly (2011) found that hindrance stressors, obstacles which prevent individuals from achieving their goals, trigger anger which in turn leads to proactive forms of counterproductive work behaviors. When coworkers are seen as detrimental to goal progress or cause anger in other ways, individuals may engage in self-starting behavior that is intended to, for example, undermine a plan, policy or project (Searle & Kelly, 2011). Negative interactions and relationships at work may thus trigger behavior which is proactive yet purely self-serving.

Conclusion

Despite the centrality of relationships to our experience of work, relationships have been traditionally placed in the background of organizational life (Ragins & Dutton, 2006). Although researchers interested in understanding proactive behavior have paid intermittent attention to the role of social context, in this chapter we have brought the interplay between workplace relationships and proactive behavior to front and center. Throughout this chapter we have attempted to provide insights on the complex web of linkages between the relational context and proactive behavior. Our dynamic model emphasizes how positive workplace relationships impact proactive goal motivation via their impact on positive psychological states, and further highlights how the nature of relationships with others can impact evaluations and outcomes of proactive behavior. Finally, the model captures ways in which proactive behaviors, in turn, have implications for the quality of relationships between colleagues. In conclusion we identify the role of relationships in organizations for "making things happen" as a promising avenue for investigation and as one worthy of further empirical research.

Acknowledgments

The first author would like to acknowledge funding received from the Irish Research Council for the Humanities and Social Sciences which aided the development of this work.

References

Ashby, F. G., Isen, A. M., & Turken, A. U. (1999). A neuropsychological theory of positive affect and it's influence on cognition, *Psychological Review*, *106*(3), 529–550. doi: 10.1037/0033-295x.106.3.529

Ashford, S. J. & Black, J. S. (1996). Proactivity during organizational entry: The role of desire for control, *Journal of Applied Psychology*, *81*(2), 199–214. doi: 10.1037/0021-9010.81.2.199

Ashford, S. J., Blatt, R., & VandeWalle, D. (2003). Reflections on the looking glass: A review of research on feedback-seeking behavior in organization, *Journal of Management*, *29*(6), 773–799. doi: 10.1016/s0149-2063_03_00079-5

Axtell, C. M., Holman, D. J., Unsworth, K. L., Wall, T. D., & Waterson, P. E. (2000). Shopfloor innovation: Facilitating the suggestion and implementation of ideas, *Journal of Occupational and Organizational Psychology*, *73*(3), 265–285. doi: 10.1348/096317900167029

Baker, W. & Dutton, J. (2006). Enabling positive social capital: in J. Dutton & B. Ragins (eds) *Exploring Positive Relationships at Work: Building a Theoretical and Research Foundation* (pp. 325–346). Mahwah, NJ: Lawrence Erlbaum.

Bandura, A. (1982). Self-efficacy mechanism in human agency, *American Psychologist*, *37*(2), 122–147. doi: 10.1037//0003-066X.37.2.122

Bandura, A. (1997). *Self-Efficacy: The Exercise of Control*. New York: Freeman.

Bandura, A. (2006). Towards a psychology on human agency, *Perspectives on Psychological Science*, *1*(2), 164–180.

Bateman, T. S. & Crant, J. M. (1993). The proactive component of organizational-behavior: A measure and correlates, *Journal of Organizational Behavior*, *14*(2), 103–118. doi: 10.1002/job.4030140202

Belschak, F. D., Den Hartog, D. N., & Fay, D. (2010). Exploring positive, negative and context-dependent aspects of proactive behaviours at work, *Journal of Occupational and Organizational Psychology*, *83*(2), 267–273. doi: 10.1348/096317910x501143

Bindl, U. & Parker, S. K. (2010). Feeling good and performing well? Psychological engagement and positive behaviors at work: in S. Albrecht (ed.) *Handbook of Employee Engagement* (pp. 385–399). Massachusetts: Edward Elgar Publishing.

Bindl, U., Parker, S. K., Totterdell, P., & Hagger-Johnson, G. (2012). Fuel of the self-starter: How mood relates to proactive goal regulation, *Journal of Applied Psychology*, *97*(1), 134–150. doi: 10.1037/a0024368

Binyamin, G. & Carmeli, A. (2010). Does the structuring of human resource management processes enhance employee creativity? The mediating role of psychological availability, *Human Resource Management*, *49*(6), 999–1024. doi: 10.1002/hrm.20397

Bolino, M. C. (1999). Citizenship and impression management: Good soldiers or good actors? *Academy of Management Review*, *24*(1), 82–98. doi: 10.2307/259038

Bolino, M. C., Valcea, S., & Harvey, J. (2010). Employee, manage thyself: The potentially negative implications of expecting employees to behave proactively, *Journal of Occupational and Organizational Psychology*, *83*(2), 325–345. doi: 10.1348/096317910X493134

Carmeli, A. (2007). Social capital, psychological safety and learning behaviours from failure in organisations, *Long Range Planning*, *40*(1), 30–44. doi: 10.1016/j.lrp.2006.12.002

Carmeli, A., Ben-Hador, B., Waldman, D. A., & Rupp, D. E. (2009a). How leaders cultivate social capital and nurture employee vigor: Implications for job performance, *Journal of Applied Psychology*, *94*(6), 1553–1561. doi: 10.1037/a0016429

Carmeli, A., Brueller, D., & Dutton, J. (2009b). Learning behaviours in the workplace: The role of high-quality interpersonal relationships and psychological safety, *Systems Research and Behavioral Science*, *26*(1), 81–98. doi: 10.1002/sres.932

Carmeli, A. & Spreitzer, G. (2009). Trust, connectivity, and thriving: Implications for innovative behaviors at work, *Journal of Creative Behavior*, *43*(3), 169–191. doi: 10.1002/j.2162-6057.2009.tb01313.x

Chan, D. (2006). Interactive effects of situational judgement effectiveness and proactive personality on work perceptions and work outcomes, *Journal of Applied Psychology*, *91*(2), 475–481. doi: 10.1037/0021-9010.91.2.475

Chen, G., Gully, S. M., & Eden, D. (2001). Validation of a new general self-efficacy scale, *Organizational Research Methods*, *4*(1), 62–83. doi: 10.1177/109442810141004

Claes, R. & Ruiz-Quintanilla, S. (1998). Influences of early career experiences, occupational group, and national culture on proactive career behavior, *Journal of Vocational Behavior*, *52*(3), 357–378. doi: 10.1006/jvbe.1997.1626

Cooper-Thomas, H. & Burke, S. (2012). Newcomer proactive behavior: Can there be too much of a good thing?: in C. Wanberg (ed.) *Handbook of Organizational Socialization*. New York: Oxford University Press.

Crant, J. M. (1995). The proactive personality scale and objective job performance among real estate agents, *Journal of Applied Psychology*, *80*(4), 532–537. doi: 10.1037/0021-9010.80.4.532

Crant, J. M. (2000). Proactive behaviour in organizations, *Journal of Management*, *26*(3), 435–462. doi: 10.1177/014920630002600304

Csikszentmihalyi, M. (1990). *Flow: The Psychology of Optimal Experience*. New York: Harper and Row.

Deci, E. & Ryan, R. (1985). *Intrinsic Motivation and Self Determination in Human Behaviour*. New York: Plenum.

Deci, E. & Ryan, R. (2000). The "what" and "why" of goal pursuits: Human needs and the self-determination of behavior, *Psychological Inquiry*, *11*(4), 227–268. doi: 10.1207/s15327965pli1104_01

Deci, E. & Ryan, R. (2002). *Handbook of Self-Determination Research*. Rochester, N.Y.: University of Rochester Press.

Den Hartog, D. N. & Belschak, F. D. (2007). Personal initiative, commitment and affect at work, *Journal of Occupational and Organizational Psychology*, *80*(4), 601–622. doi: 10.1348/096317906x171442

Den Hartog, D. N. & Belschak, F. D. (2012). *The Role of Leader Personality in Evaluating Proactive Behavior*. Paper presented at the Academy of Management Annual Meeting, Boston.

Dixon, K. & Panteli, N. (2010). From virtual teams to virtuality in teams, *Human Relations*, 63(8), 1177–1197. doi: 10.1177/0018726709354784

Dutton, J. & Ashford, S. (1993). Selling issues to top management, *Academy of Management Review*, 18(3), 397–428. doi: 10.2307/258903

Dutton, J., Ashford, S., O'Neill, R., & Lawrence, K. (2001). Moves that matter: Issue selling and organizational change, *Academy of Management Journal*, 44(4), 716–736. doi: 10.2307/3069412

Dutton, J. & Heaphy, E. (2003). The power of high quality connections: in K. Cameron, J. Dutton, & R. Quinn (eds) *Positive Organisational Scholarship* (pp. 263–278). San Francisco: Berrett-Koehler.

Edmondson, A. (1999). Psychological safety and learning behavior in work teams, *Administrative Science Quarterly*, 44(2), 350–383. doi: 10.2307/2666999

Edmondson, A., Bohmer, R., & Pisano, G. (2001). Disrupted routines: Team learning and new technology implementation in hospitals, *Administrative Science Quarterly*, 46(4), 685–716. doi: 10.2307/3094828

Fay, D. & Frese, M. (2001). The concept of personal initiative: An overview of validity studies, *Human Performance*, 14(1), 97–124. doi: 10.1207/s15327043hup1401_06

Fredrickson, B. L. (1998). What good are positive emotions? *Review of General Psychology*, 2(3), 300–319. doi: 10.1037/1089-2680.2.3.300

Frese, M. & Fay, D. (2001). Personal initiative: An active performance concept for work in the 21st century: in B. M. Staw & R. L. Sutton (eds) *Research in Organisational Behavior* (Vol. 23, pp. 133–187). Stamford CT: JAI Press.

Fritz, C. & Sonnentag, S. (2009). Antecedents of day-level proactive behavior: A look at job stressors and positive affect during the workday, *Journal of Management*, 35(1), 94–111. doi: 10.1177/0149206307308911

Fuller, J. & Marler, L. (2009). Change driven by nature: A meta-analytic review of the proactive personality literature, *Journal of Vocational Behavior*, 75(3), 329–345. doi: 10.1016/j.jvb.2009.05.008

Fuller, J., Marler, L., & Hester, K. (2012). Bridge building within the province of proactivity, *Journal of Organizational Behavior*, 33(8), 1053–1070. doi: 10.1002/job.1780

Gagne, M. & Deci, E. (2005). Self-determination theory and work motivation, *Journal of Organizational Behavior*, 26(4), 331–362. doi: 10.1002/job.322

Gittell, J. H. (2002). Co-ordinating mechanisms in care provide groups: Relational coordination as a mediator and input uncertainty as a moderator of performance effects, *Management Science*, 48(11), 1408–1426. doi: 10.1287/mnsc.48.11.1408.268

Gittell, J. H., Seidner, R., & Wimbush, J. (2010). A relational model of high-performance work systems work, *Organization Science*, 21(3), 490–506. doi: 10.1287/orsc.1090.0446

Grant, A. & Ashford, S. J. (2008). The dynamics of proactivity at work, *Research in Organizational Behavior*, 28(28), 3–34. doi: 10.1016/j.riob.2008.04.002

Grant, A., Nurmohamed, S., Ashford, S. J., & Dekas, K. (2011). The performance implications of ambivalent initiative: The interplay of autonomous and controlled motivations, *Organizational Behavior and Human Decision Processes*, 116(2), 241–251. doi: 10.1016/j.obhdp.2011.03.004

Grant, A., Parker, S., & Collins, C. (2009). Getting credit for proactive behavior: Supervisor reactions depend on what you value and how you feel, *Personnel Psychology*, 62(1), 31–55. doi: 10.1111/j.1744-6570.2008.01128.x

Greguras, G. J. & Diefendorff, J. M. (2010). Why does proactive personality predict employee life satisfaction and work behaviors? A field investigation of the mediating role of the self-concordance model, *Personnel Psychology*, *63*(3), 539–560. doi: 10.1111/j.1744-6570.2010.01180.x

Griffin, M. A., Neal, A., & Parker, S. K. (2007). A new model of work role performance: Positive behavior in uncertain and interdependent contexts, *Academy of Management Journal*, *50*(2), 327–347. doi: 10.5465/amj.2007.24634438

Hakanen, J. J. & Roodt, G. (2010). Using the job demands-resources model to predict engagement: Analysing a conceptual model: in A. Bakker & M. P. Leiter (eds) *Work Engagement: A Handbook of Essential Theory and Research* (pp. 85–101). New York: Psychology Press.

Hobfoll, S. (2002). Social and psychological resources and adaptation, *Review of General Psychology*, *6*(4), 307–324.

Hornung, S., Rousseau, D., Glaser, J., Angerer, P., & Weigl, M. (2010). Beyond top-down and bottom-up work redesign: Customizing job content through idiosyncratic deals, *Journal of Organizational Behavior*, *31*(2–3), 187–215. doi: 10.1002/job.625

Howell, J. M., Shea, C. M., & Higgins, C. A. (2005). Champions of product innovations: Defining, developing, and validating a measure of champion behavior, *Journal of Business Venturing*, *20*(5), 641–661.

Kahn, W. A. (1990). Psychological conditions of personal engagement and disengagement at work, *Academy of Management Journal*, *33*(4), 692–724. doi: 10.2307/256287

Kahneman, D. & Tversky, A. (1979). Prospect theory: An analysis of decision under risk, *Econometrica*, *47*(2), 263–291.

Kark, R. & Carmeli, A. (2009). Alive and creating: The mediating role of vitality and aliveness in the relationship between psychological safety and creative work involvement, *Journal of Organizational Behavior*, *30*(6), 785–804. doi: 10.1002/job.571

Kickul, J. & Gundy, L. K. (2002). Prospecting for strategic advantage: The proactive entrepreneurial personality and small firm innovation, *Journal of Small Business Management*, *40*(2), 85–97. doi: 10.1111/1540-627X.00042

Koestner, R. & Losier, G. F. (2002). Distinguishing three ways of being highly motivated: A closer look at introjection, identification, and intrinsic motivation: in E. L. Deci & R. M. Ryan (eds) *Handbook of Self-Determination Research* (pp. 101–121). Rochester, NY: University of Rochester Press.

Kolb, D., Caza, A., & Collins, P. (2012). States of connectivity: New questions and new directions, *Organization Studies*, *33*(2), 267–273. doi: 10.1177/0170840611431653

Lai, L., Rousseau, D., & Chang, K. (2009). Idiosyncratic deals: Coworkers as interested third parties, *Journal of Applied Psychology*, *94*(2), 547–556. doi: 10.1037/a0013506

Lind, E. & Tyler, T. (1988). *The Social Psychology of Procedural Justice*. New York: Plenum Press.

Markham, S. K. (1998). A longitudinal examination of how champions influence others to support their projects, *Journal of Product Innovation Management*, *15*(6), 490–504. doi: 10.1111/1540-5885.1560490

Maslach, C., Schaufeli, W. B., & Leiter, M. P. (2001). Job burnout, *Annual Review of Psychology*, *52*, 397–422. doi: 10.1146/annurev.psych.52.1.397

Miller, J. B. & Stiver, I. P. (1997). *The Healing Connection: How Women Form Relationships in Therapy and in Life.* Boston: Beacon Press.

Mischel, W. & Shoda, Y. (1995). A cognitive-affective system theory of personality: Reconceptualizing situations, dispositions, dynamics and invariance in personality structure, *Psychological Review*, *102*(2), 246–268. doi: 10.1037/0033-295X.102.2.246

Morrison, E. (1993). Newcomer information-seeking – Exploring types, modes, sources and outcomes, *Academy of Management Journal*, *36*(3), 557–589. doi: 10.2307/256592

Morrison, E. (2006). Doing the job well: An investigation of pro-social rule breaking, *Journal of Management*, *32*(1), 5–28. doi: 10.1177/0149206305277790

Morrison, E. & Phelps, C. (1999). Taking charge at work: Extra role efforts to initiate workplace change, *The Academy of Management Journal*, *42*(4), 403–419. doi: 10.2307/257011

Mumford, M. & Licuanan, B. (2004). Leading for innovation: Conclusions, issues, and directions, *Leadership Quarterly*, *15*(1), 163–171. doi: 10.1016/j.leaqua.2003.12.010

Mumford, M., Scott, G., Gaddis, B., & Strange, J. (2002). Leading creative people: Orchestrating expertise and relationships, *Leadership Quarterly*, *13*(6), 705–750. doi: 10.1016/S1048-9843(02)00158-3

Nahapiet, J. & Ghoshal, S. (1998). Social capital, intellectual capital, and the organizational advantage, *Academy of Management Review*, *23*(2), 242–266. doi: 10.2307/259373

Niessen, C., Sonnentag, S., & Sach, F. (2012). Thriving at work? A diary study, *Journal of Organizational Behavior*, *33*(4), 468–487. doi: 10.1002/job.763

Parker, S. (2000). From passive to proactive motivation: The importance of flexible role orientations and role breadth self-efficacy, *Applied Psychology – An International Review*, *49*(3), 447–469. doi: 10.1111/1464-0597.00025

Parker, S. (2007). *How Positive Affect Can Facilitate Proactive Behaviour in the Workplace*. Paper presented at the Academy of Management Conference, Philadelphia.

Parker, S., Bindl, U., & Strauss, K. (2010). Making things happen: A model of proactive motivation, *Journal of Management*, *36*(4), 827–856. doi: 10.1177/0149206310363732

Parker, S. & Collins, C. (2010). Taking stock: Integrating and differentiating multiple proactive behaviors, *Journal of Management*, *36*(3), 633–662. doi: 10.1177/0149206308321554

Parker, S., Williams, H., & Turner, N. (2006). Modeling the antecedents of proactive behavior at work, *Journal of Applied Psychology*, *91*(3), 636–652. doi: 10.1037/0021-9010.91.3.636

Peterson, C., Park, N., Hall, N., & Seligman, M. (2009). Zest and work, *Journal of Organizational Behavior*, *30*(2), 161–172. doi: 10.1002/job.584

Rafferty, A. & Griffin, M. (2006). Perceptions of organizational change: A stress and coping perspective, *Journal of Applied Psychology*, *91*(5), 1154–1162. doi: 10.1037/0021-9010.91.5.1154

Ragins, B. & Dutton, J. (2006). Positive relationships at work: An invitation and introduction: in J. Dutton & B. Ragins (eds) *Exploring Positive Relationships at Work: Building a Theoretical and Research Foundation* (pp. 3–28). Mahwah, NJ: Lawrence Erlbaum.

Reichers, A. E. (1987). An interactionist perspective on newcomer socialization rates, *Academy of Management Review*, 12(2), 278–287. doi: 10.1037/0021-9010.81.2.199

Rioux, S. & Penner, L. (2001). The causes of organizational citizenship behavior: A motivational analysis, *Journal of Applied Psychology*, 86(6), 1306–1314. doi: 10.1037/0021-9010.86.6.1306

Rogers, C. R. (1951). *Client-Centred Therapy*. New York: Houghton-Miffin.

Rousseau, D. (2005). *I-deals: Idiosyncratic Deals Workers Bargain for Themselves.* New York: M. E. Sharpe.

Rousseau, D., Ho, V., & Greenberg, J. (2006). I-deals: Idiosyncratic terms in employment relationships, *Academy of Management Review*, 31(4), 977–994.

Ryan, R. & Deci, E. (2000). Self-determination theory and the facilitation of intrinsic motivation, social development, and well-being, *American Psychologist*, 55(1), 68–78. doi: 10.1037//0003-066X.55.1.68

Saks, A. M. (2006). Antecedents and consequences of employee engagement, *Journal of Managerial Psychology*, 21(7), 600–619. doi: 10.1108/02683940610690169

Salanova, M. & Schaufeli, W. B. (2008). A cross-national study of work engagement as a mediator between job resources and proactive behaviour, *International Journal of Human Resource Management*, 19(1), 116–131. doi: 10.1080/09585190701763982

Schwartz, S. H. & Sagiv, L. (1995). Identifying culture-specifics in the content and structure of values, *Journal of Cross-Cultural Psychology*, 26(1), 92–116. doi: 10.1577/0022022195261007

Scott, S. G. & Bruce, R. A. (1994). Determinants of innovative behavior: A path model of individual innovation in the workplace, *Academy of Management Journal*, 37(3), 580–607.

Searle, B. & Kelly, T. (2011). *Light and Dark Sides of Proactivity: A Stressor – Emotion Approach.* Paper presented at the 9th Industrial and Organisational Psychology Conference, Brisbane.

Seibert, S. E., Kraimer, M. L., & Crant, J. M. (2001). What do proactive people do? A longitudinal model linking proactive personality and career success, *Personnel Psychology*, 54(4), 845–874. doi: 10.1111/j.1744-6570.2001.tb00234.x

Shraga, O. & Shirom, A. (2009). The construct validity of vigor and its antecedents: A qualitative study, *Human Relations*, 62(2), 271–291. doi: 10.1177/0018726708100360

Sonnentag, S. (2003). Recovery, work engagement, and proactive behavior: A new look at the interface between nonwork and work, *Journal of Applied Psychology*, 88(3), 518–528. doi: 10.1037/0021-9010.88.3.518

Spreitzer, G., Sutcliffe, K., Dutton, J., Sonenshein, S., & Grant, A. (2005). A socially embedded model of thriving at work, *Organization Science*, 16(5), 537–549. doi: 10.1287/orsc.1050.0153

Strauss, K. & Parker, S. K. (forthcoming). Effective and sustained proactivity in the workplace: A self-determination theory perspective: in M. Gagne (ed.) *The Oxford Handbook of Work Engagement, Motivation, and Self-Determination Theory*.

Tharenou, P. & Terry, D. J. (1998). Reliability and validity of scores on scales to measure managerial aspirations, *Educational and Psychological Measurement*, 58(3), 475–492. doi: 10.1177/0013164498058003008

Thompson, J. A. (2005). Proactive personality and job performance: A social capital perspective, *Journal of Applied Psychology*, *90*(5), 1011–1017. doi: 10.1037/0021-9010.90.5.1011

Tims, M., Bakker, A., & Derks, D. (2012). Development and validation of the job crafting scale, *Journal of Vocational Behavior*, *80*(1), 173–186. doi: 10.1016/j.jvb.2011.05.009

Van den Broeck, A., Vansteenkiste, M., De Witte, H., & Lens, W. (2008). Explaining the relationships between job characteristics, burnout, and engagement: The role of basic psychological need satisfaction, *Work & Stress*, *22*(3), 277. doi: 10.1080/02678370802393672

Van Dyne, L. & Ellis, J. (2004). Job creep: A reactance theory perspective on organizational citizenship behavior as overfulfillment of obligations: in J. A. M. Coyle-Shapiro, L. M. Shore, M. S. Taylor, & L. E. Tetrick (eds) *The Employment Relationship: Examining Psychological and Contextual Perspectives* (pp. 181–205). Oxford: Oxford University Press.

Van Dyne, L. & LePine, J. (1998). Helping and voice extra-role behaviours: Evidence of construct and predictive validity, *Academy of Management Journal*, *41*(1), 108–119. doi: 10.2307/256902

Vinarski-Peretz, H., Binyamin, G., & Carmeli, A. (2011). Subjective relational experiences and employee innovative behaviors in the workplace, *Journal of Vocational Behavior*, *78*(2), 290–304. doi: 10.1016/j.jvb.2010.09.005

Vinarski-Peretz, H. & Carmeli, A. (2011). Linking care felt to engagement in innovative behaviors in the workplace: The mediating role of psychological conditions, *Psychology of Aesthetics, Creativity, and the Arts*, *5*(1), 43–53. doi: 10.1037/a0018241

Wanberg, C. R. & Kammeyer-Mueller, J. D. (2000). Predictors and outcomes of proactivity in the socialization process, *Journal of Applied Psychology*, *85*(3), 373–385. doi: 10.1037//0021-9010.85.3.373

Warshawsky, N. E., Havens, D. S., & Knafl, G. (2012). The influence of interpersonal relationships on nurse managers™ work engagement and proactive work behavior, *The Journal of Nursing Administration*, *42*(9), 418–425. doi: 10.1097/NNA.0b013e3182668129

Watson, D., Clark, L. A., & Tellegen, A. (1988). Development and validation of brief measures of positive and negative affect: The PANAS scales, *Journal of Personality and Social Psychology*, *54*(6), 1063–1070. doi: 10.1037/0022-3514.54.6.1063

Wrzesniewski, A. & Dutton, J. (2001). Crafting a job: Revisioning employees as active grafters of their work, *Academy of Management Review*, *26*(2), 179–201. doi: 10.2307/259118

Xanthopoulou, D., Bakker, A. B., Demerouti, E., & Schaufeli, W. B. (2009). Reciprocal relationships between job resources, personal resources, and work engagement, *Journal of Vocational Behavior*, *74*(3), 235–244. doi: 10.1016/j.jvb.2008.11.003

7
Gender and Workplace Relationships

Barbara A. Winstead[1] and Valerie N. Streets[1]

In 2009 Winstead and Morganson published a chapter on "Gender and Relationships at Work" for Wright and Morrison's *Friends and Enemies in Organizations: A Work Psychology Perspective*. That chapter explored the complexities of studying gender and relationships at work and reviewed the research literature on the role of gender in workplace friendships, social networks, mentor relationships, cross-sex relationships, and negative relationships at work. This chapter updates what we know about these topics and expands the scope of discussion to other aspects of gender and relationships at work, including gender's role in workplace romances, leader/member relationships, virtual relationships, and relationships in family businesses. Gender is an undeniably critical factor in many aspects of the psychology of work, including the types of jobs and careers that individuals seek and receive, their promotions and career paths, and the ways in which individuals are perceived and evaluated as employees and employers. In day-to-day interactions we cannot escape the fact that we not only behave and respond in ways that are to some degree a function of our gender, but we are also perceived and responded to in ways determined in part by our gender. Psychology has a long tradition of studying sex differences and gender; and researchers have drawn numerous and sometimes contradictory conclusions about the importance of these gender differences and certainly about the sources of these differences. Despite this extensive research literature on gender, and gender and relationships in general, there is rather less on gender and relationships in the workplace.

---

[1] Department of Psychology, Old Dominion University

One can approach the study of work and organizations with a perspective that excludes gender. With job analyses, role definitions, organizational charts, etc there is an objectivity to work activities and relationships. Researchers can say that a worker (ungendered) is our focus or that an organization with clearly defined roles and relationships can be studied without regard to gender. Indeed many studies use information on the sex of participants as a covariate in their analyses. But we all live in the real world, where an aggressive, rude male boss is perceived and responded to differently than an aggressive, rude female boss. And we are likely to have a different kind of relationship with a caring, overly friendly female coworker than with a caring, overly friendly male coworker and that too will depend on our own gender. Thus, if in research on supervisor aggression or friendly coworker relations we control for gender, the full picture of the effects of gender on workplace relationships will be missed.

In the 2009 chapter we focused on relationships at work "that are voluntary and more than casual". We particularly wanted to know more about how both positive and negative relationships at work were affected by the genders of the individuals in the relationships. We focused mostly on relationships among coworkers and specifically avoided relationships defined by work roles (e.g. supervisor-supervisee). The exception to this was the section on mentoring, but there too we tried to select research studies that looked at voluntary and not organizationally prescribed relationships. In doing this, we were acknowledging that more than work happens in the workplace; it is where many individuals find meaningful social relationships. The first section of this chapter will be updates on the research and scholarly literature on workplace friendships, social networks, and mentoring relationships. In this chapter, however, we expand our view of the effects of gender on workplace relationships. We examine romantic liaisons, leader/member relationships, virtual relationships, and family relationships in the workplace from the perspective of gender. While "non-work" workplace relationships can enrich – or detract from – our work satisfaction and commitment, relationships also make up an essential part of the work we do. In every relationship gender has an effect. Although we do not examine every facet of work life, by focusing on several types of workplace relationships we expand our understanding of how gender plays a central role at work.

The interplay of gender and relationships in any context is complex. Gender itself is both a person variable (females and males differ) and a stimulus variable (females and males are perceived and treated differently). In any two-person relationship there are at least three combinations: Female-female, female-male, male-male. With any role differentiation between the individuals there are four combinations, namely female mentor-female mentee, female mentor-male mentee, male mentor-female mentee, male mentor-male mentee. Sorting out what gender differences exist in different types of relationships, considering what might affect or help explain these differences, and then what impact these differences have on the work experience of the individual, in addition to the work outcomes for the organization, is a daunting task. Nevertheless, we agree with the editors' view that relationships at work matter and, especially, that all relationships are affected in one way or another by gender.

Update on workplace relationships: Social networks and friendships

A great deal of the work on personal relationships in the workplace is research on social networks. There is less research that explicitly addresses workplace friendships. Neither of these research literatures tends to focus on gender; indeed when included, gender tends to be a covariate. That is, researchers seek to explore the functions of social networks and friendships in the workplace while controlling for the variance accounted for by gender, rather than exploring that variance. We begin by summarizing findings from the previous chapter and then considering research done in the intervening years.

A solid and well established premise in the literature on social networks and friendship is *homophily*, or the notion that "similarity breeds connection" (McPherson et al., 2001, p. 415). This, along with the fact that much of the workforce is gender segregated, means that one's social relationships in the workplace tend to be with same-sex others. On the other hand, since networks are also seen as having instrumental as well as socioemotional functions, workers also seek to network with others who have status, power, and authority. Given the tendency for men to hold positions of greater power, the homophily principle can pose a dilemma for women establishing effective social networks. Research has demonstrated that while men may seek friendship/social support *and* advice/influence from other men; women tend to find friendships with women but advice/influence from men (Ibarra, 1992, 1997; Stackman & Pinder, 1999). These outcomes are, however, influenced by the degree of sex segregation vs. integration of the workforce and the relative status of women within the workforce. Of particular note, Ely (1994) found that junior women in a law firm with more women partners had more positive relationships with both senior and junior women in the firm than women in a male-dominated firm.

Friendships in the workplace tend also to be same sex and to be described as "close" but not "best" (Markiewicz et al., 1999; Sias et al., 2003). These relationships develop into closer friendships based on personality, similarity, proximity, and shared tasks but into very close or best friends only if there are factors outside the workplace that workers share. Measures of friendship frequency or quality tend to reveal no gender differences (Markiewicz et al., 1999), although women report communicating with one another more frequently (Sias et al., 2003). Having men in one's social network and having men as higher quality friends at work is associated with higher salary. On the other hand, maintenance difficulty (relationship issues) with male friends is related to lower job satisfaction for both women and men (Markiewicz et al., 1999).

Social networks and friendships are also used to build social capital, that is the support, opportunities, and resources that are available to us through our social contacts. A distinction has been made between hard social capital (i.e. instrumental and job-related resources) and soft social capital (i.e. emotional support resources). In a sample of university faculty, van Emmerik (2006) found that although there was no gender difference in creation of soft social capital, men did create more hard social capital. This is consistent with research that shows that men are more likely to use personal contacts to find jobs (Straits, 1998) and to seek promotions (Cannings & Montmarquette, 1991). However while using these contacts, which tend to be same-sex, may be useful; Drentea (1998) found that women who use their informal networks for job searches end up in female-dominated jobs compared to women who use more formal job search methods; this pattern did not hold for men.

Recent research by McDonald (2011) focused on the connections between social networks, social capital, and job advancement. Of particular importance over one's work career is the fact that social capital is related to non-searched for job opportunities. These non-searched for opportunities are jobs that a worker learns about or is recruited for because they are known by others (through the social network) and, importantly, these jobs tend to be higher status and higher paying positions (McDonald, 2011). Analyzing data from the National Longitudinal Survey of Youth (NLSY), McDonald found that work experience and the accumulation of social capital are related to these non-searched for job opportunities for men but not for women. McDonald suggests that women's work relationships may focus more on friendship and support and less on contacts that increase job-related knowledge and resources. Women may also be excluded from homophilous male social networks (Brass, 1985; Ibarra, 1992) that provide greater access to these non-searched for job opportunities.

Curiously, although individuals with stereotypically lower status in the work world, i.e. minorities and women, often must cross race and gender boundaries to access higher status contacts, Son and Lin (2012) found that white and male respondents to the US Job Search Survey, were more advantaged than non-white or female respondents when they used cross-race and cross-gender contacts. This was particularly true for cross-gender contacts. Overall, however, this may reflect the general advantage for men and non-minorities in using social networks to seek better jobs. Compared with men, women are less likely to have high status others in their social network and tend to have less diverse networks (Brass, 1985; Ibarra, 1992; McGuire, 2002). McGuire (2002) tested two likely explanations of why women and minorities receive less instrumental help from their social networks at work: composition of the network based on position at work, and status based on gender and race. Their results indicated that women and African Americans did receive less instrumental help from their network members than men and Caucasian Americans and that women and African Americans also had network members with fewer resources that might be helpful. However, even when structural variables were controlled, women and African Americans still received less instrumental help.

In summary, women generally have less hard social capital and even when it is present it is less advantageous to them. In order to fully understand how this aspect of social capital is developed and how it functions, we must include gender in the equation.

In research explicitly on workplace friendships, Morrison (2009) also made a distinction between the "work/career assistance" and "social/emotional support" benefits that might accrue from these relationships. She found that while both women and men cited both types of benefits, women were significantly more likely than men to describe work friendship in terms of social/emotional support, whereas men were significantly more likely to cite work/career assistance. On the other hand Randel and Ranft (2007) found no gender differences in endorsement of relationship and job facilitation motivations to maintain friendships at work. The differences between these two studies may be that Morrison used an open-ended question, whereas Randel and Ranft used a Likert scale, suggesting that the support functions of workplace friendships are more likely to come to mind for women, whereas the work relevant aspects are more likely to occur to men, but women and men are equally likely to endorse these if presented with prompts.

Morrison (2009) also found that greater friendship opportunity, friendship prevalence, and workgroup cohesion tended to predict greater job satisfaction and commitment and lower intentions to leave. There was a significant gender difference in the relationship between job satisfaction and friendship prevalence such that job satisfaction and friendships were correlated for men but not for women. Morrison speculates that women's tendency to seek friends for social and emotional support, that is to "tend and befriend" (Taylor et al., 2000) when they experience stress, may mean that they form friends at work in response to a stressful or dissatisfying job, thus, negating a relationship between work friendships and job satisfaction. It may also be that women treat friendships at work as a hygiene factor, that is, a work necessity. So only in the absence of good work friends would a woman be dissatisfied, whereas for men workplace friendships act as a motivator, creating a more pleasant and satisfying job.

Although many studies have found friendships at work and social inclusion are related to positive work attitudes and job satisfaction (Berman et al., 2002), employee turnover (Maertz & Griffeth, 2004; Mossholder et al., 2005), organizational commitment (Verbeke & Wuyts, 2007) and individual and organizational productivity (e.g. Berman et al., 2002; Lin, 1999; Mehra et al., 2001; Pearce & Randel, 2004; Prusak & Cohen, 2001), an article by Song and Olshfski (2008) begins by discussing why workplace friendships might be controversial. While admitting that a friendly work setting is preferable, they also discuss the potential for friendships to lead to gossip, favoritism, or office politics that can contribute to a negative work environment. In their study they examined friendships specifically between an employee and her or his supervisor, focusing on opportunities for and quality of friendships as they related to employee's work attitudes in offices in Korea and the US. In both cultures friendship opportunity and especially friendship quality were related to employees' positive work attitudes. Interestingly in both cultures, being in the gender majority (male in Korea; female in the US) was directly related to perceived friendship opportunities. This also influenced perceptions of friendship quality. Higher friendship quality was reported by men in

Korea and by women in the US. The gender composition of the work-place and the tendency to form same-sex friendships led to somewhat different outcomes for women and men in Korea and the US, but in both cases and for women and men, opportunities for friendship and quality of the friendship with one's supervisor had a positive impact on work attitudes.

In many of the studies reviewed, the composition of the workplace plays a major role. Women and men will find socioemotional support and friendships more easily in settings where their own gender is in the majority. It is also possible that women seek and expect emotional support from their relationships at work more than men do (Morrison, 2009). The relatively higher status of men in most work settings also creates a different context for men and women seeking to build hard social capital. Whereas men can do this in a homophilous network, women must cross the gender line to network with powerful men. Perhaps women are less inclined to do this (McDonald, 2011; van Emmerik, 2006); but Son and Lin's research, showing that women are less advantaged than men even when both use cross-gender contacts, suggests that instrumental help provided to women may be less, regardless of her social capital.

Update on mentor relationships

Mentoring has also been understood as serving "hard" and "soft" func-tions, i.e. career support and psychosocial support (Kram, 1986). And, as with social networks and workplace friendships, mentor relation-ships are more commonly same-gender (Ragins & Cotton, 1999; Turban et al., 2002). Turban et al. (2002) found that while gender sim-ilarity predicts better outcomes at the beginning of a mentoring rela-tionship, this effect dissipates over time. The availability of female or male mentors is also substantially determined by the gender composi-tion of the job or profession, which is particularly an issue for women entering male-dominated professions (Kay & Wallace, 2009), but is also true for men entering professions dominated by women, e.g. young male nurses. Some researchers have found that women report less career-related mentoring than men (Koberg et al., 1994) but no differ-ences in psychosocial support (Ensher & Murphy, 1997; Koberg et al., 1994). Sosik and Godshalk (2000) found that male protégés reported more psychosocial support from female compared to male mentors and the female protégés reported more career development from male than from female mentors. Mentors tend to report that they give more psychosocial support to women protégés than to men but do not differ in provision of career-related mentoring (Allen & Eby, 2004; Burke et al., 1993). When real life conditions, such as marriage, are added to the mix, the picture becomes more complex. Olian et al. (1993) found that mentors expected the greatest rewards from married male protégés and single female protégés. Finally, simply having a male mentor, especially a white male mentor, has been shown to be an advantage in terms of salary and promotions (Dreher & Cox, 1996; Ragins & Cotton, 1999).

McKeen and Bujaki (2007) argue that in the mentoring relationship gender operates on multiple levels: the gender of the mentor and the protégé, the composition of the dyad, the culture of the organization, society and its views of women/men, and the person in her or his context. They also note that most research on mentoring takes an instrumental approach; that is, focusing on work-related outcomes of mentoring, rather than viewing mentoring as a reciprocal relationship in which both the mentor and the protégé may grow and develop. They also point out that while the gender and mentoring literature tends to assume that successful outcomes are comparable for women and men, this may not be the case if women define success in more multidimensional ways, including both career and life, more often than men do.

Since the publication of the previous chapter, a meta-analytic analysis by O'Brien et al. (2010) provides a needed summary of gender differences in mentoring. They included 40 published articles and a conference paper. They found no gender difference in reports of having a mentor nor in reports of mentoring for career development. They did find that female protégés reported more psychosocial support. There were also greater gender differences in the reports of mentors. Men were more likely than women to report serving as a mentor and men reported providing more career development mentoring whereas women reported providing more psychosocial mentoring. The relatively greater number of men in positions of power within organizations may account for these differences. But the authors also draw on relational culture theory (Fletcher & Ragins, 2007) to argue that people with less power are generally required to develop relational skills and these skills are then associated with being relatively less powerful (O'Brien et al., 2010). Thus women mentors may unintentionally provide less powerful role models. Although the mentoring literature also tends to focus on the outcomes for protégés, the lost opportunities to mentor or to provide career enhancing mentoring to protégés also may impact the later stages of the mentor's career as their protégés rise to positions that could directly influence their own success and achievements.

Kay and Wallace (2009), in a longitudinal study of lawyers, found no gender differences in obtaining a mentor, the opportunity to have multiple mentors, close relationships with mentors, mentors' level of professional status, and the perception of career and psychosocial support received from their mentors. Despite these gender similarities, the effects of mentors differed in that male protégés benefitted more than female protégés from having mentors with senior status in terms of earnings, perceived procedural justice, and work satisfaction. On the other hand, female protégés benefitted more from close mentoring relationships, in terms of earnings and career advancement; from multiple mentors in terms of work satisfaction; and from having a male mentor in terms of perceived procedural fairness.

In another sample of lawyers, Ramaswami et al. (2010b) focused on the impact of having a senior male mentor. There were no gender differences in protégés reports of having a senior male mentor. Having such a mentor, as compared to another mentor or no mentor, was related to significantly higher income and to greater satisfaction with career progress. They found that the relationship between having a senior male mentor and income and career progress satisfaction was greater for women than for men (statistically significantly for income and attaining partnership/executive positions and a trend for career progress satisfaction). Ramaswami et al. (2010b) suggest that "signaling" may account for these differences, in that having a senior male mentor signals the worthiness and legitimacy of the protégé and that a senior male mentor with a female protégé may be more visible, especially in a male-dominated profession. To explore this idea, Ramaswami et al. (2010a) surveyed midcareer managers and professionals in a range of industries. They found the expected three-way interaction between a senior male mentor, protégé gender, and male-gendered vs. gender-neutral industry. Females in male-dominated professions benefitted most from having a senior male mentor.

Ramaswami et al. (2010a, 2010b), focusing on the signaling function of mentorships, stressed the importance of having a senior male mentor in male-dominated professions, especially for women. They found no gender differences in the availability of such mentors in their sample of lawyers, although they did not explore the dynamics of these mentoring relationships. Kay and Wallace were particularly interested in mentors as social capital and especially on the impact of multiple mentors. Like many others, they found no gender differences in the presence, status, or quality of mentors, as reported by protégés, but they did find that men benefitted more than women from mentors with senior status. These were not necessarily senior *male* mentors. However, men in this sample were more likely than women to have male mentors, which may account to some degree for their finding that men were more advantaged than women by having senior mentors. For women, advantages accrued from having close relationships with mentors, multiple mentors, and a male mentor. Although the signaling function of a senior male mentor may be important for female protégés in a male-dominated workplace, the Kay and Wallace (2009) findings also suggest that the successful mentoring for women is more complex. As with social networks and friendships in the workplace the context in which mentoring occurs, the gender composition of the workforce, and the relative status of women clearly also make a difference. Finally, although research studies may include both objective (e.g. salary, promotion) and subjective (e.g. job satisfaction, perceived fairness) outcomes, they do not, as McKeen and Bujaski (2007) suggest, measure success outcomes that go beyond the career.

Update on negative relationships

As reported by Winstead and Morganson (2009), negative relationships in the workplace tend to have more severe effects for women. The greater importance placed on having friendly coworkers and supervisors by women relative to men (Konrad et al., 2000) was explored as a partial explanation for this gender difference. Additionally, the authors proposed women's relative lack of power and status as an explanation for women's increased membership in negative relationships, as they are more often the targets of aggression at work. Winstead and Morganson emphasized negative relationships that are of a hierarchical nature (e.g. dysfunctional mentorships, sexual harassment of lower-level women). As a reflection of current trends in the research, this section focuses on negative lateral relationships, as evidenced by bullying in the workplace.

Workplace bullying is an issue garnering increasing amounts of media and research attention (see Chapter 10 in this volume by Gardner et al.). It is understood as repeated, harmful mistreatment of at least one individual by another individual or group of individuals and is manifested as verbal abuse; threatening, humiliating, or intimidating conduct; and/or sabotage of one's work (SHARP, 2011).

Experiences of bullying have been reported by 35% of the US work-force, with an additional 15% witnessing bullying incidents (Workplace Bullying Institute, 2010). Data also indicate gender differences in workplace bullying, with 62% of bullies being men and 58% of targets being women (Workplace Bullying Institute, 2010). The highest prevalence of bullying is reported in male-dominated (e.g. construction workers) and female-dominated (e.g. nursing) occupations (Ortega et al., 2009). In some contexts, the target of bullying may be defined by difference and unequal power. Women, especially in male-dominated fields and positions, may have less power and status than their male coworkers, thereby relegating them to target positions (Salin, 2003; Aquino & Bradfield, 2000). The majority of workplace bullying, however, is same-gender victimization (Workplace Bullying Institute, 2010). Women are twice as likely to target female colleagues as they are male colleagues (Lutgen-Sandvik et al., 2012).

A study of Icelandic workers found no gender difference in reports of having been bullied (10.9% of workers), but men were more likely than women to report having bullied others and men were more likely than women to report having experienced behaviors that might be regarded as bullying (i.e. excessive workloads, undue criticism, and assignment of job-irrelevant tasks) (Ólafsson & Jóhannsdóttir, 2004). They also found that men were more likely than women to take an active approach to coping with unwelcome workplace experiences. Although these researchers did not consider worker status, it may be that men were more comfortable confronting bullies due to their position in the workplace.

As revealed in the Ólafsson and Jóhannsdóttir (2004) study, workers can experience (or observe) negative behaviors and may or may not label them as bullying. Salin (2009) explored this issue in terms of the gender of the target, perpetrator, and observer on an incident of persistent negative workplace behaviors. The scenario used in the study describes an individual who is socially excluded, talked about behind his/her back, given poor work assignments and denied more interesting ones. Names of the target and perpetrator were altered to manipulate gender. Male and female same-sex and male bully/female target scenarios were used in the research. A female bully/male target scenario was not included. Readers of the scenarios were asked whether the behaviors were bullying and were asked to explain the conflict and speculate on its consequences. Results revealed that female and male participants were equally likely to label the same-sex scenarios as bullying (60.6% and 51.9%, respectively) but women were more likely

(66%) than men (41.9%) to regard it as bullying when the perpetrator was male and the target, female. Note also that whereas women were more likely to regard the behaviors as bullying in the cross-sex vs. same-sex scenarios, men were less likely to regard it as bullying. In terms of anticipated consequences, neither the gender of the participant nor that of the actors in the scenarios affected the assumption that these behaviors would have a negative effect on a target's job satisfaction and desire to quit the job. Negative health outcomes were mentioned more often for female than for male targets. Women reading the scenarios were more likely than men to believe these negative behaviors would affect others in the work group and would have negative consequences for the organization. This may be because men were more likely than women to attribute the negative behaviors to something about the target and less likely than women to attribute it to something about the organization (e.g. weak leadership). Also, although male and female targets were described in the same words in the vignettes, in explaining the bullying, participants perceived male targets as being somehow different from others, but perceived female targets as provocative ("asking for" the bullying).

These studies reveal the complexities of the interaction between gender and workplace bullying. Targets may perceive negative behaviors as bullying or not (the Ólafsson and Jóhannsdóttir (2004) study suggests that men may be less likely than women to label specific behaviors as "bullying"); targets may also cope differently and target responses can also contribute to different labeling and other outcomes; observers may perceive negative behaviors differently depending on the composition of the dyad (same- vs. opposite-sex) and the gender of the target. Observers' attributions are also affected by the gender of the target. Finally, women and men vary in their perceptions, explanations, and beliefs about consequences. Moving forward, our efforts to understand and ameliorate workplace bullying should clearly take gender into account.

Romantic relationships at work

We surely form some kind of bond with others at work, whether it be networking, genuine friendship, or mentoring. But a surprising number of workplace relationships are sexual and/or romantic (see Wilson's chapter in this volume). A 2006 Society for Human Resource Management poll found that 40% of those surveyed reported having been involved in a workplace romance and an online survey of professional women found 61% reported having been romantically involved with a colleague (Gurchiek, 2005). These romantic relationships at work are, by definition, mutually desired. We do not review, in this context, the extensive literature on sexual harassment, although we will discuss to some degree the connection between broken relationships and sexual harassment charges.

Dillard et al. (1994) surveyed a random sample of adults who had observed a romantic relationship in their workplace. In cluster analyses they identified five types of relationships, including passionate love relationships (36% of the sample), defined by both love and ego motives; companionate love relationships (23%), defined by sincere affection; and fling relationships (19%), defined by ego motives and associated with illicitness and, for males, with lower levels of organizational power. The final two types were male and female utilitarian relationships. Although less frequent (8%), male utilitarian relationships are associated with male job and ego motives and female organizational power. They are not, however, associated with female ego, but rather with female love and job motives. Female utilitarian relationships (14%) are associated with female job and ego motives, greater male power, less female power, and males who are also older, better educated and better salaried. These descriptions of workplace romances suggest that most workplace romances are viewed as based on love (59%) or lust (19%) and generally speaking women and men are believed to have similar motives, including the more negative one of using relationships to get ahead at work. In the latter case, however, almost twice as many women as men are seen as being in this type of workplace romance. Although labeled "female" utilitarian relationships, these can also be seen as serving a function for the higher status male partner and are, in fact, related to the male ego motive.

Pierce et al. (1996) developed a set of propositions concerning romance in the workplace, based on theories of interpersonal attraction and love and on empirical evidence. Their proposed antecedents and consequences of workplace romance apply equally to women and men. Among their observations is that a relationship based on a love motive is likely to increase employee productivity and job involvement; whereas romantic relationships based on ego or job-related motives will show no change in productivity or job involvement (Quinn, 1977). But they also suggest that hierarchical relationships will be more deleterious than lateral romances, in part because of their impact on others, who are negatively affected by hierarchical romantic relationships (due to perceptions of likely organizational injustices and favoritism) but positively affected by lateral relationships. Despite the possibility of positive outcomes of workplace romantic relationships, responses from management do not tend to be positive. Managers may be reluctant to promote individuals involved in a workplace romance, and this is more likely to be true in a conservative as compared to a liberal work culture. And low status employees, especially women, are more likely than high status employees to be relocated or terminated.

Relatively little of the research on workplace romantic relationships has focused on gender differences in the experience of the relationships or outcomes associated with the relationship. In an early study, Dillard and Witteman (1985) interviewed a sample of workers of whom 29% had participated in a romantic relationship at work (as noted above, more recent polls found this number to be 40–61%). Romantic relationships were most likely to occur in small (i.e. 20–50 employees) organizations, but personal predictors varied by gender. Women involved in these relationships were younger, of shorter tenure, and at lower levels in the organization. Education was positively related to likelihood of romance for men but not for women. Pierce (1998), in an effort to test some of the propositions set forth by Pierce et al. (1996), surveyed graduate students employed at a university. He found, as did Powell (1986), that women held significantly more negative attitudes toward romance and sexual intimacy at work than men did. In general, however, he found that involvement in a work romance for either women or men was associated with positive feelings about one's work performance and about the job itself. Dillard and Broetzmann (1989) in a more representative sample also found that the main response to a workplace romance for both women and men was "more enthusiasm for work".

In a more recent qualitative study of romantic relationships in pubs in the United Kingdom, Riach and Wilson (2007) found that romance among the relatively young employees was considered inevitable and natural (see also Chapter 2 in this volume). Even where "rules" against certain relationships, for example, between manager and staff, were cited, these were largely ignored. But they also found that "women were consistently relegated to being the losers in romantic situations, regardless of their position" (p. 89). They were judged by a double standard regarding casual sexual behavior (good for a man, bad for a woman). But they were also judged if they expressed too much feeling about the relationship or distress at the end of a relationship, being seen as overly emotional, needy, unstable, and unable to cope. The acceptance of a highly personal relationship existing in the workplace, but the prohibition against expressing appropriately intense feelings about that relationship creates a dilemma, especially for women.

The research literature on workplace romance has also focused on the reactions of others to the romance. Dillard and Broetzmann (1989) interviewed observers as well as participants in workplace romances. Observers perceived increased enthusiasm on the part of romantic partners as a consequence of the relationship. The changes perceived, however, were affected by gender and perceived motive. Women were seen to change more than men, negatively if the romantic relationship was attributed to a job motive and positively if it was attributed to a love motive. In a recent study, Malachowski et al. (2012) found generally negative perceptions of coworkers in romantic relationships, but found no sex of romantic partner effect on these coworker perceptions. Horan and Chory (2009) similarly found no sex-of-partner effect on trust, solidarity, self-disclosure, or deception. Status, however, interacted with sex such that women dating their superiors were judged more negatively in terms of caring and trustworthiness than women dating their peers. Status did not affect perceptions of men in similar relationships. Dillard et al. (1994) also found negative perceptions of women's work performance when they were believed to be in a job-motivated, utilitarian romantic relationship. Perceptions of the work group were more negative in the case of both female and male job-motivated workplace romances, but the social climate was seen to be negatively affected only by the female job-motivated romance. Another study of coworkers' reactions used vignettes of a relationship between a younger lower-level and older, higher-level employee and manipulated the sex of the partners (Powell, 2001). Results supported previous findings of a negative impact of this sort of workplace romance. Participants attributed a job motive to the lower-level employee which was in turn associated with a belief that this was a serious problem for the organization requiring a strong managerial response and personal action. Importantly, attribution of a job motive was significantly stronger for female lower-level employees. Thus, the most negative assessments were for romantic relationships involving lower-level women with senior-level men. In general, then, coworkers may be okay with what they perceive to be a love-based lateral relationship but are unhappy with a perceived job-motivated unequal status romantic relationships, particularly if it is a less powerful woman in a relationship with a more senior man.

Clearly coworkers are inclined to view the women in these relationships negatively, but the hierarchically unequal relationship is problematic not only because it may be disruptive of the work group, but also because it raises issues of sexual harassment. Although some view these women as job motivated and seeking a utilitarian relationship to get ahead, there is also the potential in these unequal power relationships for women to be manipulated and even coerced into agreeing to a relationship they did not seek. Even after the relationship ends, the more powerful partner may behave in ways that are harassing. Although we do not review the extensive literature on sexual harassment, it is noteworthy that a 1998 Society for Human Resource Management survey found that 24% of sexual harassment claims involved previous workplace romances. In a conceptual analysis of the link between workplace romance and sexual harassment, Pierce and Aguinis (1997) proposed that a dissolved direct reporting hierarchical romance is the most likely to result in sexual harassment because these individuals must continue frequent job-related contact, a job-related motive on the part of the subordinate may lead to revenge seeking, or the supervisor may attempt unwanted sexual coercion and/or make discriminatory management decisions. Generally speaking, studies that have examined responses to vignettes have found that participants are more favorable towards the accused and less favorable towards the complainant when they have been in a previous romantic relationship (Summers & Myklebust, 1992). Perceptions are also influenced by perceived motive. Judgments of the accused are most negative when he or she is believed to have an ego motive and the complainant a love motive and most lenient when he or she has a love motive and the complainant, a job-related motive (Pierce et al., 2000). The fear of a workplace romance leading to sexual harassment claims is one of the motives for companies that attempt to establish rules or policies managing workplace romance (Boyd, 2010). A 2002 Society for Human Resource Management survey found that 95% of human resource professionals cited potential for sexual harassment claims as a reason to ban or discourage workplace romance compared to 46% concerned with lowered productivity. Some companies, unwilling to ban these relationships, have adopted a policy that requires consensual dating partners to sign a document. This too is generally an effort to avoid sexual harassment liability. Although policies banning dating, especially between employees of different rank, are often advanced with the rhetoric of protecting the less powerful, often female, employees; they seem in fact to be primarily about protecting the company against unwanted sexual harassment claims (Boyd, 2010).

Leader/member relationships

While our focus has been on mostly voluntary relationships in the workplace, we also inevitably have critical relationships with management and, as managers, with subordinates (see also Chapter 11 in this volume by Chiang and Birtch). Most of the extant research on gender and leadership emphasizes gender as it pertains to leadership style (e.g. Appelbaum et al., 2002; Eagly et al., 2003). Relatively little has been learned about the impact gender has on hierarchical relationships in the workplace. Of the literature on leader-subordinate relationships, most of the findings are contradictory in nature. Specifically, the research clusters around two major perspectives: The suggestion that leader-subordinate dyads are of the best quality when members are of the same gender, and the suggestion that female bosses can be detrimental to the advancement of female employees.

Research on gender and hierarchical relationships generally emphasizes leader member exchange (LMX) theory, which asserts that leaders and subordinates are engaged in a social exchange. Within that exchange, norms of reciprocity form in which the leader and follower provide feedback and share information (Graen & Uhl-Bien, 1995). The relationship emerges as subordinates and leaders work together over time (Wayne & Green, 1993). Because LMX theory focuses on dyadic relationships, it argues that leaders treat each subordinate in a unique manner, leading to varying degrees of perceived inclusion among employees (Graen & Uhl-Bien, 1995).

A high degree of LMX is marked by a sense of ingroup membership among followers and a sense of trust in the leader, while a low degree of LMX is characterized by a lack of interpersonal connection (Graen & Uhl-Bien, 1995). Leaders can develop different types of relationships with each member of a given workgroup, and the character of that relationship is largely centered upon the amount of negotiating latitude (i.e. flexibility in the follower's job and the leader's willingness to use position power to assist the follower) afforded to subordinates (Dansereau et al., 1975; Graen & Scandura, 1987). The quality of the leader-subordinate relationship, or LMX, has been demonstrated to affect several work outcomes. Basu and Green (1995) have empirically linked LMX to employees' attitudes toward work and overall well-being. In 1999, Epitropaki and Martin assessed a sample of administrative employees within a university setting and found manager-employee transactions to exhibit a positive correlation with organizational commitment, and very strong positive correlation with job satisfaction. The impact of gender on such outcomes has yielded mixed results, with some studies finding no support for gender as a moderator (e.g. Epitropaki & Martin, 1999; McClane, 1991), and others finding an interaction such that gender similarity strengthens the relationship between LMX and work outcomes (e.g. Ayman et al., 2004; Green et al., 1996).

Regarding gender similarity, the term relational demography is often used to describe the amount of demographic match between members of an organization (Tsui & O'Reily, 1989). From the perspective of social network theory, relational demography is essential to the attainment of high LMX (Wellman & Berkowitz, 1988). LMX consists of a social network between a leader and his or her subordinate. Quality relationships entail the sharing of resources and access to professional contacts. Such exchanges are most likely to occur among similar individuals, as they are likely to have more trust in each other and each member believes he or she knows what to expect from the other, whereas dissimilar individuals are less likely to be included because they are seen as not fitting in and their interactions with others are less predictable (Douglas, 2012; Sparrowe & Liden, 1997).

While field research in this area is often faced with the challenge of obtaining a balanced sample of male and female supervisors, several studies have found evidence in favor of gender similarity and higher LMX. For example, Varma and Stroh (2001) found a positive bias among both male and female supervisors for same-sex subordinates. This bias was exhibited in terms of ratings assigned to employees and interpersonal affect used during social exchanges. In 2003, Somech found that sex-similarity interacted with length of relationship such that, for longer relationships gender similarity was more predictive of the amount of decision-making afforded to subordinates. Maume (2011) surveyed a national sample of full-time US workers and found positive relationships between gender similarities within the dyad and outcomes such as amount of mentoring provided by the leader, level of friendship experienced, and evaluations of the subordinates. Supervisors seem to be aware of their gendered preference, as they demonstrate a preference to hire employees of the same gender (Elliot & Smith, 2004); a finding that has been shown within university settings (Pfeffer et al., 1995), law firms (Gorman, 2005), and public agencies (Baron et al., 1991). In 2007, Vecchio and Brazil studied dyads of cadet juniors and squad leaders within a US armed services training camp. Their findings generally support the case for similarity-attraction, as same-gender pairings reported higher LMX and greater levels of satisfaction than did heterogeneous pairs.

Contrary to the similarity-attraction work outlined above, other scholars have found female dyads to be toxic. Queen bee syndrome is marked by a woman supervisor's more critical treatment of female subordinates in comparison to male subordinates (Staines et al., 1973). Women who hold more traditional gender attitudes are more likely to display symptoms of the queen bee syndrome. This is because of their increased tendency to view highly qualified women as threats who are likely to be more competent, better qualified, or more popular among others in the organization (Cooper, 1997). As a result, queen bees are likely to protect their territory by withholding information and social support from female subordinates (Johnson & Mathur-Helm, 2011). This can be especially problematic because criticism of women from women is generally seen as more credible and persuasive than that from men (Sutton et al., 2006).

Stereotypical beliefs about leadership equate masculine traits (e.g. dominance, assertiveness, etc) with success (e.g. Heilman et al., 1995; Powell et al., 2002). When assuming leadership positions, women often feel pressured to adopt such traits. In order to maintain a successful image, they also feel compelled to distance themselves from female subordinates by highlighting their feminine traits in a critical manner (Ellemers et al., 2004). Queen bee syndrome has been demonstrated to emerge more often in the presence of male colleagues (Cooper, 1997), further supporting this idea. Queen bees hold themselves in high regard, and maintain standards at or above that level for female subordinates, under the mentality of "I had to work hard to get where I am, so they do too" (Snipes et al., 1988). Such women fail to acknowledge structural barriers against female career advancement, and instead subscribe to the belief that women subordinates can only blame their own shortcomings for their current position (Baumgartner & Schneider, 2010).

As with the support for gender-similarity, evidence of the queen bee syndrome has been demonstrated across contexts. Ellemers and colleagues (2004) conducted their research within an academic context and found that female professors were more inclined than male professors to rate female PhD students as less committed to their career than male students. Further supporting the queen bee theory, those female professors defined themselves in largely masculine terms, thereby distancing themselves from their gender. A 2002 sample of non-managerial employees in the US found that men with female bosses reported greater levels of supervisor support and optimism regarding their likelihood of promotion than did women with female bosses (Maume, 2011). A Dutch sample of 94 senior women in both private and public organizations revealed that women who exhibited the most negative attitudes toward female subordinates were those who endured greater levels of gender discrimination during their own career development and reported larger discrepancy between themselves and other women (Derks et al., 2011). This finding supports the notion that senior-level women develop animosity toward inferior women as a result of pursuing their own ambitions within sexist organizational cultures.

Curiously, although men's supervisory relationships with men surely range from negative to positive, there is no "syndrome" proposed to explain its nature. Perhaps this is due to the ubiquity and perceived normality of a man in a managerial position. As the presence of women in leadership positions becomes more normative (although in 2010 only 14.4% of executive officers of *Fortune* 500 companies were women), the organizational characteristics that contribute to queen bee syndrome may begin to dissipate.

Virtual relationships

Since the introduction of the Internet and the widespread, global adoption of communication technologies, much of what we think of as interpersonal interaction has changed (see Chapter 8 in this volume by Kolb). Where interpersonal contact was once primarily face-to-face or voice-to-voice, we now interact frequently with text only, using email, text, instant messages, etc to share not just reports or data, but also the question and answer, give and take, personal exchange that once would have taken place in person or by telephone. This happens in the workplace where employees are physically present, but increasingly employees work remotely or telework/telecommute. Telework grew by 61% between 2005 and 2009 (Lister & Harnish, 2011); and the US Congress has passed legislation requiring federal agencies to allow up to one day per week of telework whenever possible. Technology is also being used to provide mentoring to workers among entrepreneurs, health care workers, teachers and educators, public relations professionals, STEM (science, technology, engineering, and math) professionals and many others (Ensher & Murphy, 2007). The pros and cons of these forms of communication, work, and mentoring are being discussed and researched. The question for us is what role does gender play as we move from face-to-face and telephonic communication to virtual relationships and computer-mediated communication (CMC).

In the case of e-mentoring it has been argued that, to the extent that mentoring relationships are unavailable to some women or minorities, the availability of online mentoring helps to provide these resources. While women have not generally been found to lack access to mentors in most professions, MentorNet (http://www.mentornet.net/) is a well established network that specifically promotes diversity in engineering and science by providing an avenue for mentors and protégés to make connections. Ensher and Murphy (2007) argue that among the advantages of e-mentoring are the "equalization of status" and "decreased emphasis on demographics", such as gender or race (p. 304).

There is no body of research that focuses explicitly on gender and CMC in the workplace. Using research on gender and CMC in other contexts we establish some ideas for future research. Herring and Martinson (2004) summarize previous research on gender differences in online communication by stating: "Males make greater use of assertions, self-promotion, rhetorical questions, profanity, sexual references, sarcasm, challenges, and insults, whereas females make greater use of hedges, justifications, expressions of emotions, representations of smiling and laughter, personal pronouns, and supportive and polite language" (p. 427). Research on gender differences in instant message exchanges with a same-sex other (Baron, 2004) found women were more "talkative", i.e. took longer turns in the exchange, had longer conversations, and took more time to sign off. Women also used more formal or standard language. Research also shows that the gender of e-mail authors can be identified by others (Thomson & Murachver, 2001). This research suggests that CMC in the workplace will convey some of the language differences that women and men use in other forms of communication. On the other hand, Thomson et al. (2001) found that women and men are also greatly influenced by the linguistic style of their CMC partners. They found that both women and men were able to use styles identified with both genders and tended to accommodate to the style of their partner. To the degree that a work-related CMC has unspoken rules, i.e. no profanity, few expressions of emotion, women and men may adapt their CMC styles to fit these rules. Furthermore, the work of Thomson et al. (2001) suggests that they will also accommodate to the style of the person with whom they are communicating.

Despite potential gender differences in CMC, there has also been discussion of the potentially leveling effects of CMC. Non-verbal cues denoting status or power (dress, demeanor, even context, e.g. being at the head of the table) are absent in CMC. Although one's gender and position are likely to be known, especially in a work context, physical or visual reminders of these are often not present and, thus, their impact may be lessened. On the other hand, some have argued that without cues to other aspects of personal identity, "gender identity may be particularly salient in electronic discourse" (Thomson et al., 2001, p. 171). The gendered perception of one's coworker in face-to-face communication versus CMC, especially as they interact with different work roles and statuses, should be studied.

Much of the focus on relationships through CMC has been on the absence of non-verbal cues in this form of communication (Walther, 2012). One of the effects of absence of non-verbal cues is the dampening of the expression of emotion and affect. In some communication forums, the need to express affect that might have been conveyed non-verbally results in more direct verbal expressions. But in the work setting, less affect laden communication may be a plus and especially so for women who generally are stereotyped as the more emotional gender. The ability to edit and control CMC and its demonstrated responsiveness to the linguistic styles of others (Thomson et al., 2001) also suggest that CMC in the workplace may tend to level the playing field for women and men.

Concerns about the immediacy and effectiveness of CMC have contributed to the assumption that teleworkers may have difficulty developing and maintaining quality relationships with coworkers and supervisors. Although the relationships established in the workplace through CMC deserve further investigation, a meta-analysis of telework mostly negates this assumption. Gajendran and Harrison (2007) found a nearly zero relationship between teleworking and relationship quality with coworkers and an unexpected positive relationship between telework and quality of the employee-supervisor relationship. They also expected that more telecommuting would exacerbate negative effects. They found no impact of extent of telework on the employee-supervisor relationship, but while low levels of telecommuting had no impact on coworker relationship quality, high levels of telecommuting did have a negative impact on coworker relationship quality. Gender did not impact these outcomes but it did moderate supervisor-rated performance and perceived career prospects, such that women received higher performance ratings and had a more positive view of their career prospects. Although the meta-analysis is not a direct test of the role of gender in virtual relationships in the workplace, it tends to suggest that women may be advantaged by the greater use of technology in developing and maintaining work relationships. The possibility that some forms of technology assisted relationships may be less status conscious and less affect laden and specifically that these relationships may be advantageous to women's performance and career prospects deserves greater attention.

Virtual relationships depend to some extent on the medium by which these relationships develop. The technologies used in CMC and telework are constantly changing and it is unknown what new technologies might develop to facilitate work groups, supervision, and/or mentoring in the future. Establishing the effects of gender on these various forms of workplace communication may help us understand which modalities are most useful in creating a positive and fair work environment for both women and men.

Family relationships in the workplace

Much of the work on gender and familial relationships at work can be traced back to conflict surrounding gender roles, as issues of role conflict are especially pronounced within family businesses. This occurs as patterns of interaction within the family context spill over into the workplace (see also Chapter 12 in this volume by Ho and colleagues). About half of family businesses report tensions that result from this role spillover (Fitzgerald et al., 2001; Rosenblatt et al., 1985). This problem has been well documented for women in family businesses, as women's domestic roles and responsibilities are likely to conflict with business roles and limit the time and resources women have to dedicate to the business (Loscocco & Robinson, 1991). Such expectations of women's roles exist at the macro level, as reflected by societal attitudes, as well as at the more individual level within the family. Dumas (1990) found that socialization of new employees in the family business begins at home during early childhood via dinnertime conversations, visits to the workplace, and part-time work. These opportunities were much more present for sons of family business owners than for daughters.

Structural constraints on each gender within the workplace tend to be most strict for families that have more traditional marriages. Solomon and colleagues (2011) defined such marriages as those defined by rigid gender roles with husbands serving as the breadwinner and wives fulfilling the role of caretaker. The authors found that this strict division of labor often proved beneficial in starting a family business or starting a family, as equal attention is paid to both spheres. However, subscription to rigid gender roles becomes more problematic during later developmental phases such as appointing successors, expanding the business, and retiring. Gendered division of labor within family businesses is often maintained because married couples fear that work-related conflicts will place undue strain on their personal relationship, thereby making segregation of professional tasks more desirable (Larsen, 2006).

Role conflict poses a specific barrier to daughters of family business owners, as there is generally a great deal of resistance to appointing them as successors. This reticence toward female successors is most common among daughters, but has been reported for various female family members, such as sisters and wives (Ip & Jacobs, 2006). Furthermore, a study of family farms in New Zealand by Keating and Little (1997) found gender to be the most significant determinant of succession appointments. Gender plays a key role from a very early stage, as family business owners begin looking to their young children to assess (or encourage) interest in the business. Exclusion of daughters can occur more subtly, as daughters are often given the opportunity to work within the family business, but they are not included to the extent that other employees are (e.g. provided with formal training or placement in supervisory positions; Curimbaba, 2002; Wang, 2010).

Other barriers exist for women within family businesses on the basis of their gender. Men are considered to be better suited to lead than women, and this notion fuels the perception that businesses run by women are more prone to failure (Cole, 1997; Harveston et al., 1997). A study of ten nations (Lerner & Malach-Pines, 2011) revealed that these perceptions are often translated to attitudes among members of family businesses, as male business owners enjoy more social capital than do women. Men in these positions report a perception of better business opportunities and greater confidence in their skills and the prospects of their business than do their female counterparts. This fear of failure among female business leaders contributes to a reduced rate of innovation and involvement in management compared to that of men (Lee et al., 2010).

Despite the barriers that exist for women within family businesses, some advantages do exist. Daughters who may otherwise be excluded can get a foot in the door during times of transition or crisis for the family business. These appointments lead to such women playing a savior role and securing good standing within the business (Curimbaba, 2002). Additionally, although female managers tend to operate smaller organizations than do male managers, females have more room for growth and have yielded higher growth rates than males. Female managers of family businesses also report demographic advantages to their male counterparts, as they are generally younger, better educated, and in better health (Lee et al., 2010). Furthermore, starting a family-run business serves as an opportunity for women to make a higher salary then they would in the same industry working for another employer (Loscocco & Bird, 2012). Thus, while barriers in the form of expected gender roles do exist for women in family businesses, those that manage to cross those boundaries enjoy great success.

A great deal of the research on gender and family business is centered upon the different working strategies endorsed by men and women. A content analysis by Danes et al. (2005) found that women exhibit a more emotional style of discourse in discussing and running a family business (i.e. passionate terms, speaking about personal involvement), whereas men display a practical discourse style (i.e. discussion of planning and efficiency) balanced with the emotional style. While women tend to speak about their family business in terms of their deep involvement, often the gendered approaches to work follow the attitude inconsistency uncovered by Jurik (1998): Women are more likely than men to champion egalitarian views regarding women's involvement in the family business but are much less likely to report the business as a key component of their identity, making gender equality more difficult to achieve. Gendered management styles are also largely divided within family businesses, with masculine management being characterized as strategic, competitive, and high in central authority; while feminine management is marked by personal connections, attention to family history, and participative decision-making (Bird & Brush, 2002). As a result, women leaders often have relationship goals prioritized over maximizing profit margins and are more resistant to growth. This pattern was found across the ten nations surveyed in Lerner and Malach-Pines' study (2011).

Concrete outcomes of family businesses have received relatively little research attention within the context of gender. One such study was conducted by Danes et al. (2006), which found that gender of the owner was a significant predictor of gross sales revenue for family businesses; family businesses owned by women produced less gross revenue that those owned by men. Furthermore, gender had a moderating effect on personnel management practices (i.e. establishing personnel needs, labor costs, and performance standards; evaluating employee performance; and motivating employees) such that emphasis on personnel management yields an effect on gross revenue that is nine times greater for women than for men. Additionally, working harder and for longer hours is related to higher revenue for female owners but not male owners. Conversely, the authors found that the use of temporary help has the largest effect on revenue for male owners but has no effect for women. Lee and colleagues (2010) assessed both the perceived and actual success of family business leaders through the lens of gender. The authors found that female managers perceive their businesses as more successful than do their male equivalents; however, male managers actually report much higher profits. While such findings seem to imply that men are better suited to run family businesses, succession failure and declines of family businesses can often be attributed to the exclusion of women as successors (Miller et al., 2003). Thus, it seems that a stronger integration of women at an earlier stage would help bolster performance and the likelihood of survival for a family-run organization.

Family businesses perhaps capture the realities of gender and workplace relationships most starkly. In this arena the conflicting characteristics and demands of the traditional gender roles are clearly played out. While men are the designated breadwinner, worker, leader; women are the keepers of hearth and home. While female workers in other contexts are expected to manage their childcare and homemaking responsibilities in whatever way works for them, women in family businesses are working directly with those also concerned about the welfare of children and home. As the literature suggests, women in family business may be especially challenged in overcoming gender role expectations.

Conclusions

Work is a place in which complex and meaningful relationships occur, both positive and negative, both lateral and hierarchical; but in every case, these relationships are also gendered. Whether the relationship is same-sex or cross-sex, whether the power differential favors the man or the woman, whether the relationship is mostly work-related or personal, gender will contribute to the ways in which individuals in the relationship act and react, and gender will affect how the individuals in the relationship are perceived by others. Because relationships in the workplace also affect how individuals perceive the job itself and how satisfied, committed, and productive they are, gender and relationships in the workplace should be an ongoing focus of research in industrial/organizational psychology.

References

Allen, A. D. & Eby, L. T. (2004). Factors related to mentor reports of mentoring functions provided: Gender and relational characteristics, *Sex Roles, 50,* 129–139.

Appelbaum, S. H., Audet, L., & Miller, J. C. (2002). Gender and leadership? Leadership and gender? A journey through the landscape of theories, *Leadership & Organization Development Journal, 24,* 43–51.

Aquino, K. & Bradfield, M. (2000). Perceived victimization in the workplace: The role of situational factors and victim characteristics, *Organization Science, 11,* 525–537.

Ayman, R., Rinchiuso, M., & Korabik, K. (2004, August). *Organizational Commitment and Job Satisfaction in Relation to LMX and Dyad Gender Composition.* Paper presented at the International Congress of Psychology, Beijing, China.

Baron N. S. (2004). See you online: Gender issues in college student use of instant messaging, *Journal of Language and Social Psychology December, 23,* 397–423. doi: 10.1177/0261927X04269585

Baron, J. N., Mittman, B. S., & Newman, A. E. (1991). Targets of opportunity: Organizational and environmental determinants of gender integration within the California civil service, 1979–1985, *American Journal of Sociology, 96,* 1362–1401.

Basu, R. & Green, S. G. (1995). Subordinate performance, leader-subordinate compatibility, and exchange quality in leader-member dyads: A field study, *Journal of Applied Social Psychology, 25,* 77–92.

Baumgartner, M. S. & Schneider, D. E. (2010). Perceptions of women in management: A thematic analysis of razing the glass ceiling, *Journal of Career Development, 37,* 559–576.

Berman, E. M., West, J. P., & Richter, M. N. (2002). Workplace relations: Friendship patterns and consequences (according to managers), *Public Administration Review, 62,* 217–230.

Bird, B. & Brush, C. (2002). A gendered perspective on organizational creation, *Entrepreneurial Theory and Practice, 26,* 41–65.

Boyd, C. (2010). The debate over the prohibition of romance in the workplace, *Journal of Business Ethics, 97,* 325–338.

Brass, D. J. (1985). Men's and women's networks: A study of interaction patterns and influence in an organization, *Academy of Management Journal, 28*(2), 327–343.

Burke, R. J., McKeen, C. A., & McKenna, C. (1993). Correlates of mentoring in organizations: The mentor's perspective, *Psychological Reports, 72,* 883–396.

Cannings, K. & Montmarquette, C. (1991). Managerial momentum: A simultaneous model of the career progress of male and female managers, *Industrial and Labor Relations Review, 44,* 212–228.

Cole, P. (1997). Women in family business, *Family Business Review, 10,* 353–371.

Cooper, V. W. (1997). Homophily or the queen bee syndrome? Female evaluation of female leadership, *Small Group Research, 28*, 483–499.

Curimbaba, F. (2002). The dynamics of women's roles as family business managers, *Family Business Review, 15*, 239–252.

Danes, S. M., Haberman, H. R., & McTavish, D. (2005). Gendered discourse about family business, *Family Relations, 54*, 116–130.

Danes, S. M., Stafford, K., & Loy, J. T. (2006). Family business performance: The effects of gender and management, *Journal of Business Research, 60*, 1058–1069.

Dansereau, F. J., Graen, G., & Haga, W. J. (1975). A vertical dyad linkage approach to leadership within formal organizations: A longitudinal investigation of the role making process, *Organizational Behavior and Human Performance, 13*, 46–78.

Derks, B., Ellemers, N., van Laar, C., & de Groot, K. (2011). Do sexist organizational cultures create the queen bee? *British Journal of Social Psychology, 50*, 519–535.

Dillard, J. P. & Broetzmann, S. M. (1989). Romantic relationships at work: Perceived changes in job-related behaviors as a function of participant's motive, partner's motive, and gender, *Journal of Applied Social Psychology, 19*, 93–110.

Dillard, J. P., Hale, J. L., & Segrin, C. (1994). Close relationships in task environments, *Management Communication Quarterly, 7*, 227–255.

Dillard, J. P. & Witteman, H. (1985). Romantic relationships at work: Organizational and personal influences, *Human Communication Research, 12*, 99–116.

Douglas, C. (2012). The moderating role of leader and follower sex in dyads on the leadership behavior-leader effectiveness relationships, *The Leadership Quarterly, 23*, 163–175.

Drentea, P. (1998). Consequences of women's formal and informal job search methods for employment in female-dominated jobs, *Gender & Society, 12*, 321–338.

Dreher, G. F. & Cox, T. H., Jr. (1996). Race, gender and opportunity: A study of compensation attainment and the establishment of mentoring relationships, *Journal of Applied Psychology, 81*, 297–308.

Dumas, C. (1990). Preparing the new CEO: Managing the father-daughter succession process in family business, *Family Business Review, 3*, 169–181.

Eagly, A. H., Johannesen-Schmidt, M. C., & van Engen, M. L. (2003). Transformational, transactional, and laissez-faire leadership styles: A meta-analysis comparing women and men, *Psychological Bulletin, 129*, 569–591.

Ellemers, N., Heuvel, H. V., Gilder, D., Maas, A., & Bonvini, A. (2004). The underrepresentation of women in science: Differential commitment or the queen bee syndrome? *British Journal of Social Psychology, 43*, 315–338.

Elliott, J. R. & Smith, R. A. (2004). Race, gender, and workplace power, *American Sociological Review, 69*, 365–386.

Ely, R. (1994). The effects of organizational demographics and social identity on relationships among professional women, *Administrative Science Quarterly, 39*, 203–238.

Ensher, E. A. & Murphy, S. E. (2007). E-mentoring: Next-generation research strategies and suggestions: in B. R. Ragins & K. E. Kram (eds) *The Handbook of*

Mentoring at Work: Theory, Research, and Practice (pp. 299–322). Los Angeles, CA: Sage Publications.

Ensher, E. A. & Murphy, S. E. (1997). Effects of race, gender, perceived similarity, and contact on mentor relationships, *Journal of Vocational Behavior, 50*, 460–481.

Epitropaki, O. & Martin, R. (1999). The impact of relational demography on the quality of leader-member exchanges and employees' work attitudes and well-being, *Journal of Occupational and Organizational Psychology, 72*, 237–240.

Fletcher, J. K. & Ragins, B. R. (2007). Stone center relational cultural theory: A window on relational mentoring: in B. R. Ragins & K. E. Kram (eds) *The Handbook of Mentoring at Work: Theory, Research, and Practice* (pp. 373–400). Los Angeles, CA: Sage Publications.

Fitzgerald, M. A., Winter, M., Miller, N. J., & Paul, J. (2001). Adjustment strategies in the family business: Implications of gender and management role, *Journal of Family and Economic Issues, 22*, 265–291.

Gajendran, R. S. & Harrison, D. A. (2007). The good, the bad, and the unknown about telecommuting: Meta-analysis of psychological mediators and individual consequences, *Journal of Applied Psychology, 92*, 1524–1541.

Gorman, E. H. (2005). Gender stereotypes, same-gender preferences, and organizational variation in the hiring of women: Evidence from law firms, *American Sociological Review, 70*, 702–728.

Graen, G. B. & Scandura, T. A. (1987). Toward a psychology of dyadic organizing, *Research in Organizational Behavior, 9*, 175–208.

Graen, G. B. & Uhl-Bien, M. (1995). Relationship-based approach to leadership: Development of leader-member exchange (LMX) theory of leadership over 25 years: Applying a multi-level multi-domain perspective, *The Leadership Quarterly, 6*, 219–247.

Green, S. G., Anderson, S. E., & Shivers, S. L. (1996). Demographic and organizational influences on leader-member exchange and related work attitudes, *Organizational Behavior and Human Decision Processes, 66*, 203–214.

Gurchiek, K. (2005). Be ready for slings, arrows of Cupid in the cubicles, *HR Magazine, 50*, 36–37.

Harveston, P., Davis, P., & Lyden, J. (1997). Succession planning in family business: The impact of owner gender, *Family Business Review, 10*, 373–396.

Heilman, M. E., Block, C. J., & Martell, R. F. (1995). Sex stereotypes: Do they influence perceptions of managers? *Journal of Social Behavior & Personality, 10*, 237–252.

Herring, S. C. & Martinson, A. (2004). Assessing gender authenticity in computer-mediated language use: Evidence from an identity game, *Journal of Language and Social Psychology*, December, *23*, 424–446.

Horan, S. M. & Chory, R. M. (2009). When work and love mix: Perceptions of peers in workplace romances, *Western Journal of Communication, 79*, 349–369.

Ibarra, H. (1992). Homophily and differential returns: Sex differences in network structure and access in an advertising firm, *Administrative Science Quarterly, 37*, 422–447.

Ibarra, H. (1997). Paving an alternative route: Gender difference in managerial networks, *Social Psychology Quarterly, 60*, 91–102.

Ip, B. & Jacobs, G. (2006). Business succession planning: A review of the evidence, *Journal of Small Business and Enterprise Development, 13*, 326–350.

Johnson, Z. & Mathur-Helm, B. (2011). Experiences with queen bees: A South African study exploring the reluctance of women executives to promote other women in the workplace, *South African Journal of Business Management, 42*, 47–55.

Jurik, N. C. (1998). Getting away and getting by: The experiences of self-employed homeworkers, *Work and Occupations, 25*, 7–29.

Kay, J. E. & Wallace, J. E. (2009). Mentors as social capital: Gender, mentors, and career rewards in law practice, *Sociological Inquiry, 79*, 418–452.

Keating, N. C. & Little, H. M. (1997). Choosing the successor in New Zealand family farms, *Family Business Review, 10*, 157–171.

Koberg, C. S., Boss, R. W., Chappel, D., & Ringer, R. C. (1994). Correlates and consequences of protégé mentoring in a large hospital, *Group and Organization Management, 19*, 219–239.

Konrad, A. M., Corrigall, E., Lieb, P., & Ritchie, J. E., Jr. (2000). Sex differences in job attribute preferences among managers and business students, *Group and Organization Management, 25*, 108–131.

Kram, K. E. (1986). Mentoring in the workplace: in D. T. Hall (ed.) *Career Development in Organizations* (pp. 160–201). San Francisco: Jossey Bass.

Larsen, E. A. (2006). The impact of occupational sex segregation on family businesses: The case of American harness racing, *Gender, Work and Organization, 13*, 359–382.

Lee, Y. G., Jasper, C. R., & Fitzgerald, M. A. (2010). Gender differences in perceived business success and profit growth among family business managers, *Journal of Family and Economic Issues, 31*, 458–474.

Lerner, M. & Malach-Pines, A. (2011). Gender and culture in family business: A ten-nation study, *International Journal of Cross Cultural Management, 11*, 113–131.

Lin, N. (1999). Building a social network theory of social capital, *Connections, 22*, 28–51.

Lister, K. & Harnish, T. (2011). *The State of Telework in the U.S.* Telework Research Network. Retrieved from http://www.workshifting.com/downloads/downloads/Telework-Trends-US.pdf

Loscocco, K. A. & Bird, S. R. (2012). Gendered paths: Why women lag behind men in small business success, *Work and Occupations, 39*, 183–219.

Loscocco, K. A. & Robinson, J. (1991). Barriers to women's small-business success in the United States, *Gender and Society, 5*, 511–532.

Lutgen-Sandvik, P., Dickinson, E. A., & Foss, K. A. (2012). Priming, painting, peeling, and polishing: Constructing and deconstructing the woman-bullying-woman identity at work: in S. Fox & R. Terri (eds) *Gender and the Dysfunctional Workplace: New Horizons in Management* (pp. 61–77). Northampton, MA: Edward Elgar Publishing.

Malachowski, C., Chory, R. M., & Claus, C. J. (2012). Mixing pleasure with work: Employee perceptions of and responses to workplace romance, *Western Journal of Communication, 76*, 358–379.

Maertz, C. P. & Griffeth, R. W. (2004). Eight motivational forces and voluntary turnover: A theoretical synthesis with implications for research, *Journal of Management, 30*, 667–683.

Markiewicz, D., Devine, I., & Kausilas, D. (1999). Friendships of women and men at work: Job satisfaction and resource implications, *Journal of Managerial Psychology, 15*, 161–184.

Maume, D. J. (2011). Meet the new boss ... same as the old boss? Female supervisors and subordinate career prospects, *Social Science Research*, *40*, 287–298.

McClane, W. E. (1991). The interaction of leader and member characteristics in the leader-member exchange (LMX) model of leadership, *Small Group Research*, *22*, 283–300.

McDonald, S. (2011). What you know or who you know? Occupation-specific work experience and job matching through social networks, *Social Science Research*, *40*, 1664–1675.

McGuire, G. M. (2002). Gender, race, and the shadow structure: A study of informal networks and inequality in a work organization, *Gender & Society*, *16*, 303–322.

McKeen, C. & Bujaski, M. (2007). Gender and mentoring: Issues, effects, and opportunities: in B. R. Ragins & K. E. Kram (eds) *The Handbook of Mentoring at Work: Theory, Research, and Practice* (pp. 197–222). Thousand Oaks, CA: Sage Publications.

McPherson, M., Smith-Lovin, L., & Cook, J. M. (2001). Birds of a feather: Homophily in social networks, *Annual Review of Sociology*, *27*, 415–444.

Mehra, A., Kilduff, M., & Brass, D. J. (2001). The social networks of high and low self-monitors: Implications for workplace performance, *Administrative Science Quarterly*, *46*, 121–146.

Miller, D., Steier, L., & Breton-Miller, I. L. (2003). Lost in time: Intergenerational succession, change, and failure in family business, *Journal of Business Venturing*, *18*, 513–531.

Morrison, R. L. (2009). Are women tending and befriending in the workplace? Gender differences in the relationship between workplace friendships and organizational outcomes, *Sex Roles*, *60*, 1–13.

Mossholder, K. W., Settoon, R. P., & Henagan, S. C. (2005). A relationship perspective on turnover: Examining structural, attitudinal, and behavioral predictors, *Academy of Management Journal*, *48*, 607–618.

O'Brien, K. E., Biga, A., Kessler, S. R., & Allen, R. D. (2010). A meta-analytic investigation of gender differences in mentoring, *Journal of Management*, *36*, 537–554.

Ólafsson, R. F. & Jóhannsdóttir, H. L. (2004). Coping with bullying in the workplace: The effect of gender, age and type of bullying, *British Journal of Guidance & Counselling*, *32*, 319–333.

Olian, J. D., Carroll, S. J., & Giannantonio, C. M. (1993). Mentor reactions to protégés: An experiment with managers, *Journal of Vocational Behavior*, *43*, 266–278.

Ortega, A., Høgh, A., Pejtersen, J. H., & Olsen, O. (2009). Prevalence of workplace bullying and risk groups: A representative population study, *International Archives of Occupational and Environmental Health*, *82*, 417–426.

Pearce, J. L. & Randel, A. E. (2004). Expectations of organizational mobility, workplace social inclusion and employee job performance, *Journal of Organizational Behavior*, *25*, 81–98.

Pfeffer, J., Davis-Blake, A., & Julius, D. J. (1995). AA officer salaries and managerial diversity: Efficiency wages or status? *Industrial Relations*, *34*, 73–94.

Pierce, C. A. (1998). Factors associated with participating in a romantic relationships in a work environment, *Journal of Applied Social Psychology*, *28*, 1712–1730.

Pierce, C. A., Aguinis, H., & Adams, S. K. R. (2000). Effects of a dissolved workplace romance and rater characteristics on responses to a sexual harassment accusation, *Academy of Management Journal, 43*, 869–880.

Pierce, C. A., Byrne, D., & Aguinis, H. (1996). Attraction in organizations: A model of workplace romance, *Journal of Organizational Behavior, 17*, 5–32.

Pierce, C. A. & Aguinis, H. (1997). Bridging the gap between romantic relationships and sexual harassment in organizations, *Journal of Organizational Behavior, 18*, 197–200.

Powell, G. N. (1986). What do tomorrow's managers think about sexual intimacy in the workplace? *Business Horizons, 29*, 30–35.

Powell, G. N. (2001). Workplace romances between senior-level executives and lower-level employees: An issue of work disruption and gender, *Human Relations, 54*, 1519–1544.

Powell, G. N., Butterfield, D. A., & Parent, J. D. (2002). Gender and managerial stereotypes: Have the times changed? *Journal of Management, 28*, 177–193.

Prusak, L. & Cohen, C. (2001). How to invest social capital, *Harvard Business Review, 79*, 86–93.

Quinn, R. E. (1977). Coping with Cupid: The formation, impact, and management of romantic relationships in organizations, *Administrative Science Quarterly, 22*, 30–45.

Ragins, B. R. & Cotton, J. L. (1999). Mentor functions and outcomes: A comparison of men and women in formal and informal mentoring relationships, *Journal of Applied Psychology, 84*, 529–550.

Ramaswami, A., Dreher, G. R., Bretz, R., & Wiethoff, C. (2010a). Gender, mentoring, and career success: The importance of organizational context, *Personnel Psychology, 63*, 385–405.

Ramaswami, A., Dreher, G. R., Bretz, R., & Wiethoff, C. (2010b). The interactive effects of gender and mentoring on career attainment: Making the case for female lawyers, *Journal of Career Development, 37*, 692–716.

Randel, A. E. & Ranft, A. L. (2007). Motivations to maintain social ties with coworkers: The moderating role of turnover intentions on information exchange, *Group & Organization Management, 32*, 208–232.

Riach, K. & Wilson, F. (2007). Don't screw the crew: Exploring the rules on engagement in organizational romance, *British Academy of Management, 18*, 79–92.

Rosenblatt, P. C., de Mik, L., Anderson, R. M., & Johnson, P. A. (1985). *The Family in Business.* San Francisco, CA: Jossey-Bass, Inc.

Salin, D. (2003). Ways of explaining workplace bullying: A review of enabling, motivating and precipitating structures and processes in the work environment, *Human Relations, 56*, 1213–1232.

Salin, D. (2009). The significance of gender for third parties' perceptions of negative interpersonal behaviour: Labelling and explaining negative acts, *Gender, Work & Organization, 18*, 571–591.

SHARP (2011). *Workplace Bullying and Disruptive Behavior: What Everyone Needs to Know* (Safety & Health Assessment & Research for Prevention Report #87-2-2011). Washington: Washington State Department of Labor & Industries.

Sias, P. M., Smith, G., & Avdeyeva, T. (2003). Sex and sex-composition differences and similarities in peer workplace friendship development, *Communication Studies, 54*, 322–340.

Snipes, R. L., Oswald, S. L., & Caudill, S. B. (1988). Sex-role stereotyping, gender biases, and job selection: The use of ordinal logit in analyzing Likert scale data, *Employee Responsibilities and Rights Journal*, *11*, 81–97.

Solomon, A., Breunlin, D., Panattoni, K., Gustafson, M., Ransburg, D., Ryan, C., Hammerman, T., & Terrien, J. (2011). "Don't lock me out": Life-story interviews of family business owners facing succession, *Family Process*, *50*, 149–166.

Son, J. & Lin, N. (2012). Network diversity, contact diversity, and status attainment, *Social Networks*, *34*, 601–613.

Song, S-H. & Olshfski, D. (2008). Friends at work: A comparative study of work attitudes in Seoul city government and New Jersey state government, *Administration & Society*, *40*, 147–169.

Sosik, J. J. & Godshalk, V. M. (2000). The role of gender in mentoring: Implications for diversified and homogeneous mentoring relationships, *Journal of Vocational Behavior*, *57*, 102–122.

Sparrowe, R. T. & Liden, R. C. (1997). Process and structure in leader-member exchange, *The Academy of Management Review*, *22*, 522–552.

Stackman, R. W. & Pinder, C. C. (1999). Context and sex effects on personal work networks, *Journal of Social and Personal Relationships*, *16*, 39–64.

Staines, G. L., Tavris, C., & Jayaratne, T. E. (1973). The queen bee syndrome: in C. Tavris (ed.) *The Female Experience* (pp. 63–66). Del Mar, California: CRM Books.

Straits, B. C. (1998). Occupational sex segregation: The role of personal ties, *Journal of Vocational Behavior*, *52*, 191–207.

Summers, R. J. & Myklebust, K. (1992). The influence of a history of romance on judgments and responses to a complaint of sexual harassment, *Sex Roles*, *27*, 345–357.

Sutton, R. M., Elder, T. J., & Douglas, K. M. (2006). Reactions to internal and external criticism of outgroups: Social convention in the intergroup sensitivity effect, *Personality and Social Psychology Bulletin*, *32*, 563–575.

Taylor, S., Klein, L. C., Lewis, B. P., Gruenewald, T. L., Gurung, R. A. R., & Updegraff, J. A. (2000). Biobehavioral responses to stress in females: Tend-and-befriend, not fight-or-flight, *Psychological Review*, *107*, 411–429.

Thomson, R. & Murachver, T. (2001). Predicting gender from electronic discourse, *British Journal of Social Psychology*, *40*, 193–208.

Thomson, R., Murachver, T., & Green, J. (2001) Where is the gender in gendered language? *Psychological Science*, *12*, 171–175.

Tsui, A. S. & O'Reily, C. A. (1989). Beyond simple demographic effects: The importance of relational demography in superior-subordinate dyads, *Academy of Management Journal*, *32*, 402–423.

Turban, D. B., Dougherty, T. W., & Lee, F. K. (2002). Gender, race, and perceived similarity effects in developmental relationships: The moderating role of relationship duration, *Journal of Vocational Behavior*, *61*, 240–262.

van Emmerik, I. J. H. (2006) Gender differences in the creation of different types of social capital: A multilevel study, *Social Networks*, *28*, 24–37.

Varma, A. & Stroh, L. K. (2001). The impact of same-sex LMX dyads on performance evaluations, *Human Resource Management*, *40*, 309–320.

Vecchio, R. P. & Brazil, D. M. (2007). Leadership and sex-similarity: A comparison in a military setting, *Personnel Psychology*, *60*, 303–335.

Verbeke, W. & Wuyts, S. (2007). Moving in social circles – Social circle member-ship and performance implications, *Journal of Organizational Behavior*, *28*, 357–379.

Walther, J. B. (2012). Interaction through technological lenses: Computer-mediated communication and language, *Journal of Language and Social Psychology*, *31*, 397–414.

Wang, C. (2010). Daughter exclusion in family business succession: A review of the literature, *Journal of Family and Economic Issues*, *31*, 475–484.

Wayne, S. J. & Green, S. A. (1993). The effects of leader-member exchange on employee citizenship and impression management behavior, *Human Relations*, *46*, 1431–1440.

Wellman, B. & Berkowitz, S. D. (eds) (1988). *Social Structures: A Network Approach*. Cambridge, UK: Cambridge University Press.

Winstead, B. A. & Morganson, V. (2009). Gender and relationships at work: in R. L. Morrison & S. L. Wright (eds) *Friends and Enemies in Organizations: A Work Psychology Perspective* (pp. 139–167). Houndmills, England: Palgrave Macmillan.

Workplace Bullying Institute (2010). The WBI U.S. workplace bullying survey, *Workplace Bullying Institute Research Studies*. Retrieved from http://www.work-placebullying.org/wbiresearch/2010-wbi-national-survey/ on 1 August 2012.

8
Virtually There: The Paradox of Proximity

Darl G. Kolb

Being close to others is great. Close colleagues at work give us comfort and security when things around us are changing. We confide in close friends and they share their secrets (and gossip) with us. While we think of friends as being "near" to us, we can also stay "close" to those far away. Alternatively, we may feel "distant" from someone sitting right next to us (Turkle, 2011). This is the paradox of proximity. While both sides of the paradox have existed as long as there have been human relationships, both are accentuated in a world of increasingly ubiquitous connectivity. For instance, using Internet video calling, we can feel closer than ever to those far away. Moreover, such technologies are low cost or even free to use. Paradoxically, connective technologies make it possible to sit in the same room with people who are texting or using social media with others around the world, while ignoring those sitting right beside them! In addition to our collocated friends, social networking sites allow us to socialize virtually with just about anyone, just about anywhere. But, virtual friendships and work present both opportunities and challenges for organizations (Morrison & Wright, 2009 and other authors in this volume).

This chapter has three parts. First, I explain why distance still matters and offer a new definition of distance for a connected age. Second, I explore the paradox of proximity and offer a dynamic model of situational proximity/distance that explains how we can feel far-but-near and near-but-far. Finally, I review some of the special issues of relationships in virtual or distributed teams. Since most knowledge work is based on mediated communication (e.g. email, video conferencing,

---

[1] The University of Auckland Business School

text messaging, etc.), all work is somewhat "virtual". Therefore, the issues addressed in this chapter apply to many mediated work relationships.

Does distance still matter?

In their seminal article, entitled "Distance Matters", psychologists Olson and Olson (2000) suggest that "the reports of distance's death are greatly exaggerated" (p. 140). They suggest that,

> Even with our emerging information and communications tech-nologies, distance and its associated attributes of culture, time zones, geography, and language affect how humans interact with each other. There are characteristics of face-to-face human interac-tions, particularly the space-time contexts in which such interac-tions take place, that the emerging technologies are either pragmatically or logically incapable of replicating. Cairncross (1997/1997, 2001) (author of *The Death of Distance*) was wrong. Distance is not only alive and well, it is in several essential respects immortal (2000, pp. 140–141).

Olson and Olson are right. Their frank summation of the practical-ities of working across sites underscores distance as an enduring concept. Distance is not just about how near or far we are physically located from one another. Napier and Ferris, for example, include structural, functional, and psychological distance in their "dyadic distance" model (Napier & Ferris, 1993, p. 329). Others have focused further on the nature of psychological distance, importantly highlight-ing the subjective nature and antecedents of our perceptions of distance (Wilson et al., 2008). Moreover, these authors suggest that perceived proximity is a better predictor of the effects of distance than *merely* objective paradigm measures of physical separation (i.e. whether a colleague is down the hall or in another country). They present a compelling argument that "distance is in the eye of the beholder". Wilson and colleagues are also right.

I define distance in a connected world as connective distance (Kolb, 2007). Connective distance includes all connective absences (i.e. not available, not affordable), interruptions, and disconnects between one social actor and another, including spatial distance (down the hall, or around the world, etc.), temporal (slow transfer times, different time zones, etc.), technical problems (slow boats, missed flights, no Internet connection, etc.), security checks (spam filters, airport security lines, etc.), plus social connective gaps, including interpersonal differences (personality conflicts, different values, intentions, agendas, etc.), group issues (lack of trust, leadership, and effective communication, etc.), organizational setting (lack of flexibility, structural impediments, inadequate resources, etc.), as well as industry context (suppliers, customers, competitors, etc.), economic barriers (local, regional and national policy, trade blocs, trade barriers, etc.) cultural differences (world-views, values, belief systems, etc.), political conflict (wars, instability, uncertainty, etc.) and exclusionary philosophical perspectives (individualism, isolationism, exceptionalism, fundamentalism, etc.). Taken together, all the gaps in all of these dimensions constitute the total socio-technical distance between any two actors.

For example, a colleague who was visiting from the UK remarked on how distant she felt from her collocated PhD students (the ones in her building in the UK), while she felt normal (that is to say, no difference in proximity) with her remote Europe-based students, with whom she normally used Skype and continued to do so while travelling. In the case of the travelling colleague, her mobility created a connective gap in her place-based (face-to-face) relationship with her collocated students, but no greater connective gap with her mediated supervisions. In the situation where gaps increased, she felt distant, but where the situation presented no additional gaps, she felt as close as ever. We will return to the notion of distance-as-gaps in our theoretical model below.

Working at a distance

Summarizing Heidegger, Coyne (1997) suggests that, "Distance is a function of our caring or being concerned about aspects of the world. So that about which we care the most at any particular moment is the closest to us" (p. 505). People have felt close to distant others for centuries through media such as letter writing (Harper, 2010). But some new media, such as video calling, offer a particularly realistic sense of presence with another person. In media terms, the affordance of presence makes it feel like others are right there with us. Besides talking head videos, we can share documents. It turns out that when working online, discussing a shared object, such as a spreadsheet, slide or other visual artefact is more effective than seeing another's face. Webinars work on this principle, i.e. that a slide show or other visual graphic displayed and illustrated with a voice provides a relatively effective training milieu for many learners, especially when question-and-answer interactivity is also available (Nemiro et al., 2008).

Another revolution in staying in close contact with others is the rise and rise of mobile connectivity (Baron, 2008). Much of the knowledge-intensive and administrative work that used to revolve around the computer workstation can now be accessed on handheld smartphones, whose use is both highly promising and highly problematic for users (Baym, 2010; MacCormick et al., 2012; Mazmanian et al., 2013) as well as organizations (Perlow, 2012). The revolutionary element of the smartphone is not its mobility, but rather its enhancement of our personal connectivity, as highlighted by Manual Castells and colleagues.

The key feature in the practice of mobile communication is *connectivity* rather than mobility. This is because, increasingly, mobile communication takes place from stable locations, such as the home, work, or school. But it is also used from everywhere else, and accessibility operates at any time. So, while in the early stages of wireless communication it was a substitute for the fixed-line phone when people were on the move, mobile communication now represents the individualized, distributed capacity to access the local/global communication network from any place at any time. This is how it is perceived by users, and this is how it is used. With the diffusion of wireless access to the Internet, and to computer networks and information systems everywhere, mobile communication is better defined by its capacity for ubiquitous and permanent connectivity rather than its potential mobility (2007, p. 248) (emphasis added).

So, smartphones allow us to bring work, friends, and family relationships along with us anywhere, but more importantly, we can access those relationships at almost any time we choose. The growing challenge for both individuals and organizations is knowing when and how much to connect and disconnect (Kolb et al., 2012; MacCormick et al., 2012; Perlow, 2012; Rheingold, 2012).

GPS (Global Positioning Systems) tracking is another new technology that is already having an effect and likely to have a massive impact on the management of distributed work. Indeed, applications such as Apple's *Find Friends* are a way of monitoring within a few metres exactly where an acquaintance is located on the planet. The implications of this are still evolving, but this could become an organizational minefield for professional and/or interpersonal trust and ethics. For example, while fleet tracking, that is keeping track of where trucks travel, seems innocuous and logical, tracking your sales force with GPS devices, which are embedded in most smartphones, will present a control conundrum for managers and employees. If I can work anywhere, why do you (the organization) need or want to know where I am? Conversely, if we are paying you to work for us, don't we (organizations) have a right to know where you are?

Last but by no means least, is the dramatic rise in social networking sites as a new social place, frequented by vast numbers of the world's population. This phenomenon far exceeds the boundaries of any organization and indeed any nation. As such, organizations need to consider how to manage and negotiate individuals' use of online social media. Social networks are nothing new of course and some commentators (Rainie & Wellman, 2012) insist that despite the popular movie of the same name, Facebook is not really a social network, but rather a relatively new, Internet-enabled phenomenon, which those authors call networked individualism. Be that as it may, networking of all sorts seems to be more important than ever. But, how and why do networks make us feel close to others?

Social networks: The power of proximity

Networks – technical and/or social – have a strong impact on our experience of distance. The logic of networks is that each node has the connective possibility of connecting with each other member/node in the network, thereby exponentially increasing the reach and utility of the network (Hiltz & Turoff, 1993). Technically, for example, assuming that every member of a network has an email connection, then the time (as proxy for distance) it takes to make contact with everyone on the network is only an email away, that is to say the few seconds it takes to click on a group list and send a message. Because many members can be contacted in (essentially) the same time as it takes to reach a single member, the "network effect" compounds time-space compression effects with synchronicity effects. Metaphorically, if we can deliver 1,000 pieces of mail with the same energy as one piece of mail, we mentally calculate that we have really covered a lot of ground!

Viewing society and its social structures as networks is widely accepted (Castells, 1996, 1996/2000; Kilduff et al., 2008; Nohria & Eccles, 1992; Wellman & Berkowitz, 1988). We now take for granted many of the concepts associated with network research, from Milgram's (1967) early work on the *small world* phenomenon to the *strength of weak ties* thesis introduced by Granovetter (1973). When discussing networks, we routinely refer to strong ties (Krackhardt, 1992), centrality (Brass & Burkhardt, 1992), power (Krackhardt, 1990), and structural holes (Burt, 1992).

In network analysis, closeness is "generally calculated by summing the lengths of the shortest paths (geodesics) from a point to all other points. Direct links are counted as one step, with indirect links given proportionally less weight in the measure" (Brass & Burkhardt, 1992, p. 195). While network analysis weighting and counting links may be sufficient for examining the system as a whole, a social network also consists of "layer upon layers of relations" between actors/nodes (Kilduff et al., 2006, p. 1039), including an actor's perception of social distance. If we are interested in how actors within the network experience distance, we have to consider factors other than just the number and types of links (i.e. how many friends) they have. For example, Krackhardt and Kilduff "measured the extent to which each person in the network perceived himself or herself to be distant from every other person. Thus, our measure of social distance was a perceptual measure of how close or far ego perceived alter to be from ego" (1999, p. 774). In summary, social network research supports Wilson and colleagues' view that closeness, and proximity in general in its various dimensions, is in the eye of the beholder.

It is important to note here that, notwithstanding their mass popular appeal, the degree to which social networks actually provide much real closeness and/or tangible benefits is still open to debate. It is fine to have a wide-ranging set of contacts, but getting anything like a lunch date or job with someone becomes very difficult once you get beyond the first or second degree of separation (Fitzgerald, 2004). Moreover, what you get via close network connections can be worse than if you had used more diverse and socially distant contacts (Granovetter, 1973; Marquis, 2003; McDonald, 2003). As Watts reminds us, within networks,

> ... distance is deceiving ... We may be connected, but that doesn't make us any less foreign to each other, nor does it necessarily incline us to reach out beyond the little clusters that define our individual lives (2003, p. 300).

Summarizing the state-of-play on the matter of small worlds, Kilduff and colleagues suggest that,

> There is recent evidence that the intrinsic appeal of the idea that we are all connected in a small world network is not matched by

evidence that such clustering and small path lengths are character-istic of human communication across class and ethnic barriers (Kleinfeld, 2002). Small worlds may be less frequent in networks than previously thought (Dunne, Williams, & Martinez, 2002). Indeed, there is compelling evidence across a range of indicators that the world of social interaction between people is becoming less rather than more connected (McPherson, Smith-Lovin, & Brashears, 2006; Putnam, 2000) (Kilduff et al., 2008, p. 16).

Of course, it might be argued that networks do not need to be con-tinuously activated in order to be effective or relevant. Indeed, many networks only realize their potential under emergency or special cir-cumstances. Civil defence, emergency systems, and job seeking through friends-of-a-friend exist as latent connections until needed. In these cases, not being contacted is not necessarily a dysfunction, nor does lack of contact necessarily imply distance or isolation. In short, connectivity can be latent and/or episodic and still be effective (Kolb, 2008).

The paradox of proximity

Most of us have at times felt very distant from someone sitting near to us, say someone at a nearby workstation or sitting in the same com-puter lab. Meanwhile, at the same moment, we were chatting with someone very far away, but feel very close to that person. Wilson and colleagues (2008) have highlighted and empirically tested the paradox-ical nature of distance in organizations, namely that we can and often do feel closer to those far away from us, and vice versa. Like Kilduff and colleagues (2008), these authors suggest that what matters most is our *perception* of proximity. Rather than cognitive constructions of close and far, Wilson et al. suggest that other personal characteristics, such as personality, experience with communication media and realis-tic expectations of virtual communication and affection (*Philos*) (from Krackhardt, 1992), factor into an individual's perception of feeling close or remote from a given work associate.

Notwithstanding the strong subjective (individual perception) dimension of distance, it is nonetheless a relative and relevant concept for groups, teams and whole organizations, as collective (or configura-tions of) perceptions of being close and/or far will no doubt affect work. For example, a team with one remote member versus a team with members evenly split between two sites are likely to experience distance effects very differently. Moreover, distance is not just a concept of concern for those in remote locations. As noted above, we can feel isolated even in close quarters. Nor is distance necessarily a bad thing, in terms of performance. Depending on the nature of the task, working with distant peers may be both effective (e.g. more diverse expertise) and efficient (i.e. saving travel time and costs to and from face-to-face meetings). I will also discuss below the need for keeping our distance as connective devices and social networks seem to keep us *switched on* more and more to the extent that we need to create connective gaps.

A dynamic situational model of proximity

If we accept that new technologies are changing our perceptions of being near or far, and that mobile communications have extended the range and amount of time we can be in touch with others, no matter where they are, then how might we re-conceptualize proximity/distance? As my definition of connective distance above suggests, I view proximity/distance as a dynamic multidimensional condition of perceived remoteness or isolation, including geophysical separation, material/technical faults, delays and barriers (including speed and cost), as well as social fragmentation and/or independence. It has an *objective* basis in the physical world (i.e. travel time, no cell phone signal), coupled with *subjective* perceptions and idiosyncratic factors, including an individual's personality, personal expectations and prior experience with connective technologies. It is relative to situational elements, such as mobility and urgency, and contextual variables, including purpose and task attributes, as shown in Figure 8.1.

The core elements of this model are the situation in context, connective choices, connective gaps and the perception of those gaps. Context constitutes the general background behind specific here-and-now situations in which we find ourselves. Each situation presents some degree of connective choice. Our choices are constrained and enabled by social and technical influences, as well as individual attributes. Connective gaps are at the center of this model since in a connected world we define distance as connective gaps. Ultimately, however, it is our perception of connective gaps that constitute distance. Each of these elements will be further described below.

Context

Our experience of proximity or distance is judged in relation to the context within which we are operating (Fiol & O'Connor, 2005;

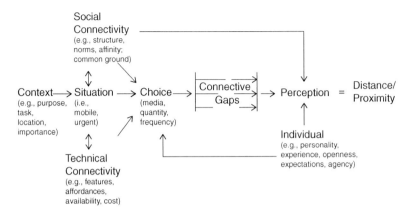

Figure 8.1 A Dynamic Model of Situational Proximity/Distance

Maznevski & Chudoba, 2000). Context includes variables such as the nature of the task (i.e. routine/novel, predictable/uncertain) and our purpose(s) for doing it. For example, project teams that are under tight deadlines to produce a high profile product will generally want the best connective technologies to match their purpose (Majchrzak et al., 2004). When high profile, important tasks encounter urgent situations, the connective choice of how and how much to connect escalates accordingly.

Situation

This is called a situational model because our perception of distance is relative to a given situation. Whereas context can be seen as a set of general conditions, a situation reflects the immediate, particular aspects of the here-and-now. Connective situations are often intensely personal and site-specific. If a friend is in a place where there is danger, and we do not receive a reply message after inquiring about their safety, we might feel desperately isolated from them. Similarly, when work situations are urgent, we often try to work closely with others, including physically coming together for face-to-face meetings and/or remaining in close contact, i.e. checking email and/or phone messages frequently. Urgency usually involves shorter time frames, i.e. expecting immediate responses and not tolerating delays or long waits. Urgent situations also affect our biological responses (i.e. anxiety, fear, anger), which in turn can modify our feelings, including those of being close or far away. We expect urgency to matter, but routine also has implications. Indeed, high levels of airport smartphone usage is often the result of boredom and/or feeling in limbo, which changes communication patterns simply because a person has time on their hands (displacement behavior). Mobility is included as a situational factor, because when colleagues are mobile their spatial location becomes dynamic, and their communication patterns often change accordingly.

Social connectivity

The *social* and *technical* dimensions in this model follow the long and well-trodden path of socio-technical systems (Barley, 1986; Bijker & Pinch, 1987; Woodward, 1958) and adaptive structuration theory (DeSanctis & Poole, 1994; Orlikowski, 1992; Yates & Orlikowski, 1992). Social structures, social ties, norms, affinity, and common ground (or the lack thereof) influence our connective choices and experience of distance. Groups and organizations, for example, often develop norms of email style (length and formality) and so our connective behaviour is guided by those social norms. We can defy these structures and write our own style of emails, but only at the risk of social isolation or sanctions (i.e. poor performance reviews).

Technical connectivity

Technologically, we can only do what technology affords us (Hutchby, 2001; Norman, 1999). For example, traditional telephones offered voice, but no video image. Early video conferencing allowed us to see one another, but was clunky and/or expensive. Then Skype enabled reasonable quality video-conferencing for free. Now, video calling is possible in handheld smartphones, so the personal computer is no longer necessary for video calls. Seeing a colleague/friend speaking live on your handheld device is a good example of what Orlikowski and Scott refer to as a sociomateriality, that is to say where the social and material worlds combine and become embedded in our lives (Orlikowski & Scott, 2008). Every connective situation is embedded in socio-technical or sociomaterial systems, constrained and enabled by the duality of structure and agency, described in the rather durable (Jones & Karsten, 2008) theory of structuration (Giddens, 1984). In other words, while technology enables our connective behaviour, it can ultimately only do what we allow it to do. Ultimately, our behaviours are not determined by the communication technologies, but by ourselves (Leonardi & Barley, 2010).

Connective choice

With the increasing pervasiveness of connective technologies, the individual has an increasing degree of connective choice or what is also called agency in sociology (Cousins & Robey, 2005; Emirbayer & Mische, 1998; Kolb, 2008). There are choices to be made around which media to use, i.e. face-to-face versus telephone versus email (Daft & Lengel, 1986). We also increasingly have to choose the frequency, quantity, and style in connecting with others. Indeed, the more connected we become, the more we as individuals must decide if, when, how, where, and how much to connect with others (Kolb et al., 2012; Kolb & Collins, 2011; Murphy, 2007). These choices impact the likelihood of connective gaps occurring as well as our perception of proximity/distance. For example, if we choose to call our children every night when travelling, then a nightly call missed (for any reason) will be perceived as a connective gap that contributes to our feeling of being distant (or travelling too much). By contrast, if we choose to normally only check work email at home periodically and seldom reply the same day, then the connective electronic and temporal gaps experienced while travelling remain normal, that is they are in line with our personal choices and the expectations of others. Increasingly in a highly connected world, we must choose to avoid hyper-connectivity by disconnecting from others and therefore create and maintain some connective gaps for personal productivity and well-being (Kolb et al., 2008; MacCormick et al., 2012; Perlow, 2012). In this sense, while staying closely involved with work, we must also learn when and how to keep our distance.

Perception

Wilson and colleagues (2008) convincingly portray distance as essentially *subjective*, varying from individual to individual, and depending largely on personal characteristics, including openness to experience (enacted as flexible, tolerant, and inquisitive in new situations) and experience with dispersed work, coupled with social factors such as depth and frequency of communication, as well as social identification, which leads to "common ground" (Olson & Olson, 2000, p. 157). Wilson et al. summarize the largely overlooked matter of personal attributes in distributed work as follows.

Although individual difference variables have received little attention in research regarding geographically dispersed teams (Martins et al., 2004), we believe that some individual characteristics affect perceptions of proximity through their influence on communication and identification. Since working at a distance has been linked to feelings of isolation and uncertainty (Kurland & Bailey, 1999), we expect that individuals whose dispositions help them cope with these conditions will be more likely to engage in communication with distant others and to identify with them. At the same time, individuals who are comfortable and accustomed to coping with virtual work will also be more likely to engage in the processes of communication and identification that will lead to increased perceived proximity with distant others (2008, p. 989).

So, while geophysical and techno-spatial realities do produce connective gaps and as such influence the psycho-social determinants of distance and isolation, ultimately distance is a subjective perception of the individual. Technical gaps may be seen to constitute an *objective* dimension within our model, i.e. fixed places remain the same spatial distance from one another and an Internet connection is either established or not and its speed can be measured in actuarial terms (though whether that speed is acceptable is subjective). The *subjective* dimension of our model is based on our individual perceptions of a given situation. If we are naturally curious, open and empathetic, working in a cohesive team with a collaborative culture, then our response to connective gaps (distance) is likely to be different than someone who feels they are working in social and technical isolation.

Individual attributes

Individual factors may lead us to make choices that mitigate connective gaps in the first place, i.e. have more friends and use more types of media, which offer connective density that allows for social and technical workarounds when gaps appear (Kolb et al., 2008). Moreover, if I choose to work relatively independently from my peers, but still deliver to my team, my connective choices may be respected without any negative effects, i.e. not being perceived as isolated from my team and not perceiving myself to be isolated (Kirkman et al., 2004). In globally distributed teams, we have found agency (choice) to be a strong predictor of team performance and innovation (Collins & Kolb, 2012a, 2012b) Indeed, besides the vagaries of technical connections (Internet speeds, phone reception, etc.), the most dynamic aspect of this model of distance and proximity is the ongoing negotiation between the individual's needs for independence and privacy (distance) versus the group's need for social cohesion (closeness).

Virtually there: Working across time and space

In this section, I present suggestions for working across distance. This is not a comprehensive or exhaustive summary, but it highlights some key relational issues when working across distance. As stated above, not everyone reading this will be working in virtual teams per se, but nearly everyone works somewhat remotely from others, even if it is just sending an email or leaving a text or voice message for someone we see regularly. Others work across great distances and multiple time zones on a regular basis. In multinational companies, for instance, working with others around the globe happens as a matter of routine. As one of the software engineers we interviewed in Boston said, in referring to her colleagues in Bangalore, "we meet all the time", without adding the fact that the software teams in each lab had never met face-to-face. Virtual is the new normal in many organizations (O'Leary & Cummings, 2007). But, notwithstanding its normalcy and new technological advances (and plummeting costs), building and maintaining relationships at a distance is not easy. So, here are some suggestions for working with others in mediated space, be it down the hall or around the world. Note that I use the terms "virtual" and "distributed" interchangeably as the notion of the purely virtual team is diminishing.

Nuance is not for the net

Those who try to be cheeky on social networking sites often find it fails and they are completely misunderstood. While strong relationships can handle almost anything, new and/or weaker ties require clarity. For example, when a distributed team is forming and its goals and direction are unclear, the standard advice is to convene a face-to-face meeting if possible. If this is not practical, then a video conference would be better than a long series of emails. Media richness theory (Daft & Lengel, 1986) suggests that the richer the medium, the better it is for conveying subtle nuances of meaning, intent, and generative thinking. This is not to suggest that face-to-face meetings are always productive (far from it), or that virtual meetings cannot be equally effective (and generally more efficient). It is just a reminder that building relationships online requires more attention to the structure (formal or informal, long or short messages), timing (rapid-fire exchanges vs. considered responses) and unintended signals (e.g. short, unedited messages may be seen as abrasive or disrespectful). The way work is organized can also be a problem. For example, when interviewing software engineers in the US and India, the latter felt they were not trusted or not given enough credit for their abilities when they were given "easy" tasks by their American counterparts. Such tasks were often quite boring. The American engineering managers, on the other hand, found more simply structured tasks easier to manage across distance, so they sent those tasks to India, not as a reflection on the abilities of their foreign peers, but just a practical way to avoid ambiguity and keep remote tasks more easily managed.

Cross-cultural issues are some of the oldest findings in the virtual team literature. For example, when highly trained aeronautical engineers from America and the United Kingdom worked together, they found huge cultural differences, even though they are ostensibly speaking the same language (Kirkman et al., 2002). It is hard to mandate cultural connections. By contrast, in our cross-cultural study of a bio-medical engineering firm (Kolb et al., 2008), we heard about a virtual team consisting of an American lab and its joint venture partner in Korea who exchanged wedding photos and other personal artefacts, which built up high levels of trust and cohesiveness, only to be crushed by a new senior executive who forbade the exchange of non-work photos and communication. The result was that both sides of the team felt frustrated and disillusioned with the project, as they were confined to solely "professional" correspondence. It is tempting to make hard and fast rules in large, bureaucratic organizations, but prescribing and/or prohibiting communication approaches is a tricky business, especially in cross-cultural contexts.

FYA: Attention isn't everything (but it's almost everything)

Information is cheap. We can find out almost anything, anytime on the Internet. We no longer need friends or colleagues to give us the answer or help us fill in the missing link in our quest for information. *Attention* is the premium thing we now desire from others. And getting it is getting much harder than it used to be. Think of a teacher trying to impart information to a class full of students who could well be sourcing more information online about the topic than the teacher has encountered in his or her lifetime. This is a scary scenario for some teachers, but may be a common experience for digital natives (those who have grown up using digital technology) (Vodanovich et al., 2010). Work reflects the same issue, but at work the information flow often includes dozens if not hundreds of emails or other electronic messages, all vying for our attention (Barley et al., 2011). The problem with too much information is that it tends to fragment our attention. Some call this multi-tasking and, although there is an ongoing debate on our human capacity to multi-task, psychologists generally agree that multi-tasking undermines task effectiveness and social connection (Atchley, 2010; Brockman, 2011; Carr, 2010).

Attention is important, as giving another person our attention signals our interest in them, which is fundamental to relationship building. Imagine trying to engage the interest of someone who is constantly interrupted or distracted by other people entering their office or by their smartphone. We used to think of the amount of time shared with others, but now the issue is more about the "mindshare" you have of another's attention, that is how much of their mental attention is focused on your shared projects and/or relationship. Getting someone's attention is not a matter of simply speaking louder. We can feign engagement, while thinking about other things (or texting under the table). One practical idea is to structure meetings (including classes) where information sharing is kept to a minimum and discussion, debate and generative dialogue engages those attending, avoiding piles of paper and long reports. Virtual meetings are often better organized than face-to-face meetings because connection time may be more costly or more tightly scheduled than face-to-face meetings. Our experience in large corporates with virtual meeting facilities has shown that participants are motivated to complete virtual meetings in a timely manner as others will be waiting for their turn with the virtual meeting rooms.

Say + Do = Trust

Want to build trust in relationships at a distance? It's simple: Do what you say you will do. The good news is that most people offer what is known as "swift trust" in many settings, including virtual ones (Meyerson et al., 1996). However, the best way to establish a more lasting version of trust is to simply deliver on what you have promised (Cummings, 2008). Essentially, without the ability to look someone in the eyes, we seek other proxies for trustworthiness. Therefore, in virtual environments, doing what you say you will do serves as an indicator of your trustworthiness. Proactively, leaders of virtual teams might say something like, "Thanks for your contact details and preferred communication methods. I will collate these and circulate them to all of you by next Monday". When this simple act is completed, i.e. a document appears in members' Inboxes the next Monday, they are able to rationally believe their leader can be trusted. Of course, over time other experiences of the leader must be consistent in order for trust to be maintained, but the point is that an easy starting point for building trust in distributed environments is delivering on our promises.

Leading online

While research on virtual teams has probably seen its peak and seems to be somewhat stagnant, research on leadership in virtual or distributed environments remains in its infancy. With some notable exceptions (Avolio et al., 2000; Weisband, 2008), much more work is needed to fully understand how to lead from a distance. Leadership is a challenging concept to measure and explore when the leadership context may be unique for each member of a virtual team or distributed organization. As noted above, more directive leadership is easiest to execute across time and space, and clear processes generally enhance trust in virtual teams (Powell et al., 2006), while more ambiguous and complex problems are much more challenging in distributed settings. One balancing act leaders have to juggle online just as they do in face-to-face environments is how long to hold open a conversation before suggesting a solution or next step, thereby closing down participation from others. On the other hand, some of the symbols of power (big office, expensive clothes) can be somewhat removed when managing first impressions with others online.

Extroverts seem to have a head start leading in the face-to-face realm, but, introverts seem to gain equality online, as they have time to compose their thoughts and contribute more equally. However, the extrovert who also communicates well in both face-to-face and online has more impact than an extrovert who eschews the online environment. In a study of young (17–28 year-old) leaders participating in an 18-month leadership development course that required both face-to-face and online activities in equal proportion, the leaders that ranked highest were those who were strong in both environments. This means that those with face-to-face (e.g. charismatic) skills were not rated to be as effective as those who had face-to-face plus online presence and participation (Kolb et al., 2009). These findings are surprising for two reasons. First, we might have expected those with high face-to-face ratings to eschew the online forums and rely on their superior face-to-face social skills. Second, we expected introverts to exceed their outgoing peers in the online environment. In fact, though competent online, the introverts did not out-shine their outgoing peers and, as mentioned above, the highest rated leaders were highly capable in both face-to-face and online environments.

Solitude vs. loneliness

Finally, when thinking about being close or far in relation to others, we must be careful to not confuse solitude and loneliness. Paradoxically, one might be physically and/or socially distant (isolated) from others, yet not feel lonely (Wright, 2009). While loneliness is a state of yearning for social contact, solitude is an individual's choice to operate independently of others or the attitude that being alone is an opportunity for reflection and/or regeneration (Kolb & Collins, 2011; Murphy, 2007). This is an important distinction as there has been considerable hand-wringing about the "Net" causing social isolation (Marche, 2012; Turkle, 2011). Yet, for many individuals, not being social is not the same as feeling isolated or lonely. They may be simply embracing and enjoying some solitude in a world of increasingly constant connectivity. Some would argue that each individual should develop a personal philosophy for living in a highly connected age (Powers, 2010; Rheingold, 2012).

Conclusion

The paradox of proximity is partly explained by Heidegger's proposition that we can always feel close to those we care about, no matter the distance between us. Most of us understand the phenomenon of "far-but-close", which means we have felt "close" to those who are far away. Some readers might relate also to feeling distant from someone who is physically near to them. This chapter further explains the paradox by examining how new connective technologies and the drive toward social networking have significantly changed our personal and work lives vis-à-vis those who are distant from us. I define distance as connective gaps between human actors and outline some of the social, technical, and contextual variables that contribute to an individual's perception of being close or far from another person. In the model presented here, connective distance (or proximity) is ultimately in the eye of the beholder.

New technologies offer increased social presence, but too much presence and/or too much social networking can also be a distraction. The connectivity conundrum is that the more connected we become, the more we need to disconnect. In situations of near-constant connectivity, "keeping our distance" (or at least some of it) is more important than ever. Moreover, while the norms of professional distance are bound to change and evolve, work can still be accomplished without one necessarily feeling close to one's work peers. Since individuals have varying tendencies toward being more or less close or distant in their relationships at work, even close-knit groups will normally have some less close members, and far-flung groups can still foster some very close interpersonal relationships.

As nearly all work is more or less mediated, the distinctions between virtual and collocated work are breaking down. Individuals will have to mindfully focus their attention on those around them, as well as those who are far away. Organizations will continue to struggle to strike the right balance between the benefits of life online, such as social net-working, and its counter-productive elements. In any collocated setting, we can witness workers sitting next to each other who rarely speak to each other, while simultaneously working closely with others around the world. Or, we can find an individual alone in a coffee shop, who is central to the success of a far-flung project team of experts located around the globe. Distance is certainly not dead, but perhaps it is changing. Leaders and managers face new challenges in a world where far is the new close and close is the new far.

References

Atchley, P. (2010). You can't multitask, so stop trying, *Harvard Business Review*, December 21. Retrieved from http://blogs.hbr.org/cs/2010/12/you_cant_multitask_so_stop_tr.html

Avolio, B., Kahai, S., & Dodge, G. (2000). E-leadership: Implications for theory, research and practice, *The Leadership Quarterly*, *11*(4), 615–668.

Barley, S. R. (1986). Technology as an occasion for structuring: Evidence from observation of CT scanners and the social order of radiology departments, *Administrative Science Quarterly*, *31*, 78–108.

Barley, S. R., Meyerson, D. E., & Grodal, S. (2011). E-mail as source and symbol of stress, *Organization Science*, *22*(4), 887–906.

Baron, N. S. (2008). *Always On: Language in an Online, and Mobile World*. Oxford: Oxford University Press.

Baym, N. K. (2010). *Personal Connections in the Digital Age*. Cambridge, UK: Polity.

Bijker, W. E. & Pinch, P. (1987). *The Social Construction of Facts and Artifacts*. Cambridge, MA: MIT Press.

Brass, D. J. & Burkhardt, M. E. (1992). Centrality and power in organizations: in N. Nohria & R. G. Eccles (eds) *Networks and Organizations: Structure, Form, and Action*. Boston: Harvard Business School Press.

Brockman, J. (ed.) (2011). *Is the Internet Changing the Way You Think?: The Net's Impact on Our Minds and Future*. New York: Harper Perennial.

Burt, R. S. (1992). *Structural Holes: The Social Structure of Competition*. Cambridge, MA: Harvard University Press.

Cairncross, F. (1997, 2001). *The Death of Distance: How the Communications Revolution is Changing Our Lives* (2nd ed.). Boston: Harvard Business School Press.

Carr, N. (2010). *The Shallows: How the Internet is Changing the Way We Think, Read and Remember*. London: Atlantic.

Castells, M. (1996). *The Rise of the Network Society*. Oxford: Blackwell.

Castells, M. (2000). *The Rise of the Network Society* (Vol. 1, 2nd edn). Oxford: Blackwell Press.

Castells, M., Fernandez-Ardevol, M., Qiu, J. L., & Sey, A. (2007). *Mobile Communication and Society: A Global Perspective*. Cambridge, MA: MIT Press.

Collins, P. D. & Kolb, D. G. (2012a). Innovation in distributed teams: The duality of connectivity norms and human agency: in C. Kelliher & J. Richardson (eds) *New Ways of Organizing Work: Developments, Perspectives and Experiences* (pp. 140–159). New York: Routledge.

Collins, P. D. & Kolb, D. G. (2012b, 7 August). *Requisite Connectivity in Distributed Teams Engaged in Exploitative and Explorative Innovation*. Presented at the meeting of the Academy of Management, Boston, MA.

Cousins, K. C. & Robey, D. (2005). Human agency in a wireless world: Patterns of technology use in nomadic computing environments, *Information and Organization, 15*(2), 151–180.

Coyne, R. (1997). Language, space and information: in P. Droege (ed.) *Intelligent Environments: Spatial Aspects of the Information Revolution* (pp. 495–517). Amsterdam: Elsevier Science.

Cummings, J. N. (2008). Leading groups from a distance: How to mitigate consequences of geographic dispersion: in S. Weisband (ed.) *Leadership at a Distance: Research in Technologically-Supported Work* (pp. 33–50). New York: Lawrence Erlbaum Associates.

Daft, R. & Lengel, R. (1986). Organisational information requirements, media richness, and structural design, *Management Science, 32*(5), 554–571.

DeSanctis, G. & Poole, M. S. (1994). Capturing the complexity in advanced technology use: Adaptive structuration theory, *Organization Science, 5*(2), 121–147.

Dunne, J. A., Williams, R. J., & Martinez, N. D. (2002). *Food-Web Structure and Network Theory: The Role of Connectance and Size*. Presented at the meeting of the National Academy of Sciences.

Emirbayer, M. & Mische, A. (1998). What is agency? *The American Journal of Sociology, 103*(4), 962–1023.

Fiol, C. M. & O'Connor, E. J. (2005). Identification in face-to-face, hybrid and pure virtual teams: Untangling the contradictions, *Organization Science, 16*(1), 19–32.

Fitzgerald, M. (2004, April). Internetworking, *Technology Review, 107*(3), 44–49.

Giddens, A. (1984). *The Constitution of Society: Outline of the Theory of Structuration*. Oxford: Polity Press.

Granovetter, M. (1973). The strength of weak ties, *American Journal of Sociology, 78*(6), 1360–1380.

Harper, R. (2010). *Texture: Human Expression in the Age of Communications Overload*. Cambridge, MA: MIT Press.

Hiltz, S. R. & Turoff, M. (1993). *The Network Nation: Human Communication Via Computer* (2nd ed.). Boston: M.I.T. Press.

Hutchby, I. (2001). Technologies, texts and affordances, *Sociology, 35*(2), 441–456.

Jones, M. R. & Karsten, H. (2008). Giddens's structuration theory and information systems research, *MIS Quarterly, 32*(1), 127–157.

Kilduff, M., Crossland, C., Tsai, W., & Krackhardt, D. (2008). Organizational network perceptions versus reality: A small world after all? *Organizational Behavior and Human Decision Processes, 107*, 15–28.

Kilduff, M., Tsai, W., & Hanke, R. (2006). A paradigm too far?: A dynamic stability reconsideration of the social network research program, *Academy of Management Review, 31*(4), 1031–1048.

Kirkman, B. L., Rosen, B., Gibson, C. B., Tesluk, P. E., & McPherson, S. O. (2002). Five challenges to virtual team success: Lessons from Sabre, Inc, *Academy of Management Executive, 16*(3), 67–79.

Kirkman, B. L., Rosen, B., Tesluk, P. E., & Gibson, C. B. (2004). The impact of empowerment on virtual team performance: The moderating effect of face-to-face interaction, *Academy of Management Journal, 47*(2), 175–192.

Kleinfeld, J. S. (2002). Could it be a big world after all?: The "six degrees of separation" myth, *Society, 39*, 61–66.

Kolb, D. G. (2007). Redefining distance: Why the world is not flat and distance can never be "dead". Symposium conducted at the meeting of the 2nd Symposium on Globally Distributed Work, Bangalore, India.

Kolb, D. G. (2008). Exploring the metaphor of connectivity: Attributes, dimensions and duality, *Organization Studies, 29*(1), 127–144.

Kolb, D. G., Caza, A., & Collins, P. D. (2012). States of connectivity: New questions and new directions, *Organization Studies, 33*(2), 267–273.

Kolb, D. G. & Collins, P. D. (2011). Managing personal connectivity: Finding flow for regenerative knowledge creation: in G. Gorman & D. Pauleen (eds) *Personal Knowledge Management: Individual, Organizational and Social Perspectives* (pp. 129–142). Surrey, England: Gower.

Kolb, D. G., Collins, P. D., & Lind, E. A. (2008). Requisite connectivity: Finding flow in a not-so-flat world, *Organizational Dynamics, 37*(2), 181–189.

Kolb, D. G., Prussia, G., & Francoeur, J. A. (2009). Leadership and connectivity: The influence of on-line activity on closeness and effectiveness, *Journal of Leadership and Organizational Studies, 15*(4), 342–352.

Krackhardt, D. (1990). Assessing the political landscape: Structure, cognition, and power in organizations, *Administrative Science Quarterly, 35*, 342–369.

Krackhardt, D. (1992). The strength of strong ties: The importance of Philos in organizations: in N. Nohria & R. G. Eccles (eds) *Networks and Organizations* (pp. 216–239). Boston, MA: Harvard Business School Press.

Krackhardt, D. & Kilduff, M. (1999). Whether close or far: Social distance effects on perceived balance in friendship networks, *Journal of Personality and Social Psychology, 76*(5), 770–782.

Kurland, N. B. & Bailey, D. E. (1999). Telework: The advantages and challenges of working here, there, anywhere, and anytime, *Organizational Dynamics, 28*, 53–68.

Leonardi, P. M. & Barley, S. R. (2010). What's under construction here? Social action, materiality, and power in constructivist studies of technology and organizing, *The Academy of Management Annals, 4*(1), 1–51.

MacCormick, J., Dery, K., & Kolb, D. G. (2012). Engaged or just connected?: Smartphones and employee engagement, *Organizational Dynamics, 41*(3), 194–201.

Majchrzak, A., Malhotra, A., Stamps, J., & Lipnack, J. (2004). Can absence make a team grow stronger? *Harvard Business Review, 82*(5), 131–137.

Marche, S. (2012, May). Is Facebook making us lonely? *The Atlantic, 309*(4), 60–69.

Marquis, C. (2003). The pressure of the past: Networking imprinting in intercorporate communities, *Administrative Science Quarterly, 48*(4), 655–689.

Martins, L. L., Gilson, L. L., & Maynard, M. T. (2004). Virtual teams: What do we know and where do we go from here? *Journal of Management, 30*(6), 805–835.

Mazmanian, M., Orlikowski, W. J., & Yates, J. (2013). The autonomy paradox: The implications of mobile email devices for knowledge professionals, *Organization Science*, forthcoming; doi: org/10.1287/orsc.1120.0806.

Maznevski, M. L. & Chudoba, K. M. (2000). Bridging space over time: Global virtual team dynamics and effectiveness, *Organization Science, 11*(5), 473–492.

McDonald, M. L. (2003). Getting by with the advice of their friends: CEO's advice networks and firms' strategic responses to poor performance, *Administrative Science Quarterly, 48*(1), 1–32.

McPherson, M., Smith-Lovin, L., & Brashears, M. E. (2006). Social isolation in America: Changes in core discussion networks over two decades, *American Sociological Review, 71*, 353–375.

Meyerson, D., Weick, K. E., & Kramer, R. M. (1996). Swift trust and temporary groups: in M. Kramer & T. R. Tyler (eds) *Trust in Organizations: Frontiers of Theory and Research* (pp. 166–195). Thousand Oaks: Sage.

Milgram, S. (1967). The small world problem, *Psychology Today, 2*, 60–67.

Morrison, R. L. & Wright, S. (eds) (2009). *Friends and Enemies in Organizations: A Work Psychology Perspective*. London: Palgrave Macmillan.

Murphy, P. (2007). You are wasting my time: Why limits on connectivity are essential for economies of creativity, *University of Auckland Business Review, 9*(2), 17–26.

Napier, B. J. & Ferris, G. (1993). Distance in organizations, *Human Resource Management Review, 3*(4), 321–357.

Nemiro, J., Beyerlein, M., Bradley, L., & Beyerlein, S. (eds) (2008). *The Handbook of High-Performing Virtual Teams: A Toolkit for Collaborating Across Boundaries*. San Francisco: Jossey-Bass.

Nohria, N. & Eccles, R. G. (eds) (1992). *Networks and Organizations: Structure, Form, and Action*. Boston, MA: Harvard Business School Press.

Norman, D. (1999). Affordance, conventions, and design, *Interactions*, May–June, 38–44.

O'Leary, M. B. & Cummings, J. (2007). The spatial, temporal, and configurational characteristics of geographic dispersion in teams, *MIS Quarterly, 31*(3), 433–452.

Olson, G. M. & Olson, J. (2000). Distance matters, *Human-Computer Interaction, 15*(2/3), 139–179.

Orlikowski, W. J. (1992). The duality of technology: Rethinking the concept of technology in organizations, *Organization Science, 3*(3), 398–427.

Orlikowski, W. J. & Scott, S. V. (2008). Sociomateriality: Challenging the separation of technology, work and organization, *The Academy of Management Annals, 2*(1), 433–474.

Perlow, L. A. (2012). *Sleeping with Your Smartphone: How to Break the 24/7 Habit and Change the Way You Work*. Boston: Harvard Business School Publishing.

Powell, A., Galvin, J., & Piccoli, G. (2006). Antecedents to team member commitment from near and far: A comparison between collocated and virtual teams, *Information, Technology & People, 19*(4), 299–322.

Powers, W. (2010). *Hamlet's Blackberry: Building a Good Life in the Digital Age.* New York: Harper Perennial.

Putnam, R. D. (2000). *Bowling Alone: The Collapse and Revival of American Community.* New York: Simon and Schuster.

Rainie, L. & Wellman, B. (2012). *Networked: The New Social Operating System.* Cambridge, MA: MIT Press.

Rheingold, H. (2012). *Net Smart: How to Thrive On-Line.* Cambridge, MA: MIT Press.

Turkle, S. (2011). *Alone Together: Why We Expect More from Technology and Less from Each Other.* New York: Basic Books.

Vodanovich, S., Sundaram, D., & Myers, M. (2010). Digital natives and ubiquitous information systems, *Information Systems Research, 21*(4), 711–723.

Watts, D. J. (2003). *Six Degrees: The Science of a Connected Age.* London: William Heinemann.

Weisband, S. (ed.) (2008). *Leadership at a Distance: Research in Technologically-Supported Work.* New York: Lawrence Erlbaum Associates.

Wellman, B. & Berkowitz, S. D. (eds) (1988). *Social Structures: A Network Approach.* Cambridge, UK: Cambridge University Press.

Wilson, J. M., O'Leary, M. B., Metiu, A., & Jett, Q. R. (2008). Perceived proximity in virtual work: Explaining the paradox of far-but-close, *Organization Studies, 29*(7), 979–1002.

Woodward, J. (1958). *Management and Technology.* London: Her Majesty's Stationary Office (HMSO).

Wright, S. L. (2009). In a lonely place: The experience of loneliness in the workplace: in R. L. Morrison & S. L. Wright (eds) *Friends and Enemies in Organisations: A Work Psychology Perspective* (pp. 10–31). London: Palgrave Macmillan.

Yates, J. & Orlikowski, W. J. (1992). Genres of organizational communication: A structurational approach to studying communication media, *Academy of Management Review, 17*(2), 299–326.

9
Collegial Relationships and Social Support in Organizations

Misty M. Bennett[1] and Terry A. Beehr[2]

Richard just started his job at a new multinational company. Although he has prior experience in his field, he has not worked at a global company before, particularly one so large. In addition his new organization utilizes a lot of teamwork, which is new to him because in his previous job he was very independent and had little contact with coworkers. He is relieved to find that his onboarding experience is pleasant, with people in his workplace being generally warm and supportive. His coworkers extend frequent invitations for him to join them for lunch and even for drinks after work, and his supervisor stops frequently to discuss how Richard is adjusting to his new job. The support that his coworkers and supervisor provide makes Richard feel welcome, and he finds that his transition to his new organization is going much better than expected.

Social contact is one of the most fundamental needs of human beings. It is not surprising, therefore, that there is an abundance of research on the topic, and that researchers generally believe that social support is beneficial and improves our well-being. Social support helped Richard in the vignette above, and many of us have had similar experiences in new jobs. Some of us may have even experienced the opposite, finding that unsupportive, sometimes hostile coworkers and supervisors can be detrimental to our satisfaction, performance, and our general well-being. This chapter considers the theory, research, and practice regarding workplace support. We will also propose areas of inquiry for which research has not yet provided answers.

---

[1] Department of Management, Central Michigan University
[2] Department of Psychology, Central Michigan University

Social support: History and origins

Maslow's Needs Hierarchy (1943) is known by introductory psychology students everywhere. The need for love and belonging is one of the basic human needs, one that drives us to search for and maintain meaningful relationships with others. Maslow considered this to be a deficiency need, along with basic physiological and safety needs, without which people would be unable to properly function, preventing them from feeling self-esteem and achievement. Indeed, sociology and anthropology, two fields from which social support research has drawn widely, have long understood the importance of belonging to social circles, and that the very survival of our species has been dependent on relationships among people. One of the fundamental elements that distinguishes human beings from other species are "prosocial emotions that promote extensive cooperation with non-kin" (Hill et al., 2009, p. 187), and this includes social support.

The fact that human beings need social support as a basic part of their survival has also widely been noted by developmental psychologists and in studies regarding infant/maternal attachment. Even some non-humans might need social contact to thrive. One famous study examined the effects of social isolation on infant rhesus monkeys (Harlow, 1965). Social isolation for six to 12 months almost completely destroyed the potential for normal social and behavioral patterns, with monkeys who had been isolated demonstrating behaviors like rocking and staring blankly ahead, running in circles, and even self-mutilation. The need for social interaction also has biological roots early in life for humans. Hormonal processes taking place during birth relate to social bonding. For instance, a mother's oxytocin, a neurotransmitter related to bonding and attachment, is released in large quantities during labor due to uterine contractions and during nursing due to nipple stimulation, a process that enhances maternal bonding with the infant (Kendrick, 2004). The infant too, while demonstrating suckling behaviors, exhibits a surge in oxytocin, which stimulates the olfactory bulb, strengthening a smell association with the infant's mother (Nagasawa et al., 2012). Thus, this neurotransmitter appears to be one biological source of social needs. Having such a strong biological drive toward attachment early in life sets the stage for social support as a basic need.

The presence of social support is therefore very important, and the absence of it can be quite detrimental. Vaux (1988) argued for the importance of social connections via a classic study of suicide by Durkheim (1897/1951), which suggested that diminished social connections to one's community were linked to suicide. More recent research has shown social support to be a buffer of the relationship between impulsivity and suicide risk, such that highly impulsive individuals who receive high levels of social support are at a lower level of suicide risk than impulsive individuals with less support (Kleiman et al., 2012).

Intuitively, humans understand the relationship between social support and well-being. The use of isolation chambers as a torture tactic and of solitary confinement as disciplinary action in our prison systems is well documented (Haney & Lynch, 1997). The early Quakers utilized isolation as a way to encourage self-reflection and penance among those who had committed trespasses, but they mostly abandoned the practice after they observed harmful effects of prolonged isolation including psychological disturbances (Miller, 1995). Even as early as the nineteenth century, the effects of isolation on prisoners was documented in medical journals of the time, describing often vivid hallucinations, delusions, apprehensions and other perceptual distortions, and even paranoia and psychosis (Shalev, 2008). Harlow himself described the isolation cells for the infant monkeys in his monkey isolation studies as a "pit of despair" (Blum, 1994). People seem to intuitively understand their own need for social support because, faced with potential stress, we often seek out others (Schachter, 1959). Both in times of stress and for the basic survival needs, it appears that social support fulfills a basic human need.

What is social support? Defining the construct

Theoretical background

Social support is a broad term used to mean different things, perhaps partly because the social support literature comes from multiple disciplines, including sociology, medicine, and psychology. Vaux (1988) attributes the beginning of the concept to Gerald Caplan, who had a varied career as a political activist and mental health advocate, John Cassel, an epidemiologist and medical physician, and Sidney Cobb, an epidemiologist who was interested in the effect that social support has on the relationship between stress and well-being. Because the origins of social support as a construct were in epidemiology, it is not surprising that early research focused on well-being, with occupational outcomes not examined until the concept developed more fully and was adopted for study by organizational psychologists. The link to epidemiology was important, however, as researchers like Cassel were able to show the important role that social support plays in the etiology of disease (e.g. 1974a, 1974b). Cobb (1976) also introduced the idea of social support as a buffer of the relationship between stressors (characteristics of or events in the work environment that are stressful) and strains (harmful effects on employee well-being), a research question that will be examined later in this chapter more fully. Caplan (1974) has one of the most frequently cited early conceptualizations of social support, describing three types: activities where support is used to help mobilize psychological resources to manage problems, support activities that help via sharing demanding tasks, and support that provides money, guidance, or similar materials to help in response to stressors. Later research examined many more conceptualizations, however, and there is still not a universally accepted definition (Beehr & McGrath, 1992).

Its multi-faceted nature makes the study of social support complicated. One could even say that support does not need to be given for it to be perceived. For example, has social support actually been given and received, or does the person just believe that support is available if he/she needs it (Lakey & Cohen, 2000)? Both of these types have been operationalized and studied in the workplace. For example, questionnaire items measuring received social support refer to someone in the workplace who helps the person, and in addition, there have been experiments in which a confederate actually helps the person. Questionnaire items measuring available support ask if there is someone in the workplace who will help with the person's problems. Studies of available support outnumber studies of support actually given and received, however. Some studies have begun to examine the relationship between the two types, examining if available support is a process variable. Received social support can predict perceptions of available social support across time (Norris & Kaniasty, 1996; Russell et al., 1997). Received support has also been shown meta-analytically to be less strongly related to mental health ($r = .12$) than perceived available support ($r = .32$) (Finch et al., 1999). Recent research still focuses on the perceptions of available support, and some of it emphasizes the role that cognition plays in the appraisal of support (e.g. Haber et al., 2007). The same support behaviors may be perceived differently depending on the characteristics of the receiver, characteristics of the provider, and characteristics of the provider-receiver relationship.

Defining Social Support

After a month on the job, the pace finally catches up to Richard and he finds himself quickly overwhelmed with too many demands. His supervisor has unrealistic expectations about his workload and is unwilling to provide clarification regarding confusing work assignments. His coworkers are still demonstrating support by inviting him to social gatherings, but they are unable to provide any instrumental support regarding his work demands. Furthermore, his coworkers are too busy with their own obligations to be able to help him. Richard is also finding that the culture of the organization is not very supportive and that he has trouble getting time off to handle personal demands. His growing work responsibilities and lack of support leave Richard feeling a growing level of job dissatisfaction. The negative feelings that Richard has toward his job begin to spill over into his personal life, and his family notices that he is more irritable and unhappy. His spouse tries to intervene by asking him to discuss how things are going at work. Richard talks briefly about his emotions toward his job but finds that this does not make him happier at work nor does it help him deal with his work demands.

The above, more pessimistic, vignette begins to demonstrate some of the various types and sources of social support. Considering this, take a second and think about the various types of support you have received in the last week. Have you had people help teach you something, help relieve responsibilities, or help by just listening? Perhaps you had someone try to help you this week and you really did not want their help or found that their "help" just left you feeling inadequate, confused, or stressed. Understanding some of the background and origin of the construct and considering your own experience of support, you may start to appreciate what we mean when we say social support is a complex construct. In fact, social support has been suggested to have a general lack of specificity in conceptualization (House & Kahn, 1985) and has even been described as a "meta-construct" by some (e.g. Heller & Swindle, 1983; Vaux et al., 1987), consisting of several different types of support that vary in terms of nature, function, and source. McIntosh (1991) notes, however, that even these dimensions upon which support may vary have not been used consistently in research and, even when the same term is used (e.g. nature of support), there is disagreement as to what these terms mean. Clarifying these terms and using them consistently is important, however, if research is supposed to be able to help drive organizational support practices.

Many lay concepts of social support are broad and include any helping behaviors from another individual. "Social support is often used in a broad sense, referring to any process through which social relationships might promote health and well-being" (Cohen et al., 2000, p. 4). Two categories of social relationship can affect health: (1) Exchange of emotional, informational, or instrumental resources in response to a need for help, and (2) processes that positively impact health due to social interactions with others that are not directly tied to a need for help. It is the former that is typically the focus of research examining social support in the workplace. A need for help, or the perception that one is in need of help, appears to be a requisite for the application and study of social support in occupational stress research.

One of the earliest definitions of social support discussed it as mental and material support one gets from the social network, which makes one feel loved, esteemed, cared for, and valued (Cobb, 1976), and these can include both appraisal (feedback from others about one's own abilities or actions) and instrumental support. Definitions of social support tend to include the quality of helping relationships or actions as well as the previously noted distinction between availability and enacted (received) support (e.g. Barrera, 1986; Haber et al., 2007; Leavy, 1983). The idea of quality is important because an employee may have many coworkers and associates, but if they do not have sufficiently intimate or high-quality relationships, then the support may not be adequate to provide any significant reduction in strains.

One of the most frequently utilized definitions for studying social support in the workplace is comprised of House's (1981) four types: (1) Emotional concern or liking, (2) instrumental aid (goods or services), (3) information, and (4) appraisal (relevant to self-evaluation). Many researchers have simplified the categories to two, instrumental and emotional support (e.g. Beehr, 1985; Thoits, 1985). Furthermore, researchers have muddled the concepts by at times combining some of the types, and at other times choosing to keep them distinct (Fenlason & Beehr, 1994), making it difficult to draw conclusions from social support research when different operational definitions are used.

McIntosh (1991) sought to clarify some of the conceptual confusion surrounding the concept of social support. Her definition was: "resources (actual or perceived by a focal person) available from one or more others to assist the focal person in the management of stress experiences and to increase the experience of well-being" (p. 202). She also proposed the following components or properties of support: Number of providers of the resource, amount of the resource available, and perceived adequacy of the resource. Interestingly, the first dimension, number of providers of support, is still an often-overlooked dimension by researchers. Perhaps because support is often viewed as a coping technique, we often think that more is better, but that may not be the case (Cohen & Wills, 1985). Adequacy of the amount of support one receives is a useful concept, as stress researchers often define job stress as a persistent level of demand that exceeds the individual's resources (such as support), leaving the person with a poor fit with their environment (e.g. French et al., 1974). In a sample of hospital nurses, the only dimension of support proposed by McIntosh (1991) that had a main effect on reducing stressors was adequacy of support. The amount of support was shown to have a buffering effect whereby more support reduced the relationship between patient death (a stressor for hospital nurses) and nurses' emotional exhaustion. Interestingly, reverse buffering effects (in which more social support strengthens instead of weakens the aversive effects of stressors on the person) were found for amount of support in the relationship of workload to emotional exhaustion as well as for support adequacy as a moderator of the relationship between workload and physical symptoms. Although a reverse buffering effect is counterintuitive, other researchers have often found reverse buffering effects of support (e.g. Deelstra et al., 2003; Devereux et al., 2009; Elfering et al., 2002), which is a topic for discussion in the next section.

Despite the several possible types of social support described above, researchers most often consider social support along two basic dimensions: Source of support (who provides it, e.g. supervisor versus spouse) and type or nature of support (e.g. instrumental versus emotional) (House, 1981; Cohen & Wills, 1985). Although we have described the various *types* of support above, we have not yet examined the *source*. In the workplace, we are often concerned with supervisor support, which is a factor in many leadership theories. Leader-Member Exchange theory (Gerstner & Day, 1997; Schriesheim et al., 1999) is a prime example. It focuses on the dyadic exchange relationship between the supervisor and subordinate. Much of the supervisor's role is support, with supervisors providing clarification on assignments, offering additional resources, or simply checking in to monitor performance. These may all be considered types of support, and although the assumed goal of support in leadership theory and research may be to enhance subordinates' performance, such support may also help reduce their stressors and/or strains. These are examples of instrumental support (i.e. they are instrumental in helping get the job done or in easing stressors). Supervisors are especially well-positioned to provide instrumental support, although they also can provide other types of support.

Coworkers are another source of support in the workplace. The nature of the relationship between an employee and a coworker is probably different from the supervisor-subordinate relationship, and so we might expect to see more forms of emotional support rather than instrumental support from one's coworkers (although they can also provide instrumental support). A longitudinal study of 2,034 employees from 21 Dutch companies found that coworkers provided more support, but supervisory support was more causally related to reducing work stressors (Marcelissen et al., 1988). Support from supervisors was found to reduce stressors such as role ambiguity, role overload, role conflict, and job uncertainty for manual laborers, which makes sense given that manual laborers are more likely to need supervisory instruction to successfully perform their job. They found hardly any causal evidence that coworker support lowered stressors. Additionally, Ng and Sorenson (2008) performed a meta-analysis of the relationships between support and work attitudes and found that perceived supervisor support was more strongly related to such work outcomes as job satisfaction, affective commitment, and turnover intention than coworker support was. Supervisors have position power over employees, and their support may be more effective as a means to reduce stressors and improve outcomes for workers than coworker support. Organizations should consider this as they design supportive interventions, and even as they select and train managers. Managers with greater emotional intelligence and both the ability and willingness to provide support may be able to help their subordinates a great deal.

A more global source of support in the workplace is the supportiveness of the whole organization, which is similar in some ways to having a supportive organizational culture. Perceived organizational support is the extent to which the organization values employees' contributions and cares for their well-being (Eisenberger et al., 1986). It is positively related to job performance (Eisenberger et al., 1990), and negatively related to absenteeism (Eisenberger et al., 1990) and turnover intentions (Guzzo et al., 1994). Perceived organizational support has been criticized more than the other sources of support, as being too conceptually muddy; some suggest that it is an employee reaction similar to organizational commitment or general job satisfaction (Shore & Tetrick, 1991) but factor analyses confirmed that perceived organizational support is distinct from organizational commitment (e.g. Eisenberger et al., 1990; Shore & Tetrick, 1991) and job satisfaction (Eisenberger et al., 1997).

In the work-family conflict literature, family-specific support is often examined (i.e. family-specific organizational support; Allen, 2001), with the idea that supervisors and organizations should provide support to help accommodate employees' various family and personal demands. A meta-analysis of the relationship between various types of organizational support and work-family conflict showed that work-family specific support (both supervisor support and organization support) was more negatively related to work-family conflict than general support was, and that work-family support from the organization was a mediator of the supervisor support-work-family conflict relationship (Kossek et al., 2011), meaning that employees who received supervisor work-family support might perceive that the whole organization supports families. Perceived organizational support, particularly family-specific support, therefore seems to be an important source of workplace support that supervisors can influence. Organizations can easily provide a measure of perceived organizational support in an annual employee opinion survey to monitor it, and could tie in interventions with supervisors to improve organizational support in their annual results.

Even though we are examining the role of support in the workplace, another important source of support for employees is from family or friends. Employees often rely on people outside the organization, especially their families, to provide them with support, particularly emotional support. Because they are not in the workplace, it is harder for them to provide the typical kinds of instrumental support that could help reduce workplace stressors. Family support has been found to be beneficial in buffering the effects of work stress (e.g. Greenglass et al., 1994), but reverse buffering effects have also been found (e.g. Lim & Lee, 2011), suggesting the relationship may be quite complex. Stoner et al. (2011) also show a complex relationship behind family support; for individuals who had low perceived supervisor loyalty yet high family support, there was a stronger relationship between a breach of the psychological contract with the organization and intention to turnover. Support from one's friends or family may thus not always have the intended effect of helping the person deal with stress; in some cases, the support might even lead to encouraging the person to find a new job with another employer, thus creating turnover from the perspective of the current employer.

Which type of support is most important?

It may be that some elements of social support are more central to its role as a coping technique and may even have a greater influence on strains. There is a general belief that emotional support is the most important or consequential aspect of support (LaRocco et al., 1980). This may be due to the fact that social support is such a humanistic concept that people immediately think of the emotional connection when they think of support, and indeed it may be that simply connecting with another individual on an emotional level is more important than providing specific or tangible assistance. Semmer et al. (2008) investigated the role of emotional support further. In a qualitative analysis of reports of support from hospital patients, they demonstrated that although the emotional component is tantamount to the success of support, even instrumental support may have an emotional component. For example, a coworker voluntarily providing instrumental support about how to use a computer program (rather than a person from IT doing this as part of their job requirements) might carry with it an emotional meaning. The recipient of support feels that the coworker who is voluntarily giving support is doing it because they care, and that emotional component might be responsible for reducing strains or reducing the stressor-strain relationship.

Social support and individual outcomes

Social support and stress: The role social support plays in the stressor-strain relationship

Stress has many different meanings and operationalizations (e.g. Beehr and Franz, 1986; Jex et al., 1992). We use the terms stressors and strains to refer to the antecedents to and consequences of the stress process, respectively. The simplest conceptualization of the relationship between social support and stressors and strains suggests three potential relationships (e.g. Beehr, 1985; House, 1981; Dormann & Zapf, 1999): 1) Social support has a direct effect on strains; 2) buffering effects, in which social support moderates the stressor-strain relationship such that stressors are less strongly related to strains in the presence of social support; and 3) social support has a direct effect on stressors (Ganster et al., 1986). The first two are the more likely and have been studied the most.

Direct effect of social support on strains

Social support can affect the stressor-strain process by directly reducing strains. This is consistent with the idea that social support is a coping method. In their meta-analysis, Viswesvaran et al. (1999) tested several models of social support and stress, and they found the most support for this model, with social support significantly leading to reduced strains ($r = -.21$). Interestingly, Marcelissen et al.'s (1988) longitudinal study found that affective strains and worry may elicit less support, which may bring into question the direction of causality in the social support-strain relationship. Do people who experience more support really have lower strains as a result, or do people who experience strains receive less support? Individuals experiencing stress might be unaware that they are making themselves unavailable to potential support givers (Beehr & McGrath, 1992). Another possible mechanism is that some stressed people may not be enjoyable to be around for people who could offer support (i.e. it is depressing to interact with depressed people).

Buffering effect of social support

By far the most popular, alluring, and complex way that social support affects the stressor-strain relationship is the process whereby social support moderates the relationship between stressors and strains. That is, high support might reduce the strength of the relationship between stressors and strains (Beehr & McGrath, 1992). Research findings have been mixed, however, with some even finding the reverse buffering effects noted earlier (e.g. Deelstra, et al., 2003; Devereux et al., 2009; Elfering et al., 2002; Glaser et al., 1999; Kaufmann & Beehr, 1986; Kickul & Posig, 2001; McIntosh, 1991). Thus it is not clear how strong the results really are for buffering effects of social support (Beehr, 1985; Beehr et al., 2000). Although the meta-analysis by Viswesvaran et al. (1999) concluded there was overall support for social support as a moderator of the relationship between stressors and strains ($R^2 = .03$), they apparently included effects of reverse buffering and buffering without regard to the direction of the moderation effect in the same calculation, resulting in over-reporting of buffering effects.

One proposal to explain the mixed findings in social support research is the matching/specificity hypothesis (Cohen and Wills, 1985), in which the type of support should be matched with the type of stressor, strain, and/or outcome. Thus more related types of support will show a stronger buffering effect, for example supervisor support will buffer the relationship between role ambiguity and job satisfaction, because they are both affected by the supervisor. Although some studies have found support for this idea (e.g. Terry et al., 1993), the meta-analysis (Viswesvaran et al., 1999) did not. Additionally, Beehr et al. (2003)

examined source congruence as a moderator (i.e. did the source of the stressor and support match?), and it made little difference in buffering effects of support on the relationship between stressors and strains.

Other effects of support

In addition to direct effects of support on strains and buffering effects of support on the relationship between stressors and strains, other models have been proposed. Social support may, for instance, reduce stressors (Kahn & Byosiere, 1992; Viswesvaran et al., 1999), which has been explained through the concept of appraisal, i.e. someone who feels supported is less likely to appraise a situation as a threat in the first place (Cohen & Wills, 1985). Another common process model is that social support may serve as a mediator of the stressor-strain relationship. Viswesvaran et al. (1999) proposed eight competing process mechanisms in total, however, and the best model was for social support directly affecting strains.

Social support and work-related outcomes

> Richard finds, in discussions with his coworkers, that he is not the only one experiencing overload and dissatisfaction. His coworkers also think that their supervisors have unrealistic expectations and frequently fail to provide clarification. The coworkers who have been there the longest say that things have always been like that. Furthermore, Richard's colleagues note that supervisors are never understanding about personal obligations and family demands and that the organizational policies do not allow for enough flexibility. Workers who do take time off for family demands never seem to be able to move up in the organization. His coworkers get Richard thinking about how negative the work environment is, which makes his dissatisfaction grow. He finds himself just going through the motions at work, unable to focus and feeling emotionally detached from his job. He starts calling in sick more frequently and begins to look for jobs elsewhere.

Now that we have looked at the various mechanisms through which social support can affect individual outcomes like health and well-being, it is also important to consider the research regarding more work-related outcomes. Even though social support researchers were initially concerned more with personal strains, a great deal of research has now examined various workplace outcomes as well.

Social support and job performance

If there is no positive impact on the "bottom line", management will be unlikely to approve programs aimed at increasing support for employees. Unfortunately, like much research on social support, the findings regarding job performance have been mixed. Social support has been shown to be related to job performance in special samples, e.g. in a sample of traffic enforcement agents, support was positively associated with productivity (i.e. number of summonses generated; Baruch-Feldman et al., 2002). There is some debate, also, about which source of support is more predictive of performance. In a sample of hospital nurses, AbuAlRub (2004) found that perceived social support from coworkers was correlated with improved job performance. Other studies suggest, however, that supervisor support was related to job performance but coworker support was not (e.g. Baruch-Feldman et al., 2002; Blau, 1981). A recent meta-analysis of coworker support and work outcomes concluded, however, that coworker support had an effect on performance even while controlling for some stressors and employee attitudes (Chiaburu & Harrison, 2008).

Social support and job satisfaction

Many individuals seek work, in part, to be connected with others socially (a latent function of work; Paul & Batinic, 2010). Some retirees even seek work after retirement (a trend termed "bridge employment", e.g. Shultz, 2003), often because they miss the social aspect of working. It makes sense, therefore, that socially connected workers are happier workers, and the literature has documented the relationship between social support and job satisfaction (e.g. Baruch-Feldman et al., 2002; Harris et al., 2001; Smith & Tziner, 1998; Winstead et al., 1995). There is again some evidence to suggest that the type and source of support is important. For instance, some studies (e.g. Bahniuk et al., 1990; Harris et al., 2007) found that instrumental support from colleagues and mentoring support were related to higher levels of job satisfaction, but coaching and collegial support were not. Regarding source of support, a meta-analysis showed that supervisor support was more strongly related to job satisfaction than coworker support was (effect size of .52 versus .37; Ng & Sorenson, 2008). Finally, a more in-depth examination of the support-satisfaction link looked for moderators. In their meta-analysis, Ng and Sorenson (2008) note that the relationships of supervisor and coworker support with job satisfaction were moderated by job type (customer-contact vs. non-customer contact jobs) but not by gender or organizational tenure; those with customer-contact jobs had a stronger relationship between support and satisfaction.

Social support and absenteeism, turnover, and burnout

Regarding negative workplace outcomes, absenteeism, turnover, and burnout are three prominent outcomes in research on social support. Burnout is a state characterized by emotional exhaustion, depersonalizing other people at work or feeling cynical about them, and feelings of low personal accomplishment (Maslach & Jackson, 1986). There is evidence that social support is negatively related to job burnout (e.g. Baruch-Feldman et al., 2002; Northrop, 1997). Regarding source of support, two studies found that family support was more closely related to job burnout than supervisor support was (among traffic enforcement agents in Baruch-Feldman et al., 2002 and among teachers in Greenglass et al., 1994). A meta-analysis by Halbesleben (2006), however, found that social support was negatively related to burnout regardless of the source of support, although work sources of support were more strongly related to exhaustion and non-work sources were more strongly related to the two other components of burnout, depersonalization, and feelings of low personal accomplishment.

Social support has also typically been a predictor of absenteeism and turnover. Regarding source of support, in their meta-analysis, Ng and Sorenson (2008) showed that supervisor support was more strongly related to turnover intentions (–.36) than coworker support (–.19). Pomaki et al. (2010) found that social support was negatively related to turnover intentions and also served as a moderator of the relationship between work demands and turnover intentions, such that having higher support reduced the relationship between work demands and turnover intentions. Finally, they found job satisfaction mediated the support-turnover intention relationship (i.e. support led to job satisfaction, which led to less turnover).

Although social support is generally thought to have a positive impact on workplace outcomes, it has sometimes been linked to a variety of negative outcomes (Harris et al., 2007), including burnout (Myung-Yong & Harrison, 1998) and depression and anxiety (El-Bassel et al., 1998; Olson & Shultz, 1994). These conflicting findings show how much we still have to discover about the complex nomological network surrounding the construct. One study suggests that providing social support in the workplace is a nuanced proposition; it can even be provided in ways that might be demeaning or unhelpful (Beehr et al., 2010). More research is needed in this area to understand the conditions in which support is perceived as being harmful instead of helpful.

Special considerations in social support

Characteristics of the recipient of support

Some research suggests that characteristics of the person receiving support can affect its availability or use (Eckenrode, 1983). People who have a positive attitude toward help, high self-esteem, are religious, and who have high moral values (Dunkel-Schetter et al., 1987), have a self-supporting personality (Xia et al., 2012), are extroverted (Swickert et al., 2002), and have an internal locus of control (VanderZee et al., 1997) tend to receive more social support or perceive its availability more.

There have been several suggested reasons for some people receiving less support. An important question is whether individuals who receive less support are going to experience more strains (as most researchers assume) or whether people who are experiencing strains are less likely to receive support. Dunkel-Schetter et al. (1987) suggest that those who report low support might be uncomfortable about receiving help, which would keep them from seeking it or may even make others less likely to volunteer it. As noted earlier, Marcelissen et al. (1988), in one of the few longitudinal field studies to examine this question, found that coworkers reduced support when strains were present (i.e. strains predicted lower support) however supervisors did not reduce support. They explained that this may be because coworkers who were giving support may be doing so voluntarily, and supervisors may be giving support because it is part of their jobs. Negative traits are typically negatively associated with support, which makes sense particularly with voluntary support. Social support has been shown to be negatively correlated to neuroticism (Swickert, 2009), pessimism (Hasan & Kathem, 2003), negative affectivity (Zellars & Perrewé, 2001), and trait anger (Baruch-Feldman et al., 2002). It may be that people are reluctant to help someone who is in a bad mood or may even fear that the person will be unpleasant toward their attempts at help. Of course, this relationship might also be spurious; negative people may simply be more negative regarding their perceptions of support.

Gender and support

Traditional gender roles suggest that women are oriented to be more social creatures. Therefore one might expect to find women receiving more support, particularly emotional support. Indeed some research has found that women are more likely to use social support to cope with work stress (e.g. Hurst & Hurst, 1997; Thompson et al., 2001). Overall, however, research on gender and social support has been mixed (Matud et al., 2003), with some finding differences in type or source of support. For example, Fusilier et al. (1986) found that women reported receiving more supervisor support but there were no differences in coworker or family support. Others failed to find any sex differences in support in the workplace (where men and women had the same job responsibilities; Baruch-Feldman et al., 2002).

Interestingly, Reevy (1995) found that sex role differences, and not sex itself, was related to the receipt of specific types of support, with femininity associated with seeking and receiving support, particularly emotional support. Masculinity was associated with seeking certain types of tangible support. In addition, Beehr et al. (2003) also found that, for people high in femininity, the relationships between social support and dissatisfaction and psychological strains were stronger. Matud et al. (2003) further give credence to the notion that sex role or gender role identity might be important, as their data supported separate models of social support for men and women; for men, support could be separated into two factors (emotional and instrumental) but women tended to generalize support. These studies highlight the need to further examine the role that sex, sex role stereotypes, and gender play on the experience of social support.

Age and support

Social support may change as we age. Antonucci (1985) discussed the idea that parents must give their children lots of support early in life but that, as the child and parent age, this balance shifts with the parent eventually having to rely on the child for support, a concept he terms "the support bank". Epidemiological research has documented a link between maintaining social contact and both mental and physical well-being (Seeman, 1996). It is important, therefore, for researchers to consider whether support changes over time so that appropriate support interventions could be designed for the elderly. Krause (1999) examined a three-year longitudinal sample of older people and found changes in received support; however these changes were not uniform or as consistent as would be expected. They were more consistent with regard to available support than received support. Krause (1999) also concluded that elderly people tend to provide less tangible support over time, but that is not true for emotional and information support, which tend to not change over time. More research is needed to uncover the nature of the changes in support, both given and received, over time for the elderly.

Culture and support

There is evidence that support experiences may differ by culture, but there is limited research in this area. Beehr and Glazer (2001) provide a literature review and contend that culture influences individuals' perceptions of the type and source of support. They propose links between Schwartz's (1994, 1999) cultural typology (conservatism vs. autonomy, egalitarianism vs. hierarchy, harmony vs. mastery) with specific types and sources of support, some of which were later tested by Glazer (2006) in a sample of over 15,000 employees in five geographic regions within a multinational company. Glazer (2006) found support for many of the propositions. Latinos, Anglos, and Western Europeans perceived more supervisor emotional support than Asians, and Anglos and Western Europeans perceived more supervisor emotional support than Eastern Europeans. Glazer (2006) explains that Anglo and Western European cultures might enjoy recognition from their supervisor more than other cultures, and that Asian cultures, which place greater emphasis on maintaining the status quo, might be uncomfortable with the imbalance created by receiving support from their supervisor in front of their colleagues. Glazer (2006) also noted that regions high in autonomy values, including Anglo and Western European countries, reported the lowest coworker instrumental support. Still further research is needed to examine cross-cultural differences in other types and sources of support.

Social support: Moving forward

The research surrounding social support is complex, as we have seen with the concepts of reverse buffering and the conflicting results surrounding gender and other concepts related to support. Instead of taking a piecemeal approach to studies, as many researchers do by examining a specific type of support with a specific outcome, more work needs to be done to understand the entire nomological network surrounding the construct. To that end, we have several suggestions for moving forward.

Antecedents of support. Studies often concern themselves with outcomes of support rather than considering what might increase support, or even what might precipitate harmful as opposed to helpful support.

Research about the characteristics of support givers and about how personal characteristics interplay with social support will help us further our understanding of its antecedents.

Available versus received support. Although received and available social support are related to each other, they may be very different and have different causes and effects. People seem to react well when they believe support is available to them, but they might react differently to support once it is offered, perhaps due to the nature or the source of the support.

Testing models of social support. As many process mechanisms have been proposed for social support (e.g. Lim & Lee, 2011; Viswesvaran et al., 1999), more studies are called for that are longitudinal in nature to help draw causal connections. Additionally, the measures that are used to study social support need to be considered, as Haber et al. (2007) found that scale-type moderated the relationship between received support and outcomes. This is concerning for researchers trying to draw conclusions across multiple studies of support. Finally, the majority of research has also relied on self-report data, even for those that distinguish between received and available support (e.g. Cohen et al., 2005). Each type might require different forms of measurement and different process models.

The buffering/reverse buffering effects of social support. Research is mixed on whether social support serves as a buffer of the stressor-strain relationship, and more investigation is needed to determine in which conditions social support improves versus worsens that relationship. One way to examine this is by looking for higher-order interactions to find additional moderators (Beehr & McGrath, 1992). Although some have tried this without success (e.g. Ganster et al., 1986), a recent study found a three-way interaction of strength of team identification, coworker support, and role stressors predicting psychological well-being (Jimmieson et al., 2010). Employees high in both support and team identification had a stronger negative relationship between role ambiguity and psychological well-being (i.e. they found a reverse-buffering effect, which was counter to their hypothesis). Additionally, more research on special populations (e.g. different cultures, genders, ages, or generations) may help further our understanding of moderators of this relationship. In other words, examining how social support might differ between and within these special groups may help us understand more about when support is helpful instead of harmful.

Practical implications and conclusion

Given the confusing and sometimes contradictory nature of the research on social support, caution should be exercised when designing interventions for practice. It is likely, overall, to have weak but beneficial effects on people's well-being, but secondary effects (e.g. reverse buffering) occasionally occur that complicate the effects of support. Lakey and Cohen (2000) stress the importance of designing social support interventions that are based on sound theory and empirically sound models, instead of intuitive models that might be easy to sell but might not get results. House (1981) and McIntosh (1991) suggest that social support has such a weak effect on reducing strains that companies are better off trying to improve work conditions to reduce stressors first. This is consistent with a preventive coping approach, with the idea that reduction of stressors means fewer strains will be present because there is no longer anything to cope with. The buffering effect, or at times, reverse buffering effect of social support is certainly complex, as McIntosh (1991) pointed out by examining higher-order moderator effects. She recommends that because sometimes too much support can be harmful, organizations should be careful before initiating any support interventions to consider the "optimum" level of support. The research we reviewed on personality characteristics suggests that the personality of the recipient needs to be taken into account as well. Finally, our examination of the research also seems to point to the greater effectiveness of supervisor versus coworker support for helping employees. Organizations should therefore consider training aimed at supervisors to encourage support-giving behaviors as opposed to general programs for all employees.

References

AbuAlRub, R. F. (2004). Job stress, job performance, and social support among hospital nurses, *Journal of Nursing Scholarship*, *36*(1), 73–78.

Allen, T. D. (2001). Family-supportive work environments: The role of organizational perceptions, *Journal of Vocational Behavior*, *58*, 414–435.

Antonucci, T. C. (1985). Personal characteristics, social support, and social behavior: in R. H. Binstock & L. K. George (eds) *Handbook of Aging and the Social Sciences* (pp. 205–226). New York: Academic Press.

Bahniuk, M. H., Dobos, J., & Hill, S. K. (1990). The impact of mentoring, collegial support, and information adequacy on career success: A replication, *Journal of Social Behavior and Personality*, *5*(4), 431–452.

Barrera, M. (1986). Distinctions between social support concepts, measures, and models, *American Journal of Community Psychology*, *14*(4), 413–445.

Baruch-Feldman, C., Brondolo, E., Ben-Dayan, D., & Schwartz, J. (2002). Sources of social support and burnout, job satisfaction, and productivity, *Journal of Occupational Health Psychology*, 7(1), 84–93.

Beehr, T. A. (1985). The role of social support in coping with organizational stress: in T. A. Beehr & R. S. Bhagat (eds) *Human Stress and Cognition in Organizations: An Integrated Perspective* (pp. 375–398). New York: John Wiley & Sons.

Beehr, T. A., Bowling, N. A., & Bennett, M. M. (2010). Occupational stress and failures of social support: When helping hurts, *Journal of Occupational Health Psychology*, 15(1), 45–59.

Beehr, T. A., Farmer, S. J., Glazer, S., Gudanowski, D. M., & Nair, V. N. (2003). The enigma of social support and occupational stress: Source congruence and gender role effects, *Journal of Occupational Health Psychology*, 8(3), 220–231.

Beehr, T. A. & Franz, T. M. (1986). The current debate about the meaning of job stress, *Journal of Organizational Behavior Management*, 8(2), 5–18.

Beehr, T. A. & Glazer, S. (2001). A cultural perspective of social support in relation to occupational stress: in P. Perrewé, D. C. Ganster, & J. Moran (eds) *Research in Occupational Stress and Well-Being* (pp. 97–142). Greenwich, CO: JAI Press.

Beehr, T. A., Jex, S. M., Stacy, B. A., & Murray, M. A. (2000). Work stressors and coworker support as predictors of individual strain and job performance, *Journal of Organizational Behavior*, 21, 391–405.

Beehr, T. A. & McGrath, J. E. (1992). Social support, occupational stress and anxiety, *Anxiety, Stress, and Coping*, 5, 7–19.

Blau, G. (1981). An empirical investigation of job stress, social support, service length, and job strain, *Organizational Behavior and Human Performance*, 27(2), 279–302.

Blum, D. (1994). *The Monkey Wars*. New York: Oxford University Press.

Caplan, G. (1974). *Support Systems and Community Mental Health: Lectures on Concept Development*. New York: Behavioral Publications.

Cassel, J. (1974a). An epidemiological perspective of psychosocial factors in disease etiology, *American Journal of Public Health*, 64, 1040–1043.

Cassel, J. (1974b). Psychosocial processes and "stress": Theoretical formulations, *International Journal of Health Services*, 4, 471–482.

Chiaburu, D. S. & Harrison, D. A. (2008). Do peers make the place? Conceptual synthesis and meta-analysis of coworker effects on perceptions, attitudes, OCBs, and performance, *Journal of Applied Psychology*, 93(5), 1082–1103.

Cobb, S. (1976). Social support as a moderator of life stress, *Psychosomatic Medicine*, 38, 300–314.

Cohen, J. L., Lakey, B., Tiell, K., & Neeley, L. C. (2005). Recipient-provider agreement on enacted support, perceived support, and provider personality, *Psychological Assessment*, 17(3), 375–378.

Cohen, S., Gottlieb, B. H., & Underwood, L. G. (2000). Social relationships and health: in S. Cohen, B. H. Gottlieb, & L. G. Underwood (eds) *Social Support Measurement and Intervention: A Guide for the Health and Social Scientists* (pp. 3–25). New York: Oxford University Press.

Cohen, S. & Wills, T. A. (1985). Stress, social support, and the buffering hypothesis, *Psychological Bulletin*, 98(2), 310–357.

Deelstra, J. T., Peeters, M. C. W., Schaufeli, W. B., Stroebe, W., & Zijlstra, F. R. H. (2003). Receiving instrumental support at work: When help is not welcome, *Journal of Applied Psychology*, 88(2), 324–331.

Devereux, J. M., Hastings, R. P., Noone, S. J., Firth, A., & Totsika, V. (2009). Social support and coping as mediators or moderators of the impact of work stressors on burnout in intellectual disability support staff, *Research in Developmental Disabilities*, 30(2), 367–377.

Dormann, C. & Zapf, D. (1999). Social support, social stressors at work, and depressive symptoms: Testing for main and moderating effects with structural equations in a three-wave longitudinal study, *Journal of Applied Psychology*, 84(6), 874–884.

Dunkel-Schetter, C., Folkman, S., & Lazarus, R. S. (1987). Correlates of social support receipt, *Journal of Personality and Social Psychology*, 53(1), 71–80.

Durkheim, E. (1951). *Suicide: A Study in Sociology*. Glencoe: The Free Press.

Eckenrode, J. (1983). The mobilization of social supports: Some individual constraints, *American Journal of Community Psychology*, 11(5), 509–528.

Eisenberger, R., Cummings, J., Armeli, S., & Lynch, P. (1997). Perceived organizational support, discretionary treatment, and job satisfaction, *Journal of Applied Psychology*, 82(5), 812–820.

Eisenberger, R., Huntington, R., Hutchison, S., & Sowa, D. (1986). Perceived organizational support, *Journal of Applied Psychology*, 71, 500–507.

Eisenberger, R., Fasolo, P., & Davis-LaMastro, V. (1990). Perceived organizational support and employee diligence, commitment, and innovation, *Journal of Applied Psychology*, 75(1), 51–59.

El-Bassel, N., Guterman, N., Bargal, D., & Su, K. H. (1998). Main and buffering effects of emotional support on job- and health-related strains: A national survey of Israeli social workers, *Employee Assistance Quarterly*, 13(3), 1–18.

Elfering, A., Semmer, N. K., Schade, V., Grund, S., & Boos, N. (2002). Supportive colleague, unsupportive supervisor: The role of provider-specific constellations of social support at work in the development of low back pain, *Journal of Occupational Health Psychology*, 7(2), 130–140.

Fenlason, K. J. & Beehr, T. A. (1994). Social support and occupational stress: Effects of talking to others, *Journal of Organizational Behavior (1986–1998)*, 15(2), 157–175.

Finch, J. F., Okun, M. A., Pool, G. J., & Ruehlman, L. S. (1999). A comparison of the influence of conflictual and supportive social interactions on psychological distress, *Journal of Personality*, 67(4), 581–622.

French, J. R. P., Jr., Rodgers, W., & Cobb, S. (1974). Adjustment as person-environment fit: in G. V. Coelho, D. A. Hamburg, & J. E. Adams (eds) *Coping and Adaptation* (pp. 316–333). New York: Basic Books.

Fusilier, M. R., Ganster, D. C., & Mayes, B. T. (1986). The social support and health relationship: Is there a gender difference? *Journal of Occupational Psychology*, 59(2), 145–153.

Ganster, D. C., Fusilier, M. R., & Mayes, B. T. (1986). Role of social support in the experience of stress at work, *Journal of Applied Psychology*, 71(1), 102–110.

Gerstner, C. R. & Day, D. V. (1997). Meta-analytic review of leader-member exchange theory: Correlates and construct issues, *Journal of Applied Psychology*, 82(6), 827–844.

Glaser, D. N., Tatum, B. C., Nebeker, D. M., Sorenson, R. C., & Aiello, J. R. (1999). Workload and social support: Effects on performance and stress, *Human Performance*, *12*(2), 155–176.

Glazer, S. (2006). Social support across cultures, *International Journal of Intercultural Relations*, *30*(5), 605–622.

Greenglass, E. R., Fiksenbaum, L., & Burke, R. J. (1994). The relationship between social support and burnout over time in teachers, *Journal of Social Behavior and Personality*, *9*(2), 219–230.

Guzzo, R. A., Noonan, K. A., & Elfran, E. (1994). Expatriate managers and the psychological contract, *Journal of Applied Psychology*, *79*(4), 617–626.

Haber, M. G., Cohen, J. L., Lucas, T., & Baltes, B. B. (2007). The relationship between self-reported received and perceived social support: A meta-analytic review, *American Journal of Community Psychology*, *39*, 133–144.

Halbesleben, J. R. B. (2006). Sources of social support and burnout: A meta-analytic test of the conservation of resources model, *Journal of Applied Psychology*, *91*(5), 1134–1145.

Haney, C. & Lynch, M. (1997). Regulating prisons of the future: A psychological analysis of Supermax and solitary confinement, *New York University Review of Law and Social Change*, *23*, 477–570.

Harlow, H. F. (1965). Total social isolation: Effects on Macaque monkey behavior, *Science*, *148*(3670), 666.

Harris, J. I., Moritzen, S. K., Robitschek, C., Imhoff, A., & Lynch, J. L. A. (2001). The comparative contributions of congruence and social support in career outcomes, *The Career Development Quarterly*, *49*(4), 314–323.

Harris, J. I., Winskowski, A. M., & Engdahl, B. E. (2007). Types of workplace social support in the prediction of job satisfaction, *The Career Development Quarterly*, *56*(2), 150–156.

Hasan, A. S. & Kathem, A. M. (2003). Optimism and pessimism in relation to test anxiety and social support, *Dirasat: Educational Sciences*, *30*(2), 290–304.

Heller, K. & Swindle, R. W. (1983). Social networks, perceived social support, and coping with stress: in R. D. Felner, L. A. Jason, J. N. Moritsugu, & S. S. Farber (eds) *Preventive Psychology: Theory, Research, and Practice* (pp. 87–103). New York: Pergamon.

Hill, K., Barton, M., & Hurtado, A. M. (2009). The emergence of human uniqueness: Characters underlying behavioral modernity, *Evolutionary Anthropology*, *18*, 187–200.

House, J. S. (1981). *Work Stress and Social Support*. Reading, MA: Addison-Wesley.

House, J. S. & Kahn, R. L. (1985). *Social Support and Health*. San Diego, CA: Academic Press.

Hurst, T. E. & Hurst, M. M. (1997). Gender differences in mediation of severe occupational stress among correctional officers, *American Journal of Criminal Justice*, *22*(1), 121–137.

Jex, S. M., Beehr, T. A., & Roberts, C. K. (1992). The meaning of occupational stress items to survey respondents, *Journal of Applied Psychology*, *77*(5), 623–628.

Jimmieson, N. L., McKimmie, B. M., Hannam, R. L., & Gallagher, J. (2010). An investigation of the stress-buffering effects of social support in the occupational stress process as a function of team identification, *Group Dynamics: Theory, Research, and Practice*, *14*(4), 350–367.

Kahn, R. L. & Byosiere, P. (1992). Stress in organizations: in R. L. Kahn & P. Byosiere (eds) *Handbook of Industrial and Organizational Psychology* (Vol. 3, 2nd ed., pp. 571–650). Palo Alto, CA: Consulting Psychologists Press.

Kaufmann, G. M. & Beehr, T. A. (1986). Interactions between job stressors and social support: Some counterintuitive results, *Journal of Applied Psychology*, 71(3), 522–526.

Kendrick, K. M. (2004). The neurology of social bonds, *Journal of Neuroendocrinology*, 16, 1007–1008.

Kickul, J. & Posig, M. (2001). Supervisory emotional support and burnout: An explanation of reverse buffering effects, *Journal of Managerial Issues*, 13(3), 328–344.

Kleiman, E. M., Riskind, J. H., Schaefer, K. E., & Weingarden, H. C. (2012). The moderating role of social support on the relationship between impulsivity and suicide risk, *The Journal of Crisis Intervention and Suicide Prevention*, 33(5), 273–279.

Kossek, E. E., Pichler, S., Bodner, T., & Hammer, L.B. (2011). Workplace social support and work-family conflict: A meta-analysis clarifying the influence of general and work-family-specific supervisor and organizational support, *Personnel Psychology*, 64, 289–313.

Krause, N. (1999). Assessing change in social support during late life, *Research on Aging*, 21(4), 539–569.

Lakey, B. & Cohen, S. (2000). Social support theory and measurement: in B. Lakey & S. Cohen (eds) *Social Support Measurement and Intervention: A Guide for Health and Social Scientists* (pp. 29–52). New York: Oxford University Press.

LaRocco, J. M., House, J. S., & French, J. R. (1980). Social support, occupational stress, and health, *Journal of Health and Social Behavior*, 21(3), 202–218.

Leavy, R. L. (1983). Social support and psychological disorder: A review, *Journal of Community Psychology*, 11, 3–21.

Lim, S. & Lee, A. (2011). Work and nonwork outcomes of workplace incivility: Does family support help? *Journal of Occupational Health Psychology*, 16(1), 95–111.

Marcelissen, F. H. G., Winnubst, J. A. M., Buunk, B., & DeWolff, C. J. (1988). *Social Science and Medicine*, 26(3), 365–373.

Maslach, C. & Jackson, S. E. (1986). *Maslach Burnout Inventory: Manual* (2nd ed.). Palo Alto, CA: Consulting Psychologists Press.

Maslow, A. H. (1943). A theory on human motivation, *Psychological Review*, 50(4), 370–396.

Matud, M. P., Ibáñez, I., Bethencourt, J. M., Marrero, R., & Carballeira, M. (2003). Structural gender differences in perceived social support, *Personality and Individual Differences*, 35(8), 1919–1929.

McIntosh, N. J. (1991). Identification and investigation of properties of social support, *Journal of Organizational Behavior*, 12, 201–217.

Miller, N. D. (1995). International protection of the rights of prisoners: Is solitary confinement in the United States a violation of international standards? *California International Western Law Journal*, 26, 139–169.

Myung-Yong, U. & Harrison, D. F. (1998). Role stressors, burnout, mediators, and job satisfaction: A stress–strain–outcome model and an empirical test, *Social Work Research*, 22(2), 100–115.

Nagasawa, M., Okabe, S., Mogi, K., & Kikusui, T. (2012). Oxytocin and mutual communication in mother-infant bonding, *Frontiers in Human Neuroscience*, 6(31), 1–10.

Ng, T. W. H. & Sorensen, K. L. (2008). Toward a further understanding of the relationships between perceptions of support and work attitudes: A meta-analysis, *Group and Organization Management*, 33(3), 243–268.

Norris, F. H. & Kaniasty, K. (1996). Received and perceived social support in times of stress: A test of the social support deterrence model, *Journal of Personality and Social Psychology*, 71(3), 498–511.

Northrop, L. M. E. (1997). Stress, social support, and burnout in nursing home staff (Doctoral dissertation). Retrieved from ProQuest Information and Learning (AAM9716373).

Olson, D. A. & Shultz, K. S. (1994). Gender differences in the dimensionality of social support, *Journal of Applied Social Psychology*, 24(14), 1221–1232.

Paul, K. I. & Batinic, B. (2010). The need for work: Jahoda's latent functions of employment in a representative of the German population, *Journal of Organizational Behavior*, 31(1), 45–64.

Pomaki, G., DeLongis, A., Frey, D., Short, K., & Woehrle, T. (2010). When the going gets tough: Direct, buffering and indirect effects of social support on turnover intention, *Teaching and Teacher Education*, 26(6), 1340–1346.

Reevy, G. M. (1995). Sex-related and gender differences in sources and types of sought and received social support (Doctoral dissertation). Retrieved from ProQuest Information and Learning (AAM9504970).

Russell, D. W., Booth, B., Reed, D., & Laughlin, P. R. (1997). Personality, social networks, and perceived social support among alcoholics: A structural equation analysis, *Journal of Personality*, 65(3), 649–692.

Schachter, S. (1959). *The Psychology of Affiliation*. Stanford, CA: Stanford University Press.

Schriesheim, C. A., Castro, S. L., & Cogliser, C. C. (1999). Leader-member exchange (LMX) research: A comprehensive review of theory, measurement, and data-analytic practices, *The Leadership Quarterly*, 10(1), 63–113.

Schwartz, S. H. (1994). Beyond individualism/collectivism: New cultural dimensions of values: in U. Kim, H. C. Triandis, Ç. Kâgitçibasi, S. Choi, & G. Yoon (eds) *Individualism and Collectivism: Theory, Method, and Applications* (pp. 85–119). Thousand Oaks, CA: Sage.

Schwartz, S. H. (1999). A theory of cultural values and some implications for work, *Applied Psychology: An International Review*, 48, 23–47.

Seeman, T. E. (1996). Social ties and health: The benefits of social integration, *Annals of Epidemiology*, 6(5), 442–451.

Semmer, N. K., Elfering, A., Jacobshagen, N., Perrot, T., Beehr, T. A., & Boos, N. (2008). The emotional meaning of instrumental social support, *International Journal of Stress Management*, 15(3), 235–251.

Shalev, S. (2008). *A Sourcebook on Solitary Confinement*. London: Mannheim Centre for Criminology, London School of Economics. Retrieved from www.solitaryconfinement.org/sourcebook

Shore, L. M. & Tetrick, L. E. (1991). A construct validity study of the Survey of Perceived Organizational Support, *Journal of Applied Psychology*, 76(5), 637–643.

Shultz, K. S. (2003). Bridge employment: Work after retirement: in G. A. Adams & T. A. Beehr (eds) *Retirement: Reasons, Processes and Results* (pp. 214–241). New York: Springer Publishing Company.

Smith, D. & Tziner, A. (1998). Moderating effects of affective disposition and social support on the relationship between person-environment fit and strain, *Psychological Reports, 82*(3.1), 963–983.

Stoner, J. S., Gallagher, V. C., & Stoner, C. R. (2011). The interactive effects of emotional family support and perceived supervisor loyalty on the psychological contract breach-turnover relationship, *Journal of Managerial Issues, 23*(2), 124–143.

Swickert, R. (2009). Personality and social support processes: in R. Swickert (ed.) *The Cambridge Handbook of Personality Psychology* (pp. 524–540). New York: Cambridge University Press.

Swickert, R. J., Rosentreter, C. J., Hittner, J. B., & Mushrush, J. E. (2002). Extraversion, social support processes, and stress, *Personality and Individual Differences, 32*(5), 877–891.

Terry, D. J., Nielsen, M., & Perchard, L. (1993). Effects of work stress on psychological well-being and job satisfaction: The stress-buffering role of social support, *Australian Journal of Psychology, 45*(3), 168–175.

Thoits, P. A. (1985). Social support processes and psychological well-being: Theoretical possibilities: in I. G Sarason & B. Sarason (eds) *Social Support: Theory, Research and Applications* (pp. 51–72). The Hague, The Netherlands: Martinus Nijhof.

Thompson, B., Kirk-Brown, A., & Brown, D. (2001). Women police: The impact of work stress on family members: in B. Thompson, A. Kirk-Brown, & D. Brown (eds) *Stress, Workload, and Fatigue* (pp. 200–210). Mahwah, NJ: Lawrence Erlbaum Associates Publishers.

Vanderzee, K. I., Buunk, B. P., & Sanderman, R. (1997). Social support, locus of control, and psychological well-being, *Journal of Applied Social Psychology, 27*(20), 1842–1859.

Vaux, A. (1988). *Social Support: Theory, Research, and Intervention.* New York: Praeger Publishers.

Vaux, A., Riedel, S., & Stewart, D. (1987). Modes of social support: The Social Support Behaviors (SS-B) scale, *American Journal of Community Psychology, 15*(2), 209–237.

Viswesvaran, C., Sanchez, J. I., & Fisher, J. (1999). The role of social support in the process of work stress: A meta-analysis, *Journal of Vocational Behavior, 54,* 314–334.

Winstead, B. A., Derlega, V. J., Montgomery, M. J., & Pilkington, C. (1995). The quality of friendships at work and job satisfaction, *Journal of Social and Personal Relationships, 12*(2), 199–215.

Xia, L. X., Liu, J., Ding, C., Hollon, S. D., Shao, B. T., & Zhang. (2012). The relation of self-supporting personality, enacted social support, and perceived social support, *Personality and Individual Differences, 52*(2), 156–160.

Zellars, K. L. & Perrewé, P. L. (2001). Affective personality and the content of emotional social support: Coping in organizations, *Journal of Applied Psychology, 86,* 459–467.

10
When Workplaces Go Sour – Bullying at Work

Dianne Gardner[1], Michael P. O'Driscoll[2], Tim Bentley[3], Bevan Catley[4], Helena D. Cooper-Thomas[5], and Linda Trenberth[6]

"[the bullying behavior] took various forms. 'It included putting fish oil in her bag, covering her with chocolate sauce, telling her that she was worthless and didn't deserve to be here, – those sorts of things' and 'they would just grab her and hold her down and put oil over her so she couldn't get away (this occurring) on three or four occasions'" (White, 2008, p. 2)

"... their bullying behaviour included the following: Greeting and acknowledging other members of the Secretariat department in a very overt manner, in order to highlight the fact that they were not speaking to me ... Excluding me from conversations ... by either talking over me or pretending they could not hear anything I said ... Waiting for me to walk past the area of the office in which they sat before bursting out laughing ... removing my name from circulation lists, hiding my post from me and removing papers from my desk... Making raspberry noises with each step I took ... Shouting to the other women 'err what's that stink in here?' and then saying 'its coming from over there' (referring to me)" (Royal Courts of Justice, 2006, p. Clause 70, pp. 20–21)

Many cases of workplace bullying are not as extreme as the two cases described above. The first example illustrates the bullying experienced

---

[1] School of Psychology, Massey University
[2] School of Psychology, The University of Waikato
[3] New Zealand Work Research Institute, Auckland University of Technology
[4] School of Management, Massey University
[5] School of Psychology, The University of Auckland
[6] Birkbeck College, University of London

by Brodie Panlock, a young employee in an Australian café. The second illustrates the experience of Helen Green, a senior employee of a large multinational bank. Both were targeted by bullies; neither received support from colleagues or managers and the outcomes were tragic. Brodie took her own life and the coroner concluded this was a direct result of the bullying. Helen experienced serious mental health problems, particularly depression, which the High Court ruled were the result of workplace bullying. This chapter will discuss what workplace bullying is and is not, its possible causes and likely effects, and solutions which organizations can implement to address it.

What is bullying at work?

Many employers and employees recognize, or should recognize, that physical assault and ritual humiliations are not acceptable at work and may be breaking the law. But what about verbal assault such as telling someone they are worthless? Does bullying have to be deliberate in order to be classified as bullying? How long must it go on for? These are difficult questions and there is little agreement about the answers. This section will outline some of our current knowledge about these issues.

A person is bullied when he or she feels that they are repeatedly subjected to negative acts in the workplace, especially when these are acts that they find difficult to defend themselves against (Einarsen et al., 1994). This definition makes several points. One important point is that bullying consists of behavior which is repeated. Although a single serious incident such as a verbal insult or physical assault might be considered to be bullying, these incidents are likely to be covered by workplace policies or legislation which explicitly address harassment or violence. The key differences between bullying, harassment, and workplace violence are the different legal frameworks. Workplace health and safety legislation in many jurisdictions does not explicitly mention workplace bullying. It is often covered implicitly by requirements for workplace hazards, including psychosocial ones, to be identified, assessed, and controlled. Subtle bullying behavior is less likely to be identified in these policies but, if repeated, it can have serious effects. While some behaviors can appear to be childish and petty, the effect of having to deal with them every day wears a target down (Royal Courts of Justice, 2006). While both of the cases above involved women targets, the bullies in one case were men and in the other both women and men. There is evidence that this kind of undermining bullying behavior can be used by both men and women bullies against men and women targets (Einarsen & Raknes, 1997).

The definition of bullying also indicates that targets feel unable to respond or defend themselves. In many cases a bully is senior to the target so the bullying involves an abuse of position power. Such bullying can be top-down, cascading through the organization (Hoel et al., 2001). But bullies can also be peers and colleagues (Hogh & Dofradottir, 2001), particularly where a group collectively bullies a weaker group or an individual. Hence a bully may be at any organizational level (Parzefall & Salin, 2010). The bully may have influence or standing through position, seniority or support from others, or may know about a target's personal situation or vulnerabilities. In general bullying involves an imbalance of power so that the bully is able to act without significant retaliation by the target. The types of power also differ for different people; those with formal management roles may be able to use their position power to bully while others may rely on others either supporting or ignoring their behavior. Over time, bullying tends to get worse as bullies experience few or no negative consequences for their behavior. Targets may feel that they cannot retaliate for fear of further victimization, of being blamed for what is happening to them, of being labeled a complainer or, in some cases, of being accused of being the bully themselves (Klein & Martin, 2011).

Bullying can be one-on-one or, as in the two illustrative cases, many-on-one. Bullies often gain allies in their bullying. Others may join in because they feel the target "deserves it" or to avoid being bullied themselves (Einarsen et al., 2011). This strengthens the bully's position, isolates the target, and reduces the chance that the target will make a complaint or that any investigation will be fair, thorough, and impartial. Because power imbalances can increase targets' feelings of helplessness as well as affecting their ability to do their work, bullying from managers can have particularly severe effects (Lutgen-Sandvik et al., 2007). This is particularly the case when economic or other factors make it difficult for a target to leave and find another job.

The definition does not state that workplace bullying has to be intentional. While bullying can arise from an intention to do harm, it can also arise from an unintentional disregard for the effects on others, for example when goal-focused behavior is aimed at achieving high levels of work performance (Parzefall & Salin, 2010). It is difficult to prove intention. Targets may be more likely to see bullying as intentional and may not be aware of any work environment pressures on the bully (Hoel et al., 1999). It is difficult to imagine that the bullies in the two cases outlined above thought their behavior was not harmful but it is unfeasible to prove they meant to do harm.

It is impossible to specify how much negative behavior is needed before it constitutes bullying. Behavior that may not trouble one person may be very upsetting to another, and most employees face at least some negative behavior in their workplaces without necessarily feeling that they are being bullied (Parzefall & Salin, 2010). Much research stipulates that a person needs to have experienced at least one negative act (selected from a checklist such as the Negative Acts Questionnaire – Revised; Einarsen et al., 2009) at least weekly over a period of time (e.g. six months) (Parzefall & Salin, 2010). Therefore, the rates of bullying found by different researchers vary depending on the criteria that are used. In addition, when people are asked to self-report whether or not they have been bullied the reported rates tend to be low, perhaps because some people do not recognize that negative behavior might constitute bullying or because they do not wish to label themselves as targets. Using the relatively strict criterion of experiencing at least two negative acts weekly for at least six months, rates of workplace bullying in New Zealand were found to be high in the health, hospitality, and education sectors; averaging 18% of the workforce (Bentley et al., 2009). Workplace bullying has been found to be high in these sectors in other countries as well, including Australia (Rutherford & Rissel, 2004), the UK (Totterdell et al., 2012), the USA (Lutgen-Sandvik et al., 2007) and Scandinavia (Einarsen et al., 2003).

In workplaces, managers are often concerned that the actions they have to take as a legitimate part of their role might be construed as bullying. Managerial behaviors related to performance management, work allocation, goal setting and rewards, and so on could be construed by some employees as bullying. This is a difficult area to address. Solutions that align with effective leadership, team development, organizational culture, justice, and fairness will be presented below.

The effects of workplace bullying

Bullying at work can severely affect targets' health and well-being causing self-doubt, anxiety, post-traumatic stress symptoms, and depression (Bond et al., 2010; Matthiesen & Einarsen, 2004). Physical health can also be affected, including an increased risk of cardiovascular disease (Tuckey et al., 2010). These effects can last five years or more (Hoel et al., 2004). The most harmful forms of bullying are those that lead targets to lose their sense of self-worth and to feel excluded, such as unfair criticism, undermining, hints they should quit, being ignored, and having their private life criticized (Hoel et al., 2004). As noted by one author "[bullies] depend on people giving up; feeling so demoralized that they cannot be bothered to fight. In the cycle of demoralization, the doubts about oneself, one's motives, what course of action to take, undermines confidence. This plays into the tyrant's hands. They rely on the target feeling that it is not worth bothering to take any action. This corrosive process can undermine individuals while they are in the organization and after they have left; its legacy living on sometimes for years" (Crawford, 1999, p. 90).

Not only targets are affected. Ripple effects can impact on families, with increased levels of work-life imbalance as targets spend more time at work trying to produce work that will satisfy a bully's increasing demands. Stress at work can spill over to home life as targets experience exhaustion, helplessness, worthlessness, confusion, and a loss of control over work priorities that are important to them (O'Connell et al., 2007). Witnesses to bullying can be badly affected by stress and anxiety (Houshmand et al., 2012; Totterdell et al., 2012), whether or not they are being bullied. Compared to those who had not witnessed bullying at work, witnesses felt more anxious, felt that their workplaces and supervisors were less supportive, were less happy with their jobs, and were more likely to want to quit (Cooper-Thomas et al., 2011). Simply working in a unit where there is bullying makes people more likely to want to leave (Houshmand et al., 2012), whether to protect themselves or to express their frustration and dislike of an organization that does not look after its staff.

Although there is no clear evidence that bullied workers go on to bully others (Lee & Brotheridge, 2006), there is no doubt that workplace relationships become severely strained (Einarsen & Raknes, 1997). In turn, organizational performance is affected as targets and witnesses take more days off, are less happy with and motivated by their jobs and more likely to leave (Houshmand et al., 2012). Even if bullying is part of a "get the job done at all costs" organizational culture, the negative effects outweigh any benefits.

Why does bullying occur?

The people

Early research concluded that targets of bullying are more likely to be anxious, lacking in self-esteem and insecure than non-targets but later work concluded that these characteristics are more likely to be the effect than the cause of bullying (Leymann, 1996). A perspective that tries to explain bullying by focusing on what targets may have in common risks unfairly blaming targets for causing their own problems. In fact, targets are often high achievers who are skilled, hardworking, truthful, competent, and bright. Brodie was "an organised, reliable and confident girl who showed compassion and cared for everyone she knew" (White, 2008, p. 1) and "Helen was an attractive, successful and confident woman" (Royal Courts of Justice, 2006, p. Clause 80, p. 24). Targets may be vulnerable for other reasons. Brodie was in a relationship with a colleague and wanted his approval and acceptance while Helen was focused on completing her six-month probation period at work. Even so, these characteristics do not necessarily cause bullying as most people want to do well at work and may want approval from others.

It is sometimes possible to distinguish between those who bully deliberately and intend to do harm (the predatory bully), those who use bullying behavior to achieve personal or work goals (the purposeful bully), and those who do not realize that their behaviors are bullying (the unaware bully). Predatory bullies often aim to demonstrate power and gain compliance from others (Einarsen, 1999). In some cases other employees may have been targeted by the same bully or group of bullies; when a new person arrives the bullies switch their bullying to the new target. Such serial bullying is severe and relatively rare; it is not often possible to know what causes it although in situations where there is ongoing serious bullying it becomes clear that the organization is not doing enough to solve problems.

Predatory or purposeful bullies may or may not fit the definition of "workplace psychopaths" (Babiak & Hare, 2006) but it is important not to characterize all bullies as psychopaths. While some bullies may set out to do harm, others use bullying behavior as a way to achieve their personal or organizational goals, these being "purposeful" bullies. Organizations with a "get the job done at all costs" culture are likely to condone bullying as long as it's seen to get results (Ferris et al., 2007). A third type is the "unaware" bully, with poor interpersonal skills, who does not realize how their behavior affects others. Linked to this are situations in which unintentional bullying can arise such as poorly designed work with unclear or conflicting demands, authoritarian or neglectful leaders, high stress, and a lack of participative decision-making (Matthiesen & Einarsen, 2007; Notelaers et al., 2009).

In general, bullying behavior arises when individuals' characteristics combine with work situations that prompt, reward or ignore bullying. While little can be done to deal with predatory bullies beyond developing effective systems to avoid recruiting them in the first place, the problems caused by purposeful and unaware or unintentional bullies can be addressed by looking at workplace factors. Bullying can be discouraged by a focus on effective leadership, empowerment, and workplace fairness (Brotheridge & Lee, 2006).

The situation

Rather than focusing on the "bad apple" approach to identifying bullies, researchers are looking at "bad barrels", or work contexts that foster and facilitate negative behavior. Targets consistently report that they have worse working conditions, more job demands such as time pressure and workloads, more role conflict, worse leadership and supervisory behavior, less information flow, less control over their work, and a worse social climate than those who have not been bullied (Tuckey et al., 2009). Organizational cultures can foster bullying by blaming targets, failing to take action or emphasizing productivity at the expense of well-being or job security (Sperry, 2009). Rapid or widespread organizational change can mean more bullying, not because change in itself is bad but because it can create confusion, uncertainty, and feelings of insecurity. Where employees are unclear about their work role and where there are conflicting demands, bullies can manipulate power structures, expand control, and act on their personal rather than work priorities (Hodson et al., 2006). This may be a sign of bullies' own uncertainties and frustrations but nevertheless it can add to targets' distress (De Cuyper et al., 2009). Restructuring and redundancies create extra stress and uncertainty, and may make targets less willing to resist bullying if they are trying to keep their jobs (Liefooghe & MacKenzie Davey, 2001). Employees who lack control over their tasks, time, and work roles often experience bullying; micro-managing can be a form of bullying in itself (Vartia, 1996). Very busy workplaces can mean that nobody has time to resolve conflicts or to identify, investigate and address negative work behaviors. A competitive and divisive culture encourages bullying and makes it difficult for targets to admit to their problems and seek support (Branch et al., 2007).

A key factor related to bullying is leadership. Destructive leadership includes behaviors such as belittling or humiliating individuals, ignoring their needs, sabotaging work efforts by withholding necessary resources, blaming others for errors or treating people unfairly (Hoel et al., 2010). It can also include unpredictable leadership which creates uncertainty about how decisions are made and the criteria for rewards and punishments (Hoel et al., 2010). Not surprisingly, destructive leadership creates a hostile work environment which gets worse over time as others copy the behavior in the belief, real or not, that it is the accepted way to get things done (Hauge et al., 2011; Hauge et al., 2007; Hoel et al., 2010). Even worse are leaders who actively join in the bullying, perhaps not realizing it is unproductive or perhaps because it appears to be an organizationally-accepted way to retain the respect of a group. If a manager engages in bullying it communicates to the target that nothing will be done to end the bullying behavior.

A different form of negative leadership is laissez-faire leadership, in which a manager avoids making important decisions, ignores conflict, waits for things to go wrong before taking action, or fails to deal with problems until they become serious (Hoel et al., 2010). Laissez-faire leadership is negligent as it indirectly condones bullying behavior and can lead to problems for individual employees and the organization as a whole. It is associated with increased bullying, not because managers directly model or encourage it but because they fail to address problems (Hauge et al., 2007; Hoel et al., 2010). Laissez-faire leaders may be weak, unwilling to stand up for themselves or their staff, may avoid getting involved, ignore reports of problems, hope problems will disappear, dismiss a problem as "not really bullying" or tell a target to ignore it. Such managers may themselves be experiencing lackluster leadership or bullying from further up the line. Organizational support systems such as Human Resources (HR) can be a key resource although small businesses may not have a formal HR function to address a complaint. In larger organizations there is likely to be a formal HR function but it may be of little help, particularly if HR see their role as supporting management rather than staff.

What can be done to reduce workplace bullying?

Resolving a serious issue like bullying requires a multi-faceted approach with effective strategies by individuals (including targets, peers, and witnesses) and by organizations including management and HR staff. A range of ideas will be presented ranging from personal coping strategies to those that are more likely to address root causes of the problem, such as attention to organizational leadership and culture.

Personal coping strategies

Individuals need strategies for dealing with stressful situations including bullying. Coping efforts typically fall into one of two categories: problem-focused coping and emotion-focused coping. Each can be effective depending on the problem and context.

Problem-focused coping strategies are intended to reduce a stressor, in this case the bullying behavior. The strategies can include trying to confront the bully about his/her actions, avoiding the bully, or gaining support and assistance from others at work. These all reflect an attempt to change the situation and its negative effects. On the other hand, emotion-focused coping does not aim to change the situation but to change emotional reactions to it. These strategies can include trying to see the situation as irrelevant ("It does not matter to me"), becoming resigned to it ("This is how it is, and there is nothing that can be done about it"), or ignoring it (Hogh & Dofradottir, 2001). These strategies do not directly aim to change the situation or reduce bullying but to change the emotions that arise from it.

Problem-focused coping efforts are generally not effective and can be associated with increased rather than decreased bullying (O'Driscoll et al., 2011). If a bully feels threatened or challenged, they may be provoked into increasing their bullying (Ólafsson & Jóhannsdóttir, 2004). Attempts to confront a bully or to complain to a bully's boss can also lead to counter-charges of bullying, in which the bully claims to be a target and then uses organizational systems, policies, and power structures against the original target (Klein & Martin, 2011). Active coping strategies like seeking counseling or outside help, or consulting HR, may be effective but are not widely used; the majority of targets take no formal action (Namie, 2007). One strategy which may be effective is to leave the organization, although this leaves the original problem unsolved. Overall, even though problem-focused coping is often effective for dealing with work stressors in general, direct efforts to counteract bullying are typically not effective.

Emotion-focused strategies such as suppressing feelings or using humor reduce the risk that the bullying will escalate but do not often resolve it (Lee & Brotheridge, 2006). Attempts to avoid or placate the bully can also worsen bullying behavior, and there is little evidence that people are able to ignore or disregard bullying behavior for long periods of time. These emotion-focused strategies take effort, and bullying behaviors over time can leave a target exhausted, demoralized, and socially isolated.

Attempts to cope with bullying often change over time. Targets may start out by trying to work harder, asking bullies to stop or reporting negative behavior, then become increasingly passive or avoidant when active strategies do not work. Passive strategies can create additional distress as feelings of helplessness increase, self-esteem deteriorates, and bullies gain confidence that their actions will not be challenged

(Dijkstra et al., 2009). Ultimately, the only viable option for many targets is to leave their job and organization, while bullies often remain in place.

Improving the workplace

While a lot is known about the factors which can foster bullying, much less is known about how to deal with it. Unfortunately there has been rhetoric but little evidence to confirm claims about effective interventions. Below we describe some approaches and discuss potential impacts.

Policy

Although many (if not most) organizations have anti-harassment policies, there is often a lack of specific reference to bullying in these policies. Several authors have suggested that policies should contain particular reference to bullying, or that organizations need to develop anti-bullying policies that are separate from their harassment policies (e.g. Salin, 2008, 2009; Vartia & Leka, 2011). Workplace bullying is an organization-level issue, not just a personal issue; it does not just arise from conflict between individuals and so it requires an organizational response.

Perhaps the most obvious place to begin is by developing documentation which outlines the kinds of interpersonal behaviors which are considered to be acceptable and unacceptable. Although violence (especially physical violence) and harassment have long been recognized as unacceptable, bullying (which some regard as a form of psychological violence) has not been made as visible. A key reason for this is that many behaviors which reflect bullying are subtle and not always observable by outsiders. While developing policies seems an obvious recommendation and is a useful start, policies alone have little impact on changing behavior (Snyder et al., 2004) unless they are supported by management and adhered to at all levels. Nevertheless, recognition of bullying in formal policy documents is a starting point for strategies to manage negative behaviors and alleviate their negative consequences (Salin, 2008).

Training

Another prominent recommendation is training. Two major reasons why people act in unacceptable ways are that they may not know the negative impact of their behavior or may not know how to behave differently. According to this logic, individuals who engage in bullying behaviors need to be informed that their actions are not acceptable and they need to be trained or coached in more appropriate ways of acting. Raising awareness of the negative consequences of behavior is presumed to be essential for changing the way a person reflects on their interpersonal interactions, and ultimately for changing behaviors. Training or coaching has been used by many organizations to deal with physical violence (Runyan et al., 2000), with some success, but its effectiveness in reducing bullying has not been firmly established. Part of the difficulty is that a "one size fits all" approach to training will not be effective; rather, the training or coaching needs to be tailored to the specific context in which the bullying is occurring and to the specific bullying behaviors being used. Training must be preceded by a risk analysis which identifies the nature of the undesirable behavior(s), the reasons why it is occurring, and the factors which may be contributing to the behavior (Vartia & Leka, 2011). Training must not be seen as a one-off solution; it needs to be integrated with an analysis of the underlying issues and any policy, structural or other changes that are required.

Mediation and counseling

Policy development and training represent the two most recommended strategies for dealing with workplace bullying. There are, however, other mechanisms which have been proposed. Some authors (Resch & Schubinski, 1996) have indicated that mediation is an effective approach to the management of bullying. Mediation entails engaging a neutral third party to referee discussions between the bully and target to help them reach a mutually-acceptable resolution. It is based on the view that bullying reflects an escalation of interpersonal conflict (Zapf & Gross, 2001) which can be addressed in the same way as other forms of conflict. Research has failed to support this approach, however, and there is little evidence that mediation achieves good outcomes for both parties. One major difficulty is that bullying reflects an imbalance of power (Salin, 2003), which means the target does not feel that he or she can negotiate with the person who is bullying them and that a bully can, in some instances, manipulate the mediation process. For this very significant reason, mediation is not often recommended for dealing with bullying in workplaces (Saam, 2010; Vartia & Leka, 2011).

Counseling has also been suggested as a way to address bullying consequences for both the target and the bully. In respect of the latter, this would fall under the category of training or coaching mentioned earlier, and its effectiveness will depend on a bully's insight and willingness to change, and on the role of situational factors in supporting bullying. Counseling for the target, however, is a different matter. Ferris (2004) indicated that counseling may help someone who has experienced bullying to deal with its negative effects. Counseling may help the target to develop problem-focused coping strategies to deal with the bully or to use emotion-focused coping to address the psychological impacts of bullying. As with mediation, however, this may be of little help unless there is a change in the bully's behavior. Given that the target may feel they have little or no control over the situation, personal coping strategies developed through counseling may be of little or no help to alleviate bullying. Moreover counseling for the target puts the onus on targets to resolve bullying problems at work. Yet responsibility rests with the organization and management to address workplace bullying (Hauge et al., 2007). Essentially this is a leadership issue, and there have been several studies on how leadership styles influence levels and outcomes of bullying (Hoel et al., 2010).

Leadership and workplace climate

Bullying comes from individual, organizational, and social factors, and one way of looking at those factors is to consider them in terms of whether they enable, motivate, or precipitate bullying. The first set of factors, enabling conditions, makes it possible for bullying to take place. These can include power imbalances, lack of negative consequences for bullying, and role models who bully (Salin, 2003). In themselves enabling conditions do not cause bullying. There also needs to be a second set of factors, namely motivating conditions which provide reasons for people to engage in bullying behavior. These could be high levels of internal competition for rewards and recognition or high levels of job insecurity. The third set of factors includes organizational restructuring, changes in the membership of a work group, increased pressure to achieve goals, fear of job loss or feelings of frustration (Salin, 2003). These factors can precipitate or trigger bullying. It is likely that the most severe bullying will take place when all three sets of factors are present (Salin, 2003).

As the factors that give rise to bullying lie within organizational systems and structures, organizational leadership plays an important role in reducing bullying. Constructive leadership motivates employees to perform at high levels, provides practical and emotional support, and deals directly with problems. In general, constructive leadership that identifies and addresses problems is associated with low levels of workplace bullying and with better outcomes for employees and organizations (Hauge et al., 2007; Hauge et al., 2011). This makes it important to develop effective leadership by appropriate selection, training, coaching, or mentoring of those in leadership positions. As well as modeling appropriate behaviors themselves, leaders need to be able to identify and attend appropriately to anti-social behaviors, including bullying.

Senior managers are responsible for creating healthy work environments through the priorities they demonstrate, through decisions on budgets, resource allocation, policies and procedures, and the relative importance of productivity and profit versus well-being (Law et al., 2011). Principles for preventing bullying include the active involvement and commitment of organizational leaders to creating and implementing policies, practices, and procedures to prevent bullying and to clarify behaviors that are acceptable at work; ensuring employees have a genuine say in decisions that affect them; and a willingness by organizational leaders to listen to and act upon concerns of staff (Bond et al., 2010; Law et al., 2011). Organizational leaders need to make it clear that negative behavior is not tolerated and this means taking corrective action to show that bullying will have negative consequences for bullies.

A team climate in which individuals work together and collaborate gives fewer opportunities for bullying and lowers the likelihood that bullying behavior will be tolerated, copied or ignored. Empowering individuals, enabling coworker support, and balancing workloads are important aspects of work which help reduce bullying and its negative impact (Brotheridge & Lee, 2006). The development of a positive work climate will go some way toward reducing the effects of bullying and other forms of anti-social behavior. In contrast, a work environment that fosters hostility and competitiveness contributes to more bullying and less well-being.

Constructive feedback in the context of group or team discussions can also help build cohesiveness and prevent problems (Arnetz & Arnetz, 2000). Good team communication can provide feedback on behavioral norms, discuss inappropriate behaviors and alternative ways of behaving, identify factors which promote or reinforce bullying, and develop strategies to address them. Open discussion of these issues can help individuals clarify what is expected of them in terms of treating other people with respect and dignity. It can also lead to agreement among team members on how to prevent bullying and deal with situations in which it occurs. This can give individuals confidence to bring bullying out into the open where it can be resolved. These approaches have led to positive changes in organizations which previously experienced bullying (Mikkelsen et al., 2011; Salin, 2008).

While we know a great deal about workplace characteristics that are related to bullying, it is a complex picture and no single explanation is enough on its own to explain why bullying occurs. It is an interaction between the characteristics of bullies and targets and the situations they work in. When work environments are stressful and unsatisfactory, people experience frustration and stress but this does not necessarily cause people to become bullies or targets. This means that finding solutions is not easy. It is important to focus on work situations and conditions and to avoid blaming individuals, whether bullies or targets.

Future research on workplace bullying

Over the past 15 years there has been a plethora of research on the predictors and consequences of bullying at work. Considerable knowledge has been acquired on the factors which cause bullying in organizational settings, including personal attributes (of both perpetrators and targets), as well as the psycho-social and other outcomes of bullying, including stress, emotional disturbance, dysfunctional performance at work, and ultimately productivity. There is no shortage of information on these issues, so there is little need for further confirmation of factors related to the occurrence of bullying and its consequences.

There is an urgent need, however, for systematic research on other fronts. One of these is the need to examine the processes by which bullying unfolds over time. Typically, research has examined bullying and its correlates using cross-sectional research designs, which treat bullying as a static phenomenon. Such research does not enable an examination of unfolding processes, which are vital to the understanding of how bullying occurs and its impacts. Longitudinal investigation of bullying will allow researchers to investigate changes in social relationships over time, and will enhance our understanding of early interventions to help deal with conflict and bullying.

Although there have been numerous discussions on organizational responsibilities to reduce bullying, little systematic research has been conducted on organizational interventions and their effectiveness. Organizational culture and climate can contribute to bullying if they promote competitiveness or hostility between organizational members, and destructive or laissez-faire management is also related to bullying

(Hauge et al., 2011). Although these associations are well known, less is known about how to build respect, collaboration, and collegiality within organizations. Longitudinal research (over a span of years rather than weeks or months) is needed to evaluate the effectiveness of organizational initiatives. To date there has been limited research on bullying interventions and most has taken a very short-term focus (Saam, 2010). Multiple research methods are needed, including surveys at all organizational levels, interviews with key people, and collection of objective data such as performance, absenteeism and turnover statistics.

While it is clear that the reduction of bullying requires concerted organizational intervention, there is a need for longitudinal research on personal strategies which can help people reduce the negative impacts of bullying. Problem-focused coping is typically viewed as the most effective approach to stress management in general (Dewe et al., 2010), but in some cases it can increase rather than reduce bullying (Ólafsson & Jóhannsdóttir, 2004). Little is known about how to make personal coping strategies more effective, and there is an ongoing need for evidence-based ways to help individuals deal with bullying.

Another issue that deserves attention is differences in "perspectives" on bullying. Following Karl Weick's (1995) notion of sense-making in organizations, it is important to probe different perceptions and interpretations in order to understand the "why" of bullying as well as its prevalence and contributing factors. Most studies have focused on the self-reported experiences of targets and, sometimes, witnesses of bullying (for example, Hansen et al., 2006). There has also been a focus on downward bullying (from managers to subordinates) but much less on upwards bullying in which staff bully managers or supervisors (Branch et al., 2007; Wallace et al., 2011). In order to develop effective preventative strategies, it is important to explore how different groups perceive and interpret bullying behaviors.

These additional research areas will not be easy to investigate. There are many obstacles to the systematic and reliable evaluation of organizational interventions, as has been well documented in the literature on stress management for example. Nevertheless, it is essential to confront these challenges in order to increase our understanding of bullying and develop more effective ways to counteract anti-social behaviors.

Conclusion and recommendations

In this chapter we have endeavored to outline some of the major consequences of work-related bullying, along with some possible methods for dealing with this serious social problem which occurs in many organizations. As we have noted, bullying can have significant negative consequences, not just for the individuals who experience it directly (the victims), but also for other people in an organization (for example, coworkers and others who observe bullying occurring), and for the organization as a whole. The negative effects of bullying on people's job satisfaction, work engagement, and commitment to their organization can be felt throughout a workplace and can ultimately be detrimental to the overall performance and productivity of a firm or company.

We have also discussed some of the circumstances which can lead to the occurrence of bullying. A consistent theme in research on this issue is that bullying is not simply one person's anti-social behavior toward another person, but can also reflect a climate of competitiveness, hostility and lack of cooperativeness between people. When leaders (managers) adopt a laissez-faire approach, that is "turn a blind eye" to bullying, this can serve to not only permit its occurrence but can even foster more bullying to occur. Leadership therefore plays a very important role in either promoting or preventing workplace bullying. One of the strongest recommendations, therefore, is that organizational managers, who have the power and authority to instigate changes within their organization, must strive to develop a culture (or climate) where bullying is not just abhorred but also has negative consequences for individuals who engage in this undesirable social behavior. Managers must figuratively "take the bull(y) by the horns" and endeavor to prevent bullying, or at the very least deal with it when it does occur.

Above we have referred to training as one mechanism for changing peoples' (anti-social) behaviors. Training will be successful, however, only if there is motivation and willingness to change. Hence managers need to inculcate the value of collegiality and cooperation in employees, and develop an organizational culture where the norm is collaboration rather than competition. Rewarding collegial behaviors is an important component of addressing bullying and other anti-social behaviors such as harassment and interpersonal conflict generally.

We also suggested that developing anti-bullying policies is an important first step toward reduction of bullying. However, it is only a first step and must be supported by managers and supervisors modeling appropriate behavior and attending to the behaviors of others in a constructive way. Showing employees that alternative approaches, other than bullying, will be more effective in achieving work goals is critical. In so far as employees often imitate the actions of managers, it is up to the latter to enact policies in their own behaviors.

In conclusion, workplace bullying must be viewed as more than just an escalation of conflict between two individuals. Rather, there are multiple reasons, some of them systemic, for the display of bullying behaviors, and we need to move beyond treating these simply as problems at the individual level (either the bully or the victim). The mechanisms outlined above, when used in conjunction with each other, will enable organizations to be proactive in addressing this insidious problem.

Some further information on workplace bullying

There are numerous sources of additional sources of information on the manifestations of bullying in workplaces and suggestions on how to deal with bullying. In addition to the plethora of research and academic journal articles on this issue, below we list a few more general sources which complement the material we have presented in this chapter. These are just suggestions, and other relevant information can be obtained from websites as well as print media.

Caponecchia, C. & Wyatt, A. (2011). *Preventing Workplace Bullying: An Evidence-Based Guide for Managers and Employees*. Crows Nest, Australia: Allen & Unwin.

Einarsen, S., Hoel, H., Zapf, D., & Cooper, C. L. (eds) (2011). *Bullying and Harassment in the Workplace: Developments in Theory, Research and Practice* (2nd ed). Boca Raton, Florida: CRC Press.

Needham, A. W. (2003). *Workplace Bullying: The Costly Business Secret*. Auckland: Penguin.

Needham, A. W. (2008). *Courage at the Top: Igniting the Leadership Fire*. Auckland: Penguin.

Two networks which provide communication opportunities for workplace bullying researchers and practitioners are:

International Association for Workplace Bullying and Harassment (www.iawbh.org)

Australasian Workplace Bullying Research Network (awb-research@explode. unsw.edu.au)

The following website has resources to help organizations address bullying and related issues:

Workplaces against Violence in Employment: www.wave.org.nz.

References

Arnetz, J. & Arnetz, B. (2000). Implementation and evaluation of a practical intervention programme for dealing with violence towards health care workers, *Journal of Advanced Nursing, 31*, 668–680.

Babiak, P. & Hare, R. D. (2006). *Snakes in Suits: When Psychopaths Go to Work.* New York: HarperCollins.

Bentley, T., Catley, B., Cooper-Thomas, H., Gardner, D., O'Driscoll, M., & Trenberth, L. (2009). Understanding stress and bullying in New Zealand workplaces: Final report to OH&S steering committee (pp. 1–100). Wellington, NZ: Health Research Council/New Zealand Department of Labour.

Bond, S. A., Tuckey, M. R., & Dollard, M. (2010). Psychosocial safety climate, workplace bullying, and symptoms of posttraumatic stress, *Organization Development Journal, 28*(1), 37–56.

Branch, S., Ramsay, S., & Barker, M. (2007). Managers in the firing line: Contributing factors to workplace bullying by staff – An interview study, *Journal of Management and Organization, 13*, 264–281.

Brotheridge, C. M. & Lee, R. T. (2006). Examining the relationship between the perceived work environment and workplace bullying, *Canadian Journal of Community Mental Health, 25*(2), 31–44.

Cooper-Thomas, H. D., Catley, B. E., Bentley, T. A., Gardner, D. H., O'Driscoll, M. P., & Trenberth, L. (2011). *Is There a Double Whammy from Being an Observer and a Target of Workplace Bullying?* Paper presented at the Symposium conducted at the 9th Industrial and Organisational Psychology Conference, Brisbane, Australia.

Crawford, N. (1999). Conundrums and confusion in organisations: The etymology of the word "bully", *International Journal of Manpower, 20*(1/2), 86.

De Cuyper, N., Baillien, E., & De Witte, H. (2009). Job insecurity, perceived employability and targets' and perpetrators' experiences of workplace bullying, *Work & Stress, 23*(3), 206–224.

Dewe, P. J., O'Driscoll, M. P., & Cooper, C. L. (2010). *Coping with Work Stress: A Review and Critique.* Chichester, UK: Wiley-Blackwell.

Dijkstra, M. T. M., De Dreu, C. K. W., Evers, A., & van Dierendonck, D. (2009). Passive responses to interpersonal conflict at work amplify employee strain, *European Journal of Work and Organizational Psychology, 18*(4), 405–423.

Einarsen, S. (1999). The nature and causes of bullying at work, *International Journal of Manpower, 20*(1/2), 16.

Einarsen, S., Hoel, H., & Notelaers, G. (2009). Measuring exposure to bullying and harassment at work: Validity, factor structure and psychometric properties of the negative acts questionnaire-revised, *Work & Stress, 23*(1), 24–44.

Einarsen, S., Hoel, H., Zapf, D., & Cooper, C. L. (eds) (2003). *Bullying and Emotional Abuse in the Workplace: International Perspectives in Research and Practice.* London: Taylor & Francis.

Einarsen, S., Hoel, H., Zapf, D., & Cooper, C. L. (eds) (2011). *Bullying and Harassment in the Workplace: Developments in Theory, Research, and Practice* (2nd ed.). Boca Raton, FL, USA: Taylor & Francis.

Einarsen, S. & Raknes, B. (1997). Harassment in the workplace and the victimization of men, *Violence and Victims, 12*(3), 247–263.

Einarsen, S., Raknes, B., & Matthiesen, S. (1994). Bullying and harassment at work and their relationships to work environment quality: An exploratory study, *European Work & Organizational Psychologist*, 4(4), 381.

Ferris, G., Zinko, R., Brouer, R. L., Buckley, M. R., & Harvey, M. G. (2007). Strategic bullying as a supplementary, balanced perspective on destructive leadership, *Leadership Quarterly*, 18(3), 195–206.

Ferris, P. (2004). A preliminary typology of organisational response to allegations of workplace bullying: See no evil, hear no evil, speak no evil, *British Journal of Guidance & Counselling*, 32(3), 389–395.

Hansen, Å. M., Hogh, A., Persson, R., Karlson, B., Garde, A. H., & Ørbæk, P. (2006). Bullying at work, health outcomes, and physiological stress response, *Journal of Psychosomatic Research*, 60(1), 63–72.

Hauge, L. J., Einarsen, S., Knardahl, S., Lau, B., Notelaers, G., & Skogstad, A. (2011). Leadership and role stressors as departmental level predictors of workplace bullying, *International Journal of Stress Management*, 18(4), 305–323. doi: 10.1037/a0025396

Hauge, L. J., Skogstad, A., & Einarsen, S. (2007). Relationships between stressful work environments and bullying: Results of a large representative study, *Work & Stress*, 21(3), 220–242.

Hodson, R., Roscigno, V. J., & Lopez, S. H. (2006). Chaos and the abuse of power, *Work & Occupations*, 33(4), 382–416.

Hoel, H., Cooper, C. L., & Faragher, B. (2001). The experience of bullying in Great Britain: The impact of organizational status, *European Journal of Work & Organizational Psychology*, 10(4), 443–465.

Hoel, H., Faragher, B., & Cooper, C. L. (2004). Bullying is detrimental to health, but all bullying behaviors are not necessarily equally damaging, *British Journal of Guidance & Counselling*, 32(3), 367–387.

Hoel, H., Glaso, L., Hetland, H., Cooper, C. L., & Einarsen, S. (2010). Leadership styles as predictors of self-reported and observed workplace bullying, *British Journal of Management*, 21, 453–468. doi: 10.1111/j.1467-8551.2009.00664.x

Hoel, H., Rayner, C., & Cooper, C. L. (1999). Workplace bullying, *International Review of Industrial and Organisational Psychology*, 14, 195–230.

Hogh, A. & Dofradottir, A. (2001). Coping with bullying in the workplace, *European Journal of Work & Organizational Psychology*, 10(4), 485–495.

Houshmand, M., O'Reilly, J., Robinson, S., & Wolff, A. (2012). Escaping bullying: The simultaneous impact of individual and unit-level bullying on turnover intentions, *Human Relations*, 65(7), 901–908. doi: 0.1177/0018726712445100

Klein, A. & Martin, S. (2011). Two dilemmas in dealing with workplace bullies: False positives and deliberate deceit, *International Journal of Workplace Health Management*, 4(1), 13–32. doi: 10.1108/17538351111118572

Law, R., Dollard, M., Tuckey, M. R., & Dormann, C. (2011). Psychosocial safety climate as a lead indicator of workplace bullying and harassment, job resources, psychological health and employee engagement, *Accident Analysis & Prevention*, 1782–1793. doi: 10.1016/j.aap.2011.04.010

Lee, R. T. & Brotheridge, C. (2006). When prey turns predatory: Workplace bullying as a predictor of counteraggression/bullying, coping, and well-being, *European Journal of Work & Organizational Psychology*, 15(3), 352–377.

Leymann, H. (1996). The content and development of mobbing at work, *European Journal of Work & Organizational Psychology, 5*(2), 165–185.

Liefooghe, A. P. D. & MacKenzie Davey, K. (2001). Accounts of workplace bullying: The role of the organization, *European Journal of Work & Organizational Psychology, 10*(4), 375–392.

Lutgen-Sandvik, P., Tracy, S. J., & Alberts, J. K. (2007). Burned by bullying in the American workplace: Prevalence, perception, degree and impact, *Journal of Management Studies, 44*(6), 837–862.

Matthiesen, S. & Einarsen, S. (2004). Psychiatric distress and symptoms of PTSD among victims of bullying at work, *British Journal of Guidance & Counselling, 32*(3), 335–356.

Matthiesen, S. & Einarsen, S. (2007). Perpetrators and targets of bullying at work: Role stress and individual differences, *Violence and Victims, 22*(6), 735–753.

Mikkelsen, E. G., Hogh, A., & Puggaard, L. B. (2011). Prevention of bullying and conflicts at work: Process factors influencing the implementation and effects of interventions, *International Journal of Workplace Health Management, 4*(1), 84–100.

Namie, G. (2007). The challenge of workplace bullying, *Employment Relations Today, 34*(2), 43–51. doi: 10.1002/ert.20151

Notelaers, G., De Witte, H., & Einarsen, S. (2009). A job characteristics approach to explain workplace bullying, *European Journal of Work and Organizational Psychology, 19*(4), 487–504. doi: 10.1080/13594320903007620

O'Connell, P. J., Calvert, E., & Watson, D. (2007). Bullying in the workplace: Survey Reports 2007. In T. E. a. S. R. Institute (ed.). Ireland: The Department of Enterprise, Trade and Employment.

O'Driscoll, M. P., Cooper-Thomas, H. D., Bentley, T., Catley, B., Gardner, D. H., & Trenberth, L. (2011). Workplace bullying in New Zealand: Work attitudes and performance, coping and organizational responses, *Asia Pacific Journal of Human Resources, 49*(4), 390–406.

Ólafsson, R. & Jóhannsdóttir, H. L. (2004). Coping with bullying in the workplace: The effect of gender, age and type of bullying, *British Journal of Guidance & Counselling, 32*(3), 319–333.

Parzefall, M.-R. & Salin, D. (2010). Perceptions of and reactions to workplace bullying: A social exchange perspective, *Human Relations, 63*(6), 761–780. doi: 10.1177/0018726709345043

Resch, M. & Schubinski, M. (1996). Mobbing: Prevention and management in organizations, *European Journal of Work & Organizational Psychology, 5*(2), 295–308.

Royal Courts of Justice (2006). Case No: TLQ/05/0753. Before: The Honourable Mr Justice Owen. Between: Helen Green and DB Group Services (UK) Limited.

Runyan, C., Zakocs, R., & Zwerling, C. (2000). Administrative and behavioral interventions for workplace violence prevention, *American Journal of Preventive Medicine, 18*, 116–127.

Rutherford, A. & Rissel, C. (2004). A survey of workplace bullying in a health sector organisation, *Australian Health Review, 28*(1), 65–72.

Saam, N. J. (2010). Interventions in workplace bullying: A multilevel approach, *European Journal of Work and Organizational Psychology, 19*(1), 51–75. doi: 10.1080/13594320802651403

Salin, D. (2003). Ways of explaining workplace bullying: A review of enabling, motivating and precipitating structures and processes in the work environment, *Human Relations, 56*(10), 1213–1232.

Salin, D. M. (2003). Ways of explaining workplace bullying: A review of enabling, motivating and precipitating structures and processes in the work environment, *Human Relations, 56*(10), 1213–1232.

Salin, D. M. (2008). The prevention of workplace bullying as a question of human resource management: Measures adopted and underlying organizational factors, *Scandinavian Journal of Management, 24*(3), 221–231.

Salin, D. M. (2009). Organisational responses to workplace harassment, *Personnel Review, 38*(1), 26–44.

Snyder, L. A., Chen, P. Y., Grubb, P. L., Roberts, R. K., Sauter, S. L., Swanson, N. G., & Pamela, L. P. a. D. C. G. (2004). Workplace aggression and violence against individuals and organisations: Causes, consequences and interventions, *Research in Occupational Stress and Well Being, 4*, 1–65.

Sperry, L. (2009). Mobbing and bullying: The influence of individual, work group, and organizational dynamics on abusive workplace behavior, *Consulting Psychology Journal: Practice and Research, 61*(3), 190–201.

Totterdell, P., Hershcovis, M. S., Niven, K., Reich, T. C., & Stride, C. (2012). Can employees be emotionally drained by witnessing unpleasant interactions between coworkers? A diary study of induced emotion regulation, *Work and Stress, 26*(2), 112–129.

Tuckey, M. R., Dollard, M., Hosking, P. J., & Winefield, A. H. (2009). Workplace bullying: The role of psychosocial work environment factors, *International Journal of Stress Management, 16*(3), 215–232. doi: 10.1037/a0016841

Tuckey, M. R., Dollard, M., Saebel, J., & Berry, N. M. (2010). Negative workplace behaviour: Temporal associations with cardiovascular outcomes and psychological health problems in Australian Police, *Stress and Health, 26*, 372–381.

Vartia, M. (1996). The sources of bullying – Psychological work environment and organisational climate, *European Journal of Work & Organizational Psychology, 5*(2), 203–214.

Vartia, M. & Leka, S. (2011). Interventions for the prevention and management of bullying at work: in S. Einarsen, H. Hoel, D. Zapf, & C. L. Cooper (eds) *Bullying and Harassment in the Workplace: Developments in Theory, Research, and Practice* (2nd ed., pp. 359–380). Boca Raton, FL, USA: Taylor & Francis.

Wallace, B., Johnson, L., & Trenberth, L. (2011). Bullying the boss: The prevalence of upward bullying behaviours, *Australian and New Zealand Journal of Organisational Psychology, 3*(1), 66–71.

Weick, K. E. (1995). *Sense-Making in Organizations.* Thousand Oaks, CA: Sage.

White, P. (2008). Record of investigation into death: Case No: 3625/06. Melbourne, Australia: State Coroner, Victoria.

Zapf, D. & Gross, C. (2001). Conflict escalation and coping with workplace bullying: A replication and extension, *European Journal of Work & Organizational Psychology, 10*(4), 497–522.

11

Understanding Leading, Leader–Follower Relations, and Ethical Leadership in Organizations

Flora F. T. Chiang[1] and Thomas A. Birtch[2]

Introduction

Leaders hold the power to influence followers within and beyond organizational boundaries. Leaders, whether leading from spiritual, authentic, or servant models, can motivate individuals and teams in a desired direction; cultivate constructive interpersonal relations; promote higher standards of conduct and performance; create a caring and supportive organizational culture; and encourage a range of other positive employee and organizational outcomes. They can also inspire employees to volunteer and take part in community outreach initiatives and other forms of civic and social responsibility. However, as the popular business press and scholars in the fields of work psychology, organizational behavior, and interpersonal relations all too often remind us, such influence is not necessarily always positive. Abusive, despotic, and toxic behaviors, misconduct, and other ethical failings of leaders may not only be detrimental to the well-being, behaviors, and performance of followers but may also adversely impact other members of an organization, customers, suppliers, and the broader society in general. For these reasons, scholars and practitioners alike have been attempting to better understand how leader-follower relations might be improved and the role that ethical leadership can play in helping to mitigate deviant and counterproductive behaviors in the workplace. Consider the following scenario:

> Vincent heads a high profile department in a large Chinese service organization and directly oversees and manages several of its well

[1] Hong Kong Baptist University
[2] University of Cambridge

established programs. At the insistence of the executive arm of the organization, Vincent's department is charged with making a final attempt to revitalize a new program that is pending cancellation due to low customer demand and various operational complexities (e.g. coordination with overseas partner organizations). Walter is hired in part to help revitalize the new program and in part to perform duties for other departments in the organization. Vincent (Chinese) and Walter (American) are from different cultural backgrounds. The well established programs that Vincent manages compete for customers with the new program. They are fully staffed with experienced management teams, unlike the new program which suffers from severe resource constraints – both staffing and financial. Due to uncertainty surrounding its future and in order to cut costs, Vincent terminated all staff previously dedicated to the new program, leaving Walter the only individual responsible for its day-to-day operations (albeit in a fractional capacity). Such staffing cuts were made despite its heavy workload, special operating requirements, and development needs relative to the well established programs. In fact, its workload had more than doubled from the previous year.

1. When Walter was hired, he was not informed about the problematic history of the new program (e.g. customer quality and resource limitations) or its negative stigma within the organization. To take up the position, Walter had to resign from a senior role in government and relocate overseas.

2. Although ultimately responsible for looking after the new program, Vincent lacked basic knowledge about its heavy workload, special operating requirements, and development needs. Vincent also refused to take part in the new program's activities or to provide any assistance or professional guidance to Walter. Staff from the other well established programs were also prevented by Vincent from providing assistance to the new program, even in their own personal volunteer capacities (e.g. after regular working hours).

3. Given the heavy workload, special operating requirements, and development needs of the new program, Walter made several requests to Vincent for additional staffing and resources. Vincent's refusal, however, meant that Walter was forced to work extraordinarily long hours on the new program in addition to performing his other duties for the organization. This included working evening and weekends, and often through the night and

on public holidays for special activities and events related to the new program. It also meant that Walter was forced to use his own personal funds and financial credit to support the new program's activities, including hosting major events with partner organizations that required multi-city accommodation, transportation, workshops, and venue and meal arrangements for approximately 100 international guests.

4. In spite of such obstacles, in the months that followed, Walter achieved several noteworthy outcomes and milestones for the new program (e.g. a doubling of customers and industry accolades) and gained praise from colleagues and the news media. He further prevented the cancellation of the new program by helping to negotiate an agreement with partner organizations to extend its life for an additional five years. Doing so prevented a major competitor of the organization from becoming involved in the new program and with its partner organizations. Walter also arranged and obtained external funding for a series of special community outreach events designed to benefit the organization and local community.

5. Following an incident, Walter informed Vincent that he had been verbally and physically abused by a colleague, Mary, a long standing senior staff member in the department and also under Vincent's supervision. Vincent excused Mary's behavior as "just her style" and took no disciplinary action.

6. At the time of his annual performance review, Vincent rated Walter's performance in relation to his duties for the new program as satisfactory. Walter also excelled in his other duties for the organization, as demonstrated by winning an employee performance award and being invited to take up other opportunities in various departments. However, Walter later learned that Vincent had been undermining his reputation by making false and misleading statements about his work performance to colleagues and others. Worried about his future under Vincent's leadership, Walter attempted to transfer to another position in the organization but was blocked by Vincent.

7. Walter also learned that Vincent withheld important feedback from problematic customers preventing him from responding or taking appropriate action to resolve the matter in an open and transparent fashion. The new program had been plagued by poor customer behavior and several recent incidents led Walter to call for a code of conduct to be established with partner

organizations. Other members of the organization were also adversely affected by the poor behaviors of customers from the new program. Attempts to raise such concerns with Vincent were met with resistance. Vincent made it clear to Walter that his only concern was about obtaining sufficient customers for the new program and that any other concerns or issues were unimportant and unworthy of further discussion.

8. After close to a year's employment and in need of some rest and recuperation from the excessive working hours, Walter applied for his annual leave entitlement prior to its expiration and during the most suitable period in the new program's work schedule. Walter also arranged for another senior and experienced department head to act on his behalf during his intended leave period. However, Vincent rejected Walter's application and threatened that should he insist on taking his annual leave entitlement that he would risk losing his job. Walter subsequently resigned.

As incredible as the above scenario sounds, such circumstances are hardly new or exclusive to Vincent and Walter and can occur and propagate in any organization if left unchecked. Not only does the scenario reflect the negative consequences of poor leader-follower relations and unethical leadership but it illustrates the interconnected web of leader relations and influence within and beyond organizational boundaries. More specifically, the scenario raises several important questions about leader-follower relations and ethical leadership relevant to today's organizational and economic context. How can organizations function effectively when leader-follower relations are obstructed? How do leaders influence followers and others' well-being, behaviors, and performance? What constitutes an ethical leader and how is it important? How should organizations respond when a leader's actions and behaviors become potentially damaging to relations with followers and other members of the organization as well as to the organization's reputation with customers, suppliers, and in the community? Answers to such questions represent important pathways toward improving our understanding about leader-follower relations and, in particular, the implications associated with ethical leadership.

This chapter reviews recent scholarly work on leader-follower relations and ethical leadership. Such a review is important because successful leadership has been shown to engender both high quality relationships (Fletcher, 2007) and ethical components (Brown & Treviño, 2006). As the chapter unfolds, we also revisit our scenario in the hope that we stimulate further thinking about its implications for theory and practice. The chapter begins with a brief introduction to leadership, how it is defined, and the importance of relationships. Although leaders may exist independently of formal work roles and responsibilities, our main emphasis here is on managerial leadership in the context of formal organizations. Next, we explore the powerful influence of leaders on their followers and the dimensionality of leader relations. In particular, we identify relational interactions at both the micro-process (vertical and internal) and macro-process (horizontal and external) level. Understanding leadership and its relational context is important for several reasons. First, the influence and effectiveness of a leader cannot be assessed independently of relationships, since followers and other members of organizations are required to work together to get things done in organizations (Fletcher, 2007). Second, relationships are not confined solely to leader-follower dyads. They can include a wider array of ties with both internal and external stakeholders (Maak & Pless, 2006). Third, relationships are not always the same or equal with all subordinates. In-group and out-group differentiation (Liden et al., 2006) affects the symmetry and balance of relationships. Lastly, relationships form part of a social influence process, which is highly dependent on one's resources, influence, and power in relation to others (Brass & Burkhardt, 1993). Simply put, influence and power may be more salient in one context than another (e.g. hierarchical design versus team-oriented design). Moreover, since relationships are interactive processes not static entities (Uhl-Bien, 2006), relationships can be affected not only by prior interactions but also anticipated future interactions (Hinde, 1997). The discussion that follows is primarily concerned with enriching our understanding of ethical leadership and its implications to organizations, an especially important subject given its increasing attractiveness to modern organizations. Since leadership involves the process of getting things done through followers (Carmeli et al., 2012; Fletcher, 2007), leaders' individual values and attitudes toward followers and how they relate, interact, influence, manage, and leverage relationships are of paramount importance to organizations wishing to instill an organizational culture that values ethical behaviors. Lastly, the chapter closes by making some suggestions for possible directions in future research.

244 Leadership in Organizations

Deconstructing leading, leader relations, and ethical leadership

Defining leadership

Leadership has been defined and conceptualized in different ways depending on the criteria used and area of interest (Yukl, 2013). While early conceptualizations emphasized the content (e.g. dispositions, traits, skills, behaviors) and context (e.g. contingency factors) of leadership, more recently its relational aspects have been receiving heightened attention (see Uhl-Bien (2006) for a comprehensive review). Such advances in the literature are not surprising considering that, according to Pearce et al. (2007), leadership is "a concept of relationship; it assumes the existence of some people who follow one or more others ... There can be no leadership if there is just one person" (p. 287). As Mehra et al. (2006) similarly contend, "leaders do not lead in a social vacuum: They are embedded in ongoing systems of interpersonal relationships, or social networks, with subordinates, peers, and superiors" (p. 64). Uhl-Bien (2006) further defined leadership as "a social influence process through which emergent coordination (i.e. evolving social order) and change (e.g. new values, attitudes, approaches, behaviors, and ideologies) are constructed and produced" (p. 655). In the same vein, Cunliffe and Eriksen (2011) conceptualized leadership as "a way of being and relating with others, embedded in everyday experience and interwoven with a sense of moral responsibility" (p. 1432). As these conceptualizations imply, leadership is an important social influence process embedded in relationships. It is through this social influence process that leaders acquire and leverage the support and resources of their followers to accomplish goals and objectives.

Understanding leader relations and the power to influence

Leadership involves influence and that influence resides in and emanates from interactions with others. A leader's relations can be both internal (e.g. peers and subordinates) and external (e.g. customers and suppliers) to the organization, depending on job nature and position. The importance of relationships to leading has long been advanced by studies of leadership behavior, including those relating to leaders who possess a strong human relations focus and show consideration, respect, support, and concern for others (Bowers & Seashore, 1966; Stogdill et al., 1962) as well as those who achieve trust and high quality work relationships (Graen & Uhl-Bien, 1995). Leaders better able to develop and nurture relationships are thought to garner greater influence.

The ability to build and leverage relationships is often deemed to be at the heart of a leader's effectiveness (Mehra et al., 2006; Uhl-Bien, 2006). Since organizations are no longer purely hierarchical (i.e. leaner and flatter organizations), leaders can no longer rely solely on leader-centric authority and top-down approaches to influence. Such organizational developments necessitate that leaders "work in and through relationships" to achieve objectives (Fletcher, 2007, p. 348). At the same time, organizations have also become more knowledge-based, team-oriented, and interconnected. Given that resources, such as knowledge and capabilities, reside in individuals, leaders must find ways to leverage those resources through relationships and network ties in order to accomplish goals and objectives. Merely initiating structure, providing direction, and coordination are no longer sufficient (Krackhardt & Hanson, 1993).

> Walter, as a leader of the new program, was able to build relationships with other members in the organization that proved essential to gaining access to much needed resources and support and that eventually helped achieve a number of milestones (e.g. staff volunteer efforts, cross-departmental collaboration and support).

As the above suggests, a leader's effort represents a "bundle" of individual efforts (Maak & Pless, 2006). Through this process of bundling, the relations of leaders with their followers and others not only serve as important sources of influence (Sparrowe & Liden, 2005), relational identification (Sluss & Ashforth, 2007), and social support (Amabile et al., 2004), but enable them to overcome and by-pass formal structural constraints imposed by organizational bureaucracy (Pfeffer, 1992). Imagine if you are a leader who has good relationships with your followers (subordinates). If things go wrong, you will likely be more able to solicit their support and gain early insights into their attitudes and opinions about the situation. Maintaining close connections with followers may also make it easier to uncover the roots of counterproductive behaviors and influence the dispersion and diffusion of ethical values and norms. Ties to the upper echelons in an organization can also provide an early forecast about future strategic directions. Good connections with stakeholders can help maintain or re-build trust and improve public relations during times of crisis. Hence, stronger leader relations are likely to enhance the richness of communication and level of information processing as well as the degree of social bonding, trust, and emotional and cognitive connection (Gittell & Douglass, 2012, p. 711) essential to establishing and fostering ethical characteristics in an organization.

> Vincent had developed long standing ties and relations with a range of organizational members (including upper echelons) through his active leadership role and involvement on cross-departmental executive committees. Such relations made it possible for Vincent to distort facts about the new program and divert attention away from his failings in relation to his managing of the well established programs (e.g. sharp declines in customers, the loss of an international certification, problems associated with a poorly planned and implemented restructuring). By contrast, Walter was a new employee, his duties were divided between departments, he did not have any formal subordinates (i.e. worked independently on the new program), and given his extraordinary workload was virtually precluded from developing a broad range of ties or relationships with other members of the organization.

The dimensionality of relationships

According to Uhl-Bien (2006), an individual is relational if he/she "likes people and thrives on relationships" (p. 654). This suggests that relationships entail values and attitudes toward people – the purpose of life (Klinger, 1977), the basic need to belong (Baumeister & Leary, 1995), and the intrinsic values of people (Bateson, 1980). Being sensitive to the needs of others, caring for others, treating others justly and fairly, and showing respect to others represent basic foundations for a relationship. Thus, relationships can be considered a process through which a leader can gain benefits, either extrinsically (e.g. valuable information and resources), or intrinsically (e.g. social support, affection, and belonging) (Podolny & Baron, 1997).

When two or more individuals come into contact with one another or interact, a relationship forms. The nature of the relationship depends on the interacting parties' roles and positions and the context in which the relationship takes place. For example, an individual can be both a leader and follower depending on who he/she interacts with. An individual can also be a leader (e.g. supervisor or manager) at work and a friend outside the workplace. Relationships at work can be based on a formal employment contract, defined by hierarchy and work roles (e.g. supervisor versus subordinates), personal and informal (e.g. friendship), or expanded and negotiated role responsibilities (i.e. extra task role) (Northouse, 2013). They can also be vertical (upward and downward) and horizontal (multi-directional), internal and external, and person- or process-focused. Hence, the nature and composition of relationships can differ markedly.

Relational interactions and microprocesses (vertical and internal)

A dominant relationship-based logic to understanding leadership found in the literature is the notion of leader-member exchange (LMX) (Liden et al., 1997). Originating from vertical-dyad-linkage (VDL) theory (Dansereau et al., 1975), LMX is primarily concerned with vertical dyadic working relationships between a leader (supervisor) and his/her followers (subordinates) (Dienesch & Liden, 1986). Central to the theory is the idea that leaders develop different exchange relationships (LMX differentiation) with their followers, in which the quality of the relationship differently impacts leader-member outcomes (Gerstner & Day, 1997). A valued social exchange between a supervisor and subordinate is thought to represent a high quality LMX (Liden et al., 1997), which is characterized by mutual trust, liking, obligations, respect, support, and reciprocity and is found to elicit many profound and desirable outcomes (e.g. job satisfaction, affective commitment, organizational citizenship behavior) (see Dulebohn et al., 2011 and Ilies et al., 2007 for good reviews).

A positive relationship between leader and follower is an important relational aspect of the concept of ethical leadership. According to Brown and Treviño (2006, p. 603), "ethical leaders are exemplary models who care about and maintain positive relationships with their subordinates". Ethical leaders are viewed by followers as ethical people who are honest, trustworthy, fair, and care about the well-being of their employees and value their opinions – all of which are important components of high quality relationships (Brown & Treviño, 2006; Brown et al., 2005). The positive effects of ethical leadership on employee outcomes can be promoted via social exchange. When employees perceive that their leaders act in their best interest and are considerate, they reciprocate with higher levels of loyalty, emotional connection, and mutual support (Erdogan et al., 2006). They are also more likely to engage in prosocial as opposed to counterproductive behavior (Brown & Treviño, 2006). Mahsud et al. (2010) found that leaders with strong ethical values use more relations-oriented behaviors (e.g. empowering, supporting, developing). They also found that ethical leadership is positively associated with LMX. Dadhich and Bhal (2008) proposed the differential effects of ethical leadership and LMX on two different outcomes: ethics (a leader's honesty, whistle-blowing, and trust) and work-related (a leader's work effectiveness, satisfaction with the leader, and employee's extra effort), respectively. Ethical leadership was found to affect both ethics- and work-related outcomes similar to LMX, leading to the conclusion that the appraisal of leaders is influenced not only by on-the-job interactions with the leader (affective appraisal) but also by normative ethical conduct (cognitive appraisal). Tumasjan et al. (2011) further found that leaders who are considered more ethical by their subordinates receive higher LMX ratings. In Walumbwa et al.'s (2011) study, LMX was found to be an important mediating factor for explaining the ethical leadership-employee performance relationship. What these studies propose is that rather than relying on positional authority, ethical leaders who are able to demonstrate their ethical personal qualities and develop meaningful interpersonal relationships that go beyond simple economic and transactional relationships are more likely to engender a higher quality of social exchange (LMX), which is based on trust and positive relationships (Brown & Treviño, 2006; Walumbwa & Schaubroeck, 2009).

A second noteworthy relationship-based approach found in the literature is relational leadership theory (RLT). Uhl-Bien (2006) conceptualized relational leadership as both an entity (person-focused) and relational (process-focused) perspective. The former is said to emphasize an individual's attributes and behavioral styles as they engage in interpersonal relationships, while the latter takes a process view of relationships with leaders as they evolve. As Fletcher (2007) posited, the concept of relational leadership has become more explicit as a model of leadership effectiveness. Emerging research on relationship-based leadership is calling for expansion beyond the leader-follower dyad (Graen, 2006; Offstein et al., 2006), recognizing that leadership can occur in any direction. Other leadership constructs, such as follower-centered leadership (Shamir et al., 2007), distributed leadership (Ancona & Bresman, 2007), connective leadership (Lipman-Blumen, 1992), and shared leadership (Pearce & Conger, 2003) similarly recognize the importance of the relational aspects of leadership. The heart of relational leadership is to develop "shared goals, shared knowledge, and mutual respect, fostering attentiveness to the emerging situation and to one another" (Gittell & Douglass, 2012, p. 720). This shift in emphasis has led to a growing scholarly interest in process-oriented relational aspects of leadership (Fletcher, 2007; Uhl-Bien, 2006) and social networks (Balkundi & Kilduff, 2005; Friedrich et al., 2009).

Vincent's primary influence was restricted to that offered by his position of authority, since he was unable to create valued social exchanges, as reflected by his poor relationships with professional staff in the organization and partner organizations.

Relational interactions and macroprocesses (horizontal and external)

While LMX theory draws attention to the importance of relationships, particularly dyadic exchange relationships between leaders and followers, such exchanges and interpersonal relationships can be extended to those between leaders and other social interacting parties, such as peers and superiors (Tangirala et al., 2007), stakeholders (Maak & Pless, 2006), and individuals in other organizations (Barden & Mitchell, 2007). A social network is represented by sets of actors and ties between actors (Scott, 2000). From a network perspective, a leader is part of, and embedded in, a web of network tie relationships that influence his/her effectiveness both within and across organizations. The central premise is that network ties (connections) constitute social and relational capital and resources that provide value-added economic returns (Burt, 2000). Unlike LMX, social network theories position leaders as "key to managing and sustaining the relationships between environmental, social and organizational network elements" (Cunliffe & Eriksen, 2011, p. 1429). In other words, this view moves away from microprocess relational interactions and "individualist, essentialist, and atomistic explanations" toward more macroprocess "relational, contextual, and systemic understandings" of relational interactions (Borgatti & Foster, 2003, p. 991). Hence, network theory offers a more contextual approach to examining leaders' relationships (Venkataramani et al., 2010).

An emphasis on ties and relations between actors is the most important feature of network research (Au et al., 2009). Ties "serve as conduits for the flow of interpersonal resources" (Balkundi & Harrison, 2006, p. 50). Network resources are rooted in relationships and relationships constitute important network resources. Networks between individuals are developed through high quality interpersonal exchanges and shared resources. Central to network and social relationships are the concepts of content (i.e. nature of resources/relations exchanged) and structure (i.e. pattern of relations) (Borgatti & Everett,

1999). Two important types of content are instrumental and expressive network relations (Ibarra, 1993). Instrumental relations involve the exchange of knowledge, information resources, and work-related advice, emerge from formal relationships (e.g. leader-subordinate), and provide task-related resources needed for effective work performance (Seibert et al., 2001). Expressive relations, on the other hand, are affect-related and involve the exchange of friendship and social support characterized by higher levels of affect, closeness, and trust more so than those that are exclusively instrumental (Ibarra, 1993; McGuire, 2007).

By contrast, the structural dimension of networks reflects the overall pattern of relationships among contacts and the degree of interconnectedness in a network (Nahapiet & Ghoshal, 1998). Key structural characteristics include density (extensiveness of contact), centrality/periphery (position), weak/strong ties (tie strength), embeddedness (prior relationships among contacts), range (degree of diversity), and structural holes (social gaps between connections). Moreover, such structural features have important implications for leader's effectiveness (Balkundi & Harrison, 2006; Kilduff & Tsai, 2006). In their meta-analysis on the relationship between leader and team networks and team performance, Balkundi and Harrison (2006) found that a leader's centrality was related to the team's task performance. Mehra et al. (2006) also found that leaders' centrality in external and internal friendship networks was related to both economic performance of their units and their personal reputation as leaders. Sparrowe and Liden (2005) found that leaders' sponsorship and their centrality in the advice network shape the influence members gain through their LMX relationships.

Within this stream of studies, leveraging network resources must be accompanied by strong relational and exchange components (Nahapiet & Ghoshal, 1998). Unlike other types of resources, network resources are derived from the advantages (e.g. information) individuals obtain from their relationships with others (Brass, 1984). In this sense, leaders are not atomized decision-makers but rather influenced by a network of relationships (Hoang & Antoncic, 2003). Since network resources are rooted and embedded in, and mobilized through relationships, a leader's ability to recognize and interpret relevant characteristics of a social network (network cognition), and her/his ability to access, interact with, and influence others is important to obtaining these resources (Kilduff & Tsai, 2006). Armed with useful relationships, a leader with high network ties can more readily gain access to a broader base of information, mobilize personal influence, build coalitions, and access valuable resources that reduce transaction costs (Williamson, 1987). Thus, this stream of research draws on the importance of relational network resources in explaining leadership outcomes (e.g. Balkundi & Harrison, 2006; Mehra et al., 2006). Most research on social networks in organizations has focused on individual work-related outcomes, such as promotion and extrinsic and intrinsic career success (Ng et al., 2005). In the context of leadership, social network research has often been approached from the stakeholder perspective (Maak & Pless, 2006). To our knowledge, empirical studies that link the network approach to ethical leadership in an organizational setting are sparse.

> Walter was able to establish ties and create a network with senior leaders from industry and government that enabled him to help offset some of the resource constraints and limitations imposed by Vincent. Such network ties and relationships, especially those beyond Vincent's authority, enabled Walter to achieve a range of milestones in the new program's development.

To summarize, LMX focuses mainly on the quality of relationships (usually a single relationship between a leader and follower) while network theory considers both the content (the repertoire of network relationships) and structure of relationships as valued resources that a leader can draw on through his/her position in the network. Both perspectives are relationship-based, with LMX focusing on the "formally constituted vertical dyad" and network resources on "emergent or informal networks of relationships" (Sparrowe & Liden, 2005, p. 506). In the context of leadership, LMX theory suggests that high quality LMX offers valued resources to leaders that allow them to affect important work outcomes while network theory suggests that network relationships provide leaders with valued resources that can enhance their LMX (Venkataramani et al., 2010). In the context of ethical leadership, it is through these relationships and interactions that a sense of ethical responsibility can be fostered and upheld, as we shall now elaborate.

Ethical leadership and its relational implications

According to Maak and Pless (2006), leadership takes place in relationships – they are at the "centre of leadership" and ethics is at the "heart of leadership" (p. 101). As empirical studies have shown, ethical leadership is positively correlated with a range of relational elements, such as leader consideration, interactional fairness, idealized influence, trust, and high LMX quality (e.g. Brown et al., 2005; Mayer et al., 2009; Neubert et al., 2009). In other words, an ethical leader connects others with ethical values and beliefs, manages with integrity, and leads with trust.

Ethical leadership has been examined from prescriptive, philosophical, and empirical perspectives (Avey et al., 2012). Unlike other leadership constructs (e.g. authentic, spiritual, transformational), which also entail ethical components (Brown & Treviño, 2006), ethical leadership is more specific (ethic-specific) and issue-oriented (in response to scandals). It encompasses traits (e.g. honesty, integrity, and trustworthiness), behaviors (e.g. altruistic, interactional fairness, empathy, role-modeling), situations (e.g. ethical climate, moral intensity of the issue), contingencies (e.g. the appropriateness of decisions in terms of ethical consequences), and both transactional (e.g. rewards and punishment) and relational (e.g. caring, supportive, and trust) components (Treviño et al., 2003; Yukl, 2013).

Since ethical issues are often ambiguous and contentious in nature, the study of ethical leadership in its own right is highly important. Such dynamics also make relationships that establish emotional, cognitive, and behavioral connections important. For example, according to attachment theory, in highly uncertain situations, individuals often turn to and are more attached to close others for advice, guidance, assistance, and support (Bowlby, 1982). There are strong motivations for followers (subordinates) to seek security and safety from significant close others (leaders) to reduce anxiety associated with uncertainty (Neubert et al., 2009). Treviño (1986) argued that during such occasions individuals often turn to leaders for ethical guidance.

> By condoning Mary's inappropriate behavior, Vincent negatively impacted safety, security, and anxiety in the organization and left such behaviors to propagate, be repeated, and mimicked. Mary's continued abusive behavior led to other employees' resignations and turnover. A lack of ethical oversight also meant that such poor and unethical behaviors even materialized during interactions with customers.

Moreover, according to social learning and identity theories, individuals learn by observing and modeling the behavior of their attractive role models (Bandura, 1986). Being highly visible figures in organizations, ethical leaders can increase moral awareness and set normative standards and goals (Kidwell & Bennett, 1993; Neubert et al., 2009).

They can also inspire followers to cognitively align with their ethical beliefs and values (Zhu et al., 2011). Setting good examples fosters morally right or ethical behaviors. Followers mimic and role-model the behaviors of their leaders by observing and emulating how they act and behave, and learn what behaviors are (un)acceptable in their workplace (Bandura, 1986). Strong identification also increases followers' likelihood of emulating their leaders' behavior. The motivation to comply with, imitate, and model ethical leaders is based on the desire to identify with their leader. Followers are also more likely to identify with and emulate those leaders perceived as consistent and trustworthy (Grojean et al., 2004; Brown et al., 2005). Research has shown that salient social identities can be powerful in motivating behavior (Turner et al., 1994) and provide a basis for social judgment, influence, trust, and cooperation (Haslam, 2004; Tyler & Blader, 2000). Hence, ethical leadership should promote positive workplace relationships and behaviors, particularly since followers model attractive leader behaviors, are inspired by their leader's normative standards and values, and are motivated to comply and identify with and act in alignment with approved norms and expectations of their leaders (Grojean et al., 2004).

Although defining ethical leadership is difficult as there is "no ethically neutral ground" (Yukl, 2013, p. 329), a commonly adopted definition is provided by Brown et al. (2005). These scholars define ethical leadership as "the demonstration of normatively appropriate conduct through personal actions and interpersonal relationships, and the promotion of such conduct to followers through two-way communication, reinforcement, and decision-making" (p. 120). This conceptualization entails two important mechanisms through which ethical leaders influence followers' ethical behaviors. The first is through personal qualities and actions, either serving as an ethical example (being a moral person) or by actively managing morality (being a moral manager) (Treviño et al, 2000) whereas the second takes place through interpersonal relationships, for example, treating people fairly and communicating about ethics (Brown & Treviño, 2006; Mayer et al., 2012). Although there are subtle differences in the definitions of moral and ethical behavior, we use the terminology interchangeably.

Being a moral person versus being a moral manager

Values determine an individual's behavior and attitudes toward people in general. Values of an ethical leader include altruism, honesty, empathy, fairness, caring, and trust and entail the "moral person"

254 *Leadership in Organizations*

component (Brown & Treviño, 2006). Leadership involves personal influence and inspiration (Yukl, 2013). The ethical values of leaders are manifested through their relations-oriented behaviors with followers (subordinates) (Mahsud et al., 2010), such that they are more likely to treat others justly and with respect, empower followers, and use two-way communication and participation to promote ethical norms (Brown et al., 2005). To the extent that ethical leaders create a fair, caring, and positive work environment and when ethical norms and behaviors are made salient to followers by ethical leaders (e.g. through role modeling), followers should become more mutually dependent and cooperative and less likely to exhibit dishonest actions or harm others (De Hoogh & Den Hartog, 2008). Empirical research suggests that ethical leadership is positively associated with prosocial and helping behaviors (Kacmar et al., 2011) and negatively associated with counterproductive behaviors and interpersonal relationship conflict in the workplace (Mayer et al., 2012). When followers feel connected to their ethical leaders, they are obliged to show ethical concern (Glover, 2000).

By refusing to provide guidance to Walter or assist with the new program's activities, Vincent intentionally obstructed goals of the organization. Preventing other followers' involvement, whether formal or voluntary, signaled that the new program was not valued. Vincent also made false and misleading statements to other members in the organization about Walter's performance, contrary to objective facts. To further undermine Walter's reputation and the goodwill that he had established, Vincent withheld information about customers with a problematic history of poor behavior. This effectively prevented Walter from being able to deal with matters in an open and transparent manner and promoted an environment of wild speculation. Vincent further denied Walter's request for annual leave, despite being informed by Walter about his health concerns. He further threatened Walter's job. At the same time, Vincent condoned the misconduct of his other followers. Vincent's actions were unethical.

While being a moral person reflects the values and qualities of the ethical leader, being a moral manager reflects the means and practices by which ethical leaders promote ethical conduct at work. In addition to being an ethical role model, ethical leaders promote ethical norms in organizations by openly and explicitly talking about ethics, empowering employees, seeking justice, being accountable for actions, and establishing ethical standards and ethical norms of conduct via reinforcement mechanisms (Brown et al., 2005; Brown & Treviño, 2006). Ethical leaders enact and enforce organizational practices, policies, and procedures that encourage and facilitate the display of ethical behavior, thereby reducing the likelihood of unethical conduct. For example, setting ethical reward and performance criteria signals to organizational members the importance of various moral values and ethical behaviors (see Chiang & Birtch, 2012 for a discussion about the differential effects of rewards). When employees learn that ethical and unethical behaviors are evaluated, rewarded or punished, and reinforced or prohibited, they are more likely to engage in or refrain from appropriate or deviant behaviors (Brown et al., 2005; Mayer et al., 2009).

> Neither Vincent nor the organization in our scenario had established mechanisms or practices for dealing with unethical behavior. As a consequence, not only were Vincent's unethical actions and behaviors allowed to flourish but so too were those of his followers (subordinates). Contrary to Vincent, when Walter was personally subjected to and also witnessed other organizational members being exposed to unprofessional conduct and the poor behavior of customers, Walter's reaction was to take steps to ensure that such behaviors were mitigated in future, including the establishment of a "code of conduct" and reporting incidents to senior management.

Being a moral person, by setting personal examples and possessing virtues such as caring, fairness, and honesty, and being a moral manager, by establishing transparent, consistent, and open communication of ethical expectations through transactional mechanisms, ethical leaders create a relational climate that is psychologically safe (Walumbwa & Schaubroeck, 2009), meaningful and fulfilling (Avey et al., 2012), and based on interactional justice (Neubert et al., 2009). By emphasizing the importance of ethical values and the potential consequences of violating them through punishment, leaders possess the ability to make ethical standards salient to followers (Treviño et al., 2006).

Interpersonal relationships

Ethical leaders not only influence organizational members through "demonstration of normatively appropriate conduct through personal actions" but also through "interpersonal relationships" (Brown et al.,

2005, p. 120). Individuals also learn from their interactions and experiences with others (Bandura, 1986). Frequent and close interactions facilitate the establishment of relationships in the workplace. Individuals are more aware of the moral nature of issues from someone who is close (proximal) to them (Jones, 1991). Close interaction and relationships also increase attention to the preferences of others (Sally, 2000) as well as sensitivity to their needs (Smith, 1966), the result being that each party places a positive value on the outcomes of the other (Bolton & Ockenfels, 2000). Further, when the strength of a relationship increases so too does the possibility of moral inclusion (Brass et al., 1998). Studies have shown that individuals are more likely to identify and empathize with those that they feel close to (Turban et al., 2002). They are also more likely to form higher-quality relationships with those they perceive they have more in common with (Schaubroeck & Lam, 2002).

Although both social learning and social identity theories imply close interpersonal relations between leader and follower, the extent of role modeling behavior depends on the nature and quality of the relationship. Social exchange theory (Blau, 1964) is more directly linked to the interactional processes of ethical leadership. Interactions that constitute relationships are characterized by a degree of trust, mutuality, and reciprocity. Social exchange theory (Blau, 1964) proposes that behavior is the result of an exchange process. The norm of reciprocity (Gouldner, 1960) requires that if one exchange partner does something beneficial for the other, that the other has an obligation to reciprocate with desirable behavior (Cropanzano & Mitchell, 2005). Because ethical leaders are likely to engender high levels of trust and fairness (Brown & Treviño, 2006), and be considerate, supportive, and concerned for their followers' well-being (Brown et al., 2005), followers should feel accountable and indebted, thereby reciprocating such treatment by exhibiting ethical behaviors and refraining from deviant behaviors that would be detrimental to the organization. When employees feel supported by their leaders, they also exhibit greater dedication, satisfaction, affective commitment (Toor & Ofori, 2009), and citizenship behavior (Euwema et al., 2007). Moreover, they are less likely to act counterproductively or unethically (Mayer et al., 2009). Perceptions about the quality of social interactions are necessary antecedent cognitions preceding workplace behaviors. Violation results in negative norms of reciprocity or "sentiments of retaliation" in which "the emphasis is placed not on the return of benefits but on the return of injuries" (Gouldner, 1960, p. 172).

Walter worked hard to establish good interpersonal relations with others, especially given the stigma attached to the new program. Albeit eventually thwarted by Vincent, Walter was able to involve a range of colleagues in the new program that had previously refused involvement. Walter also attempted to act as an agent of change by providing assistance to Vincent and his other followers in relation to the well established programs, although the anticipated reciprocity was never forthcoming.

High quality relationships not only rely on reciprocity but also on norms associated with trust and justice. Trust is an important relational exchange between parties and has a powerful impact on relationships. Empirical studies linking ethical leadership and trust are scant. One exception is Den Hartog and De Hoogh (2009) who provide evidence suggesting that perceived ethical leader behavior (measured as perceived fairness and integrity behavior) is positively associated with followers' trust in management and colleagues, although the effect is stronger for trust in management than in colleagues. To explain this finding, the authors concluded that the trust effect may extend from the leaders to their coworkers (positive association).

While social learning and identity theories explain how leader role modeling shapes norms for employee ethical behaviors, the exchange perspective explicates how reciprocity and fair treatment create the norms for future exchange relationships that drive ethical behaviors. Although they focus on different aspects of influence, one feature in common is that they are concerned about relationships, with the former emphasizing the strength of relationships and the latter the exchange component of relationships. By emphasizing fair treatment, listening to follower concerns (Brown & Treviño, 2006), providing job autonomy (Piccolo et al., 2010), the right to a voice in decision-making (Brown et al., 2005), and empowering followers (De Hoogh & Den Hartog, 2008; Resick et al., 2006), ethical leaders can foster a work environment that is based on interactional fairness and justice (Neubert et al., 2009) in which followers perceive a sense of belonging and optimism about their leader and organization (De Hoogh & Den Hartog, 2008).

Directions for future research

Despite many important advances in leader-follower relations and ethical leadership research, there is still much to learn (Brown &

Mitchell, 2010). First, while the extant literature has emphasized the impacts of ethical leadership on attitudinal (e.g. affective commitment) and behavioral outcomes (e.g. organizational citizenship behavior), empirical evidence linking ethical leadership with follower relational outcomes (e.g. relationship quality, trust, fair treatment) remains insufficient. Neglecting the relational context of ethical leadership limits our ability to understand the influence process of ethical leadership, its antecedents, and its consequences.

Second, little prior research explicitly examines the influence of (un)ethical leadership on "dark side", counterproductive, and deviant workplace behaviors (Detert et al., 2007). According to Brown and Mitchell (2010), the "dark sides" of organizational behavior (both destructive leader and destructive follower behaviors) should be incorporated in the study of ethical leadership. As discussed above, a leader's influence on follower behaviors can be significant. Thus, how this influence is exercised is important. As our scenario illustrates, leaders can exploit relations with followers and influence them to do things contrary to their better judgment (e.g. work extraordinary work hours to compensate for severe resource constraints imposed by an incompetent, complacent, or self-interested leader, such as Vincent). Leaders can even influence followers and others to engage in "crimes of obedience" (Hinrichs, 2007, p. 69).

> Vincent was able to influence the human resources department to agree that Walter's leave would somehow be damaging to the new program's operations, even though Walter had openly expressed health concerns and arranged for a suitable acting replacement during his intended leave. The act of denying annual leave entitlement even contradicted labor laws.

Hence, further research is needed to better understand, compare, and contrast the influence of ethical versus unethical leadership (Detert et al., 2007). As Brown and Mitchell (2010) asserted "much more research is needed to uncover the dynamics of leadership and ethics – from both a positive and negative angle" (p. 591).

Third, the primary focus in the extant literature is on the main effects of ethical leadership (Brown et al., 2005; Detert et al., 2007; Mayer et al., 2009; Zhu et al., 2011). Absent are investigations about potential mediating processes and boundary conditions for ethical leadership (Mayer et al., 2009). As this chapter suggests, a relational approach to ethical leadership requires greater attention. The link between ethical leadership and job behaviors can depend on the content and context of relationships between a leader and follower. Walumbwa et al. (2011) drew on social exchange and social identity theories to propose that ethical leaders are able to develop meaningful interpersonal relationships, trust, and fairness with their followers, which translate into high LMX and organizational identification, and ultimately employee performance. Thus, followers of ethical leaders can be intrinsically motivated by the effect of positive social relationships.

Fourth, to more fully understand the effects of ethical leadership, future research should also examine boundary conditions. For example, we know relatively little about how the relational context can be used to explain the more or less favorable effects of ethical leadership and how to differentiate follower behaviors between ethical and unethical leaders. Cognitive and affective appraisal of leaders' and/or followers' behaviors can be affected not only by their normative values but also by the nature of their relationships. A strong relationship is often associated with more favorable evaluations between dyadic partners (Andersen & Chen, 2002). For instance, when ethical leaders have strong relationships with followers, they are less likely to make negative internal attributions about their followers' wrongdoings (Steiner, 1997). Similarly, followers are more likely to rationalize or neutralize the negative attributes of their leaders' unethical behavior (Tumasjan et al., 2011). Hence, strong relationships may lead to greater levels of rationalization, which results in more lenient evaluations of in-group leaders/followers versus out-group leaders/followers even following moral transgression. This provides a possible explanation for Vincent's apparent acceptance of a senior staff member's (Mary) (in-group) abusive behavior in our scenario.

Fifth, ethical leadership entails both "moral person" and "moral manager" components. An ethical leader should also be a "social and relational person and manager". It is likely that some ethical leaders may be more proficient than others at motivating and regulating ethical behaviors. Hence, relational skills (e.g. social skills, emotional intelligence, and the effective use of feedback) may represent important boundary conditions (Uhl-Bien & Maslyn, 2003). Recent research on political skill echoes such arguments (Wei et al., 2012). Following such logic, the impact of ethical leadership on relational outcomes is likely to be stronger when leaders possess greater social skills than their counterparts (e.g. the ability to utilize and leverage social capital and influence others either through upward appeal or coalition influence) (Ferris et al., 2005).

Finally, we suggest that future research should also explore the impact of culture and other contextual factors (e.g. institutions) and how these might affect the influence of (un)ethical leadership on follower relations. Current research provides only a limited and fragmented view of how cultural differences between leaders and followers might impact their relational context and therefore the ability to establish and motivate ethical norms and behaviors. When a leader and follower come from different cultural backgrounds, as exemplified by our scenario about Vincent (Chinese, collectivist culture) and Walter (American, individualistic culture), how might cultural differences affect their perceptions and relationships?

> When Walter attempted to discuss staffing shortages, resource constraints, and incidents involving misconduct and poor behavior with other leaders (mainly Chinese) in the organization, he was frequently referred back to Vincent and advised that Vincent was responsible for overseeing all decisions and addressing matters relating to the new program. Although expatriate leaders acknowledged such obstacles and issues, they similarly felt compelled to conform to the Chinese style of hierarchy. Being considered as an out-group member, Walter felt powerless and excluded. When Walter was abused by Mary, an in-group member of Vincent, Vincent simply excused Mary's behavior. To add to the cultural complexity associated with operating the new program, its majority of customers and partner organizations were from different cultures and countries. Such cultural characteristics meant that standards of conduct and behavior were subject to a variety of different interpretations.

Since ethical issues are embedded in situation and context, what is considered ethical in one culture may not necessarily be considered ethical in another. When conflicts do arise, we could ask; which is more important – ethical or relational considerations? Do strong relationships undermine or facilitate ethical behaviors? These issues are particularly relevant to multinational corporations in which employees, customers, and other interacting parties come from diverse cultural backgrounds.

Conclusion

As this chapter advances, a clearer understanding of leader-follower relations and the implications of ethical leadership is not only vital to improving our understanding of how, why, and through what relational content, processes, and context ethical leadership relates to follower workplace behavior but is also essential to selecting, developing, and motivating ethical leaders, a goal that is high on the agenda of most organizations.

Following Walter's resignation, Vincent took up responsibilities for managing the new program until the role was assumed by new leadership. The new program was eventually provided with a team of dedicated staff and additional resources. However, in the years that followed it has yet to develop much beyond Walter's early achievements. The community outreach initiatives established by Walter have also ceased. Walter was eventually required to take legal action to recover his losses associated with unpaid annual leave, unpaid work performed on holidays, and other financial losses. Vincent's abusive behavior towards another staff member became public through reports in local news media. Vincent continues to be employed by the organization.

References

Amabile, T. M., Schatzel, E. A., Moneta, G. B., & Kramer, S. J. (2004). Leader behaviors and the work environment for creativity: Perceived leader support, *The Leadership Quarterly*, *15*, 5–32.

Ancona, D. & Bresman, H. (2007). *X-teams: How to Build Teams that Lead, Innovate and Succeed*. Boston: Harvard Business School Publishing.

Andersen, S. M. & Chen, S. (2002). The relational self: An interpersonal social–cognitive theory, *Psychological Review*, *109*(4), 619–645.

Au, K., Ren, B., & Birtch, T. A. (2009). China's business network structure during institutional transitions, *Asia-Pacific Journal of Management*, *26*, 219–240.

Avey, J. B., Wernsing, T. S., & Palanski, M. E. (2012). Exploring the process of ethical leadership: The mediating role of employee voice and psychological ownership, *Journal of Business Ethics*, *107*, 27–34.

Balkundi, P. & Harrison, D. (2006). Ties, leaders, and time in teams: Strong inference about network structure's effects on team viability and performance, *Academy of Management Journal*, *49*, 49–68.

Balkundi, P. & Kilduff, M. (2005). The ties that lead: A social network approach to leadership, *The Leadership Quarterly*, *16*(6), 941–961.

Bandura, A. (1986). *Social Foundations of Thought and Action*. Englewood Cliffs, NJ: Prentice-Hall.

Barden, J. Q. & Mitchell, W. (2007). Disentangling the influences of leaders' relational embeddedness on interorganizational exchange, *Academy of Management Journal*, *50*(6), 1440–1461.

Bateson, G. (1980). *Mind And Nature: A Necessary Unity*. New York: Bantam.

Baumeister, R. F. & Leary, M. R. (1995). The need to belong: Desire for interpersonal attachments as a fundamental human motivation, *Psychological Bulletin*, *117*, 497–529.

Blau, P. M. 1964. *Exchange and Power in Social Life.* New York: John Wiley.

Bolton, G. & Ockenfels, A. (2000). A theory of equity, reciprocity, and competition, *American Economic Review, 90,* 166–193.

Borgatti, S. P. & Everett, M. G. (1999). Models of core/periphery structures, *Social Networks, 21,* 375–395.

Borgatti, S. P. & Foster, P. (2003). The network paradigm in organizational research: A review and typology, *Journal of Management, 29,* 991–1013.

Bowers, D. G. & Seashore, S. E. (1966). Predicting organizational effectiveness with a four factor theory of leadership, *Administrative Science Quarterly, 11,* 238–263.

Bowlby, J. (1982). *Attachment and Loss: Vol. 1 Attachment* (2nd ed.). New York: Basic Books.

Brass, D. J. (1984). Being in the right place: A structural analysis of individual influence in an organization, *Administrative Science Quarterly, 29,* 518–539.

Brass, D. J. & Burkhardt, M. E. (1993). Potential power and power use: An investigation of structure and behavior, *Academy of Management Journal, 36,* 441–470.

Brass, D. J., Butterfield, K. D., & Skaggs, B. C. (1998). Relationships and unethical behavior: A social network perspective, *Academy of Management Review, 23,* 14–31.

Brown, M. E. & Mitchell, M. S. (2010). Ethical and unethical leadership: Exploring new avenues for future research, *Business Ethics Quarterly, 20*(4), 583–616.

Brown, M. E. & Treviño, L. K. (2006). Ethical leadership: A review and future directions, *Leadership Quarterly, 17,* 595–616.

Brown, M. E., Treviño, L. K., & Harrison, D. A. (2005). Ethical leadership: A social learning perspective for construct development and testing, *Organizational Behavior and Human Decision Processes, 97,* 117–134.

Burt, R. S. (2000). Decay functions, *Social Networks, 22*(1), 1–28.

Carmeli, A., Tishler, A., & Edmondson, A. C. (2012). CEO relational leadership and strategic decision quality in top management teams: The role of team trust and learning from failure, *Strategic Organization, 10,* 31–54.

Chiang, F. & Birtch, T. A. (2012). The performance implications of financial and non-financial rewards: An Asian Nordic comparison, *Journal of Management Studies, 49*(3), 538–570.

Cropanzano, R. & Mitchell, M. S. (2005). Social exchange theory: An interdisciplinary review, *Journal of Management, 31,* 874–900.

Cunliffe, A. L. & Eriksen, M. (2011). Relational leadership, *Human Relations, 64,* 1425–1449.

Dadhich, A. & Bhal, K. T. (2008). Ethical leader behaviour and leader–member exchange as predictors of subordinate behaviours, *Vikalpa, 33,* 15–25.

Dansereau Jr., F., Graen, G. B., & Haga, W. J. (1975). A vertical dyad linkage approach to leadership in formal organizations, *Organizational Behavior and Human Performance, 13,* 46–78.

Detert, J. R., Trevino, L. K., Burris, E. R., & Andiappan, M. (2007). Managerial modes of influence and counterproductivity in organizations: A longitudinal business-unit-level investigation, *Journal of Applied Psychology, 92,* 993–1005.

De Hoogh, A. H. B. & Den Hartog, D. N. (2008). Ethical and despotic leadership, relationships with leader's social responsibility, top management team effectiveness and subordinates' optimism: A multi-method study, *The Leadership Quarterly*, *19*, 297–311.

Den Hartog, D. N. & De Hoogh, A. H. B. (2009). Empowering behaviour and leader fairness and integrity: Studying perceptions of ethical leader behaviour from a levels-of-analysis perspective, *European Journal of Work and Organizational Psychology*, *18*(2), 199–230.

Dienesch, R. M. & Liden, R. C. (1986). Leader-member exchange model of leadership: A critique and further development, *Academy of Management Review*, *11*, 618–634.

Dulebohn, J. H., Bommer, W. H., Liden, R. C., Brouer, R. L., & Ferris, G. R. (2011). A meta-analysis of antecedents and consequences of leader-member exchange: Integrating the past with an eye toward the future, *Journal of Management*, *38*, 1715–1759.

Erdogan, B., Liden, R. C., & Kraimer, M. L. (2006). Justice and leader–member exchange: The moderating role of organizational culture, *Academy of Management Journal*, *49*, 395–406.

Euwema, M. C., Wendt, H., & Van Emmerik, H. (2007). Leadership styles and group organizational citizenship behavior across cultures, *Journal of Organizational Behavior*, *28*(8), 1035–1057.

Ferris, G. R., Treadway, D. A., Kolodinsky, R. W., Hochwarter, W. A., Kacmar, C. J., Douglas, C., & Frink, D. D. (2005). Development and validation of the political skill inventory, *Journal of Management*, *31*, 126–152.

Fletcher, J. K. (2007). Leadership, power, and positive relationships: in J. E. Dutton & B. R. Ragins (eds) *Exploring Positive Relationship at Work: Building a Theoretical and Research Foundation* (pp. 347–371). Mahwah, NJ: Lawrence Erlbaum Associates, Inc.

Friedrich, T. L., Vessey, W. B., Schuelke, M. J., Ruark, G. A., & Mumford, M. D. (2009). A framework for understanding collective leadership: The selective utilization of leader and team expertise within networks, *The Leadership Quarterly*, *20*, 933–958.

Gerstner, C. R. & Day, D. V. (1997). Meta-analytic review of leader-member exchange theory: Correlates and construct issues, *Journal of Applied Psychology*, *82*, 827–844.

Gittell, J. H. & Douglass, A. (2012). Relational bureaucracy: Structuring reciprocal relationships into roles, *Academy of Management Review*, *37*(4), 709–733.

Glover, J. (2000). *Humanity: A Moral History of the 20th Century*. New Haven, CT: Yale University Press.

Gouldner, A. W. (1960). *The Psychology of Behavioral Exchange*. Reading, MA: Addison-Wesley.

Graen, G. B. (2006). Post Simon, March, Weick, and Graen: New leadership sharing as a key to understanding organizations: in G. Graen & J. A. Graen (eds) *Sharing Network Leadership* (Vol. 4, pp. 269–279). Greenwich, CT: Information Age Publishing.

Graen, G. B. & Uhl-Bien, M. (1995). Relationship-based approach to leadership: Development of leader-member exchange (LMX) theory of leadership over 25 years: Applying a multi-level multi-domain perspective, *The Leadership Quarterly*, *6*, 219–247.

Grojean, M. W., Resick, C. J., Dickson, M. W., & Smith, D. B. (2004). Leaders, values, and organizational climate: Examining leadership strategies for establishing an organizational climate regarding ethics, *Journal of Business Ethics, 55*, 223–241.

Haslam, S. A. (2004). *Psychology in Organizations: The Social Identity Approach* (2nd ed.). London: Sage.

Hinde, R. A. (1997). *Relationships: A Dialectical Perspective.* Hove, UK: Psychology Press.

Hinrichs, K. T. (2007). Follower propensity to commit crimes of obedience the role of leadership beliefs, *Journal of Leadership and Organizational Studies, 14*, 69–76.

Hoang, H. & Antoncic, B. (2003). Network-based research in entrepreneurship: A critical review, *Journal of Business Venturing, 18*, 165–187.

Ibarra, H. (1993). Personal networks of women and minorities in management: A conceptual framework, *Academy of Management Review, 18*, 56–87.

Ilies, R., Nahrgang, J. D., & Morgeson, F. P. (2007). Leader-member exchange and citizenship behaviors: A meta-analysis, *Journal of Applied Psychology, 92*, 269–277.

Jones, T. M. (1991). Ethical decision making by individuals in organizations: An issue-contingent model, *Academy of Management Review, 16*, 366–395.

Kacmar, K. M., Bachrach, D. G., Harris, K. J., & Zivnuska, S. (2011). Fostering good citizenship through ethical leadership: Exploring the moderating role of gender and organizational politics, *Journal of Applied Psychology, 96*, 633–642.

Kilduff, M. & Tsai, W. (2006). *Social Networks and Organizations.* London, England: Sage Publications.

Kidwell, R. E., Jr. & Bennett, N. (1993). Employee propensity to withhold effort: A conceptual model to intersect three avenues of research, *Academy of Management Review, 18*, 429–456.

Klinger, E. (1977). *Meaning and Void: Inner Experiences and the Incentives in People's Lives.* Minneapolis: University of Minnesota Press.

Krackhardt, D. & Hanson, J. (1993). Informal networks: The company behind the chart, *Harvard Business Review, 71*, 104–111.

Liden, R. C., Sparrowe, R. T., & Wayne, S. J. (1997). Leader-member exchange theory: The past and potential for the future: in G. R. Ferris & K. M. Rowland (eds) *Research in Personnel and Human Resources Management* (Vol. 15, pp. 47–119). Greenwich, CT: JAI Press.

Liden, R. C., Erdogan, B., Wayne, S. J., & Sparrowe, R. T. (2006). Leader–member exchange, differentiation, and task interdependence: Implications for individual and group performance, *Journal of Organizational Behavior, 27*, 1–24.

Lipman-Blumen, J. (1992). Connective leadership: Female leadership styles in the 21st century workplace, *Sociological Perspectives, 35*, 183–203.

Maak, T. & Pless, N. M. (2006). Responsible leadership in a stakeholder society: A relational perspective, *Journal of Business Ethics, 66*, 99–115.

Mahsud, R., Yukl, G., & Prussia, G. (2010). Leader empathy, ethical leadership, and relations-oriented behaviors as antecedents of leader-member exchange quality, *Journal of Managerial Psychology, 25*, 561–577.

Mayer, D., Kuenzi, M., Greenbaum, R., Bardes, R., & Salvador, M. R. (2009). How low does ethical leadership flow? Test of a trickle-down model, *Organizational Behavior and Human Decision Processes, 108*, 1–13.

Mayer, D. M., Aquino, K., Greenbaum, R. L., & Kuenzi, M. (2012). Who displays ethical leadership, and why does it matter? An examination of antecedents and consequences of ethical leadership, *Academy of Management Journal*, 55(1), 151–171.

McGuire, G. M. (2007). Intimate work, *Work and Occupations*, *34*, 125–147.

Mehra, A., Dixon, A. L., Brass, D. J., & Robertson, B. (2006). The social network ties of group leaders: Implications for group performance and leader reputation, *Organization Science*, *17*, 64–79.

Nahapiet, J. & Ghoshal, S. (1998). Social capital, intellectual capital and the organizational advantage, *Academy of Management Review*, *23*, 242–266.

Neubert, M. J., Carlson, D. S., Kacmar, K. M., Roberts, J. A., & Chonko, L. B. (2009). The virtuous influence of ethical leadership behavior: Evidence from the field, *Journal of Business Ethics*, *90*, 157–170.

Ng, T. W. H., Eby, L. T., Sorensen, K. L., & Feldman, D. C. (2005). Predictors of objective and subjective career success: A meta-analysis, *Personnel Psychology*, *25*, 367–408.

Northouse, P. G. (2013). *Leadership: Theory and Practice* (6th ed.). Thousand Oaks, CA: Sage.

Offstein, E. H., Madhavan, R., & Gnyawali, D. R. (2006). Pushing the frontier of LMX research: The contribution of triads: in G. Graen & J. A. Graen (eds) *Sharing Network Leadership* (Vol. 4). Greenwich, CT: Information Age Publishing.

Pearce, C. L. & Conger, J. A. (2003). All those years ago: The historical underpinnings of shared leadership: in C. L. Pearce & J. A. Conger (eds) *Shared Leadership: Reframing the Hows and Whys of Leadership* (pp. 1–18). Thousand Oaks, CA: Sage Publications.

Pearce, C. L., Conger, J. A., & Locke, E. A. (2007). Shared leadership theory, *Leadership Quarterly*, *18*, 281–288.

Pfeffer, J. (1992). *Managing with Power*. Boston, MA: Harvard Business School Press.

Piccolo, R. F., Greenbaum, R., Den Hartog, D. N., & Folger, R. (2010). The relationship between ethical leadership and core job characteristics, *Journal of Organizational Behavior*, *31*, 259–278.

Podolny, J. M. and Baron, J. N. (1997). Resources and relationships: Social networks and mobility in the workplace, *American Sociological Review*, *62*, 673–693.

Resick, C. J., Hanges, P. J., Dickson, M. W., & Mitchelson, J. K. (2006). A cross-cultural examination of the endorsement of ethical leadership, *Journal of Business Ethics*, *63*, 345–359.

Sally, D. F. (2000). A general theory of sympathy, mind-reading, and social interaction with an application to the Prisoners' Dilemma, *Social Science Information*, *39*, 567–634.

Schaubroeck, J. & Lam, S. S. K. (2002). How similarity to peers and supervisor influences organizational advancement in different cultures, *Academy of Management Journal*, *45*, 1120–1136.

Scott, J. (2000). *Social Network Analysis: A Handbook*. London, England: Sage.

Seibert, S. E., Kraimer, M. L., & Liden, R. C. (2001). A social capital theory of career success, *Academy of Management Journal*, *44*, 219–237.

Shamir, B., Pilai, M., Bligh, M., & Uhl-Bien, M. (eds) (2007). *Follower-Centered Perspectives of Leadership*. Greenwich, CT: Information Age Publishing.

Sluss, D. M. & Ashforth, B. E. (2007). Relational identity and identification: Defining ourselves through work relationships, *Academy of Management Review*, *32*, 9–32.

Smith, H. C. (1966). *Sensitivity to People*. New York: McGraw-Hill.

Sparrowe, R. T. & Liden, R. C. (2005). Two routes to influence: Integrating leader–member exchange and social network perspective, *Administrative Science Quarterly, 50*, 505–535.

Steiner, D. D. (1997). Attributions in leader–member exchanges: Implications for practice, *European Journal of Work and Organizational Psychology, 6*, 59–71.

Stogdill, R. M., Goode, O. S., & Day, D. R. (1962). New leader behavior description subscale, *Journal of Psychology, 54*, 259–269.

Tangirala, S., Green, S. G., & Ramanujam, R. (2007). In the shadow of the boss's boss: Effects of supervisors' upward exchange relationships on employees, *Journal of Applied Psychology, 92*, 309–320.

Toor, S. R. & Ofori, G. (2009). Ethical leadership: Examining the relationships with full range leadership model, employee outcomes, and organizational culture, *Journal of Business Ethics, 90*, 533–547.

Treviño, L. K. (1986). Ethical decision making in organizations: A person–situation interactionist model, *Academy of Management Review, 11*, 601–617.

Treviño, L. K., Hartman, L. P., & Brown, M. (2000). Moral person and moral manager: How executives develop a reputation for ethical leadership, *California Management Review, 42*, 128–142.

Treviño, L. K., Brown, M., & Hartman, L. P. (2003). A qualitative investigation of perceived executive ethical leadership: Perceptions from inside and outside the executive suite, *Human Relations, 55*, 5–37.

Treviño, L. K., Weaver, G. R., & Reynolds, S. J. (2006). Behavioral ethics in organizations: A review, *Journal of Management, 32*, 951–990.

Tumasjan, A., Strobel, M., & Welpe, I. (2011). Ethical leadership evaluations after moral transgression: Social distance makes the difference, *Journal of Business Ethics, 99*, 609–622.

Turban, D. B., Dougherty, T. W., & Lee, F. K. (2002). Gender, race, and perceived similarity effects in developmental relationships: The moderating role of relationship duration, *Journal of Vocational Behavior, 61*, 1–23.

Turner, J. C., Oakes, P. J., Haslam, S. A., & McGarty, C. (1994). Self and collective: Cognition and social context, *Personality and Social Psychology Bulletin, 20*, 454–463.

Tyler, T. R. & Blader, S. L. (2000). *Cooperation in Groups: Procedural Justice, Social Identity, and Behavioral Engagement*. New York: Psychology Press.

Uhl-Bien, M. (2006). Relational leadership theory: Exploring the social processes of leadership and organizing, *Leadership Quarterly, 17*, 654–676.

Uhl-Bien, M. & Maslyn, J. M. (2003). Reciprocity in manager-subordinate relationships: Components, configurations, and outcomes, *Journal of Management, 29*, 511–532.

Venkataramani, V., Green, S. G., & Schleicher, D. J. (2010). Well-connected leaders: The impact of leaders' social network ties on LMX and members' work attitudes, *Journal of Applied Psychology, 95*, 1071–1084.

Walumbwa, F. O. & Schaubroeck, J. (2009). Leader personality traits and employee voice behavior: Mediating roles of ethical leadership and work group psychological safety, *Journal of Applied Psychology, 94*(5), 1275–1286.

Walumbwa, F. O., Mayer, D. M., Wang, P., Wang, H., Workman, K., Christensen, A. L. (2011). Linking ethical leadership to employee performance: The roles of leader–member exchange, self-efficacy, and organizational identification, *Organizational Behavior and Human Decision Processes*, 115, 204–213.

Wei, L. Q., Chiang, F., & Wu, L. Z. (2012). Developing and utilizing network resources: Roles of political skill, *Journal of Management Studies*, 49, 381–402.

Williamson, O. E. (1987). Transaction cost economics: The comparative contracting perspective, *Journal of Economic Behavior & Organization*, 8(4), 617–625.

Yukl, G. (2013). *Leadership in Organizations* (8th ed.). Upper Saddle River, NJ: Pearson.

Zhu, W., Riggio, R. E., Avolio, B. J., & Sosik, J. J. (2011). The effect of leadership on follower moral identity: Does transformational/transactional style make a difference? *Journal of Leadership and Organizational Studies*, 18, 150–163.

12
Relationships in Family Business: The Paradox of Family Organizations

Marcus Ho[1], Christine Woods[2], and Deborah Shepherd[2]

Anthony Washington, the scion of Pacific Wide, a well-known family business in New Zealand, pondered the email in front of him. "Are you thinking of coming back? It would be a good time – Dad".

Established in 1988, the Pacific Wide Group is a privately owned family company. As a leading exporter and importer of soil-less growing media such as sphagnum moss, processed pinus radiata bark and coir, Pacific Wide has an international reputation for quality standards and an international group of companies from Chile to Sri Lanka. Pacific Wide encompasses activities from securing raw resources to direct delivery of products and information. Anthony grew up around the business and began his career working for Pacific Wide. After flourishing in the role and completing a sizeable project successfully, he suggested formalising the arrangement and his role in the company. Clive Washington, his father and founder of Pacific Wide, replied: "No, go out and get a job". Anthony did just that and after four years achieved promotion and success in the organization where he was employed. Now as he thought about the message from his father, the family business exerted a great pull on his emotions and aspirations.

The family business presents a unique context in which to examine relationships in organizations. Family businesses, with the resulting intersection of family members, the family, and the business (Shepherd & Haynie, 2009), have sparked great interest among academics because

[1] Management Department, AUT University
[2] Management Department, The University of Auckland

of the theoretical and practical insights for entrepreneurship and business that they offer (Milton, 2008; Shepherd & Haynie, 2009). The ubiquitous nature of family businesses, the significant contribution family businesses make to many economies globally (Neubauer & Lank, 1998), and their impact on mainstream management thought (Colli, 2003) makes family businesses an important context for examining relationships. For example, family owned businesses tend to dominate the business landscape in many western economies (Brice & Richardson, 2009; Colli, 2003; Villalonga & Amit, 2010) and are the primary drivers of entrepreneurial activities, corporate growth, and economic development (Rogoff & Heck, 2003). Recent research has also shown that family businesses, in contrast to popularly held belief, tend to outperform other, non-family businesses (Anderson & Reeb, 2003).

Aside from the traditional notions of differences in succession and governance issues, family businesses must effectively deal with the changing role of family members, politics, and values (Davis et al., 2010). Added to this, the changing demographics and social changes that see the family business as raison d'être for opportunity and entrepreneurship (Aldrich & Cliff, 2003), the rich tapestry of family businesses, and their significant impact in the overall landscape of business and society is worthy of theoretical and practical examination. Familial relationships are an important and critical feature of the family business. Family businesses tend to differ from their non-family counterparts in terms of their intangible resources such as social capital, capabilities, access to financial capital, organizational structures, entrepreneurial orientation, risk taking, and innovations (Acquaah, 2012; Naldi et al., 2007). Underlying many of these differences and capabilities are the relationships that exist within the company such as the sharing of values and knowledge and the creation of a "family" culture within the business. Thus, family businesses have been described appropriately as, "complex, dynamic, and rich in intangible resources" (Habbershon & Williams, 1999b, p. 3). The very nature of relationships in family business invites paradox as a central feature. In starting and working in a family business, there is an acceptance of paradox in terms of relationships, systems, and work activities. The central premise of this chapter is to highlight the paradoxes inherent in relationships in family business and to use paradox as an organizing framework for understanding family business. We highlight these paradoxes by introducing the family business as a meta-system, then consider the nature of paradox, followed by an exploration of the advantages and disadvantages of relationships that highlight these paradoxes, and lastly offer a framework for understanding relationships and paradox in family business. We interweave these ideas through several vignettes of Pacific Wide, a family business where paradoxes within relationships can be observed.

A framework for understanding family business: Definitions, models, and systems

There are many different kinds of family business. Not only is the family business diverse, but definitions in the literature are similarly contentious. While there is debate over the precise definition of the family business, most definitions generally include family members owning and running a venture (Heck & Trent, 1999; Rogoff & Heck, 2003). Further definitions have included aspects of "familiness" such as defining "kin" (Colli, 2003) as well as including the extent and nature of family control (Chrisman et al., 2003). In addition, family businesses are diverse; ranging from businesses of husband-wife partnerships, family franchises, to intergenerational large enterprises. One of the most widely cited definition from the literature identifies family businesses as those that have: 1. Top management identifying the business as a family business; 2. more than 50% of shares or equity owned by a single family group; 3. one or more members of the management group drawn from the "owning" family and; 4. intergenerality (Westhead et al., 2002). From the brief description above, family business have a range of diversity and can include businesses which run the gamut from spousal partnerships, long term intergenerational businesses, and lifestyle small businesses. The type of definitions used often depends on the level of analysis and the type of businesses of interest.

In this chapter, we explore relationships in family business and highlight some of the inherent paradoxes underpinning family relationships within family business. In a recent article reflecting on family business research, Zahra and Sharma (2004) challenge researchers in the field to seek a better understanding of the challenges faced by family business owners and managers. They suggest that probing the paradoxes observed in family business can lead to fruitful avenues for research and practice. To that end, we utilize a case study to highlight the paradoxical nature of the family business and to provide real examples of the nature of these relationships in the family business. In doing so, we hope to make practical suggestions for dealing with the "unique characteristics that accompany family ties in organizations" (Cruz et al., 2012, p. 65).

Understanding relationships in the family business: A model of family business and the importance of relationships

Clive Washington, Anthony's father, and founder and group managing director of Pacific Wide, harboured great expectations for his children. Early in 1988, a few months after the New Zealand stock market crashed in October 1987, Clive, the General Manager at Country Traders Ltd, was working with a team of 50 staff, exporting bark primarily into the Japanese market. He arrived at work one day and received word that Country Traders was going into receivership.

"Basically, when the receiver was appointed, we had no jobs, and all of these customers were just going to be let down. So I said to the accountant at Country Traders, we've got nothing to lose. I've got all the customers overseas – how about we contact them all over the weekend, and I'll explain to them what has happened. If we've got a fair bit of support out there, I'll source the product and we'll keep going."

Even with a strong customer base, times were still tough. "Cash flow was dreadful. The more products we'd shift the more profit we made, the worse the cash flow problem got!" Despite the teething problems of being a new business owner, Clive saw potential and opportunities in the business. Shortly after buying over Country Traders, Clive saw an opportunity to expand the business. In early 1989 Clive set up CoastPak Holding to export sphagnum moss, an increasingly popular growing medium. Having built his business from these turbulent times, Clive ensured his children were interested in the business and harboured a private expectation and desire of their future within the business.

As the above vignette demonstrates, businesses may often start with an eye towards long term succession. Often this is associated with the maxim of "who better to get involved, and to trust, than family members?" (Getz et al., 2003). As the criteria for family businesses demonstrate, family businesses, with the main involvement of family members and family control, can have many advantages. Recent research has shown that succession and continued family control in a firm can be productive for business (Zellweger et al., 2012). This is no small point, as the longevity of family ownership in a business can be beneficial due to the associated long term perspective and unique strategic positioning (Zellweger, 2007). In addition, family control in business has been linked to fewer agency problems (such as acting in the best interest of other parties rather than one's own) and higher firm values, highlighting the role and benefits of family relations in the business (Anderson & Reeb, 2003). Research has also found that the family values and relationships of family businesses can positively affect the resource inventory and usage of their firms, indicating the critical role of managerial control and relations (Arregle et al., 2007; Habbershon & Williams, 1999a). In addition, continued family control and management can promote new entrepreneurial activity and the innovation essential for long term strategy and viability of the firm (Kellermanns & Eddleston, 2006; Nordqvist & Melin, 2010). The research mentioned briefly above provides insights into how families are able to make a positive contribution to their firms and, in addition, that active involvement of family in management is positive for the firms (Anderson & Reeb, 2003). Aside from the traditional notions of differences in succession and governance issues, family businesses must also effectively deal with the changing role of family members, politics, and values (Davis et al., 2010).

In contrast to the positive advantages that family businesses enjoy from their relationships, family businesses, and the family relationships inherent within them, are also known for their negative outcomes such as nepotism (Cruz et al., 2012; Lee et al., 2003; Salvato et al., 2012), conflict (Kidwell et al., 2012; Shepherd & Haynie, 2009), equity issues (Carsrud, 2006; Masulis et al., 2011; Patel & Fiet, 2011) and inherent sense of rebellion and entitlement (Chrisman & Patel, 2012; Eddleston et al., 2012). Relationships in family business are theoretically rich as organizational and work practice phenomena. Family businesses as organizations embody the paradoxes of organizations; that is, they are replete with inconsistencies, theoretical contradictions, and oppositions. Relationships in the family business often have complex meanings, with organizational features producing theoretical paradoxes which are interesting and thought provoking. Thus, what the advantages and disadvantages of relationships in family business show is that such businesses are inherently contradictory and paradoxical.

While realizing that paradox has been investigated in the realm of organizational theory for at least 50 years (e.g. Handy, 1976; March & Simon, 1993; Mintzberg et al., 1976) it has yet to be applied to family business although there have been calls to examine these paradoxes (e.g. Zahra & Sharma, 2004). Paradox has several levels of meaning; in general conversation it can be thought of "as an information umbrella for interesting and thought-provoking contradictions of all sorts ... a paradox is something which grabs our attention, a puzzle needing a solution" (Poole & van de Ven, 1989, p. 563). More formally, a paradox indicates "contradictory yet interrelated elements – elements that seem logical in isolation but absurd and irrational when appearing simultaneously" (Lewis, 2000, p. 760). The literature clearly portrays family businesses as having their own unique characteristics and dynamics brought about by the intersection of family and business, quite different to non-family business and warranting their own field of research (Chrisman et al., 2010; McAdam et al., 2010; Moores, 2009). Therefore, we posit the idea that family firms are inherently paradoxical, as relationships within the family contain all kinds of paradoxes, from the mutually supportive yet competing rivalry of sibling relationships to the love and hate relationships that husband and wife partnerships may have within a family business. "The more turbulent the times, the more complex the world, the more the paradoxes" (Handy, 1976, p. 17). Using a lens of paradox is by no means a new or unexplored phenomenon within the world of business research, having been explored namely in the domain of organizational theory research and finding renewed attention in our present turbulent environment (e.g. Leana & Barry, 2000; Schultze & Stabell, 2004; Gupta et al., 2006; Lok, 2006; Mintzberg, 2009; Farjoun, 2010; Bendixen & Luvison, 2010; Smith & Lewis, 2011).

However, in order to understand where paradox arises in the family business it is important to understand how family businesses can be understood. While there is no unified paradigm for studying the area of family business, the overlapping circles model of family business has become a common starting point for showing the important domains in family business (Habbershon et al., 2003). Figure 12.1 shows the interrelationship of business and family.

Based on a systems perspective, three overlapping circles or subsystems are represented; these are family, ownership, and business/management. The overlapping circles model was extended by Gersick et al. (1997) into a life cycle developmental model. For two decades the three circles model has been the standard theoretical model "for picturing family and business as interlinking systems that explain the competitive tensions in strategy making" (Habbershon et al., 2003, p. 453). Thus, the model has been central to the understanding of family business. However, for the same period of time, the limitations to this model have also been discussed. Central to this discussion has been the assertion that the model fails to take into account the dynamic nature

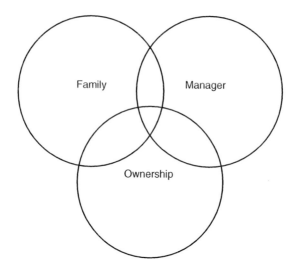

Figure 12.1   Three Overlapping Circles Model
Source: Habbershon et al., 2003.

of family business (Hoy & Verser, 1994). Further, the model provides little space for understandings of entrepreneurial processes and activities; entrepreneurial issues are left implicit within the growth models and generally only related to the business founder and the start-up phase (Johannission, 2002; Fletcher, 2004). While the overlapping circles model provides a useful conceptual platform, Hoy and Verser argue that it "barely touches on the true complexity of the firm" and does not adequately address the dynamics of how issues within the circles and between the circles overlap (1994, p. 16). They suggest that critical strategic management issues for family firms are located at the nexus of the three circles, and often the model simply provides static, descriptive pictures of the interaction. The outcome is that strategic management of family firms "focuses on a series of internal negative trade-offs to manage the overlap between family and business rather than a process for finding the systemic synergy that can lead to strategic competitiveness for the firm" (Habbershon et al., 2003, p. 454). With these criticisms in mind, a more unified systems model was developed to include the systems dynamic of the overlapping circles model more broadly, integrating and showing how events in one part feed through into other subsystem components. Therefore, in order to understand the outcomes of family business, it is essential to understand the relationships within the family business.

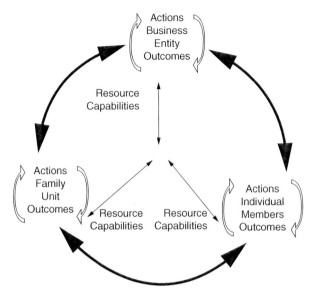

Figure 12.2 Three Subsystems of Family-Based System Resources, Capabilities, and Outcomes
Source: Habbershon et al., 2003.

The work by Habbershon and Williams (1999) provides a useful framework for understanding the dynamics of relationships in the family business. Habbershon and Williams (1999) suggest that the unique systemic family influences can be examined through an analysis of the resources and capabilities of the family firm. To that end, Habbershon et al. (2003) develop a unified systems perspective demonstrating how parts of the family business system interact to generate idiosyncratic antecedents to firm performance (Figure 12.2).

The idiosyncratic bundle of resources and capabilities result from systems interaction between the family unit, the business, and individual family members. This bundle is referred to as the "familiness" of the firm. They focus on the dynamic interactions that occur and on the circular feedback processes with continuous influences; this contrasts to the overlapping circles model where subsystem analysis results in isolated points of influence. Thus, family businesses are unique in that their relationships may become a central resource and allow a more central role for interactions around relationships and resources in the family business. From a systems perspective, a social system model must "show how the systemic infusions of the system are a product of the continuous interactions of the parts" (Habbershon et al., 2003, p. 454). They focus on a metasystem: the family business social system. This metasystem is comprised of three subsystems: the controlling family unit, the business entity, and the individual family members. These three subsystems create chains of interactions; the systemic interactions are complex and dynamic, drawing on and bringing about the emergence of intangible and tangible resources and capabilities that serve to create transgenerational wealth creation.

Thus this signifies that, in order to understand the system level of outcomes, there needs to be an understanding of the interaction of people within the family business. While the above model (Figure 12.2) focuses on the strategic management perspective and remains broad in its focus to capture the systemic influences of the model, it remains a useful theoretical framework for our understanding of the demands of family, business, and individuals. The model of family business shows the different levels of analysis and the importance of interactions in understanding the family business, however the actual interactions occurring between specific stakeholders such as family members, employees, and customers have not been examined in detail. Thus there is an opportunity to frame the relationships in family business into the wider analysis of the business metasystem. This is addressed through chains of interactions, giving rise to the idiosyncratic resources and capabilities unique to the enterprising family that is in turn thought to link to performance. The enterprising family must pay attention to competitive advantage and the "source of sustained wealth creation" (Habbershon et al., 2003, p. 462). As the relationships and the interactions of family, business, and the wider family business framework are taken into account, the greater the amount of paradox, contradictions, and inconsistencies that will be embodied in the relationships. Therefore a useful way through this, as indicated earlier, is to delineate the concept of relationships in family business through examining the paradoxes within them.

Paradox and the family business

The paradox offers a useful framework for moving beyond oversimplified, polarised understandings of organisations to explore the complexity, diversity and ambiguity inherent in organisational activity (Cameron & Quinn, 1988).

Paradoxes comprise a wide variety of contradictory yet interwoven elements that might include perspectives, feelings, messages, demands, identities, interests, or practices. They are constructed by actors to make sense of a complex, ambiguous and ever changing world and come about through some form of reflection or interaction that reveals the juxtaposition of elements that do not sit comfortably together (Lewis, 2000; Ford & Hackoff, 1988). Pertinent to the study of family businesses are social paradoxes; these types of paradoxes are concerned with "tensions and oppositions between well-founded, well-reasoned, and well supported alternative explanations of the same phenomenon. When juxtaposed, they present a puzzle to the theorist, because each side seems valid, yet they are in some sense incompatible or hard to reconcile" (Poole & van de Ven, 1989, p. 565).

Poole and van de Ven (1989, pp. 565–567) propose four ways of relating to social paradoxes.

1) Opposition: Accept the paradox and use it constructively
The paradox is accepted and no attempt is made to resolve it; rather we learn to live with it. The ambiguity within the paradox is considered with the two opposing parts of the paradox kept separate and their contrasts appreciated.

2) Spatial separation: Clarify levels of analysis
Paradoxes are resolved by clarifying the levels of analysis and the links between them. It is assumed that one part of the paradox operates at one level while the other part of the paradox operates at the other level. Examples of such distinctions include: Individual-social; micro-macro; individual-business.

3) Temporal separation: Take time into account
One part of the paradox is assumed to be relevant during one time period; the other part is assumed to hold during a different time period. One of the key challenges from this perspective is where and when the transition point occurs.

4) Synthesis: Introduce new terms to resolve the paradox
This approach assumes that the paradox arises because of conceptual limitation. With synthesis new perspectives or concepts are introduced to overcome the limitations of assumptions made.

All four approaches can be combined; for example accepting the paradox can serve as a first step to pursuing one of the other approaches. We suggest that the interplay of paradoxes within the family business can play themselves out as virtuous and vicious spirals across time and levels, and thus provide a lens for understanding relationships in family business. We utilise the case of Pacific Wide to frame the paradox of relationships in family business and revisit these approaches to dealing with paradox at the end. These vignettes will serve to illustrate the different points of paradox examined in this chapter.

The paradox of relationships in family business

Several years after the email to his son, Clive collapsed in his office with severe chest pain after returning from an overseas trip. The stress of running the business combined with a significant amount of overseas travel was taking its toll. Anthony, worried about his father, made a commitment to come on board the following year. He and Clive talked seriously about how this might work. A Sri Lankan partnership had been established, a Chilean partnership was progressing smoothly, and a new bark plant in New Zealand had been started. The company was moving to a new level. Anthony was not moving to the business just to help out his Dad – he chose Pacific Wide because of the opportunity it offered. Anthony came to Pacific Wide with a vision of what he wanted to do in the company. He and Clive had talked about the opportunities over the years, so each understood where the other was coming from. The vision developed and changed as did the father and son, talking on a daily basis, planning and developing opportunities. Everybody in the business had a chance to pitch their ideas and have them taken seriously. It was still a struggle to get everybody to understand the focus, the direction, and the intention, but they made progress. However, Anthony has noticed a new problem: "Dad and I are almost in sync now; we really know what is going on with each other, and I think that may create a bit of a problem. We now know where each other is heading so much that we're not communicating that to everybody else all the time."

Anthony and Clive spent a good deal of time and energy developing and building a working relationship based on good communication and trust. This is enabling a successful transition to occur in the business whereby leadership is being carefully managed and transferred. However, with the success of this transition comes the potential for a vicious spiral to arise. The more "in sync" they are, the more excluded others in the organization can become. With an implicit understanding now developing between the two, it is essential that what is implicit between them is communicated in an explicit way to others in the organization.

Strong family bonds, which can be said to be characterized by trust and commitment, are a key element of family business (Eddleston et al., 2012). The literature on family business finds that a powerful ingredient is the family culture, which tends to promote trust and commitment. Studies have found that family businesses are likely to have open communication, quick decision making, and a strong culture of understood norms and values, leading to increased trust and commitment (Chua et al., 2009; Eddleston & Kellermanns, 2007; Miller & Le Breton-Miller, 2006). The distinct characteristics of family businesses and the ability to foster relationships within the organization has seen the topics of trust and commitment discussed under theoretical approaches such as stewardship theory (Davis et al., 2010; Eddleston et al., 2012); leadership (Banalieva & Eddleston, 2011; Chung & Chan, 2012; Hernandez, 2008; Nicholson, 2008); and agency theory (Cruz et al., 2010; Miller et al., 2010; Rama, 2012; Roida & Sunarjanto, 2012).

The paradox of trust and commitment: Positive outcomes

We look first at trust in more detail. Trust has been seen as a central feature of family business because it occurs in a context of communities with "naturally occurring trust relations (Fukuyama, 1995) including a "particular proclivity to invoke trust as a governance mechanism" (Eddleston et al., 2010, p. 1044). Trust is a psychological state that has been defined as an individual's willingness to be vulnerable and expect that an exchange partner will not behave opportunistically (Baron, 2008; Eddleston et al., 2010; Mayer et al., 1995). Researchers believe that trust in the family business may form the basis for understanding a range of outcomes including the range of behaviors, strengths, and weaknesses observed in the family firm (Corbetta & Salvato, 2004; Sundaramurthy, 2008). Further, others believe that the concept of trust may serve as an organizing framework for understanding relationships in family business (Cruz et al., 2010; Eddleston et al., 2010). Given that family businesses have multiple reasons for being in business other than financial gain, such as having a closer relationships between family members and clear succession (Orth & Green, 2009), they have often been viewed as being more trustworthy (Sundaramurthy, 2008). In fact, research bears this out with studies showing that consumers perceive family business to be far more trustworthy than non-family business (Corbetta & Salvato, 2004; Cruz et al., 2010; Sitkin & Roth, 1993; Steier, 2001). Other research has shown that family offers a great source of support, resources and goodwill for family founders (Kwan et al., 2012; Zahra, 2012; Zellweger et al., 2012). This is thought to be integrated into family business systems through the close family relationships and the inherent trust associated with these relationships. Tagiuri and Davis (1996) refer to this as "family language" and point to the close sharing of information or as an effect of less "information asymmetry" in the exchange relationships. Moreover, Daily and Dollinger (1992) show that family businesses also tend to have a flatter organizational structure and lower monitoring and control costs.

> Clive gave Anthony a "one pager" soon after he arrived in the business telling him about a French customer of the Sri Lankan operations who had noted the number of tomatoes grown in New Zealand, and expressed an interest in importing them. Anthony had his first start up:
>
> "Gro Pacific has been my baby ... Rather than as a wing of Pacific Wide, it was set up as a separate enterprise – in a trust. It's been good, and important to the Group. ... The great thing is you've got the backing of the other companies within the Group, so that you do not have to go through the strain of that business alone. We've been able to do it properly as well. We haven't had to cut the corners that Dad had to when he set up Pacific Wide."

In addition to trust, commitment in the family business has also been seen as a strong point of relationships in the family business (Davis et al., 1997; Poutziouris, 2001; Tagiuri & Davis, 1996). Commitment is "viewed as a partisan, affective attachment to the goals and values of an organization, to one's role in relation to goals and values, and to the organization for its own sake, apart from its purely instrumental worth" (Buchanan, 1974, p. 533). As pointed out earlier, given that family business values are closely aligned with the values and beliefs of the family itself, it is not surprising to find that commitment to family relationships are closely aligned to the commitment with the family business (Davis et al., 2010; Hernandez, 2008). Commitment through the family is seen as advantageous for the family business and its standing strategically (Zahra et al., 2008). How family members are involved in the family business and how leadership is enacted become important precursors to the performance of these family businesses (Eddleston & Kidwell, 2012). In addition, Corbetta and Salvato (2004) postulate that prosocial behavior in family business is easier as elements such as mutual trust, intra-familial altruism, and clan-based collegiality are easier to establish in family business due to the involvement of family members. Others have determined that prosocial behavior in family business is the result of agency costs such as asymmetric altruism, the separation of ownership and management, conflict of interests between owners and lenders, and conflict of interests between dominant and minority shareholders (Chrisman et al., 2004). Because family firms are a context in which the norms of kinship may dominate relational exchanges (Stewart, 2003), Sharma and Irving (2005) propose four bases of successor commitment to a family firm, namely affective (based on perceived desire), normative (based on perceived sense of obligation), calculative (based on perceived opportunity costs involved), and imperative (based on perceived need). This model of successor commitment to the family business allows an integration and understanding of how family relationships and commitments are translated into management philosophy. Various studies have found that the translation of family commitment to the family business is often characterized by the business into a highly participative workplace with open communication, worker empowerment, and the establishment of trust (Davis et al., 1997; Davis et al., 2010). Despite the trust and commitment that family businesses can engender, the paradox of family relationships within the business is that these relationships can also breed rivalry and inequity in the family business.

The paradox of trust and commitment: Negative outcomes

While Anthony's transition was not all plain sailing, the shift to Pacific Wide was successful, with one exception – his relationship with Clive's second in charge (2IC) Jane Smith. While the partnership helped build Pacific Wide's success, there were downsides. The 2IC kept very strict discipline over everybody who worked in the business and staff tended to play Clive and Jane off against each other. The two did not talk as often as they perhaps needed and so they did not always check what was happening in the business.

However, Jane gave Anthony a lot of support until he started stepping on her toes, doing things differently. The office atmosphere soured. One day she and Clive had a more severe clash than normal. When Anthony intervened suggesting the need for more professionalism in the relationship between them, Jane handed in her resignation. While this had happened before, this time there was one difference – Anthony and Clive both accepted it.

While relationships in family business offer many advantages, paradoxically, they can also breed negative consequences. Studies often view nepotism, preservation of the status quo, and expropriation of non-family shareholders as main rationales for succession within the family (Fukuyama, 1995; Morck et al., 1988). The involvement of the family thus produces situations for family businesses that may have unintended consequences. Conversely, Birley (2001) has described that, for some family members, the "the family business has become the family prison" (p. 63). Negative relationships in the family business can arise because of jealousies, rivalries, favoritism, and the distribution of power among family members. While family relationships are frequently enduring between family members, the overlap of business and family can change the dynamics of the relationship. One way to make sense of the various outcomes of relationships in family business, and to start understanding the paradoxes of family ties, is through the study of Birley et al. (1999) who identified distinct clusters of attitudes about the family business. Their study showed that there are three distinct attitudes to family involvement in the family business which include: "family in" groups who were clear that their children should be involved in the business at a young age and successors should be chosen from the family; "family out" groups that were opposed to family involvement beyond the current incumbents and "family-business juggler" groups who did not express strong views on any of the issues but were finding balance between family and business. Their international study, conducted over 16 countries, also concluded that family business ownership attitudes were far more important in describing family business than traditional methods of equity and managerial control. Thus, the intention to involve family in the business may be a good starting point for understanding the genesis of relationships in the family business.

> Early in the business Clive was feeling the weight of the odds against him. Although he saw almost limitless potential for growth, the daily grind of running a business was wearing him down. In those days, Clive struggled with the disciplines of managing the day-to-day running of the business, although he knew the usefulness. Business discipline was brought into the business by Clive's 2IC, Jane. He credits her meticulous bookkeeping with getting Pacific Wide through those early crisis-riven days. Clive describes her contribution as bringing tight administration to the business and a strong control of the finances. Therefore, the day Anthony accepted her resignation, Clive had grave reservations. The leaving date was arranged but Clive started losing his nerve and said he

couldn't survive without her, pressuring Anthony to ask her to stay.

These attitudes towards family involvement may breed the kinds of paradoxical relationships among family members in the family business. For example, founders of family business may be reluctant to hand over managerial responsibility to their offspring as they may feel that their children have not developed the required managerial capabilities (Birley, 2001). Indeed the literature on family business demonstrates that the attitudes and reasons behind how involved the family is in starting the business, and its eventual evolution, has a huge impact on firm outcomes such as the kind of organizational culture that emerges, the strategies pursued, who is in succession, and the management style and values (Eddleston et al., 2010). Meanwhile studies have found that barriers to family relationships in a family business include rivalries, work-life balance spillover, and succession problems (Birley, 2001; Bocatto et al., 2010; Lam, 2011; Lumpkin & Brigham, 2011; Mehrotra et al., 2011; Vera & Dean, 2005; Zahra et al., 2007). In addition, while family ties enhance formal and informal knowledge sharing in family businesses, Zahra et al. (2007) found that these jealousies, rivalries, and the concentration of power distributions acted to stifle this knowledge sharing. One of the most examined dynamics of family business is the place of conflict within the family and the business (Daily & Dollinger, 1993; Harvey & Evans, 1994; Kellermanns & Eddleston, 2004; Shepherd & Haynie, 2009). Just as close bonds between family members can also enhance the sharing of information and streamlining of decisions, conflict can also arise and can relate to anything from critical issues such as succession, to mundane decisions such as hours of operations. The spillover effects of family and business can also present a source of conflict. These conflicts stem from the close intersection of family members, the family, and the business (Shepherd & Haynie, 2009).

The paradox of family relationships: Parent-child and sibling relationships in the business

As suggested above, positive outcomes can come from having family member being involved in the business, however, the paradox of these relationships is that while family members can contribute to the organization, conflicts are central to the family business. Parasuraman et al. (1996) have shown that conflict between family members contributes to stress and satisfaction in business owners, a finding that is replicated in other studies. For example, Karofsky et al. (2001) demonstrated that conflict between family members is positively associated with anxiety and frustration while another study showed that business owners who face significant conflict experience anxiety and business dissatisfaction (Smyrnios et al., 2003). Van der Heyden et al. (2005) suggested that the conflict that ensues among family members arises because of the different criteria (need, merit, and equality) that impacts on the distributive justice that is felt among family members in a family business. They suggest that "the family firm tests the limits of distributive justice because the business family faces a dual challenge that goes beyond the allocation of particular ownership or management rights. Not only must the family design and operate a business system that creates value for its customers, employees, shareholders, and family members, it must also sustain the system beyond the horizons of the current actors toward further shareholders, next-generation family members, and future employees" (p. 7).

Within this context, possibly the most explored family relationships in the family business is the relationships between parents and their offspring, particularly in the context of succession (Schröder et al., 2011). Stavrou and Swiercz (1998) provide a model of family succession that is useful in conceptualizing the succession of family members (particularly children) into the business. They conceptualized the entry into the family business as a developmental process that includes socialization influences starting as early as adolescence. In their three level intergenerational transition model, potential successors in the pre-entry stage are associated with the family business through activities such as family discussions and part-time employment. The second level is when the potential successor enters the firm as full-time employee. The third level entails the appointment of the offspring to the leadership position and responsibilities within the family firm. In terms of the children's involvement in the family business, the stronger the parents' succession preference and preparation, the more likely adolescents are to join the family firm compared to starting their own business or entering other employment (Schröder et al., 2011). Despite this, conflict issues can arise as a result of the family system and have spillover effects on the family business (Cosier & Harvey, 1998).

Aside from the conflicts and problems observed from parental relationships (e.g. Leaptrott & McDonald, 2008; Santiago, 2011; Stavrou, 1999), problems also emerge from sibling relationships. Bernstein (2012) describes sibling rivalry quite distinctively, "experts say it remains one of the most harmful and least addressed issues in a family. We know it when we see it. Often, we deeply regret it. But we have no idea what to do about it" (p. D1). Furthermore, these relationships in family business can be prone to infighting and conflict (Friedman, 1998; Gerstner, 2000). Early research in this area shows that different siblings such as daughters and younger sons have lower positions and confront unique challenges in the family business (Barnes, 1988). This, she postulates, can be the direct result of the incongruity of family business and family hierarchy. Unfortunately, aside from one study (e.g. Friedman, 1991), relationships between family and siblings (or other members of the same generation) have received little attention. As demonstrated above, anecdotal evidence exists although a theory of sibling behavior in family firms still remains to be developed (Handler, 1991). Some have observed that rivalry is a natural extension in the family business; however, the natural bonds of family serve to keep conflict and negative outcomes small. Friedman (1991) has suggested that, despite this, rivalries do occur and there are many reasons as to why it comes to affect the family businesses. For example, he suggests that intersibling comparisons, mode of justice (equity versus equality), and parental role in conflict resolution all play an important part on the effects of sibling relationships in the family business. Intersibling comparison is the tendency of family members to compare siblings in a family. Mode of justice refers to the perceptions of justice in how siblings feel they are treated by their parents (Bryant, 1982; Friedman, 1991). Parental role in conflict resolution refers to the parental interference in siblings' attempts at resolving conflicts. Thus conflict management in the family business is aimed at reducing the effects of the rivalry in terms of inequity and equality (Friedman, 1991; Friedman, 1998).

Thus, it is clear from the studies reviewed above that, if we are to take the relationships among family members in the family business as a paradox, there are many contradictions and inconsistencies that arise when working with family members in a family business. Working with family can engender feelings of protectiveness-competition, favoritism-equality, and entitlement-meritocracy. Expecting that these paradoxes be resolved or disappear is to deny the complex nature of the family-business-individual subsystems described in our definition of the family business metasystem. To be in a family business is to accept that paradoxes will occur for family members. Such relationships are not static and clearly evolve throughout the evolution of the family-business-individual subsystems. Thus, paradox exists at different levels of the metasystem and integrates throughout the subsystems.

Ways to address the paradox in the family metasystem

Accepting Jane's resignation was the only time Clive and Anthony seriously disagreed over anything and in hindsight Anthony describes it as the best decision he has made and Clive agrees. The staff accepted the change and in many ways welcomed it. The culture of the organization was changing due to Anthony's professional discipline and more democratic, as opposed to directive, approach.

What are we then to make of the paradoxical relationships in the family business? On the one hand, relationships among family can be good, productive, and advantageous. On the other hand, it can also turn out bad, disruptive, and contentious. As discussed above, relationships in the family business are a paradox and there are many ways in which we can understand the role of paradox within relationships in the family business. While Poole and Ven de Ven's (1989) four approaches to paradox were detailed to address paradox in organizational theory, they are of particular relevance in the paradoxes observed in family business. Is the relationship between family members in the family business a paradox of opposition, spatial separation, temporal separation, or synthesis (Poole & Ven, 1989)? Or is it a simultaneous integration of all four paradoxes? In order to come close to examining the paradox of the family relationship in family business, we need to examine each in detail. In Pacific Wide, Anthony is torn by the two messages he receives from his family, particularly his father. On the one hand, the message from his father was to make it on his own. But after success outside the family business, he was expected to return. This paradox may be resolved by thinking of the close relationships between the two family members where knowledge and information sharing exists and is in constant flux (Chirico & Salvato, 2008; Giovannoni et al., 2011; Pérez Rodríguez & Basco, 2011). The mixed messages from Clive to Anthony in the opening vignette demonstrate that relationships can be a temporal paradox where context and situation at different points of the family members life stage and the business lifecycle are important (Colli, 2012; Pagliarussi & Rapozo, 2011; Yan & Sorenson, 2006).

Our second main paradox in the relationships of family members occurs when seemingly consecutive advantages and disadvantages exist in having family members become involved in the family business. In Pacific Wide, when Anthony returns to the family business, there is simpatico between him and his father in terms of the direction and vision for the business. Anthony and Clive spent a good deal of time and energy developing and building a working relationship based on good communication and trust. Despite this, the administration and running of the business became a source of tension and conflict in the management of the family business. How then should we understand the paradox of having the same understanding and yet disagreeing on the direction of the business? The closest type would be to assess the paradox as an opposition and a spatial separation (Poole & Ven, 1989). It is accepted in the literature that relationships among family members can be simultaneously both close and contentious (Steier, 2001; Sundaramurthy, 2008). As an opposition paradox, existing family relationships are what make the relationships in the family business interesting and evolving. The relationship between Anthony and Clive may be dichotomous and full of contradictions (Floyd & Morman, 2003; Schwartz, 1996). On the other hand, by examining the relationship in the family business as a spatial separation, one can understand the links between the levels of analysis which may make the paradox understandable. For example, in Pacific Wide, utilizing the father-son relationship may be a potentially useful way to understand the conflicted yet close relationship between Clive and Anthony (Haberman & Danes, 2007). Indeed, specifying the levels of analysis is a particularly fruitful way of understanding the relationship paradox in the family business (Eddleston & Kidwell, 2012; Friedman, 1991; Handler, 1991; Xiaowei & Chi-Nien, 2005).

Our last paradox consists of the impact of the relationships between family members and the impact on the business. Clive's reluctance to let the 2IC go was reinforcing a vicious cycle supporting the view that reactions to paradox can often be defensive, "clinging to past understandings to avoid recognizing their cognitive and social foibles" (Lewis, 2000, p. 763). However, for Anthony, the tension served as "a trigger for change" (Lewis, 2000, p. 763). While the paradox of "historical success sowing the seeds for future failure" is apparent, perhaps just as paradoxical, is that conflict was essential in breaking the cycle and creating a more democratic and positive culture of inclusion. Such synthesis of concepts and paradox may require further investigation in the literature. As presented in this chapter, relationships in the family business are starting to make an impact into the general management and strategy literature. Table 12.1 details the four approaches to paradox in organizations and how it applies to Pacific Wide.

Family business is replete with paradoxes and is therefore an area of great synthesis and conceptual development (Berrone et al., 2012;

Table 12.1   Four Ways to Address Paradox (Poole & Ven, 1989) and Examples from the Pacific Wide Case Study

Paradox	Method for working with paradox	Example in Pacific Wide
Opposition	Accept the paradox and use it constructively	Clive wanted Anthony to be part of the business but Anthony had to prove himself that he was able to do business … away from the family business
Spatial Separation	Clarify levels of analysis	Agreement between Clive and Anthony on vision and direction of business yet there was a difference of opinion on its operations and staffing
Temporal Separation	Take time into account	How business was run between Clive and Jane versus how business was run between Anthony and 2IC
Synthesis	Introduce new terms to resolve the paradox	Reluctance to let go of what worked in the past vis-à-vis Clive vs what new ways of working Anthony brings to the company

Litz et al., 2012; Strike, 2012). To that end, it has been suggested that family business research could benefit further from integrating family sciences research, developing innovative measures, adopting rich longitudinal methodologies, and including more diverse subjects and samples (Litz et al., 2012). As can be seen from Table 12.1, showing the approaches to paradox by Poole and Ven de Ven (1989), there are ways in which the paradox in family business can be resolved, understood or merely accepted. For example, in opposition, we see that Anthony accepted the challenge of proving himself by working for other companies before being offered the role in the family business. This example highlights the acceptance of the paradox and using it constructively. For many reasons, Anthony felt that by working for other businesses before working for the family business, not only would it allow him consideration of other career/vocational options outside of the family business, it would build his capabilities and develop his access to resources independent of the family business. This enabled Anthony to capture the capabilities and networks required to continue the success of the family business.

The spatial separation approach to paradox is seen by the sharing of a vision between the father and son in Pacific Wide alongside differing perspectives on how to achieve this vision. As seen from the vignettes, while Clive and Anthony agreed on the overall direction and vision for the family business, there was significant disagreement on the operations of the business. This example can be clearly understood as a level of analysis problem in which contradictions can co-exist because of the levels from which these paradoxes exist. Taking into account the family metasystem (Habbershon & Williams, 1999b), paradoxes will exist at the individual, family, and business levels. Such inconsistencies are part and parcel of the relationships within the family business and family members can produce unexpected results and even contribute to the conflicts found in the family business. Recognition of the levels through which these paradoxes emerge may be a way in which to understand and perhaps resolve the cognitive dissonance that arises because of this paradox. In the Pacific Wide case, Clive and Anthony were able to navigate through the subs system paradoxes toward an overall shared vision of the family business. Thus, overall family trust and also the relationship of father and son helped Clive and Anthony to navigate the paradoxes they encountered to take mutually acceptable actions and decisions. For example, Clive accepting Anthony's decision about the 2IC (Jane) after her resignation. Such paradoxes operate in organizational life and approaching it through a levels of analysis approach allows for the lessening of cognitive dissonance around the paradox encountered.

Temporal separation as a way to understand paradox was highlighted by how historical trajectories are established in the business (DiMaggio & Powell, 1983). The relationship between Clive and his 2IC (Jane) had worked well and the working relationship had evolved systems and behaviors that became the norm. With the arrival of Anthony taking over most of Clive's responsibilities, this relationship was disrupted and the changed environment created conflict between Anthony, Clive, and Jane. This had a significant impact on Jane who was familiar with Clive's "way of doing things" as opposed to Anthony's different style of management. Temporal separation suggests that one side of the paradox holds for a certain point in time and the opposing side of the paradox holds for a different point in time. In Pacific Wide, the arrival of Anthony represented a paradox for Jane who felt conflict and had to deal with the paradox of managing Clive and Anthony. Thus, the paradox could not be resolved and Jane decided to leave.

The synthesis approach to paradox can be observed in Pacific Wide where Anthony was integrated into the company, and his effect on the culture of the company and its employees. The entry of Anthony, at a high level in the family business, introduced new management and many other changes into the organisation. Change in organizations is always a time of paradox for employees. Some manage this change by leaving (e.g. 2IC), some deal with the effects on their emotions, participation, and psychological contracts with the company (Bordia et al., 2011; Dahl, 2011; De Vos & Freese, 2011; Freese et al., 2011), while others form new meanings around the actions and behaviors or to synthesize the paradoxes observed. This highlights that paradoxes in organizations may not be conducive to solutions, rather, that paradox may just need to be understood and accepted. In addition, decisions and actions can be made when an understanding of the paradox is accepted. In the case of Pacific Wide, while the changes with the entry of Anthony into the company caused many disruptions and paradoxes in its processes, some in the management team and employees were able to deal with the contradictions in management style by creating new ideas and terms about the new manager. Solutions such as executive onboarding (Ndunguru, 2012) and strategies by businesses to aid in organizational change are ways in which organizational change can help in dealing with the paradoxes observed.

Conclusion

In this chapter, we have explored the importance of understanding relationships in the family business. Through the lens of the family metasystem and paradox, we have explored the ways in which relationships in family business become complex yet dynamic subsytems that create conflict and contradictions. Although we have highlighted the paradoxes in the vignettes introduced throughout this chapter, we have remained silent on how individuals, families, and family business can find solutions to the paradoxes observed in family business. The nature and process of paradox is that while there may be ways in which paradoxes can be resolved (such as the four approaches framework presented, this may not be possible as paradoxes are paradoxes because they are inherently abstract and contradictory. Rather, the management of the emotions, dissonance, and acceptance may be the way forward for untangling the paradoxes observed in relationships.

References

Acquaah, M. (2012). Social networking relationships, firm-specific managerial experience and firm performance in a transition economy: A comparative analysis of family owned and nonfamily firms, *Strategic Management Journal*, *33*(10), 1215–1228.

Aldrich, H. E. & Cliff, J. E. (2003). The pervasive effects of family on entrepreneurship: Toward a family embeddedness perspective, *Journal of Business Venturing*, *18*, 573–596.

Anderson, R. C. & Reeb, D. M. (2003). Founding-family ownership and firm performance: Evidence from the S&P 500, *Journal of Finance*, *58*, 1301–1328.

Arregle, J.-L., Hitt, M. A., Sirmon, D. G., & Very, P. (2007). The development of organizational social capital: Attributes of family firms, *Journal of Management Studies*, *44*, 73–95.

Banalieva, E. R. & Eddleston, K. A. (2011). Home-region focus and performance of family firms: The role of family vs non-family leaders, *Journal of International Business Studies*, *42*(8), 1060–1072.

Barnes, L. (1988). Incongruent hierarchies: Daughters and younger sons as company CEOs, *Family Business Review*, *1*(1), 9–21.

Baron, R. A. (2008). The role of affect in the entrepreneurial process, *Academy of Management Review*, *33*(2), 328–340.

Bendixen, M. & Luvison, D. (2010). The behavioral consequences of outsourcing: Looking through the lens of paradox, *Journal of Applied Management and Entrepreneurship*, *15*(4), 28–52.

Bernstein, E. (2012). Bonds/On relationships: Sibling rivalry grows up – Adult brothers and sisters are masters at digs; finding a way to a truce, *Wall Street Journal*, D.1. New York, N.Y., United States.

Berrone, P., Cruz, C., & Gomez-Mejia, L. R. (2012). Socioemotional wealth in family firms: Theoretical dimensions, assessment approaches, and agenda for future research, *Family Business Review*, *25*(3), 258–279.

Birley, S. (2001). Owner-manager attitudes to family and business issues: A 16 country study, *Entrepreneurship: Theory & Practice*, *26*(2), 63–76.

Birley, S., Ng, D. W. N., & Godfrey, A. (1999). The family and the business, *Long Range Planning*, *32*(6), 598–608.

Bocatto, E., Gispert, C., & Rialp, J. (2010). Family-owned business succession: The influence of pre-performance in the nomination of family and nonfamily members: Evidence from Spanish firms, *Journal of Small Business Management*, *48*(4), 497–523.

Bordia, P., Restubog, S. L. D., Jimmieson, N. L., & Irmer, B. E. (2011). Haunted by the past: Effects of poor change management history on employee attitudes and turnover, *Group & Organization Management*, *36*(2), 191–222.

Brice, W. D. & Richardson, J. (2009). Culture in family business: A two-country empirical investigation, *European Business Review*, *21*, 246–262.

Bryant, B. K. (ed.) (1982). *Sibling Relationships in Middle Childhood*. Hillsdale, NJ: Erlbaum.

Buchanan, B. (1974). Building organizational commitment: The socialization of managers in work organizations, *Administrative Science Quarterly*, *19*, 533–546.

Cameron, K. & Quinn, R. (eds) (1988). *Organizational Paradox and Transformation*. Cambridge, MA: Ballinger.

Carsrud, A. L. (2006). Commentary: "Are we family and are we treated as family? Nonfamily employees' perceptions of justice in the family firm": It all depends on perceptions of family, fairness, equity, and justice, *Entrepreneurship: Theory & Practice*, *30*(6), 855–860.

Chirico, F. & Salvato, C. (2008). Knowledge integration and dynamic organizational adaptation in family firms, *Family Business Review*, *21*(2), 169–181.

Chrisman, J. J. & Patel, P. C. (2012). Variations in R&D investments of family and nonfamily firms: Behavioral agency and myopic loss aversion perspectives, *Academy of Management Journal*, *55*(4), 976–997.

Chrisman, J. J., Chua, J. H., & Litz, R. (2003). A unified systems perspective of family firm performance: An extension and integration, *Journal of Business Venturing*, *18*, 467–472.

Chrisman, J. J., Chua, J. H., & Litz, R. A. (2004). Comparing the agency costs of family and non-family firms: Conceptual issues and exploratory evidence, *Entrepreneurship Theory & Practice*, *28*(4).

Chrisman, J., Kellermans, F., Chan, K., & Liano, K. (2010). Intellectual foundations of current research in family business: An identification and review of 25 influential articles, *Family Business Review*, *23*(1), 9–26.

Chua, J. H., Chrisman, J. J., & Bergiel, E. B. (2009). An agency theoretic analysis of the professionalized family firm, *Entrepreneurship Theory and Practice*, *33*(2), 355–372.

Chung, H.-M. & Chan, S.-T. (2012). Ownership structure, family leadership, and performance of affiliate firms in large family business groups, *Asia Pacific Journal of Management*, *29*(2), 303–329.

Colli, A. (2003). *The History of Family Business, 1850–2000*. New York: Cambridge University Press.

Colli, A. (2012). Contextualizing performances of family firms: The perspective of business history, *Family Business Review*, *25*(3), 243–257.

Corbetta, G. & Salvato, C. (2004). Self-serving or self-actualizing? Models of man and agency costs in different types of family firms: A commentary on comparing the agency costs of family and non-family firms: Conceptual issues and exploratory evidence, *Entrepreneurship Theory and Practice*, *28*, 355–362.

Cosier, R. A. & Harvey, M. (1998). The hidden strengths in family business: Functional conflict, *Family Business Review*, *11*(1), 75–79.

Cruz, C. C., Gomez-Mejia, L. R., & Becerra, M. (2010). Perceptions of benevolence and the design of agency contracts: CEO-TMT relationships in family firms, *Academy of Management Journal*, *53*(1), 69–89.

Cruz, C., Justo, R., & De Castro, J. O. (2012). Does family employment enhance MSEs performance?: Integrating socioemotional wealth and family embeddedness perspectives, *Journal of Business Venturing*, *27*(1), 62–76.

Dahl, M. S. (2011). Organizational change and employee stress, *Management Science*, *57*(2), 240–256.

Daily, C. M. & Dollinger, M. J. (1992). An empirical examination of ownership structure in family and professionally managed firms, *Family Business Review*, 5(2), 117–136.

Daily, C. M. & Dollinger, M. J. (1993). Alternative methodologies for identifying family- versus non-family managed businesses, *Journal of Small Business Management*, 31, 79–90.

Davis, J. H., Allen, M. R., & Hayes, H. D. (2010). Is blood thicker than water? A study of stewardship perceptions in family business, *Entrepreneurship: Theory & Practice*, 34(6), 1093–1116.

Davis, J., Schoorman, F., & Donaldson, L. (1997). Toward a stewardship theory of management, *Academy of Management Review*, 22(1), 47–74.

De Vos, A. & Freese, C. (2011). Sensemaking during organizational entry: Changes in newcomer information seeking and the relationship with psychological contract fulfilment, *Journal of Occupational & Organizational Psychology*, 84(2), 288–314.

DiMaggio, P. & Powell, W. W. (1983). The iron cage revisited: institutional isomorphism and collective rationality in organizational fields, *American Sociological Review*, 48, 147–160.

Eddleston, K. A., Chrisman, J. J., Steier, L. P., & Chua, J. H. (2010). Governance and trust in family firms: An introduction, *Entrepreneurship: Theory & Practice*, 34(6), 1043–1056.

Eddleston, K. & Kellermanns, F. W. (2007). Destructive and productive family relationships: A stewardship theory perspective, *Journal of Business Venturing*, 22, 545–565.

Eddleston, K. A., Kellermanns, F. W., & Zellweger, T. M. (2012). Exploring the entrepreneurial behavior of family firms: Does the stewardship perspective explain differences? *Entrepreneurship: Theory & Practice*, 36(2), 347–367.

Eddleston, K. A. & Kidwell, R. E. (2012). Parent-child relationships: Planting the seeds of deviant behavior in the family firm, *Entrepreneurship: Theory & Practice*, 36(2), 369–386.

Farjoun, M. (2010). Beyond dualism: Stability and change as a duality, *Academy of Management Review*, 35(2), 202–225.

Fletcher, D. E. (2004). Organisational (re) emergence and entrepreneurial development in second-generation family firm, *International Journal of Entrepreneurial Behaviour and Research*, 10(1/2), 34–48.

Floyd, K. & Morman, M. T. (2003). Human affection exchange: II. Affectionate communication in father-son relationships, *The Journal of Social Psychology*, 143(5), 599–612.

Ford, J. D. & Backoff, R. W. (1988). *Organizational Change In and Out of Dualities and Paradox*. Cambridge, MA: Ballinger.

Freese, C., Schalk, R., & Croon, M. (2011). The impact of organizational changes on psychological contracts: A longitudinal study, *Personnel Review*, 40(4), 404–422.

Friedman, S. D. (1991). Sibling relationships and intergenerational succession in family firms, *Family Business Review*, 4(1), 3–20.

Friedman, S. E. (1998). *The Successful Family Business*. Chicago: Dearborn Publishing.

Fukuyama, F. (1995). *Trust*. New York: Free Press.

Gersick, K. E., Davis, J. A., Hampton, M. M., & Lansberg, I. (1997). *Generation to Generation: Life Cycles of the Family Business*. Boston, MA: Harvard Business Press.

Gerstner, U. (2000). The Successful Family Business (Review), *Family Business Review, 13*(1), 80.

Getz, D., Carlsen, J., & Morrison, A. (2003). *The Family Business in Tourism and Hospitality*. Wallingford, UK: CABI Publishing.

Giovannoni, E., Maraghini, M. P., & Riccaboni, A. (2011). Transmitting knowledge across generations: The role of management accounting practices, *Family Business Review, 24*(2), 126–150.

Gupta, A. K., Smith, K. G., & Shalley, C. E. (2006). The interplay between exploration and exploitation, *Academy of Management Journal, 49*(4), 693–706.

Habbershon, T. G. & Williams, M. L. (1999). A resource-based framework for assessing the strategic advantages of family firms, *Family Business Review, 12*, 1–25.

Habbershon, T. G., Williams, M. L., & MacMillan, I. C. (2003). A unified system perspective of family firm performance, *Journal of Business Venturing, 18*, 451–465.

Haberman, H. & Danes, S. M. (2007). Father-daughter and father-son family business management transfer comparison: Family firo model application, *Family Business Review, 20*(2), 163–184.

Handler, W. C. (1991). Key interpersonal relationships of next-generation family members in family firms, *Journal of Small Business Management, 29*(3), 21–32.

Handy, C. (1976). *Understanding Organizations*. London: Penguin.

Harvey, R. & Evans, R. (1994). Family business and multiple levels of conflict, *Family Business Review, 7*, 331–348.

Heck, R. & Trent, E. (1999). The prevalence of family business from a household sample, *Family Business Review, 12*, 209–224.

Hernandez, M. (2008). Promoting stewardship behavior in organizations: A leadership model, *Journal of Business Ethics, 80*(1), 121–128.

Hoy, F. & Verser, T. G. (1994). Emerging business, emerging field: Entrepreneurship and the family firm, *Entrepreneurship: Theory & Practice, 19*(1), 9–23.

Johannisson, B. (2002). Energising entrepreneurship. Ideological tensions in the medium-sized family business: in D. E. Fletcher (ed.) *Understanding the Small Family Business* (pp. 46–57). London: Routledge.

Karofsky, P., Millen, R., Yilmaz, M. R., Smyrnios, K. X., Tanewski, G. A., & Romano, C. A. (2001). Work-family conflict and emotional well-being in American family businesses, *Family Business Review, 14*, 313–324.

Kellermanns, F. W. & Eddleston, K. A. (2006). Corporate entrepreneurship in family firms: A family perspective, *Entrepreneurship Theory and Practice, 30*, 809–830.

Kellermanns, F. & Eddleston, K. (2004). Feuding families: When conflict does a family firm good, *Entrepreneurship Theory and Practice, 28*, 209–228.

Kidwell, R., Kellermanns, F., & Eddleston, K. (2012). Harmony, justice, confusion, and conflict in family firms: Implications for ethical climate and the "Fredo Effect", *Journal of Business Ethics, 106*(4), 503–517.

Kwan, H. K., Lau, V. P., & Au, K. (2012). Effects of family-to-work conflict on business owners: The role of family business, *Family Business Review, 25*(2), 178–190.

Lam, W. (2011). Dancing to two tunes: Multi-entity roles in the family business succession process, *International Small Business Journal*, *29*(5), 508–533.

Leana, C. R. & Barry, B. (2000). Stability and change as simultaneous experiences in organizational life, *Academy of Management Review*, *25*(4), 753–759.

Leaptrott, J. & McDonald, J. M. (2008). Entrepreneurial opportunity exploitation and the family: Relationship-based factors that affect the adult child's decision to jointly participate with parents in a new venture, *Entrepreneurial Executive*, *13*, 101–115.

Lee, K. S., Lim, G. H., & Lim, W. S. (2003). Family business succession: Appropriation risk and choice of successor, *Academy of Management Review*, *28*(4), 657–666.

Lewis, M. (2000). Exploring paradox: Toward a more comprehensive guide, *Academy of Management Review*, *25*(4), 760–776.

Litz, R. A., Pearson, A. W., & Litchfield, S. (2012). Charting the future of family business research: Perspectives from the field, *Family Business Review*, *25*(1), 16–32.

Lok, J. (2006). Steps towards a theory of institutional stability and change as dialectically related opposites, *Academy of Management Meeting Proceedings*, August 2006. Retrieved from http://search.ebscohost.com/login.aspx?direct=true&db=bth&AN=27175652&site=ehost-live doi:10.5465/ambpp.2006.27175652

Lumpkin, G. T. & Brigham, K. H. (2011). Long-term orientation and intertemporal choice in family firms, *Entrepreneurship: Theory & Practice*, *35*(6), 1149–1169.

March, J. G. & Simon, H. (1993). *Organizations* (2nd ed.). Cambridge, MA: Basil Blackwell.

Masulis, R. W., Pham, P. K., & Zein, J. (2011). Family business groups around the world: Financing advantages, control motivations, and organizational choices, *Review of Financial Studies*, *24*(11), 3556–3600.

Mayer, R. C., Davis, J. H., & Schoorman, R. D. (1995). An integrative model of organizational trust, *Academy of Management Review*, *20*, 709–734.

McAdam, R., Reid, R., & Mitchell, N. (2010). Longitudinal development of innovation implementation in family-based SMEs: The effects of critical incidents, *International Journal of Entrepreneurial Behaviour & Research*, *16*(5), 437–456.

Mehrotra, V., Morck, R., Shim, J., & Wiwattanakantang, Y. (2011). Must love kill the family firm? Some exploratory evidence, *Entrepreneurship: Theory & Practice*, *35*(6), 1121–1148.

Miller, D. & Le Breton-Miller, I. (2006). Family governance and firm performance: Agency, stewardship and capabilities, *Family Business Review*, *XIX*(1), 73–87.

Miller, D., Le Breton-Miller, I., & Lester, R. H. (2010). Family ownership and acquisition behavior in publicly-traded companies, *Strategic Management Journal*, *31*(2), 201–223.

Milton, L. P. (2008). Unleashing the relationship power of family firms: Identity confirmation as a catalyst for performance, *Entrepreneurship: Theory & Practice*, *32*(6), 1063–1081.

Mintzberg, H. (2009). *Managing*. New York: Berrett-Koehler Publishers.

Mintzberg, H., Raisinghani, D., & Theoret, A. (1976). The structure of unstructured decision processes, *Administrative Science Quarterly*, *21*, 192–205.

Moores, K. (2009). Paradigms and theory building in the domain of business families, *Family Business Review*, *22*, 167–180.

Morck, R., Shleifer, A., & Vishny, R. W. (1988). Management ownership and market valuation: An empirical analysis, *Journal of Financial Economics, 20,* 293–315.

Naldi, L., Nordqvist, M., Sjöberg, K., & Wiklund, J. (2007). Entrepreneurial orientation, risk taking, and performance in family firms, *Family Business Review, 20*(1), 33–47.

Ndunguru, C. A. (2012). Executive onboarding: How to hit the ground running, *Public Manager, 41*(3), 6–9.

Neubauer, F. & Lank, A. G. (1998). *The Family Business: Its Governance for Sustainability.* London: Macmillan Press.

Nicholson, N. (2008). Evolutionary psychology, organizational culture, and the family firm, *Academy of Management Perspectives, 22*(2), 73–84.

Nordqvist, M. & Melin, L. (2010). Entrepreneurial families and family firms, *Entrepreneurship & Regional Development, 22*(3), 1–29.

Orth, U. R. & Green, M. T. (2009). Consumer loyalty to family versus non-family businesses: The roles of store image, trust and satisfaction, *Journal of Retailing and Consumer Services, 16,* 248–259.

Pagliarussi, M. S. & Rapozo, F. O. (2011). Agency relationships in a Brazilian multifamily firm, *Family Business Review, 24*(2), 170–183.

Parasuraman, S., Purohit, Y. S., Godshalk, V. M., & Beutell, N. J. (1996). Work and family variables, entrepreneurial career success, and psychological well-being, *Journal of Vocational Behavior, 48,* 275–300.

Patel, P. C. & Fiet, J. O. (2011). Knowledge combination and the potential advantages of family firms in searching for opportunities, *Entrepreneurship: Theory & Practice, 35*(6), 1179–1197.

Pérez Rodríguez, M. J. & Basco, R. (2011). The cognitive legitimacy of the family business field, *Family Business Review, 24*(4), 322–342.

Poole, M. & Ven, A. v. d. (1989). Using paradox to build management and organisation theories, *Academy of Management Review, 14*(4), 562–578.

Poutziouris, P. (2001). The views of family companies on venture capital: Empirical evidence from the UK small to medium-size enterprising economy, *Family Business Review, 14*(3), 277–291.

Rama, M. (2012). *Corporate Governance and Corruption: Ethical Dilemmas of Asian Business Groups* (Vol. 109, pp. 501–519). Springer Science & Business Media B.V.

Rogoff, E. G. & Heck, R. K. Z. (2003). Evolving research in entrepreneurship and family business: Recognizing family as the oxygen that feeds the fire of entrepreneurship, *Journal of Business Venturing, 18*(5), 559–566.

Roida, H. Y. & Sunarjanto, N. A. (2012). Family ownership type and the international involvement of SMEs: Empirical study of agency theory in East Java Indonesia, *Chinese Business Review, 11*(2), 224–232.

Salvato, C., Minichilli, A., & Piccarreta, R. (2012). Faster route to the CEO suite: Nepotism or managerial proficiency? *Family Business Review, 25*(2), 206–224.

Santiago, A. L. (2011). The family in family business: Case of the in-laws in Philippine businesses, *Family Business Review, 24*(4), 343–361.

Schröder, E., Schmitt-Rodermund, E., & Arnaud, N. (2011). Career choice intentions of adolescents with a family business background, *Family Business Review, 24*(4), 305–321.

Schultze, U. & Stabell, C. (2004). Knowing what you don't know? Discourses and contradictions in knowledge management research, *Journal of Management Studies, 41*(4), 549–572.

Schwartz, H. S. (1996). The sin of the father: Reflections on the roles of the corporation man, the suburban housewife, their son, and their daughter in the deconstruction of the patriarch, *Human Relations, 49*(8), 1013–1013.

Sharma, P. & Irving, P. (2005). Four bases of family business successor commitment: Antecedents and consequences, *Entrepreneurship Theory and Practice, 29*(1), 13–33.

Shepherd, D. & Haynie, J. M. (2009). Family business, identity conflict, and an expedited entrepreneurial process: A process of resolving identity conflict, *Entrepreneurship: Theory & Practice, 33*(6), 1245–1264.

Sitkin, S. B. & Roth, N. L. (1993). Explaining the limited effectiveness of legalistic "remedies" for trust/distrust, *Organization Science, 4*, 367–392.

Smith, W. K. & Lewis, M. W. (2011). Toward a theory of paradox: A dynamic equilibrium model of organizing, *Academy of Management Review, 36*(2), 381–403.

Smyrnios, K. X., Romano, C. A., Tanewski, G. A., Karofsky, P. I., Millen, R., & Yilmaz, M. R. (2003). Work-family conflict: A study of American and Australian family businesses, *Family Business Review, 16*, 35–51.

Stavrou, E. T. (1999). Succession in family businesses: Exploring the effects of demographic factors on offspring intentions to join and take over the business, *Journal of Small Business Management, 37*(3), 43–61.

Stavrou, E. T. & Swiercz, P. M. (1998). Securing the future of the family enterprise: A model of offspring intentions to join the business, *Entrepreneurship Theory and Practice, 23*, 19–39.

Steier, L. (2001). Family firms, plural forms of governance, and the evolving role of trust, *Family Business Review, 14*, 353–367.

Stewart, A. (2003). Help one another, use one another: Toward an anthropology of family business$, *Entrepreneurship Theory and Practice, 27*(4), 383–396.

Strike, V. M. (2012). Advising the family firm: Reviewing the past to build the future, *Family Business Review, 25*(2), 156–177.

Sundaramurthy, C. (2008). Sustaining trust within family businesses, *Family Business Review, 21*, 89–102.

Tagiuri, R. & Davis, J. A. (1996). Bivalent attributes of the family firm, *Family Business Review, 9*(2), 199–208.

Van der Heyden, L., Blondel, C., & Carlock, R. S. (2005). Fair process: Striving for justice in family business, *Family Business Review, 18*(1), 1–21.

Vera, C. F. & Dean, M. A. (2005). An examination of the challenges daughters face in family business succession, *Family Business Review, 18*(4), 321–345.

Villalonga, B. & Amit, R. (2010). Family control of firms and industries, *Financial Management, 39*, 863–904.

Westhead, P., Cowling, M., Storey, D. J., & Howorth, C. (eds) (2002). *The Scale and Nature of Family Business*. London: Routledge.

Xiaowei, L. & Chi-Nien, C. (2005). Keeping it all in the family: The role of particularistic relationships in business group performance during institutional transition, *Administrative Science Quarterly, 50*(3), 404–439.

Yan, J. & Sorenson, R. (2006). The effect of Confucian values on succession in family business, *Family Business Review, 19*(3), 235–250.

Zahra, S. (2012). Organizational learning and entrepreneurship in family firms: Exploring the moderating effect of ownership and cohesion, *Small Business Economics, 38*(1), 51–65.

Zahra, S. A. & Sharma, P. (2004). Family business research: A strategic reflection, *Family Business Review, 17*(4), 331–346.

Zahra, S. A., Hayton, J. C., Neubaum, D. O., Dibrell, C., & Craig, J. (2008). Culture of family commitment and strategic flexibility: The moderating effect of stewardship, *Entrepreneurship: Theory & Practice*, *32*(6), 1035–1054.

Zahra, S. A., Neubaum, D. O., & Larrañeta, B. (2007). Knowledge sharing and technological capabilities: The moderating role of family involvement, *Journal of Business Research*, *60*(10), 1070–1079.

Zellweger, T. (2007). Time horizon, costs of equity capital, and generic investment strategies of firms, *Family Business Review*, *20*, 1–15.

Zellweger, T. M., Nason, R. S., & Nordqvist, M. (2012). From longevity of firms to transgenerational entrepreneurship of families: Introducing family entrepreneurial orientation, *Family Business Review*, *25*(2), 136–155.

Index

Printed and bound by CPI Group (UK) Ltd, Croydon, CR0 4YY